KU-659-671

2nd Edition

Sociology & Social Work

Jo Cunningham & Steve Cunningham

Los Angeles | London | New Delhi
Singapore | Washington DC

Series Editors:
Jonathan Parker and Greta Bradley

Learning Matters
An imprint of SAGE Publications Ltd
1 Oliver's Yard
55 City Road
London EC1Y 1SP

SAGE Publications Inc.
2455 Teller Road
Thousand Oaks, California 91320

SAGE Publications India Pvt Ltd
B 1/I 1 Mohan Cooperative Industrial Area
Mathura Road
New Delhi 110 044

SAGE Publications Asia-Pacific Pte Ltd
3 Church Street
#10–04 Samsung Hub
Singapore 049483

© 2014 Jo Cunningham and Steve Cunningham

First published in 2008 by Learning Matters Ltd.
Second edition 2014 by SAGE/Learning Matters.

Apart from any fair dealing for the purposes of
research or private study, or criticism or review,
as permitted under the Copyright, Design and
Patents Act 1988, this publication may be
produced, stored or transmitted in any form,
by any means, only with the prior permission
in writing of the publishers, or in the case of
reprographic reproduction, in accordance with
the terms of licences issued by the Copyright
Licensing Agency. Enquiries concerning
reproduction outside these terms should be sent
to the publishers.

Editor: Luke Block
Production controller: Chris Marke
Project management: Deer Park Productions,
Tavistock, Devon
Marketing manager: Tamara Navaratnam
Cover design: Wendy Scott
Typeset by: C&M Digitals (P) Ltd, Chennai, India
Printed in Great Britain by CPI Group (UK) Ltd,
Croydon, CR0 4YY

Library of Congress Control Number: 2014940525

British Library Cataloguing in Publication Data

A catalogue record for this book is available from
the British Library.

MIX
Paper from
responsible sources
FSC
www.fsc.org   FSC® C013604

CANTERBURY CHRIST CHURCH UNIVERSITY LIBRARY
361.
3o1
CuN

3607547259

ISBN 978-1-4462-6667-0 (pb)
ISBN 978-1-4462-6666-3 (hb)

At SAGE we take sustainability seriously. Most of our products are printed in the UK using FSC papers and boards.
When we print overseas we ensure sustainable papers are used as measured by the Egmont grading system.
We undertake an annual audit to monitor our sustainability.

Contents

Acknowledgements

We would like to thank Helen Fairlie from Learning Matters at Sage, for her patience and encouragement.

Thanks also go to the very many students we have taught, past and present, for their never-ending enthusiasm and willingness to share their views and experiences.

Introduction

We are delighted to have been given the opportunity to update this textbook. It seems remarkable to us that almost six years have now passed since the publication of the first edition. Clearly much has happened in the intervening period. On a personal level, we are obviously a little older, and, we hope, perhaps a little wiser. Remarkably, our son is now in the final year of his A Level studies and is on the verge of enrolling on a politics degree at university himself. Needless to say, he decided to study sociology as one of his A Level subjects (nothing to do with us, of course!). Outside of our professional lives, our interests remain much the same and tend to revolve around the respective football teams that we support, Preston North End (Steve) and Burnley (Jo). On a professional level, we continue to teach at the University of Central Lancashire, where our enthusiasm for promoting and teaching sociology to students on our various social work programmes remains undiminished. The intervening years have also seen us publish another book, which focused upon another one of our passions – social policy (Cunningham and Cunningham, 2012). It was while we were working on the finishing touches to that text that our publisher asked us if we would be interested in writing a second edition of our sociology book, which, of course, we were. The original book was, to our pleasant surprise, more successful than we could have hoped for, receiving favourable reviews from both our academic peers and students. It is, though, the positive reaction from students, both at our own university and elsewhere, which has brought us the most satisfaction. From the outset, we wanted to write a text that would provide an accessible, engaging introduction to the importance of sociology to social work and we hope we were successful in achieving this aim.

Since 2008, much has happened, economically, politically and in the sphere of social work practice and education, which leads us to believe that a second edition is necessary. For example, in 2008 the economic, political and social work landscape was very different to that which prevails today. The book was written in a relatively benign, pre-economic crisis period, when politicians of all political shades seemed committed, albeit to varying degrees, to utilising public expenditure to tackle social problems. Politically, Labour governments had been in power for more than ten years. While the ideological trajectory of some of their initiatives was open to question, Labour governments did devote considerable resources to funding programmes designed to promote 'inclusion' and mitigate economic and social inequality. Labour also sought to enhance the status of the social work profession, through the introduction of an honours degree-level social work qualification and a concerted campaign to increase and improve the levels and quality of recruitment. Meanwhile, back in 2008, David Cameron, the leader of the Conservative Party, was busily detoxifying his party's 'nasty' image, hinting at an ideological shift towards a more 'inclusive', 'compassionate' form of conservatism that genuinely cared about social justice.

Six years on, we are faced with a rather different landscape. The economic crisis which began in 2007/8 ushered in an economic recession, the likes of which had not been seen since the 1930s. Unemployment has soared and real incomes have plummeted, exacerbating the extent and nature of many of the social problems that we discussed in the first edition of this text. In the political sphere, Labour failed to win an overall majority in the 2010 General Election and a Conservative/ Liberal Democrat administration was formed. This Conservative-dominated Coalition immediately committed itself to an unprecedented level of public expenditure cuts, slashing spending on welfare programmes, at a time when social need was at its greatest for decades. The ideological climate has changed too. As unemployment, poverty and exclusion have increased, 'behavioural', 'pathological' interpretations for economic and social problems have re-emerged with a vengeance. Of course, as we showed in the first edition to this book, senior politicians and the media were not averse to blaming individuals and families themselves for the difficulties that befell them in the pre-economic recession era. Indeed, the UK has a long, undistin- guished history of holding vulnerable people morally culpable for their fate, blaming them for the circumstances within which they find themselves. Welfare recipients, in particular, have always been treated with suspicion, accused of being 'irrespon- sible', 'idle' or 'feckless' (see Cunningham and Cunningham, 2012). However, the intensity and ferocity of such accusations have gathered at an unprecedented pace, largely encouraged by senior Coalition Ministers. Hence, since 2010, we have seen little evidence of the kind of 'compassionate conservatism' that was intimated by Cameron when his party was in opposition. Although 'social justice' and even 'compassion' have occasionally been invoked by Coalition Ministers to justify their welfare reforms, their variants of 'social justice' and 'compassion' are tainted with 'moral underclass discourse'. Reducing the incomes of welfare recipients has thus been presented as a 'caring', 'morally invigorating' exercise; it constitutes part of a 'responsibilisation' process that will, ultimately, improve the quality of the lives of those who are temporarily, and 'necessarily' plunged into hardship. Social policy has, therefore, taken a distinct, rightward, neo-liberal twist.

Of course, the social work profession has not been immune to the rightward, ideo- logical shift that has taken place since 2008, and nor have service users themselves. On a practice level, the local authority budget cuts imposed by the Coalition have left local authority social service departments starved of funds. Staffing levels have inevitably suffered, increasing the already heavy pressures social workers face in meeting the needs of service users. At the same time, local authorities have been forced to respond to expenditure reductions by cutting service user provision. Hence, despite a backdrop of growing demand for social care among the over-65s, between 2009/10 and 2012/13, there was a 26 per cent reduction in the number of older people receiving publicly funded support in the community (Ismail et al., 2014). Other services user groups have faced similar reductions in services, a phenomenon that has inevitably impacted negatively on health, psychological and social well-being. Meanwhile, the social work profession has itself been targeted by Coalition Ministers, who have expressed a desire to see the development of a less social science-based, more 'judgemental', skills-focused form of social work education and practice. As we explained in the previous edition, this is not a particularly novel development, but as we show in this updated book, the level of intensity of the criticism the profession has faced is quite unique, as is the apparent determination among Ministers to push through fundamental reforms to social work education. Ironically, this has occurred at a time when the profession itself, in the form of The College of Social Work, has reaffirmed its commitment to embedding an understanding of social justice across all aspects of social work training. As social work academics who are passionate advocates of sociology, we are obviously concerned about future developments and, in part, this new edition seeks to re-emphasise the invaluable contribution sociology makes to the social work curriculum.

Why sociology?

Sociology has been taught in British universities for over 100 years. As well as being delivered as a 'stand-alone', specialist subject, an element of sociological content can be found on the syllabi of numerous degree courses. Sociology also often features strongly on many professional training programmes, including accountancy, teaching, journalism, health professions and, of course, social work. The popularity and influence of sociology to such a wide range of disciplines and professions serves to emphasise its importance and standing as an academic subject in universities. Its attraction stems from its core subject matter. Sociology seeks to provide us with explanations for a broad range of social phenomena and societal trends. Hence, sociological research can provide accountants with indications as to how consumers may react to increases in prices, or variations in tax rates. It can provide teachers with an understanding of why children from deprived backgrounds tend to do less well at school than their better-off counterparts. Sociology can assist in showing journalists how inaccurate media representations of particular social groups can lead to stereotyping and stigmatisation. In addition, it can help health professionals understand why society is characterised by social class variations in life expectancy, health and mortality. We examine the relevance of sociology to social work in greater detail in Chapter 1, but hopefully you can already see the potential of the discipline to help inform the social work curriculum. For example, as we explain in Chapter 2, the lives of many of the service users that we work with are structured by the poverty that they experience. It is, therefore, crucial that we are able to understand some of the complex factors that contribute to poverty, as well as the ways in which it can constrain life chances and opportunities, contributing to the difficulties service users face. Sociology can help inform this understanding, encouraging us to challenge some of the common-sense assumptions that tend to govern thinking around poverty. Social work practice can also be enhanced by gaining an appreciation of the factors that affect educational opportunities. It is useful for social workers to understand why looked-after children do not fare as well in the education system as their non-looked-after peers. Likewise, the fact that children from minority ethnic group backgrounds are far more likely to be excluded from school than white British children is also a trend of concern. These are important issues, and sociology can help us gain an appreciation of the causal factors that shape these trends.

Although the attractions of sociology are more widely acknowledged within social work and academia today, this has not always been the case. For instance, on 22 August 1902, *The Times* published a letter from a correspondent identified only as a 'Sociologist'. The letter lambasted the British educational establishment for its failure to acknowledge the important role the emerging academic discipline of sociology could perform in facilitating an understanding of the social problems that gripped the country at the turn of the twentieth century. This was a time, it should be remembered, when the pioneering poverty surveys of Charles Booth and Seebohm Rowntree were laying bare the depth of urban squalor and poverty, provoking the consciences of Victorian Britain. It was also a time when embryonic social work, under the auspices of the Charity Organisation Society (COS), remained gripped with pathological explanations for social and economic ills. In keeping with the prevailing philosophies of the day, as well as the COS's own moralistic philosophy, students were taught that poverty, squalor and other social and economic evils were a result of the ignorance or inappropriate behaviour of the poor. The author of the letter to *The Times* made reference to the possibility of an alternative approach to comprehending social problems: one based upon a more scientific, sociological understanding of the urban poor's plight. However, he feared England was falling behind other nations in grasping the explanatory potential of sociology. This was, the author felt, particularly unfortunate in the light of overwhelming evidence that social problems were not inevitable or untreatable:

> The time has now arrived when an old school economist who holds to the irremediable character of social evils is looked upon much as would be a physician who should reiterate the view that once prevailed that plagues and pestilences are wholly beyond the reach of human art to arrest, remove or prevent. Those who perceive these deeper truths of society, whatever they may call themselves, are sociologists, and their number and importance are increasing very rapidly.

Quite how readers of *The Times* reacted to the revelation that sociologists were, as a species, on the verge of multiplying enormously in number is not altogether clear. Neither do we know what the response was to a second letter to *The Times*, published on 22 September 1903, which pleaded for its readers to donate £10,000 for the setting up of a school of sociology in London. The reaction, we suspect, was not one of enormous enthusiasm. Nonetheless, a school of sociology, which went under the name the London School of Economics (LSE), was created very soon after. Of course, the LSE has today evolved into a citadel of first-class social science research and teaching, justifiably attracting plaudits from governments and academics around the world. Its days of having to rely for its funding on pleas for cash in national newspapers are long gone. However, things did not initially go particularly smoothly for this embryonic school of sociology. The LSE's first annual report, for example, talked about the need to dispel the fog of indifference that seemed to surround its endeavours. Sociology, the report went on, was not at present popular and the calibre of the students they were attracting was not altogether good. Many of their students were inclined to pessimism and disillusionment, unable to grasp the explanatory potential of sociological research and teaching (*The Times*, 7 December 1904). In fact, their lack of enthusiasm may have resulted from the somewhat underwhelming, uninspiring nature of the early curriculum offered by the school of sociology. As Jones (1983) has shown, in its early incarnation its provision remained tainted with the COS's moralistic philosophies. Students continued to be taught that poverty and destitution resulted from a lack of morality or foresight rather than a lack of material resources. Accordingly, its courses focused upon the benefits of self-help and thrift, while bemoaning the idleness, profligacy and drinking habits of the 'lower orders'.

It was not until the creation of the Department of Social Science and Administration at the LSE in 1912 that a genuinely sociologically informed social work curriculum began to emerge. Clement Attlee, then a social worker, but a future Labour Prime Minister, was one of the Department's early appointments. He, and other formidable appointees, such as RH Tawney and TH Marshall, believed that social work students needed to be provided with a much broader, sociological, political education which, when taught alongside their practical vocational studies, would leave them better equipped to assist the individuals and families they would be working with (Cunningham and Cunningham, 2012). Attlee's 1920 book, *The Social Worker*, represented a passionate manifesto for the development of a more sociologically based form of social work training. The social worker, Attlee (1920, p241) argued, should be a 'social investigator', a 'pioneer', and indeed an *agitator, who has some clear conception of what society he wishes to see produced*. However, attempts to establish sociology as an academic discipline did not always run smoothly. In 1904, the chair of the first meeting of the LSE's Sociological Society, the Liberal MP James Bryce, stated that he believed the subject *had a great and useful future* ahead of it, but bemoaned the lack of interest in the discipline within academia. He argued that *there ought to be chairs and lectureships in sociology in our universities* (*Manchester Guardian*, 1904). It would, though, be a while before sociology would succeed in infiltrating the upper echelons of academia, something that clearly vexed the sociological community at the time. As Dr AJ Carlisle, a member of the Sociological Society stated somewhat bitterly in 1922: *The dreadful word 'sociology', if uttered at Oxford at all, is spoken in a whisper, while 'psychology' is ever mentioned*. Carlisle made these comments at a week-long conference the Society had organised at Oxford University. According to the *Manchester Guardian*, the sociologists received a *cordial and helpful* welcome on arrival, *but Oxford's suspicion and scepticism in reference to sociology was markedly, if jocularly, displayed* throughout the week's proceedings (*Manchester Guardian*, 1922).

These early, passionate defences of the discipline do have something of a contemporary resonance. The difficulties the pioneers of sociology experienced in getting the subject taken seriously sound familiar to us as sociologists today, for although the discipline is now widely accepted in further and higher education, it has always struggled to get itself taken seriously 'out there' in the 'real' world. Indeed, we sociologists have often found ourselves at the butt of what 'we in the trade' regard as unwarranted jokes and humour. By way of example, some of you may remember the British

Telecom 'ology' advert shown in 1988 starring Maureen Lipman as 'Beattie', the doting grandma. She received a phone call from her distraught grandson, who told her that he had failed all his exams. For those of you who did not see the advert, here is an extract from it:

> Beattie (receiving the phone call while baking a cake): *Anthony? Ooh, congratulations on your exam results.*
>
> Anthony (sitting sulking on the bottom of his stairs at home): *Grandma, I failed.*
>
> Beattie (sits down, shocked): *What do you mean, you failed?*
>
> Anthony: *I mean I failed!* (he then goes through all the 'real' academic subjects he has failed)
>
> Beattie: *You didn't pass anything?*
>
> Anthony: *Pottery!* (he says this sulkily)
>
> Beattie (her spirits pick up): *Pottery's very useful... Anthony, people will always need plates! Anything else?*
>
> Anthony: *Sociology!* (he almost spits this out, the tone of his voice illustrating the lack of 'worth' he attaches to the subject).
>
> Beattie (unaware of the 'uselessness' of a sociology qualification): *An 'ology'! He gets an 'ology' and he says he's failed!? You get an 'ology' and you're a scientist!*

The joke, of course, was on poor Beattie, who was daft enough to even think that an 'ology' was a serious subject, and worthy of congratulation. Indeed, in Anthony's eyes sociology came even further down the pecking order than pottery, as evidenced by the fact that he mentioned it last.

As well as having to respond to ridicule, sociology has also been criticised for contributing to moral breakdown and as being a bastion of unhinged, militant, left-wing revolutionaries. In 1969, for example, the Pope blamed sociology for generating moral uncertainty, describing it as socially very dangerous and accusing it of undermining the Catholic faith (*The Times*, 4 December 1969). At the same time, the study of sociology was blamed for encouraging campus riots, anti-Vietnam war protests, and later in the 1970s, it was linked to a propensity to commit terrorist acts. The discipline has been a particular target for conservatives on the 'right' of the political divide, many of whom see it as a destabilising influence. One such commentator, David Marsland, once said that sociology students were *being systematically de-skilled for effective work and trained (by deliberate intent or by default) to be critical saboteurs of Britain as it is, and as most people want it to be* (cited in Bossley, 1987). They were invariably being taught, argued another right-wing commentator, by *an ignorant rabble lost in jargon, fired by doctrine and profoundly hostile to all forms of authority and power* (Scruton, 1985). It is perhaps for this reason that sociology has also been blamed, particularly by right-wing politicians and commentators, for indoctrinating social work students with left-wing dogma and thus 'subverting' the social work curriculum. The following extract is fairly typical in this respect:

Fifty years ago, social workers (whether voluntary or professional) tended to be sensible middle-aged folk who had a certain air of authority ... 'The cruelty man' at the NSPCC as the child welfare officer was colloquially known was ... often a former policeman or a military man who didn't put up with any nonsense ... Then came the Sixties and Seventies. The nature of social work changed ... Out went the experienced former coppers ... In came a generation of well-meaning young sociologists who had studied social scientists ... They believed ... that the old approach to the disadvantaged was dated. They also disapproved of the Sally Army's simple morality about right and wrong. To them, there was no right or wrong way of doing things in a pluralist society ... But this simplistic ideology failed to make allowance for the fact that society contains a minority of sadistic and uncontrolled individuals who require authoritarianism and discipline ... So, out with the textbooks and in with a bit of decent, robust, common sense (Kenny, 2003, p8).

Certainly, sociologists have often been motivated as much by a desire to change society as they have to explain it, and in this sense they are often driven by passion and a clear sense of purpose. Karl Marx, one of the 'founding fathers' of sociology, was deeply moved by the exploitation and endemic poverty suffered by the working classes in the nineteenth century, and in his work he sought to set out the path towards a society that would be free of social and economic ills. Many sociologists since, while not necessarily subscribing to Marx's ideas, have been influenced by a similar desire to initiate progressive change. It is perhaps this that often leads to charges of political bias and subjectivity. However, as you will see as you work your way through this text, there is no one 'truth', or 'correct' explanation for social and economic problems. There are different, competing interpretations and there are as many influential sociologists of the 'right' as there are of the 'left'. Rather than this being a handicap, for us as teachers of sociology this is one of the subject's most endearing features. Helping students negotiate these different explanations for social phenomena, watching them grapple with interpretations of social problems with which they were previously unfamiliar, and seeing them challenge their preconceived views is fascinating and rewarding. Indeed, while writing both editions of this book, we have revisited our own first encounters with sociology. Although we discovered the discipline at different periods in our lives, its impact and influence upon both of us was the same. Sociology opened up a new outlook on the world for us, challenging taken-for-granted assumptions that we had held for years, and providing interpretations of social phenomena that helped us situate our viewpoints and experiences.

Most of all, though, our passion for sociology stems from the fact that it offers insights into and explanations for the problems that social workers have to deal with on a day-to-day basis. Surely, as professionals who are positioned at the 'front line' of efforts to deal with poverty, social exclusion, educational disadvantage, unemployment, youth offending, community breakdown and other social ills, there is a compelling case for us to take an interest in attempts to explain these phenomena. Of course, that is not to say that sociology can find all the answers to all the social problems and issues that we discuss in this book. At the very least, though, we hope that it can inform your understanding of the issues and help you develop a sociological imagination which can in turn help shape your practice. As social workers, you will be working with vulnerable, marginalised individuals and groups of people, and we feel that it is crucial that you can see beyond crude, inaccurate and stereotypical representations, which fail to acknowledge what are often the social causes of oppression.

The book has been carefully mapped to the Professional Capabilities Framework for Social Workers in England and will help you to develop the appropriate standards at the right level. These standards are:

- **Professionalism**

  Identify and behave as a professional social worker, committed to professional development.

- **Values and ethics**

  Apply social work ethical principles and values to guide professional practice.

- **Diversity**

  Recognise diversity and apply anti-discriminatory and anti-oppressive principles in practice.

- **Rights, justice and economic wellbeing**

  Advance human rights and promote social justice and economic wellbeing.

- **Knowledge**

  Apply knowledge of social sciences, law and social work practice theory.

- **Critical reflection and analysis**

  Apply critical reflection and analysis to inform and provide a rationale for professional decision-making.

- **Intervention and skills**

  Use judgement and authority to intervene with individuals, families and communities to promote independence, provide support and prevent harm, neglect and abuse.

- **Contexts and organisations**

  Engage with, inform, and adapt to changing contexts that shape practice. Operate effectively within your own organisational frameworks and contribute to the development of services and organisations. Operate effectively within multi-agency and inter-professional settings.

- **Professional leadership**

  Take responsibility for the professional learning and development of others through supervision, mentoring, assessing, research, teaching, leadership and management.

  References to these standards will be made throughout the text and you will find a diagram of the Professional Capability Framework in an Appendix on page 263.

Chapter 1 of the book begins by explaining the relevance of sociology to social work. As well as drawing your attention to the structures and influences that shape people's experiences and life chances (such as social class, socialisation, education, gender, race and religion), we introduce you to a range of core perspectives that sociologists use to explain society, including functionalism, Marxism, symbolic interactionism and postmodernism.

Chapter 2 moves on to examine the extent and nature of poverty in the UK. As we will show, social work service users are among the most impoverished people and for many of them poverty defines their lives. Here we examine the extent of poverty, and explanations that have been advanced to account for it. We also assess the role of social work in relation to poverty.

Chapter 3 focuses on the concept of social exclusion and its relevance to social work. The chapter considers the evolution of the concept and looks at its influence on policy debates in the UK. It goes on to assess different interpretations of social exclusion and examines the relative influence of each of these on recent policy and practice.

The family is one of the core institutions in society and it is often the site of social work interventions. In addition, the family, or more accurately family breakdown, has been popularly portrayed as the cause of a range of social ills. Chapter 4 examines these claims by looking at recent trends in family life and assessing different sociological and feminist perspectives on the family. In addition, it considers the possibilities for developing a feminist approach to social work practice.

Like 'the family', the 'community' often figures prominently in debates about social problems, welfare and social work. Chapter 5 examines sociological perspectives on community. It looks at different definitions of 'community' and assesses the implications of each for social work practice. The chapter also considers the assumptions underpinning recent initiatives that have been geared towards restoring 'community' in deprived areas.

The problems faced by many groups of social work service users can sometimes be compounded by the marginalisation and stigma that result from inaccurate, exaggerated levels of concern surrounding the 'threat' they are said to pose. Chapter 6 looks at the sociological concept of moral panics, assessing its potential for helping us to explain the exaggerated levels of concern that sometimes surround certain social groups and problems. We examine how moral panics can emerge and the functions that they have been said to perform.

It is widely acknowledged that there is a link between educational attainment and future life chances. However, children's experiences of compulsory education in the UK differ. Some groups of children, for example, are more likely to be excluded from school than others. In addition, not all children are afforded the same levels of educational opportunity. Chapter 7 provides compelling evidence of educational inequality and examines the different sociological explanations that have been advanced to account for it.

Chapter 8 is a new chapter that focuses upon social class and, importantly, the demonisation of sections of the working class. We examine the differential impact that social class has on life chances and consider why it is important for social workers to have an awareness of social class.

The book concludes with an overview of the role of sociology in social work training. As we will show, historically, the inclusion of sociology as a core subject on the social work curriculum has been contested. However, we are firmly convinced of the need for a sociological perspective in social work training, and we end the book with a plea – that you, as future social workers, seek to understand the environmental and structural factors that underpin and shape the lives of the service users you work with. Only then will you be able to move beyond a narrow 'blaming' perspective, and gain a fuller, holistic understanding of the wider structural factors that constrain experiences and opportunities.

Chapter 1

Developing a sociological imagination: Debunking society

A C H I E V I N G   A   S O C I A L   W O R K   D E G R E E

This chapter will help you to develop the following capabilities from the **Professional Capabilities Framework:**

- **Professionalism**
  Demonstrate ability to learn using a range of approaches.

- **Knowledge**
  Demonstrate an initial understanding of the application of research, theory and knowledge from sociology, social policy, psychology, health and human growth and development to social work.

- **Rights, justice and economic wellbeing**
  Understand the principles of rights, justice and economic wellbeing, and their significance for social work practice.

It will also introduce you to the following standards as set out in the 2008 social work subject benchmark statement:

5.1.1 Social work service, service users and carers.
5.1.4 Social work theory.

Introduction

This chapter encourages you to understand the concept of the sociological imagination in relation to your own lives and those of social work service users. As both the Health and Care Professions Council (HCPC) Standards of Proficiency for Social Work, and The College of Social Work (TCSW) Professional Capabilities Framework suggest, social workers need to understand how knowledge from sociology and other disciplines can help us make sense of social work practice. The importance of this cannot be over-emphasised – social work is a profession and, as such, it must be informed by a coherent knowledge base. The discipline of sociology has much to contribute to the social work profession because it provides theories which challenge the 'taken for granted' assumptions that may underpin common sense. This is important for social workers who are required to critically reflect upon their practice to ensure that it is ethically informed, takes account of equality and diversity and contributes to the pursuit of social justice. This chapter introduces the core sociological concepts of 'structure' and 'agency' and examines their relevance to social work. It goes on to introduce theories of Marxism, Functionalism, Symbolic Interactionism and Postmodernism and suggests ways in which they can assist social workers to understand the world in which they live and work. A range of practice examples and exercises will be used to encourage you to 'debunk society' and question common sense assumptions, which may lead to oppressive and pathologising practice if they are left unchallenged.

The sociological imagination

Arguably, learning to think sociologically is one of the most important skills social workers can bring to their practice. A sociological perspective encourages social workers to critically unpack taken for granted assumptions about social life, enabling them to develop skills which allow them to link issues occurring in the lives of service users to an understanding of the 'bigger picture', or broader underpinning context. This is imperative if social workers are to avoid falling into the trap of inappropriately *blaming* service users for the circumstances they find themselves in. By adopting a 'sociological imagination', social workers are assisted to understand the social basis of many issues that face service users in the context of a society that is fundamentally unequal and unjust. Social workers have a professional and ethical responsibility to promote social justice and this can only be achieved by working for change on a structural level as well as on an individual level. This does not abdicate service users from a sense of personal responsibility. We are not suggesting that child abuse, for example, is acceptable or is somehow the responsibility of some mysterious social structure. Rather, the message is that thinking sociologically allows social workers to resist the temptation to pathologise or blame individuals for circumstances that may be beyond their control. It is imperative that social workers understand how the social conditions in which some people live can contribute to many of the issues that they face. Baldwin puts this rather well when he states:

> A practice based on social justice will ... shift the basis for such practice from individual pathology to the pathology of social systems. An understanding that recognises that some behaviour is logical within pathological social systems is much less likely to result in stigmatising and scapegoating approaches to individuals, and families within their communities.

> (Baldwin, cited in Lavalette, 2011, p201)

Consequently, throughout this book, we urge social work students to develop and hone a sociological imagination and ensure that their practice is based upon an unequivocal commitment to the pursuit of social justice and social work values.

The term 'sociological imagination' was coined by the flamboyant American sociologist C. Wright Mills to refer to the ability to link what happens in individuals' lives, to the social structures of the wider world. He talked about how the 'private troubles of men' effectively trapped them in their lives, as they were only able to understand their *immediate personal difficulties* rather than understanding what was happening to them with reference to the histories in which they lived.

> *It is the idea that the individual can understand his own experience and gauge his own fate only by locating himself within his period, that he can know his own chances in life only by becoming aware of those of all individuals in his circumstances.*

(Mills, 1959, p12)

It is worth noting that Mills wrote at a time when language tended to be rather sexist. As you will see, Mills talks about 'men' although he is in fact referring to all human beings. He stresses the importance of understanding individual issues with reference to the experiences of others in the same social group. For example, rather than conceptualising in individual terms the specific experiences of someone who is experiencing periods of low mood and depression after they were made redundant, Mills suggests that in order to gain a fuller understanding, we should locate that person's experiences within a broader awareness of the social, economic and historical circumstances of the day. So, rather than focusing solely upon the person's depression and failure to cope, attention might also turn to wider issues such as the causes and consequences of unemployment. This may seem contrary to other teachings in social work which generally tend to begin from the fundamental assumption that social workers should treat all people as individuals. We need to take care here, as one position does not necessarily exclude the other. Clearly, it is extremely important that social workers do indeed relate to service users individually and recognise that everybody's circumstances and experiences are different. However, while ensuring that we are respecting individuals and taking time to understand each person's very particular circumstances, it is also important, as Mills suggested, for social workers to locate service users within an understanding of the *bigger picture*. In other words, social workers need to use their sociological imagination to situate individuals within analyses of broader social structures and to comprehend the social processes which shape their lives.

If we draw upon our sociological imagination then, 'personal troubles' become reconfigured as 'public issues':

> *It is by means of the sociological imagination that men now hope to grasp what is going on in the world and to understand what is happening in themselves.*

(Mills, 1959, p14)

You may have come across a similar idea from feminist writings, where the phrase 'the personal is political' is used to explain how the individual experiences of women's oppression are rooted in the structures, legislation, culture and economics of centuries of patriarchy, or male domination. Whether you agree with this position or not, the point to understand here is that although the troubles of individuals are inherently personal and unique, they occur within a specific set of political, social and economic circumstances which shape and to some extent define the lives of individuals. Sociologists disagree on the extent to which society defines or constrains the lives of individuals and we will give more consideration to this debate later in this chapter. For now, however, we wish to turn our attention to thinking sociologically and developing a sociological imagination. Peter Berger (1963) suggests that sociology enables us to *see the general in the particular:* in other words, thinking about how the *general* categories into which we fall, (for example, white, female, working class) shape our *particular* life experiences. Berger makes the case for deconstructing or debunking 'the familiar' in order to see the world differently.

ACTIVITY **1.1**

Debunking society

You should do this exercise individually and then discuss some of the issues raised, in small groups. Thinking about Berger's view that sociology helps us to see how the 'general' shapes the 'particular', spend some time debunking the particular of your life from a sociological perspective. As a student who has recently started a social work degree, think about what 'general' factors led to you commence social work training. How did some or all of the factors listed below influence, help, or hinder you?

- *The social class you were born into.*
- *Area of living/neighbourhood.*
- *Culture.*
- *Socialisation/norms/values.*
- *School – including the school you went to, messages from teachers, peer groups, streaming/ ability groups.*
- *Language.*
- *Gender.*
- *Ethnicity.*
- *Religion.*
- *Ability and disability.*
- *Family.*
- *Economy.*
- *Politics/policy.*
- *Groups and interaction.*

By doing this exercise, you will have hopefully had the opportunity to really think about the 'taken for granted' of your life. Very often, the factors that make up our individual biographies are unquestioned by us, as these become the 'facts of our lives', the things we take for granted. Studying sociology can often have the effect of illuminating our lives in ways that perhaps we have not thought of before. It enables us to ask *why?* Once you have started to develop a sociological imagination, you will probably find yourself becoming passionate about the subject and wanting to learn more and more. As Berger (1963) suggests, *sociology is ... a passion. The sociological perspective is more like a demon that possesses one, that drives one compellingly, again and again, to the questions that are its own* (p36).

Once you have begun to challenge the familiar of your own life and see beyond the immediate reality that presents itself, you will begin to recognise and understand some of the factors that have shaped or constrained your path through life so far. It is not uncommon for students in our sociology classes who have returned to education after an unhappy time at school, to tell us that they have gone through their lives without really questioning what they have been told about their own academic ability. Once they have begun to deconstruct their lives more, they have been able to recognise how factors such as their social class, ethnicity, gender or other 'general' categories have significantly impacted upon their particular experiences. Perhaps this is true for you too. Possibly by the time you come to the end of the sociology module on your course, you will feel as though you are looking at your own life in a very different way, almost as if someone had turned the light on for you! You may be wondering why we have asked you to spend so much time thinking about your own lives so far, rather than using examples of service users. Mills is helpful here when he makes the point that those who think sociologically should not split their work from their lives, and implores that they use their life experience in their intellectual work. Understanding our own biographies in sociological terms then, equips us to more effectively comprehend the lives of those we work with.

Structure and agency

Sociologists are interested in looking at the patterns, processes and structures of social life, and the relationship between these and members of society. One of the most exciting, yet most daunting aspects of sociology for those who are new to it is that there are many different ways of looking at the world sociologically. Later in this chapter, we will introduce you to different sociological perspectives and consider some of the issues relevant to these. One core issue of debate for sociologists is to analyse the extent to which society shapes and controls what individuals do, versus the extent to which human beings are the architects of their own lives. This is referred to as the structure/agency debate. At its simplest, this considers whether it is the entity *Society* that determines, influences and constrains individuals over and above all other factors, or whether *Individuals* create and shape their own destiny by making choices, decisions and taking action in order to affect their own unique path through life.

Structural perspectives are those that adopt a macro level of analysis to emphasise the significant influence of Society in individuals' lives. In other words, although we go about our lives in various ways, structural sociologists argue that the underpinning structures or formations in society ultimately shape and constrain individuals. Peter Berger (1963) uses the analogy of society being like a great puppet theatre, with individuals merely conforming to a pre-written script, *the structures of society become the structures of our own consciousness... Society penetrates us as much as it envelops us* (p140). Berger here is suggesting that individuals are so shaped by factors such as gender, social class, ethnicity and the structures and formations that are embedded within organisations in society, that over time these things become part of our everyday thinking – they become our unquestionable normality and part of the fabric of our lives.

So, although we might make an individual decision to become a student on a social work course, or buy a large house, or stay at home to look after our children, structural sociologists purport that these 'individual' decisions are in fact *constrained* decisions that are ultimately shaped by factors such as class, gender and ethnicity, and that our decisions are actually a product of Society shaping our identity and consciousness, controlling the strings of the puppets in the great societal puppet theatre.

Agency perspectives, on the other hand, emphasise the free will of the individual to act upon their environment, to interpret their reality, make decisions and choose their own paths throughout life. Agency perspectives adopt a micro view of the world; therefore they are interested in individual experiences rather than in viewing society as a total entity that somehow has the ability to shape people's lives. Berger returns to his analogy of the puppet theatre to explain this:

> *We locate ourselves in society and thus recognise our own position as we hang from its subtle strings. For a moment, we see ourselves as puppets indeed. But then we grasp a decisive difference between the puppet theatre and our own drama. Unlike the puppets, we have the possibility of stopping in our movements, looking up and perceiving the machinery by which we have been moved.*

(p198)

The suggestion here is that individuals are able to act upon society and transform it. Rather than being puppets that unwittingly conform to a pre-written script, individuals are themselves involved in consciously writing their own script as they create and recreate society each and every moment of the day.

The structure/agency debate concerns not only the importance attributed to the respective influence of individuals and society, but also influences the ways in which sociologists go about their business. Sociologists who engage in a structural level of debate do not focus upon the small-scale experiences of individuals, rather they are interested in learning quantitatively about patterns, structures and formations in society, whereas sociologists who prioritise agency are very much concerned qualitatively with the experiences of individuals.

Sociological perspectives

Macro approaches

There are a number of different ways of thinking about society and the way in which it operates. We have already identified the structure/agency debate and the core difference between the two positions. It is now important to refine this further as we approach some of the main sociological perspectives. Structural approaches then, refer to sociological perspectives which examine society as a whole and regard the organisation and structure of society as determining, or at least greatly influencing, the lives of individuals. Within this broad approach, however, there are two very distinct ways of conceptualising the world; these are perspectives based upon either consensus or conflict.

Consensus perspectives begin from the assumption that there is general agreement between members of society, who live together in co-operation with others. To this end, members of society have a strong sense of shared social values, which enables there to be order and stability in social life.

Conflict theories on the other hand, believe that there are vast inequalities of power within society that significantly determine life chances. Society comprises different groups, which are essentially in conflict with one another.

Consensus theory: introducing functionalism

Perhaps the best place to begin when getting to grips with understanding functionalism is to borrow a well-rehearsed analogy from biology. Just as biologists understand the ways in which different bodily organs such as the heart, brain, kidneys, lungs and so on, perform a specific function to keep the human body alive, functionalists suggest the same is true with society. Its different components work in harmony with one common end, the survival and well-being of the whole. Social institutions such as the family, religion, education, the political system, the economy and the legal system exist because they perform important tasks which contribute to the maintenance and well-being of society. According to Auguste Comte (1798–1857) who is largely credited with originating of the term 'sociology' in 1839 and who influenced the development of the functionalist perspective, society is a system of interrelated parts each of which relies upon other parts (or sub-systems) for efficient functioning. For example, the education system is dependent upon the family to produce effectively socialised children who understand the early rules of school; the economy relies upon the education system to produce suitably educated and trained individuals to perform certain tasks so that jobs are filled by appropriately skilled workers; the family depends upon the economy to enable it to earn a livelihood to support family members, and so on.

Just as the main aim of the human body is to stay alive, survival is also the key goal of society. Talcott Parsons (1951) used the term 'social equilibrium' to describe the ways in which healthy societies work to attain a state of harmony or balance. Whenever there is change in one sub-system, this is usually matched by changes in another. One example of this can be found in the societal response to changing attitudes towards gay and lesbian relationships. As late as 1967 homosexuality was illegal in Britain, however, over time archaic views towards gay and lesbian relationships have inevitably had to shift. This has been reflected in changes to social institutions (or sub-systems) such as the legal system which now acknowledges the legal basis of same sex relationships; some religious institutions which now permit gay marriage; the family which may now consist of same sex couples; and the education system which no longer prohibits any discussion of same sex relationships. From a functionalist perspective this gradual process of social change, though not without controversy, has resulted in social equilibrium being restored.

Parsons was influenced by Emile Durkheim (1858–1917), who argued that social order is crucial for any society to exist. Central to this is the existence of shared values, or value consensus, without which individuals would pursue their own interests and chaos would ensue (Durkheim, 1972).

ACTIVITY 1.2

Pause for a minute to think about social order. We tend to take this for granted, only perhaps recognising its existence when things go wrong and stability is disrupted. Try to write down three examples of instances where social order has been disrupted, either locally, nationally or internationally, and think about the consequences. What happened? What was the effect of the disruption? How were things brought under control again?

You may have come up with examples such as the situation in Iraq following the displacement of Saddam Hussein in 2003; or protests in the UK against the introduction of student tuition fees. More recently, you may recall vivid pictures on the TV and in newspapers of the riots that spread across Britain in the summer of 2011, where the nation watched as tall, majestic buildings burnt to the ground and prolific looting occurred in central London, Manchester and other towns and cities across the UK. If we think about the first example in Iraq, images of violence and confusion come to mind. Looting was commonplace as it was unclear who, if anyone, held authority, as the scenes on television depicted chaos and near anarchy. In his day, Durkheim used the term *anomie* to refer to a state where the norms governing social behaviour had broken down, as was the case in Iraq in 2003.

Durkheim made the assumption that for any group to live co-operatively, social order was essential. There also needed to be common agreement among group members upon how to behave towards each other, and consensus about what their priorities should be. Durkheim referred to this as the 'collective conscience'. He suggested that members of society normally co-operated with one another in order to pursue shared goals. Durkheim noted some differences, however, between pre-industrial and industrial society. In primitive society people worked together on the land producing what they needed to subsist. Durkheim believed that a collective conscience emerged out of tradition, morality, shared beliefs and values that largely developed from people sharing similar lives and roles within communities. He called this 'mechanical solidarity'. However, he intimated that as industrial society developed and became more complex, mechanical solidarity would inevitably break down and a new social order would develop. Over time, Durkheim suggested that as working processes became more complex, individuals began to work away from the home and became involved in more specialised tasks and roles. Consequently individuals were dependent upon one another, because nobody could produce everything they needed in order to survive in modern society. Durkheim suggested that such interdependence generated what he termed 'organic solidarity', where bonds were based upon differences and co-dependence, rather than upon similarity and co-existence. Despite the fact that society is more complex and fragmented than in pre-industrial times, Durkheim argued that a strong sense of commonality and shared values remained, constituting the collective conscience that is fundamental to the survival and smooth running of society.

The collective conscience both constrains and obliges individuals to act in certain ways. The shared understandings that emerge unite members of society in a unified whole and enable them to live co-operatively. Hence it is useful to think of the collective conscience as being rather like a 'social glue' that binds members of society together. According to the functionalist perspective, all social relationships are structured and underpinned by the shared norms and values which are transmitted from one generation to the next via the socialisation process.

ACTIVITY 1.3

Try to list as many examples as you can of factors that might constitute the 'collective conscience' or 'social glue' in contemporary society. In other words, what shared values exist?

You may have identified examples such as the value of human life; being safe; law and order; loyalty and faithfulness; valuing people's rights to their property; and so on. Depending upon your religious beliefs, you may identify some of these values as being present in religious teachings. In summary, shared norms and values perform a powerful social cohesion function for members of society, acting as a form of social control by perpetuating norms which are designed to curb certain behaviours. This is central in understanding functionalist thinking.

Functionalists do recognise that conflict can occur within society; however, they see it as being the result of temporary disturbances or 'blips' in the system, which are usually quickly corrected. A relatively recent example of such a disturbance would be the riots of summer 2011 that we mentioned earlier. Sociologists from this perspective might view the riots as being a temporary but nonetheless threatening phenomenon. Hence it was clear to see how social institutions including the media, politicians, government, forces of law and order quickly acted to restore equilibrium and reinforce the collective conscience. Functionalists accept that differences of interest exist but see the bigger picture as being one where shared values overwhelmingly predominate. They contend that all groups benefit if society runs smoothly. Furthermore, if people step out of line, society needs to have adequate means of ensuring that anti-social behaviour is dealt with and conformity re-established. This is important for the 'greater good' and for the equilibrium in society to be maintained.

Functionalism is often criticised for being deterministic in that it denies the existence of free will and choice, preferring to regard individuals as passive recipients of whatever the 'system' serves them. This is contested by social action theorists who, as we shall see later, reject the deterministic stance of structural theories, and contest the idea that systems possess qualities which can act upon individuals, preferring to see individuals as architects of their own lives. Additionally, functionalism has been criticised for its basic belief that shared values exist in society. As we shall see later in this chapter, Marxists argue that shared values are in fact bourgeois values that serve the interests of the ruling class rather than everyone in society. Furthermore, some critics maintain that contemporary Britain is a diverse society in which different values coexist.

A functionalist perspective of social work
For functionalists, the social work profession is one of the sub-systems of society that fulfils certain functions and plays an important role in maintaining the whole. Martin Davies (1994) uses the analogy of social workers being like motor mechanics who

perform an important role in the maintenance of society, and are pivotal in assisting marginalised individuals to be better integrated. The emphasis is upon *assisting service users to adjust* by educating them, helping them to change and supporting them to fit into mainstream society more effectively. The social worker is performing a useful role, to all intents and purposes smoothing over the rough edges around the periphery of society. Drawing upon the work of Parsons, social workers can be regarded as assisting those who have been 'incorrectly socialised' to fit back into society, so that they can engage in effective role performance. Individuals who are mentally ill, for example, need help to get better so that they can play a full role in society. Social work from this point of view should be actively involved in curbing deviant behaviour and thereby contributing to the smooth running and successful functioning of the social system. Similarly, parents who fall short of 'good-enough parenting' should be assisted to perform the parenting role more effectively; their children who have experienced 'faulty socialisation' should be helped to relearn the norms and values of mainstream society in order to become good citizens of the future. The Coalition government's 'Troubled Families' initiative, which we examine in greater detail in Chapter 3, is an example of an approach which is, arguably, informed by such a perspective.

Clearly, this view is open to much criticism as it effectively locates the source of all problems as being quite firmly with the individual, requiring him or her to change in order to be a fully functioning part of society, rather than seeing the system as being in any way culpable. However, it could be argued that much state-sponsored social work is premised upon the principle of assisting service users to fit into society, while those who do not are subject to the more coercive social control functions of the social work role. This can be seen particularly in the fields of mental health, childcare and youth justice, where social workers are empowered to implement legislation which curtails and controls individual 'dysfunctions'.

CASE STUDY

Paul is a 25-year-old man who works in a packing factory. He works long hours, mostly on night shifts, doing work that he finds largely unfulfilling, for which he gets paid the minimum wage. He has had a great deal of time off sick recently due to being depressed and feeling anxious. Paul's poor mental health began 12 months ago following the death of his parents in a car crash and the subsequent break-up of his relationship six months afterwards. Paul's wife was pregnant when his parents were killed, but after their death, Paul wanted nothing more to do with her or the baby. It was just too painful; he did not want to know the child if his parents could not know their grandchild. Since the break-up, however, Paul has felt unable to cope and has been very confused. Recently he has been wandering through town late at night muttering to himself. Last night, he was picked up by the police who found him on a high bridge in a distressed state. He was taken to the local hospital and agreed to be admitted as a voluntary patient.

Adopting a functionalist perspective, think about how Paul's circumstances might be considered. What would be the role of the social worker?

A functionalist analysis to this case would consider that Paul's behaviour is somewhat deviant, because it is preventing him from participating in society. He is unable to fulfil his designated social roles, of worker, father or husband. Paul's illness is costing society, both in terms of the health care he requires and because he is not contributing to the upbringing of his newborn baby. A functionalist perspective would suggest that Paul must be taken care of by society in order to bring him back into the parameters of normality. The social worker would therefore have a responsibility, along with health care professionals, to help Paul become well again. Effective intervention would hopefully assist Paul to work through his loss and become reintegrated into society. It is hoped that he would return to work, possibly reunite with his wife and baby, or at least contribute to their lives financially.

Although this is a slightly exaggerated analysis, you will hopefully be able to understand how a functionalist perspective regards individuals who deviate from socially agreed norms, and understand how social work is regarded as being a key component part of society and performs an important function for the well-being of the whole.

Conflict theories: introducing Marxism

In contrast to the above, conflict theories regard society as being characterised not by harmony and consensus, but by conflict. It is considered that conflict is a common and persistent feature in society, with some groups having clear and distinct advantages and power over others. Although there are a number of views encapsulated within this perspective, the best known and most influential is Marxism.

The work of Karl Marx (1818–83) has been immensely significant in shaping social theory. Marx was a German political activist who dedicated his life to writing about the social class system and the endemic inequalities that permeated the lives of ordinary working people. He lived during a time when capitalism was beginning to emerge on a global scale. Marx was deeply uncomfortable with what he saw on a daily basis: people whose lives were blighted by poverty and despair, coexisting with those whose lives were characterised by opulent riches and affluence. Marx was very concerned by the conditions of the poor and believed there could be a fairer, more equal form of society (Wheen, 2000).

Marx and social change

Marx was interested in how societies developed and evolved. He noted that in primitive societies members of society coexisted, sharing the production of food and material goods. There was no private property and no one owned the 'means of production'; rather, hunters and gatherers sourced from nature what they needed to sustain life in a truly 'classless society' (Marx and Engels, 1969). As time moved on, however, society began to produce more goods than were needed to survive and so people began trading with one another. Production gradually became more specialised and a division of labour

(Continued)

(Continued)

began to emerge; rather than families producing everything themselves that they required for survival, they could trade with others to ensure they had everything they needed. This meant that some people were able to achieve a surplus of wealth or a profit.

The ownership of private property gradually began to emerge and there was a need to secure clear lines of heritage through the emergence of the modern family so that property and wealth could be securely passed on. Over time, a class of successful owners of the means of production became economically and socially distinct from ordinary working people.

Famously, Marx and Engels wrote: The history of all hitherto existing society is the history of class struggles *(1969, p40). Marx suggested that in order to understand any period in history, it was necessary to understand the antagonism between oppressing and oppressed classes and the ongoing struggle between them. Simply put, Marx believed that inequalities in wealth necessarily generated tensions which ultimately led to conflict, and that this eventually brought about social change. This was true of both ancient society where the struggle was between masters and slaves, and feudal society where the struggle was between lords and serfs. Much of Marx's work, however, was dedicated to analysis of capitalist society, the form of economic and social system that we live in today, where the struggle is between the bourgeoisie (or ruling class) and the proletariat (or working class).*

Marx argued that capitalist society was an inherently unequal system that was defined by the infrastructure of the economy (or the 'base' of society). Like consensus perspectives, Marx also regarded society as comprising interrelated parts, but the key difference was that Marx asserted that it was the economy (or the 'base') that strongly shaped all other components. In other words, the ways in which material goods were produced significantly influenced the rest of society. In capitalism, the economy is based around ownership of private property and it is this arrangement that, according to Marx, determines the operation of all other social institutions such as the political system, religion, the media, the family, the education system and so on. Marx referred to these components as the superstructure.

ACTIVITY 1.4

Sometimes students tell us they find it difficult to understand Marx's concepts. However, if we take some time out to unpack some of his ideas, you will see that they are in many ways relevant to our own lives today. This activity is designed to help you begin to understand for yourself some of the concepts and terms used.

In simple terms, capitalism can be defined as a form of economic system in which there is private ownership of the means of production, or industry.

Try to think of some of the major corporations that exist today that employ workers in return for a wage. In order to help you compile your list you might want to think about any soft drinks companies that you have bought a can from this week; any fast food place you have been to; the chocolate bars you have eaten; the fashion designers you buy your clothes from; the make of your MP3 player; the designer of your computer system or mobile phone and so on.

You will often hear on the news when companies announce their profits. Alternatively have a look on the internet. What levels of profits do they make? How do you think they generate their profits?

How are you influenced by capitalism? You may wish to think of the way in which the advertising industry influences us to buy things, or you may wish to have a look through any glossy magazine lying around and see how cars, fashion and music are portrayed. What are the subtle and not so subtle means by which we as consumers contribute to the profits of large corporations?

By doing this exercise you will have hopefully begun to demystify some of Marx's ideas. You will probably have begun to recognise that society today is organised in such a way that some very wealthy people own large, multinational corporations that make significant amounts of money each year, and that they do this by using many persuasive techniques to encourage us to buy their products. The pursuit of profit is key and there are many examples where this has taken precedence over more ethical concerns. You may recall for example a large well-known coffee company in 2012 using loopholes to avoid paying the correct amount of tax. This company effectively increased their own profits, thereby withholding money that would have otherwise gone to the government to pay for public services for the benefit of all. There have been many other examples where the profit motive has predominated over public interest. Notably, a well-known clothing company launched an investigation in 2010 after it was discovered that its products were manufactured using child labour. The production process had been outsourced to countries where regulation is poor and labour cheap. In the 12 months prior to writing the book, the electronics giants Samsung, Apple and Nintendo, the clothing retailer H&M and the chocolate corporation Nestlé were all implicated in child labour scandals (Cunningham and Lavalette, 2014). While writing this second edition, our newspapers and TV channels were full of stories about horsemeat being found in processed foods in Britain. A Marxist analysis of this would focus upon the corporate crime being committed here, whereby consumers are exploited in the ruthless pursuit of profit, as producers have substituted a more expensive product (beef or lamb) with the significantly cheaper product of horse. Importantly, the manufacturers that failed to label their products accurately as containing horsemeat were actively concealing this in order to maximise their profit. It is debatable the extent to which High Street retailers were aware of this; however, by failing to check and secure the source of their produce, arguably they were complicit in the duping and mass exploitation of their consumers.

Now we will carry on to begin to understand more of Marx's ideas. Marx identified two main groups in capitalist society; the bourgeoisie, who owned the means of production (in the present day these are wealthy individuals such as the Richard Bransons or Bill Gates of the world), and the proletariat or workers, who sell their labour to the bourgeoisie in return for a wage. An important point to understand is that the wage paid to the proletariat or workers is far less than the profit generated by them. In other words, although it is the workers that through their own hard effort, blood, sweat and tears physically produce goods such as aeroplanes, cars, clothes, food, and so on, the wages they are paid in return are relatively low when compared with the amount of money the goods are sold for, thereby generating a healthy profit or 'surplus value' for the capitalist class. Thus, importantly, Marx argued that an exploitative relationship occurs, with the bourgeoisie exploiting the proletariat.

Marx noted, however, that the workers accepted this situation unquestioningly most of the time, and that this was due to a number of complex reasons. Essentially, he argued, the proletariat have been socialised to believe that this is the 'way of the world' – that the bourgeoisie are rightfully in their privileged positions because they have worked hard to get there, they are naturally bright, good leaders and deservedly high status, powerful and well-paid businessmen and women. Similarly, workers are socialised to believe that they are also in their rightful positions. This may have occurred through the education system where powerful messages are perpetuated around ability, or it may have occurred through religious belief systems, which tend to portray inequality as being the will of a supreme being. Some of you will be familiar for example with the words of the well-known hymn 'All things bright and beautiful' which go like this: *The rich man in his castle, the poor man at his gate,* God made them high and lowly *and ordered their estate* [our emphasis]. You can see here how the message is transmitted that God has created some of us privileged and others of us not. Another means by which the bourgeoisie 'manufacture consent' is by seeking to foster divisions within the proletariat. As we show in later chapters, attempts have undoubtedly been made to stigmatise and demonise certain sections of the working class in a way that leads them to turn against each other, mitigating against collective oppositional action. Marx uses the term 'false class consciousness' to describe the way that the proletariat are subtly coerced to accept the *status quo* and are unaware of their true class position.

Furthermore, Marx argued that norms and values, which form the backbone of society and are promoted by its key institutions, are in fact, ruling-class norms and values. Marxists are critical here of functionalist thinking which regards shared norms and values as being applicable to all members of society; by contrast, Marx argues that in fact such values actually serve to maintain and perpetuate the unequal social system. Marxists refer to the set of beliefs and ideas which prop up the system as 'ideologies'. In Britain and America, for example, there is an emphasis on material possessions, freedom and working hard. These values are extended to all members of society in subtle ways through the media, the education system, the family and other components of the superstructure. Marx argues that such values contribute to the dominance of the bourgeoisie or ruling class, as they subtly ensure that the proletariat continue to work hard for their wages, to buy as many material goods as they can afford in the belief that they are living free and privileged lives. In reality, however, their hard work directly creates profit for the wealthy owners of the means of production, ensuring that they get richer, while the workers buy back the material goods that they in the first place have created. They do this under the belief that they are free, yet in reality they are slaves of the ruling class.

Marx developed the important concept of *alienation* to describe the way in which advanced productive processes in capitalism isolate workers both from their labour and from their true selves. Marx argued that in capitalist society, technology had replaced human beings in most aspects of production, such that workers were effectively machine operatives rather than skilled craftsmen and women. Marx suggested that this changed the very nature of work from being creative and fulfilling to being largely dull and monotonous. Workers on assembly lines were separated entirely from the end product of their labour and were likely to be entirely unfulfilled by their role in the process. Importantly, they were also separated from each other by the noise and speed of the production line. Thus Marx argued that workers would return home dehumanised and alienated from their work, from other workers and from themselves, *physically exhausted and mentally debased* (cited in Bottomore, 1963, p124).

Marx believed, however, that at some point in history the proletariat would ultimately come to see the true nature of their exploitation, and would join together in a state of true class consciousness and revolt. He argued that *the proletarians have nothing to lose but their chains* (Marx and Engels, 1969, p96) and that they would eventually unite to overthrow the system that had always oppressed them and replace it with a fairer communist society in which private property would be abolished and collective ownership would replace capitalism, where no one social group would exploit another.

Marxism has often been criticised for being inaccurate, as most of the regimes set up in Marx's name have been discredited and have ultimately collapsed. It is often argued that far from a revolution occurring, any sense of conflict has been weakened by the ideological attacks on the trade union movement and the legislative restraints that were placed on industrial relations in the 1980s. Like functionalism, Marxism is often regarded as being deterministic, as its basic premise is that economic forces differentially determine the social position of members of society. Social action theories reject this presumption, arguing that members of society engage in conscious human action, which has the possibility of transcending social arrangements. Finally, Marxism is criticised by for being overly focused upon class, at the expense of other social divisions such as gender or race.

It is worth noting that in recent years Marxism has enjoyed something of a renaissance. The recent global economic crisis has led to a renewed interest in Marx's critique of capitalism, as more widespread economic divisions become apparent and contradictions in the system have become more glaring. In a book entitled *Why Marx was right*, Terry Eagleton (2011, p195) notes *capitalism is perfectly capable of collapsing under its own contradictions without even the slightest shove from its opponents. In fact, it came fairly near to doing so just a few years ago.*

A Marxist perspective of social work

A Marxist analysis of social work begins from the starting point that social work is essentially part of the state apparatus, and as such reflects and reinforces the interests of the ruling class. Marxists dismiss claims that the state in capitalist societies is a neutral entity that reflects the interests of all citizens, making decisions in an objective, unbiased manner. Rather, they argue that the state always acts in the interests of the bourgeoisie, including when it intervenes to provide welfare services. Marxists perceive social work as performing two key functions – a 'legitimation' function and an 'accumulation' function. By legitimation, Marxists mean that social work serves an ideological role, creating the image of a caring capitalism, interested in the welfare of its citizens. Social work is the compassionate, civilised face of welfare and is seen by many as an example of society's preparedness to care for and support some of its most vulnerable members. Needless to say, Marxists perceive this image of social work to be a myth. Social work also performs an 'accumulation' function – for example, social workers are integrally involved in assisting people with 'the problems of living' which might otherwise prevent them from fulfilling roles as members of the workforce. Consequently, through discharging some of its 'welfare' functions, social work indirectly serves to accumulate and enhance profits of the capitalist class, as workers are able to fulfil their role in the workplace. In this sense, social work is a component of the welfare state which performs a palliative role in capitalist society, tending to some of the worst excesses of capitalism while simultaneously maintaining the system unchanged. Like functionalists, Marxists highlight the social control role of social work, but rather than perceiving this as being necessary for the whole of society, they argue that it is predominantly groups that are already excluded and marginalised that find themselves on the receiving end of harsh and punitive measures of social control. Thus, according to Marxists, much of the social work role is based around social control and surveillance and the blaming of individuals:

> For many ... social work remains as the last safety net. But it is a safety net with many holes, and one that comes at a high price. For many, to call upon the social services – or, more accurately, to be referred to them, since the vast majority of clients do not go willingly but are sent by the courts or other state welfare agencies – it is surrender...often the best that is on offer is friendly advice; at worse a moral condemnation – backed up by extensive powers.

(Jones and Novak, 1999, p80)

Marxists argue that poverty structures the lives of many service users, and social workers need to understand this. However, rather than working to address poverty, they suggest that social workers tend to be ignorant of it and work around and within poverty, rather than empowering service users to take action to bring about change. It is recognised that much (though by no means all) of social work is state sponsored and statutory in nature therefore, by definition, social workers are constrained in bringing about any real change. Utilising Davies's analogy of the motor mechanic, social workers are at best tinkering around the edges of the vehicle, rather than recognising that it is a new vehicle altogether that is needed. Marxist writers call for more consciousness-raising approaches that genuinely seek to empower service users to be active in their communities to bring about collective change. Radical social work in the 1970s began to adopt community approaches that sought to use collective action to raise consciousness. However, this was soon to be constrained by the advent of managerialism in the 1980s and 1990s where state social work became more tightly regulated and proceduralised. More recently, academics influenced by Marxism have developed a manifesto calling for a new approach to social work. It argues that *the need for a social work committed to social justice and challenging poverty and discrimination is greater than ever* (Jones et al., 2004, p1) and suggests that the profession can learn much from the service user movement which has developed innovative approaches to change, such as collective advocacy.

CASE STUDY

Revisiting the case study of Paul

Let us return briefly to the case study of Paul that we considered in the previous section. How would a Marxist analysis of Paul's circumstances differ from a functionalist analysis?

Marxists would be more likely to see that Paul's depression was influenced by his working conditions. They would argue that the long hours that Paul put in at the packing factory had left him demoralised and alienated. Marxists would point to the bourgeoisie having little or no interest in human suffering; Paul is first and foremost a worker and a producer of wealth. Social work would be regarded by Marxists as having a role to play in assisting Paul to return to good health. The sooner he is able to resume his work, the better. The social work profession is regarded somewhat cynically as part of the state apparatus which performs various social control functions to ensure that capitalist society continues and functions to generate optimum profit for the ruling classes.

Again, this is a somewhat simplistic analysis; however, hopefully you will understand how different perspectives adopt distinct ideological views on individuals who deviate from their social roles and come to the attention of the social work profession.

Micro social action approaches

Both functionalism and Marxism are macro, structural theories which are concerned with the way in which society constrains individuals' lives. There are a range of approaches that are critical of the idea that structures influence and shape what individuals do. These are generically referred to as micro, social action perspectives and are concerned with the concept of 'agency' or the capacity of individuals to act upon the environment. The German sociologist Max Weber was significant in contributing to a theory of social action and was influential in the development of many subsequent schools of thought that shared basic assumptions about the primacy of the individual in creating society. Weber argued that in order to understand the social world, sociologists should begin by attempting to understand the subjective meanings that underpin human behaviour. He utilised the German term *verstehen* to emphasise the need to understand the social world from the point of view of those in it. He was critical of suggestions that sociologists could study the social world in the same way that scientists studied the natural world and stressed the need for sociologists to put themselves in the position of those being studied to really appreciate the subjective meanings behind experience. The concept of *verstehen* is consistent with the underpinning ethos of social work, which stresses the need for empathy and understanding of service users. For example, if a social worker visits a service user one day and discovers him or her frantically cleaning the house, the worker would need to understand whether the cleaning was because the service user had important guests coming to stay for the weekend, or as a displacement activity to avoid writing an essay for the college course they were enrolled on, or a sign of obsessive compulsive disorder, or something completely different altogether. In this example, you can see how the subjective meaning of the action is key to understanding. *Verstehen* then, is a process that social workers use in their practice daily. This concept marks a distinct shift away from the ideas articulated by functionalism and Marxism, and has influenced the subsequent development of other micro theories.

Introducing symbolic interactionism

Symbolic interactionism is a micro, 'agency' theory which is concerned with the small-scale interactions that take place between individuals and with the meanings and interpretations that people give to action. Key writers such as George Herbert Mead, Charles Horton Cooley, William Isaac Thomas, Herbert Blumer and Erving Goffman have made a significant contribution to symbolic interactionism.

Symbolic interactionism is critical of structural perspectives that suggest that human beings are passive recipients of the hand that society deals them. It rejects claims that actions are determined by social forces, and by adopting the analogy of a game of cards, symbolic interactionists suggest that although individuals might be dealt a hand of cards by society, the individual *chooses* how to play those cards, *interprets* the meaning of the hand dealt to them, *decides* what moves to make, how to interpret the rules of the game and indeed, whether to play the hand at all. This differs from structural perspectives that regard individuals' lives as being shaped and determined by the hand that was dealt them by society.

Symbolic interactionists begin from the position that human beings differ from animals in one important respect – that they have the ability to think and reflect upon experience. Mead (1934) suggested that thinking was simply an *internalised or implicit conversation of the individual with himself* (p47). This enables individuals to test out situations in their own minds, as well as to interpret symbols in the social world and apply meanings to them. This is the basis of all interaction, and ultimately the basis of all society. We live in a symbolic world, in which symbols and gestures have shared meanings. Common meanings are passed on through the socialisation process, so it is likely that if you see someone waving at you, or sticking their thumb up, or possibly making a rude gesture to you, you will know what is being communicated; you may not know why, but you are able to hypothesise in an internal conversation with yourself about the meaning of the gesture and possibly even the motive. However, the meanings of symbols may generate different interpretations to different people. Blumer (1969) sums this up: *A tree will be a different object to a botanist, a lumberman, a poet and a home gardener* (p11). This links with Weber's concept of *verstehen* that we discussed earlier: it is important to be able to understand things from the point of view of the other person. Meanings are context specific. For example, the act of shooting someone dead may command a sense of outrage and revulsion on the streets of Manchester, but may generate feelings of bravery, heroism and duty if carried out in times of war. The act is the same, but the interpretation of the act and the subsequent meaning applied to it are very different. Similarly, it is unlikely that anyone would be too fazed by a topless woman on a beach in Greece; however, if the same woman walked topless down a local high street in Britain, it is highly likely she would generate an altogether different reaction. Meanings are also subject to change over time; for example, we may make an initial judgement about someone but later refine our view of them.

Symbolic interactionists note the power of symbols to communicate different messages; for example, someone who drives a Porsche communicates a different image to someone who drives a Vauxhall Corsa. As a student on a social work course, it is important that you reflect upon the way that you communicate to people, both in terms of the way you present, the clothes you wear, and the language you use, as we are all communicating things all of the time, even when we do not intend to.

For symbolic interactionists then, it is the interpretation of meanings and the billions of micro interactions that take place every minute of the day that constitute society. Individuals constantly create and re-create 'society', rather than 'society' existing as an objective entity endowed with the ability to act upon its members.

The concept of 'self' holds central importance to symbolic interactionists, who argue that, unlike animals, all human beings have a self. Mead (1934) suggests that this is evident when we consider that individuals can undergo experience and be aware of that experience. They have the capability to reflect and be aware of how they present to others. Mead suggests that individuals have what he refers to as an 'I' and a 'Me'. The 'I' is the part of the self which stems from basic impulses; it is the instinctual inner self that is to a large extent unpredictable. You may recall a situation where you appeared to act spontaneously almost on instinct or 'gut feeling'. Mead suggests that it is in the 'I' that our true selves are located, raw, undeveloped and unrefined. The 'Me' however, is the part of the self which receives information from the outer world. It is the more developed and refined part of the self which curbs our basic impulses by receiving feedback from others which allows individuals to live comfortably within society. Mead says that an ongoing internal dialogue takes place between the 'I' and the 'Me', with the result being the *social self*, which is constantly being developed and defined.

Similarly, Cooley (1902) utilises the term 'looking-glass self' to describe the ways that we see ourselves based upon or reflecting how we think others see us. The three components of this are:

- how individuals are able to imagine how they appear to others;

- how they are able to imagine how others judge the way they appear;

- how individuals develop feelings as a result, often of pride or mortification.

It might help here to give an example. Lucy goes out with her friends one night; she consumes some alcohol and feels sociable and amusing. Lucy is quite 'loud', laughing a lot, telling jokes and generally being the centre of attention. At the time, she is confident that she is coming over as being funny and the life and soul of the party. She imagines that she is popular and vivacious. Lucy goes home to bed, wakes up the next morning with a hangover, and more importantly with utter feelings of horror that she was so loud and brash. She is mortified and feels a great deal of shame and embarrassment. Lucy decides that she is not a good person and that everyone must have been talking about her. She decides to stay in for a while. This example should help you to understand how the 'looking-glass self' contributes to the development of the self concept, or the way that people feel about themselves. You may consider that this is overly psychological in nature. However, importantly, symbolic interactionists are making the point that individuals navigate their way through society by interacting and negotiating meanings with others and that central to this is the way in which individuals' sense of self interacts with and is shaped by others.

Insights for social work

Interactionists are concerned with how actions come to be defined in a certain way and the *processes* that are involved. This is particularly significant for social workers who often work with individuals who have labels attached to them, and of course, social workers may be involved themselves in assigning labels to individuals. An important consideration is how some individuals come to be defined as 'unfit parents', 'delinquent', or 'mentally ill' for example, whereas others do not. A whole range of factors are important here, including the preconceived ideas, experiences and values of those applying the label. According to symbolic interactionists, a process of negotiation occurs between the 'actors' or individuals involved in the scenario, who are continually involved in interpreting actions and then constructing definitions and meanings. The concept of 'labelling' is important (Becker, 1963); this refers to the process whereby labels (or categories) are applied to individuals, which evoke certain images and stereotypes. A self-fulfilling prophecy may occur whereby individuals take on the characteristics of the labels assigned to them and start acting accordingly. These ideas are looked at more fully in Chapter 6 in relation to youth crime and asylum, but here we want to use mental health as an example to help you make sense of interactionist thinking and labelling theory.

Thomas Szasz (1972) makes the radical proposition that in fact there is no such thing as mental illness *per se;* rather he suggests that 'mental illness' is more accurately behaviour that others disapprove of, which becomes labelled in a particular way. He argues that:

> Mental illness is a myth. Psychiatrists are not concerned with mental illness and their treatments. In actual practice, they deal with personal, social and ethical problems of living.

(1972, p269)

Szasz claims that 'mental illness' must be considered within an understanding of the social context in which it occurs. He rejects any biological basis to mental illness and queries the use of the term 'illness' altogether. He draws attention to the process by

20

which doctors over the years have treated people who act strangely 'as if they were ill', and he claims that over time the 'as if' has been dropped and people are now treated as ill, thereby creating the myth of mental illness. In reality then, people who present with 'mental illness' are really showing outward effects of a range of problems that arise throughout life, but they are doing so in ways that generate a social response of disapproval. Szasz draws attention to the subtleties of social construction and the ways in which meanings are derived: *If you talk to God, you are praying; if God talks to you, you have schizophrenia. If the dead talk to you, you are a spiritualist, if you talk to the dead, you are a schizophrenic* (1973, p113). He suggests, for example, that the 'mental illness' called 'depression' is in reality a dramatisation of not being happy. In other words, it is about how experience is defined and classified. Szasz attacks the power of psychiatrists to construct *illness* and refers to this role as being one of 'social manipulator' that punishes, coerces, incarcerates and classifies patients.

Szasz's work has been the subject of a great deal of criticism, in particular from medical professionals who argue that there is a medical basis for many forms of mental illness and that denying the existence of such could lead to some patients being untreated.

Although controversial, Szasz's ideas have been supported by others who broadly fall within the interactionist paradigm. Edwin Lemert (1972) for example, writing about paranoia, argued that rather than being a form of illness, paranoia is best understood in relation to the process and relationships that surround it. He discusses the ways in which people who are 'paranoid' or suspicious interact with others. Let us consider an example of Fred, who starts a new job in an office. Fred is uneasy around people, which contributes in turn to other people feeling uneasy around Fred; no one in the office can quite put their finger on it, but they find him slightly 'hard work'. Fred is invited to the office Christmas party but declines because he feels the night would be an ordeal. The others are slightly relieved that Fred does not attend and next time there is a social night out, they do not invite Fred as they assume he will not go anyway. Fred, however, is aware of the night out and feels excluded because he was not invited. He reacts against this by becoming even more uncomfortable around his colleagues, and avoiding them by not going to the staff room at all during lunch; he hardly speaks to his colleagues now because he feels so alienated. This new reaction from Fred provides justification for his colleagues to further exclude him as they assume he is a loner at best, or is dowright rude at worst. The colleagues start to discuss Fred's strange behaviour, but they do so covertly, to prevent any further reaction. Fred is aware that others are talking about him and starts to feel paranoid. Far from being a 'mental illness', Lemert would argue that Fred's paranoia is based in reality – he *is* being talked about. This has developed out of the social interactions in his workplace.

Let us pause here and assume that Fred's feelings of paranoia become quite serious and lead him to take time off work and eventually to attend the GP's surgery, where he breaks down and tells the doctor how he feels. The doctor in turn might tell Fred that he is suffering from paranoia. Fred, however, decides to take positive action and leave his job to work elsewhere. Largely because of his experiences in the first workplace, Fred begins his new job once again feeling uneasy and worrying about being excluded. His lack of confidence contributes to a similar scenario arising. A vicious circle has developed here for Fred who begins to live up to the label of 'paranoid'.

Lemert is keen to stress, however, that rather than having any medical basis, the label 'paranoid' has been constructed out of social processes and relationships. He recognises that individuals can be stigmatised by public labelling and refers to this as secondary deviance; in other words, it is not the original act that was a problem, but the public reaction to it. In Fred's case, it was the interrelated chain of events that led to his 'paranoia', but the label applied to him classifies him as being 'mentally ill'.

By considering the application of some of the core principles to mental illness, you will hopefully be able to make sense of symbolic interactionism, which is very different to the structural theories that we have so far considered. A symbolic interactionist analysis of social work would be concerned with the individual or micro interactions that take place between social workers and their service users. The principle of *verstehen* is at the centre of practice, emphasising the importance of understanding issues from the viewpoint of the service user. As we have seen, attention to process is important, particularly as social workers hold potentially powerful roles that are capable of assigning labels.

Our students sometimes become confused by this perspective, as they fall into the trap of thinking that symbolic interactionists would blame service users for their own predicaments because it is as a result of their own free will that they have become involved in challenging life circumstances. This is not a correct assumption. Symbolic interactionists should not be confused with sociologists such as Charles Murray whose ideas we look at in the next chapter. Rather, symbolic interactionists are concerned only with the way that meanings are applied, negotiated and constructed to create and recreate society. For social workers, this perspective is highly relevant when we consider the process of labelling and self-fulfilling prophecies. It is not a blaming perspective.

Symbolic interactionism can be criticised, however, for failing to take account of structure when considering human interaction. To deny that social structures impact upon individuals' experiences is regarded by structural sociologists as being naive at best and negligent at worst. Symbolic interactionists have also been criticised for explaining why people act in certain ways in the first place; by overly concentrating upon social reaction, they fail to explain the original act. Ironically, symbolic interactionism has also been criticised for failing to acknowledge more 'microscopic' features such as the 'unconscious', and factors like emotions, motivations and intentions. Nevertheless, symbolic interactionism is useful for practitioners to help them understand social processes and the construction of a range of social issues.

Reconciling structure and agency – a way forward for social workers?

Although this chapter has broadly separated sociological theories into those which fall under 'structure' and those which fall under 'agency', this dichotomy is to an extent academic for social workers, who may find it more useful to adopt a more eclectically informed approach to their practice. Giddens (1984) uses the concept *structuration* to identify the mutuality of structure and agency; he argues that each is dependent upon and mutually reinforcing of the other. In other words, billions of social actions carried out by billions of individuals create and maintain structures, and simultaneously it is through structures that social actions occur. Although his work has been criticised for lacking an adequate theoretical base, Giddens does offer the possibility of reconciling structure and agency. We began this chapter by arguing that it was essential for social workers to develop a sociological imagination, and by suggesting that they need to be able to locate firstly themselves in the 'bigger picture', but also importantly, be able to locate their service users. Central to this is undoubtedly an understanding of structure. Social workers must have a clear understanding of the unequal nature of society and the way that this impacts upon the lives of service users. However, it is also important for social workers to understand the micro-level issues that are important in service users' lives. Another way of thinking about this is that for some service users, micro-level issues are likely to be individual manifestations of inequality. The social work value base is premised upon the fact that social workers should treat people as individuals and respect individual circumstances, and clearly this is extremely important. However, our view is that this should be done within an understanding of the context of the system that people live their lives in.

Both micro and macro perspectives offer valuable insights for social workers who intervene with individuals, but who must do so reflectively and critically, taking into account the impact of structure. However, it would be inappropriate to conclude this chapter without considering more recent developments in sociology. In the final section, we introduce you to some of the key ideas of postmodernism.

Postmodernism

The label 'postmodernism' is one of a number of different terms which have been used to describe the same, or a broadly similar set of processes. Some writers, for example, prefer to use the terms post-Fordism, post-industrialism and post-structuralism to refer to the same set of changes and developments, all of which are said by some sociologists to be characteristic of a movement from the 'modernist' era to a new 'postmodern' era.

Clearly, when we talk about post-something or other, we are referring to a later period, a later social order, or a later event. For example, the term 'post-Second World War' is used to refer to the period after the Second World War. In a similar vein, the term postmodernism is used to denote a period, an era, after 'modernism' – hence postmodernism. It might, therefore, be a good idea to begin by looking at the key characteristics of 'modernism', and then we will be in a better position to understand and assess the changes and developments which supposedly led to the development of a 'postmodern' society. It is perhaps worth pointing out that many of the claims made by advocates of postmodernism have not remained uncontested, not least because they challenge the foundations of many key sociological thinkers.

What is modernism?

The modernist period is said to have been characterised by a shift away from explanations of social life that were based on tradition or religion, and movement towards a belief in reason, rationality and the potential of human beings to shape the world and discover universal truths. Hence, the modernist era is said to have been symbolised by a belief in the validity of 'big', overarching political and sociological theories, which purported to be able to explain the world and point the way to a better future. This was, in short, a period when it was assumed that humankind could control the natural world through rational thought and planning, and that it was possible to consciously design a better society. As we have seen, the founding thinkers of sociology sought to provide holistic explanations for how societies work, based upon the notion that it was possible to provide a 'universal' grounding for truth and/ or develop a universal strategy that would lead to human emancipation. Although interpretations of the world varied, all were convinced that they could explain past and future patterns of human development. Postmodernists, such as Jean-Francois Lyotard (1984) refer to the theories of those such as Durkheim, Weber and Marx as 'grand narratives', or 'metanarratives'. How then does the new 'postmodern' era that we are said to be living in now differ from the 'modernist' period?

Postmodernist thought

According to postmodernists, the postmodern world is characterised by a loss of faith in 'grand narratives'. As Fiona Williams (1992) explains, with postmodernism there is:

> *an indifference to grand theory – the meta narratives – of either classic Marxism or Parsonian functionalism, or indeed any theory which seeks to establish a total picture or to suggest forms of universalism, determinism, or truth.*

> (p206)

One of the main reasons that postmodernists dismiss the validity of 'grand narratives' is their belief that they are based upon a 'single truth' and that their implementation will often involve the suppression of 'other truths'. At worst, the dogged pursuit of a 'utopia' through a set of universal principles may lead to oppression or totalitarianism, as evidenced in former communist countries, where political freedom and the rights of minorities were sacrificed in the name of the 'common welfare'. At best, the pursuit of an emancipatory strategy, based on a universal grounding for truth (that is, a particular set of ideas and beliefs), may mean that in the quest for the 'common good', particular needs are ignored and not met. Hence, postmodern critiques of welfare and social work have, with some justification, drawn attention to the postwar British welfare state, where a universal 'one size fits all' model of welfare delivery failed to acknowledge or meet the *particular* needs of *particular* welfare users, such as women, minority ethnic groups, older people and disabled people.

The potential for diverse and particular needs to be subsumed by the universalism of grand narratives is a theme that runs throughout postmodernist approaches to welfare and social work. In this sense, as Ferguson (2006) notes, the attractions of postmodernism are obvious. 'Mass', ideologically driven welfare policy failed to acknowledge the voices, desires and needs of some groups of service users, and postmodernist perspectives, with their celebration of fragmentation and particularism, offer us the basis for a new politics. The changes described by postmodernism should, it could be argued, therefore be welcomed and embraced by policy-makers and practitioners. The fragmentation of political life, epitomised by the shift towards self-organisation and self-advocacy among different groups of service users, should be celebrated. Recognition can now be given to those voices that have hitherto been ignored. Commitment to old-style universalism should be abandoned in favour of more specialised, targeted services developed to take account of the diverse needs of 'newly enfranchised' particular groups. In short, the new 'postmodern' world in which we are living should be embraced with enthusiasm.

Discussion

Postmodernism's claims concerning the demise of 'grand narratives' seem to be accurate. Internationally, the ideas of Marx have been discredited with the fall of communism, while domestically, the UK Labour Party appears to have dropped its commitment to socialism in favour of a pragmatic, non-ideological 'what works' approach.

However, the contribution of postmodernism to sociology and social welfare and social work is a matter of dispute. Postmodernism is perceived by some theorists as being premature in its belief in the demise of grand narratives. Marxists, in particular, dispute this latter claim. Alex Callinicos (1989), a prominent Marxist critic of postmodernism, argues that postmodernism's celebration of the 'local' has led it to miss the 'big picture' and hence fail to acknowledge the devastating impact that recent social, economic and political changes have had on huge sections of the population. Postmodernism, he argues, has little to say about what really are the key developments affecting contemporary capitalist societies. In the economic sphere, these include the wholesale transfer of manufacturing industries to developing countries, the end of full employment, and the growth in low-paid, insecure work. In the 'social' sphere, they include the retrenchment of social rights, the infusion of market principles into welfare services, and a more explicit focus on disciplining the poor in social welfare and social work. These developments should, Callinicos insists, be seen precisely for what they are – attempts by capitalists and their political representatives to do what they have always done: maximise profits, cut public expenditure and control the working population. Ruling-class interests are the real driving force behind such changes, and in this sense, postmodernists are naive and premature to talk of the demise of Marxism's potential. It is, Marxists insist, an odd time to be debating the obsolescence of a class-based explanation for social and economic change, when over the past 30 years economic and social policies in the UK have contributed to, on the one hand, staggeringly increased incomes for the rich, yet on the other hand, a massive increase in insecurity, and poverty among the working class.

Postmodernism's celebration of political fragmentation that has accompanied the emergence of new social movements and 'issue politics' has also been criticised. Few would dispute that in the past, the claims of such groups have often been ignored by both the labour movement and established political parties. Nor is the recent positive contribution made by new social movements to politics, social policy and social work a matter of contention. However, some theorists have pointed to what they see as the 'dangers' of political fragmentation. The pursuit of sectional interests can, for example, lead particular social groups to fail to acknowledge their shared interests, or their common sites of oppression. Marxists, for instance, argue that there is a common obstacle to the pursuit of effective civil rights for disabled people, black people and women – that is, employers and their pursuit of profit. Organisations representing business such as the Confederation of British Industry and the Institute of Directors have consistently opposed the introduction of anti-discriminatory legislation for these social groups on the grounds of cost. The danger, Marxists argue, is that the fragmented nature of the strategies and demands of new social movements can, firstly, prevent them from acknowledging their 'common enemy', and secondly, dilute their overall political influence and leverage. Political fragmentation can also be used by governments to divide groups whose interests are, in reality, very much the same. As Ferguson (2006) points out, *it can allow governments, whose overriding concern is limiting welfare expenditure, to play one group off against another as they squabble over the limited resources on offer* (p172).

In conclusion, postmodernism is accused by its critics of failing to adequately explain the changes it identifies, having an inadequate grasp of the power relations that underpin those changes, and in doing so acting as an inadvertent 'ideological smoke-screen', obscuring the very real political interests that are driving policy.

CHAPTER SUMMARY

Incorporating a sociological perspective to social work practice enables social workers to locate service users within an understanding of the 'bigger picture' or context in which they live. This is important so that social workers can recognise the structural underpinnings of many of the issues and problems that service users present with. The Structure/Agency debate in sociology analyses the extent to which society constrains the lives of individuals, versus, the extent to which human beings shape and control their own lives. Although there are very many differing sociological perspectives, this chapter has chosen to focus upon Functionalism, Marxism, Symbolic Interactionism and Postmodernism.

FURTHER READING

For students who are new to sociology, there are a range of textbooks available that introduce you to the discipline, including **Haralambos, M and Holborn, M** (2013) *Sociology, themes and perspectives.* 8th edition. London: Collins; and **Giddens, A** (2013) *Sociology.* 7th edition. Cambridge: Polity Press.

For a comprehensive consideration of key debates and theoretical concepts, see **Ritzer, G** (2010) *Sociological theory.* 8th edition. Maidenhead: McGraw-Hill.

Chapter 2

Poverty and social work service users

ACHIEVING A SOCIAL WORK DEGREE

This chapter will help you to develop the following capabilities from the **Professional Capabilities Framework:**

- **Professionalism**
  Describe the role of a social worker.

- **Values and ethics**
  Understand the profession's ethical principles and their relevance to practice.

- **Rights, justice and economic wellbeing**
  Understand the principles of rights, justice and economic wellbeing, and their significance for social work practice.

- **Interventions and skills**
  Demonstrate the ability to engage with people in order to build compassionate and effective relationships.

It will also introduce you to the following standards as set out in the 2008 social work subject benchmark statement:

3.1.1 **Social work services and service users.**
3.1.4 **Social work theory.**
3.1.5 **The nature of social work practice.**

Introduction

Poverty is a key and defining feature in the lives of many social work service users. This chapter considers debates about the nature of poverty in modern 'developed' societies, and examines different sociological explanations for the causes of poverty. You will be encouraged to examine your own values and beliefs about poverty and the implications of these for practice. The chapter will discuss the impact that poverty has on people's lives and then, drawing upon parallel social work theories, it will consider practical and empowering approaches for working with service users whose lives are blighted by poverty.

The relevance of poverty for social workers

Those who use, and are required to use, social work services continue overwhelmingly to be poor and disadvantaged.

(Smale et al., 2000, p18)

Social work service users are among the most impoverished people in Britain and for many of them, poverty defines their lives. The relationship between poverty and social work is not new, yet it is one that remains understated and implicit in social work training courses and practice. Certainly, poverty provides the *context* for other factors that can increase the likelihood of contact with social services. For example, unemployment, inadequate housing, low income and social isolation can be contributory factors in causing problems such as family break-up and conflict, poor health, stress, and difficulties in caring for children and other dependents. Similarly, poverty can increase the likelihood of children experiencing maltreatment and being looked after by care services; of older adults going into residential care; and of admission to a psychiatric ward (Hooper et al., 2007; Blood, 2010; Mind 2011; Smale et al., 2000; Social Exclusion Unit, 2004b). Much social work practice therefore takes place within and around poverty. One major criticism of the social work profession is that social work often intervenes with individuals and families without attempting to effect change on a more societal level. However, given the frequently devastating consequences of poverty, arguably it is not sufficient to adopt a stance of passive acceptance and to work around poverty. Later on in this chapter, we will be considering ways of working with service users which offer opportunities to challenge the structures which constrain their life chances and choices. We need to begin, however, by considering what we understand the term poverty to mean and by examining sociological explanations for its existence.

Definitions of poverty

There is no consensus over what constitutes poverty. For some, such as Bartholomew (2006), poverty means a lack of basic necessities, such as food, clothing and shelter. In academic and policy terms, this is often referred to as *absolute poverty*. This takes no account of prevailing living standards. The emphasis is on basic physical needs (rather than cultural or social needs). Absolute definitions, therefore, provide a very meagre view of poverty; for example, a young homeless person who has occasional access to a hostel where she or he can obtain a meal, a bed and charitable clothing, would not be considered poor if a strict absolute definition of poverty was applied. Similarly, a family of five living in damp, overcrowded housing on a deprived estate, relying upon benefits to survive, and having to make choices between food and heating would not be considered to be in poverty. In both these cases, individuals have access to the basic requirements to sustain life, and hence they are not considered poor. If we accept this as a legitimate definition of poverty, then very few people are poor in Britain today.

You can perhaps see how absolute definitions of poverty can be attractive to politicians who may want to underestimate levels of poverty, or even deny its existence. For example, in the 1980s and 1990s Conservative ministers used absolute definitions to refute claims that Britain had a significant poverty problem and that their policies had led to increased levels of poverty. The problem of poverty was 'defined away'. Poverty simply did not exist and in policy-making terms there was no need to do much about it.

Food banks

Since we wrote the first edition of this chapter, the issue of absolute poverty has re-emerged on the policy agenda. Nowhere is this more evident than in the rise of the food bank phenomenon, with large numbers of people in Britain now reliant upon charitable food donations to sustain them and their families. The Trussell Trust (2014) noted that the number of people dependent upon food banks had tripled in the last 12 months, evidencing a clear relationship between recent welfare cuts and absolute poverty. In order to access food banks, people need to be referred by professionals such as social workers, GPs or health visitors.

We will examine the phenomenal rise in food banks in greater detail in the Community chapter (Chapter 5). However, we would like you to start to think about the issue of food poverty in this chapter. Have a look at the quotes below:

> The explosion in food poverty and the use of food banks is a national disgrace, and undermines the UK's commitment to ensuring that all citizens have access to food – one of the most basic human rights.

> (Cooper and Dumpleton, 2013, p6)

> Families are experiencing distress and humiliation as they have to turn to food banks to meet their basic need. The social injustice of having to rely on food aid is strongly felt by those compelled to turn to food banks.

> (Cooper and Dumpleton, 2013, p6)

Contrast these quotes with the former Education Secretary, Michael Gove's view about the use of food banks after he visited one in his constituency in September 2013. Gove said that food bank use was

> ... often as a result of some decisions that have been taken by those families which mean that they are not best able to manage their finances. (Gove, House of Commons Hansard, 9 September 2013: Column 681)

In other words, Gove was articulating a view that reliance upon food banks was linked inextricably to poor decision-making by families and an inability to budget.

ACTIVITY 2.1

What do you think about the recent increase in food banks? In this task we would like you to access a recently published joint report from Church Action on Poverty and Oxfam, entitled Walking the breadline: The scandal of food poverty in twenty-first century Britain, *analysing the extent and nature of food poverty. The report is widely available on the internet*

(Continued)

(Continued)

and is in accessible format. Once you have read the report, we would like you to utilise the information it contains to assess the above interpretations of the rapid increase in food banks. You might also want to undertake a newspaper database search, examining the plethora of recent articles about food poverty.

As the above activity makes clear, absolute poverty is not a 'thing of the past' in Britain. However, the use of absolute definitions of poverty have been heavily criticised for failing to take into account the prevailing living standards of the day. Most now accept that relative definitions of poverty are more appropriate indicators for measuring poverty in developed countries such as the UK. Peter Townsend provided the classic definition of relative poverty in his 1979 book, *Poverty in the United Kingdom*:

> Individuals, families and groups in the population can be said to be in poverty when they lack the resources to obtain the types of diets, participate in the activities and have the living conditions and amenities which are customary, or at least widely encouraged or approved, in the societies to which they belong. Their resources are so seriously below those commanded by the average individual or family that they are, in effect, *excluded from ordinary living patterns, customs and activities*.

(Townsend, 1979, p31; emphasis added)

As can be seen from the above quote, relative definitions are much broader than absolute ones. The emphasis is on the 'types of diets' that are 'customary' (rather than food needed to secure life), and living standards and conditions that are 'encouraged or approved of' (rather than a mere roof over the head, or clothes provided by a charitable organisation). In short, this definition encompasses more than the basic necessities to sustain life – rather it is about fitting into society. If we adopt a relative definition, therefore, significantly more people are in poverty in Britain today. In policy-making terms, poverty becomes a 'problem' and there is more pressure for governments to do something about it.

One of the difficulties with relative definitions of poverty, however, is that when it comes to creating a precise 'poverty line' there is considerable scope for disagreement and controversy. While we may agree it is desirable that poverty lines take into account prevailing standards of living, we might not agree about exactly what living conditions, patterns and amenities should be considered 'customary'. How do we determine who is 'excluded from ordinary living patterns, customs and activities'? For example, should an individual or family that does not have sufficient income to enable them to access a television, a telephone, or presents for their children on special occasions be considered 'poor'? *'Consensual' relative definitions* of poverty seek to overcome such difficulties by seeking to establish what 'most' people think is an acceptable standard of living (hence the term 'consensual'), and then assessing the numbers of people living below that standard. The 2013 Poverty and Social Exclusion Survey was one such study.

RESEARCH SUMMARY

The Poverty and Social Exclusion Survey

The Poverty and Social Exclusion Survey (PSE Survey) gathered together a representative sample of the population in 2012 and placed in front of them a series of cards, each of which had written on it a particular good or service – for example, 'television', 'access to the internet', 'holiday once every two years'. People were then asked to place the cards into two piles; in one pile, goods and services they considered to be 'socially perceived necessities' (that is, not necessities needed to sustain life, but goods and services needed for people to participate in what Townsend refers to as 'ordinary living patterns, customs and activities'). In the other pile, they were asked to place those items they did not consider to be 'socially perceived necessities'. If more than half of the people in the survey said a particular good or service (for instance, a television) was a socially perceived necessity, the authors of the survey included it in their basket of goods and services that all families should be able to afford to purchase or access.

The authors of the PSE Survey then used their basket of socially perceived necessities as a yardstick to assess the extent of poverty in Britain. They decided that if an individual or family lacked three or more of their socially perceived necessities because they could not afford them (not because they did not want them – some people might not want a television), then they could be considered to be in poverty. The study found that 33 per cent of the population were lacking three or more socially perceived necessities because they could not afford them. Hence, 33 per cent of the population were in poverty and were experiencing 'significant difficulties'. It is worth noting that the research took place before the 'austerity' benefit cuts implemented by the Coalition Government came into force and so the impact is likely to be even greater. Interestingly, the impact of the recession seems to have reduced minimum expectations – so, for example, being able to afford to give presents to family and friends once a year (such as at Christmas or on birthdays) was not considered necessary in the 2012 study, whereas it was in all previous studies. The survey found that the situation was much worse today than it was in 1983 when the first survey was carried out, and that many more children than previously live 'impoverished and restricted lives' (p2).

ACTIVITY 2.2

In this exercise we want you to try replicating the PSE Survey. Listed below are a range of goods and services. Get together with fellow students and, as a group, try dividing the list into two categories: 'socially perceived necessities' and 'not socially perceived necessities'. While doing so, discuss the relative merits of each. You may wish to think about what you would not want to be without.

• Access to the internet	• Attending weddings/funerals
• A television	• Washing machine
• A telephone	• Medicines prescribed by doctor
• Toys for children	• Fresh fruit and vegetables daily
• Regular savings of £20 per month (for rainy days or retirement)	• Holiday away from home once a year without relatives
• Christmas presents for children	• Two pairs of all-weather shoes
• Birthday presents for children	• Car
• A warm coat	• A fridge
• Attending a place of worship	• Curtains or blinds at the window
• Dictionary	• Dressing gown
• Roast joint or vegetarian equivalent	• MP3 player
• Going to the pub once a fortnight	• Carpets in living room and bedrooms

At the end of this exercise, you will probably have become aware of the contentious nature of establishing a precise relative poverty line!

It is partly a result of the controversy over establishing a precise relative definition of poverty that some have advocated the use of *income-based relative definitions*. With income-based relative definitions, an assessment is made as to what percentage of average income is needed to secure a decent 'socially acceptable' standard of living, and people living on incomes below that standard are considered to be in poverty. It is a 'relative' definition because it tracks average income and hence takes into account general improved standards of living. For example, let us say (hypothetically) that in 2014 average income was £500 per week, and that it was determined that an income of at least 60 per cent of average income was necessary to secure a decent 'socially acceptable' standard of living. Here, the poverty line would be £300 per week (because this is 60 per cent of 500). If, however, in 2015, average income increased to £1000 per week, the poverty line for that year would increase to £600 (because this is 60 per cent of 1000). The advantage of this kind of definition of poverty is that it ensures that the poverty line keeps track with average standards of living – as the living standards of those on average incomes improve, so too do the living standards of those on poverty-line incomes. Another advantage is that this definition sidesteps debates about what goods and services are 'appropriate', one of the main drawbacks of consensual, relative definitions of poverty.

The Child Poverty Action Group (CPAG), and other groups that campaign on behalf of people on low incomes, have long called for poverty to be measured using income-based relative definitions. Significantly, Labour governments between 1997–2010 chose to adopt such an approach, defining poverty (as our example did above) as the numbers of individuals living on incomes that are below 60 per cent of median earnings. This definition was not randomly chosen; it was and remains an internationally recognised method of assessing poverty, which allows comparisons to be made over time and between different countries. It is, according to UNICEF (2012, p11), a definition over which *there is widespread agreement in principle*.

As we explain below, it seems that the Coalition government is seeking to relegate the importance of income-based definitions in favour of 'less precise' indicators. However, at the time of writing, the 'official' poverty rate is still calculated using an income-based relative definition. To give you some idea as to the monetary equivalent of this measurement, in 2009/10 a lone parent with two children, one aged 14 and the other over 14, was in poverty if his or her income was below £257 per week (£13,347 per year) after housing costs. The poverty line for a couple with two children, one aged 14 and the other over 14, was £346 per week (£17,992 per year) (CPAG, 2013).

Using this definition of poverty, we can estimate the extent of poverty and assess how poverty levels have changed over the past 25 or so years.

- In 1979, 13 per cent of people in the UK were living on below 60 per cent of median income after housing costs.

- By 2010/11, 21 per cent of people (13 million) were living on below 60 per cent of median income after housing costs (Cribb et al., 2012).

Clearly, a huge increase in poverty occurred in Britain between 1979 and 2010/11. However, the indicators suggest that the risk of poverty is not shared equally. Economic status (whether a person is employed or not), ethnicity, age and household structure all influence the experience of poverty. As the Child Poverty Action Group (2013) point out, in 2009/10:

- Families containing at least one disabled family member were 30 per cent more likely to be living in poverty than families without any disabilities.

- People from minority ethnic group backgrounds were 64 per cent more likely to live in poverty than average.

- Lone parents were twice as likely to live in poverty as two parent families.

- Children are more likely to be in poverty than other sections of the population. In 2009/10, 29.1 per cent of children were living in poverty, compared to 22.2 per cent of the population generally.

(CPAG, 2013; Cribb et al., 2012)

These different levels of poverty are a reflection of the wider structural disadvantage and sometimes discrimination that these groups face. In recent years, particular international and domestic attention has been devoted to the poverty experienced by children in developed countries such as the UK. We now turn to examine in more detail the extent and impact of child poverty in the UK, as well as police responses to it.

Child poverty

The right of children to access an acceptable standard of living is enshrined in the 1989 UN Convention on the Rights of the Child (UNCRC), Article 27 of which states that *children should have access to a standard of living adequate for their physical, mental, spiritual, moral and social development*. Article 11 goes on to stipulate that children should have a right to *the continuous improvement of living conditions*. The inclusion of these clauses in the UNCRC, both of which emphasise the need to maintain children's *relative* living standards, reflects a growing international recognition of the detrimental impact of poverty on children's lives in developed countries. The UN argues that poverty is morally unacceptable and that, for social justice reasons, 'rich' nations such as the UK should develop poverty reduction strategies. As UNICEF argue, it is *fundamental to shared concepts of progress and civilisation that an accident of birth should not be allowed to circumscribe the quality of life* (UNICEF, 2000, p3).

Impact of child poverty: A social justice-based case for action – Research round-up

Over the past two decades, numerous studies have drawn attention to the negative impact poverty has on the life chances of children. Tess Ridge (2011) has analysed the findings from a range of qualitative research with low-income children and parents over a ten-year period. Ridge found that for some children going without food, bedding, towels and other everyday items was common, as was restricted access to toys, leisure goods and activities, and the latest fashion items. However, she found that in addition to factors like this, poverty had other less tangible outcomes – children who lived in poverty often experienced anxiety, unhappiness and insecurity in their friendships. Poverty placed a strain upon making and maintaining friendships as children were unable to join in or keep up with their peers. The barriers to participation experienced by children placed a particularly heavy emotional toll upon them which resulted in feelings of humiliation and shame.

> Poverty brings both uncertainty and insecurity, and it can penetrate deep into social and interpersonal relationships, sapping self-esteem and undermining children's confidence (p76).

Additionally, poverty also impacted upon the home environment children experienced, with parents commonly feeling high levels of anxiety and pressure, as well as emotions such as anger, frustration and personal shame. Where parental stress levels were high children were often found to be negotiating complex family relationships and managing emotional situations that placed a burden upon them.

Since the publication of Ridge's findings, a number of other surveys have shown how poverty continues to blight the lives of children. In 2013, The Children's Society published Through Young Eyes, *a piece of research that was based upon 2,000 interviews with children themselves. This found that children who described themselves as poor were* much more likely than other children to report bullying, problems in their friendships, unhappiness with their home, and to have lower self-esteem and lower aspirations for the future (p9). *The sheer extent to which poverty impacts negatively on children's experiences was* reflected in the respective answers that 'poor' and 'non-poor' children gave to a series of questions about different aspects of their lives:

% saying that they ...	Non-poor children	Poor children
... do not feel safe at home	2%	23%
... do not have a lot to be proud of	3%	27%
... do not think their friends treat them well	2%	17%
... do not have enough choice how to spend their time	6%	35%
... do not always feel positive about the future	5%	35%
... do not feel safe at school	5%	25%
... feel that their health is bad or very bad	5%	21%
... have been bullied more than 3 times in the past 3 months	9%	37%

(Pople et al., 2013)

A 2012 survey undertaken by Save the Children, which involved 1,504 children aged 8–16, also highlighted the negative impact poverty had on poor children's experiences of childhood. It also illuminated the extent to which children themselves showed an acute awareness of the financial difficulties facing their families. More than a half (52 per cent) of children in poverty reported that shortages of money made their parents unhappy, anxious or stressed, while over a third (36 per cent) said their families were struggling to pay bills. Fifty-three per cent of children in poverty stated that they themselves were worried and anxious about their families not having enough money to get by. This research, like that conducted by the Children's Society, argued that the poverty these children faced was not inevitable. It shouldn't happen here in the UK in 2012, stated Fergus Drake, Director of Save the Children UK. If we fail to act now, we risk betraying the dreams and talents of an entire generation (Whittam, 2012, p1).

Such calls to reduce and eliminate child poverty on social justice grounds certainly carry considerable force. However, the increased international attention devoted to child poverty has also been prompted by a growing recognition that it is linked to a range of other negative, costly social and economic problems and behaviours, both in childhood and later life. As UNICEF (2000, p3) point out, *many of the most serious problems facing today's advanced industrialized nations have roots in the denial and deprivation that mark the childhoods of so many of their future citizens.* In this sense, developed countries have been encouraged to act on child poverty for more self-interested reasons; put simply, tackling child poverty will help diminish the incidence and costs of other, related social and economic problems. A more recent UNICEF (2012, p1) report has reiterated the *economic* case for tackling child poverty, insisting that nations that failed to do so would pay a *very significant price – in reduced skills and productivity, in lower levels of health and educational achievement, in increased likelihood of unemployment* and welfare dependence, in the higher costs of judicial and social protection systems, and in the loss of social cohesion. One should perhaps not under-estimate the strength of such appeals. For instance, one influential Coalition government report estimated that the costs of dealing with the consequences of child poverty were between £11.6 and £20.7 billion in 2006/07 (Field, 2010). A more recent estimate suggests the costs could be as high as £29 billion per year, £15 billion of which is spent on the additional social service, criminal justice and educational support needed by 'poor' children (Hirsch, 2013).

Such inducements to tackle the problem of child poverty have particular relevance to the UK, for it is renowned for having one of the worst child poverty records of all comparable developed countries. For example, between 1979 and 1996/7, child poverty increased dramatically, from 14 per cent (1.9 million) to 34.1 per cent (4.3 million). Throughout this period, Conservative governments reacted to criticisms of their record by simply rejecting the definitional basis for the child poverty estimates and denying its existence. Their stance was epitomised by the refusal of John Major's government to participate in the UN's *International Year for the Eradication of Poverty* programme in 1996. Peter Lilley, then Minister for Social Security, simply claimed that poverty was essentially a third world phenomenon; the UK had *social protection systems to prevent poverty and maintain living standards*, and hence nobody was 'poor' (Brindle, 1996, p15). Not surprisingly, the government's dismissal of the concept of 'relative' poverty was widely condemned by child welfare agencies and organisations, and even David Cameron has subsequently accepted that Conservative administrations during this period *were wrong to declare the end of poverty* (cited in Helm, 2006). The 'legacy' of this approach was documented in a UNICEF (2000) 'league table' of child poverty in rich nations, which was based on data gathered in the mid-1990s. It ranked the UK twentieth out of 23 countries, with only Italy, the United States and Mexico having worse child poverty records.

Child poverty: Labour's strategy (1997–2010)

The election of a Labour government in 1997 heralded a dramatic shift in UK government policy towards child poverty, and in 1999 Tony Blair made a speech committing his government to eradicating it within a generation (by this, he meant by 2020). It would be incorrect to assume that social justice concerns alone were responsible for this shift. Labour ministers were well aware of the social and economic costs of the UK's 'child poverty problem' and this too shaped their determination to act. A number of interim targets were set – the reduction of child poverty by a quarter by 2004 and by 50 per cent by 2010. The government also announced that trends in child poverty would, in future, be monitored more thoroughly and in a number of ways, including through the use of similar methods to the PSE survey. Moreover, for the purposes of its targets, Labour embraced the 60 per cent income-based relative definition of poverty outlined above, a decision which was widely accepted as being ambitious and progressive. Admittedly, the overarching aim – to *eradicate* child poverty – was subsequently diluted somewhat. For instance, Labour ministers claimed that reducing child poverty to 10 per cent by 2020 could be interpreted as having 'eliminated' child poverty, because it would bring the UK in line with countries such as Sweden, which have the best records in the world. However, despite this 'tinkering' with the target, we should not underestimate the significance of the commitment Blair made in 1999. During his speech, he described it as 'historic' and indeed it was. No previous UK government had ever defined child poverty, let alone set targets for eliminating it. If achieved, it had the real potential to transform the living conditions, life chances and opportunities of millions of children. Moreover, Labour enshrined these targets in law in the 2010 Child Poverty Act, which, unless the Act is repealed, means that all future UK governments are committed to achieving them within the set timescales.

By the time Labour lost the election in 2010, all the existing indicators suggested that Blair's 'historic' aim, *for ours to be the first generation to end child poverty*, would not be achieved (Hirsch, 2009). Child poverty had certainly reduced between 1997–2010 – from 4.3 to 3.6 million children – but none of the government's interim targets were met, nor was its 2020 target likely to be achieved. Analyses of why this was the case focused upon a number of factors. First, the government wrongly assumed that getting parents into work would lead to a substantial fall in child poverty. As an all-party House of Commons Department for Work and Pensions Select Committee (2008) inquiry noted, 50 per cent of poor children lived with a parent who was *in work*, and without higher wages and more adequate in-work financial support, children in these families would continue to experience poverty. The Committee also pointed to the low benefit levels provided to parents who, for whatever reason, were unable to work, which failed to provide them with an income which was above the poverty line. It recommended a review into the way adult benefits were calculated, with a view to ensuring that they kept pace with median earnings. The high costs of childcare in the UK were also cited as a key impediment to tackling child poverty, and again, the Committee called for measures to be introduced to reduce the financial burden of childcare on working families.

Despite Labour's apparent failure to achieve its targets, its efforts to measure and tackle child poverty did receive plaudits both domestically and internationally. Regarding Labour's definition of child poverty, UNICEF (2005, p15) described the indicators it had chosen to use as *transparent, credible and not so complex that the monitoring of progress becomes either impossible or ensnared in too much detail*. While noting that the UK still had one of the highest child poverty rates in Europe, it also welcomed the reductions in child poverty that had occurred, noting the continuous downward trajectory in the numbers of poor children.

The Coalition and child poverty

As already noted, the 2010 Child Poverty Act enshrined Labour's child poverty targets in law and the Coalition government is currently legally committed to achieving them. However, the election of the Coalition has signalled a shift in the UK's record on, and approach to, child poverty. First, in a reversal of the trend under Labour governments, child poverty rates are now projected to rise by at least one million by 2020 (CPAG, 2013). As the influential Institute for Fiscal Studies point out, this increase is *in large part due to cuts in benefits and tax credits being implemented as part of the fiscal consolidation* (Cribb et al., 2013, p53). Its assessment of the impact of these cuts is blunt: *The supposedly binding target of 'eradicating' child poverty by 2020 will not be achieved*. As a critical joint report written by the UK's Children's Commissioners (2011) emphasised, the impact of the government's austerity policies on children themselves is likely to be equally bleak, as many more children will be denied the same opportunities to secure 'inclusion' as their more affluent peers:

> *In 2008, we stated in our joint report that we considered it unacceptable that a country as wealthy as the UK had 3.8 million children (one in three) living in relative poverty. As this report outlines, this figure has not changed. In fact, there is now a very real danger that this figure will increase. The ... reduction in support for childcare, the impact of the ... cap on benefit levels and the introduction of conditionality in benefit payments have the potential to drive more vulnerable children, young people and their families into poverty. We therefore strongly urge the UK Government to reconsider the impact of these reforms.*

(p4)

Rather than reconsidering its welfare reforms, the Coalition has responded by seeking to re-frame the child poverty debate, by claiming that childhood deprivation has little to do with a lack of income, and shifting the focus away from structural explanations for child poverty. Indeed, it is claimed by the Coalition that initiatives based upon such interpretations, which have been geared towards boosting family incomes through tax credits or the benefit system, may have increased child poverty, by sapping initiative and reinforcing a 'cycle of dependency' within families:

> *... we believe that the aims of the Child Poverty Act – to dramatically reduce levels of child poverty in the UK – will not be achieved through simply throwing money at the perceived symptoms. This approach has been exhausted, not only failing to turn the tide on income poverty, but worse still, exacerbating the problem by suppressing incentives to work and keeping families in cycles of entrenched deprivation.*

(HM Government, 2011, p4)

To a government that is ideologically committed to cutting state support and reinforcing personal responsibility for welfare, the suggestion that 'money does not matter' is politically convenient, but as we saw in our research round-up, this is not supported by the evidence. More recently, such claims have been repudiated by the findings of an exhaustive Joseph Rowntree Foundation-funded survey of 46,668 poverty studies, which came to the conclusion that there *was abundant evidence ... that money makes a difference to children's outcomes. Poorer children,* the authors concluded, *have worse cognitive, social-behavioural and health outcomes in part* because they are poorer, *and not just because poverty is correlated with other household and parental characteristics* (original emphasis) (Cooper and Stewart, 2013, pp4–5).

On a related point, we have witnessed a reinforcement of pathological interpretations for social ills, including child poverty. As we show in our social exclusion chapter (Chapter 3), these never entirely disappeared under Labour governments, but they are now being utilised by Coalition ministers with a renewed level of intensity. In relation to child poverty, the emphasis has now clearly shifted away from *income* to a focus upon *behaviour and lifestyle choices*. This is apparent in the following quote taken from the introduction to the Coalition's *Independent review on poverty and life chances*:

> *I no longer believe that the poverty endured by all too many children can simply be measured by their parents' lack of income. Something more fundamental than the scarcity of money is adversely affecting the lives of these children. Since 1969 I have witnessed a growing indifference from some parents to meeting the most basic needs of children, and particularly younger children, those who are least able to fend for themselves. I have also observed how the home life of a minority but, worryingly, a growing minority of children, fails to express an unconditional commitment to the successful nurturing of children.*

> (Field, 2010, p16)

This message – that the causes of poverty lie 'within' rather than 'without' – has a long historical pedigree. In the UK, it can be traced as far back as the Poor Law Amendment Act (1834), which sought to reinforce a pathological, morally judgemental perception of the poor (see Cunningham and Cunningham, 2012). More recently, its roots can be found in a distortion of the culture of poverty theory that emerged in 1966 from Oscar Lewis and to which we will turn later in this chapter. Suffice to say for now, the Coalition government is hostile towards any definition of poverty that places emphasis upon the unequal structure of British society or the paucity of welfare benefits and low wages (and therefore upon the accountability of Governments), preferring instead to embrace measurements that focus upon the 'failings' and 'weaknesses' of people in poverty. As Lansley (2013, p15) notes, the rhetoric has become more 'anti-poor' than 'anti-poverty'; *there has been a sharp shift in philosophy towards poverty, one that has shifted sharply away from Labour's 'welfarist' approach to a much more 'individualistic' model, one more in tune with the views of the 1980s.*

Finally, the Coalition has signalled its dissatisfaction with Labour's income-based definition of child poverty and its preference for what it refers to as a more 'multidimensional measure' that moves the focus away from 'income' and on to somewhat vague, indeterminate 'behavioural' indicators such as parental skills, family stability and worklessness. Of course, this is entirely in keeping with its embrace of 'individual' interpretations of poverty. At the time of writing, the outcome of the government's 'official consultation' on child poverty measurements, which began in November 2012, is not yet clear. What has become evident, though, is the strength of support for the existing income-based method of measuring poverty among child welfare professionals and agencies. The following comments, made by the Children's Commissioner for England (2013), were representative of those made by other authoritative, interested organisations, including the Joseph Rowntree Foundation and the Child Poverty Action Group:

> *Poverty is multidimensional, but can be most easily measured and understood in terms of a lack of money and low income ... the pre-eminence of income measures in assessing poverty must not be lost nor downgraded ... OCC believes that the Government must support and continue to use* the current child poverty measures set out in the Child Poverty Act 2010. [original emphasis]

As we have sought to emphasise throughout this chapter, 're-defining' poverty is not without policy or practice implications. Put simply, if, as a result of 're-definition', fewer children are officially recognised as being in poverty, then there will be less pressure on governments to act to reduce it. Just as importantly, fewer resources will be devoted to tackling child poverty, as well as the problems that are associated with it. In addition, of course, re-definition could be used as an opportunity by the government to 'tweak' the targets in the Child Poverty Act, making them easier to achieve. Some child poverty campaigners have interpreted the government's review of child poverty measurement as an effort to do just that. They see it as a politically motivated attempt by the government to dilute the targets enshrined in the Child Poverty Act, at a time when child poverty is expected to rise as a direct result of its austerity agenda. As Lansley (2013, p15) argues, *Ministers, it seems, have been trying to find a way of redefining poverty downwards, simply by adopting new measures associated with lower rates of poverty*.

Hopefully, you will now have some understanding of the significance of the 'definitions' debate. Ultimately, the answer to the question 'how many poor people are there in the UK today' depends on the definition of poverty adopted. If poverty is defined in 'absolute' terms, as it was in the 1980s and the 1990s by Conservative ministers, then very few people are poor. Likewise, the kinds of 'multidimensional' indicators favoured by the Coalition may make child poverty more difficult to gauge. They are also likely to lead to a significant under-estimation of 'structural' child poverty and a reinforcement of pathological interpretations of the phenomenon.

The 'definitions debate' is therefore important, and its relevance for helping us to understand levels of poverty and policy responses should not be underestimated. That said, we do need to be aware that the overwhelming focus placed on the question of definitions, both within academic literature and policy debates, can act as a 'smoke-screen', diverting attention away from the devastating consequences of poverty. Hence, while books, academic journals and government consultation exercises deliberate the relative merits of competing definitions, the experiences of the millions of people living through the hardships that poverty generates can remain largely unnoticed. It is to the experiences of those living in poverty that our discussion now turns.

The impact of poverty on people's lives

As trainee social workers it is important that you take some time to think about what it means to live in poverty and consider the impact upon people's lives and well-being. We would like you to complete the following exercise as a way of doing this.

CASE STUDY

Gemma is a 29-year-old woman who lives with her three children in rented accommodation. Recently she has been using the local food bank to help her feed her family as the cost of food is just too high, with her rent being so expensive. Her home is damp and cold and in a poor state of repair. Gemma claims benefits and cannot afford to adequately heat her home. She would like to move out of the flat as she is unhappy there; she finds it gloomy and depressing, and does not know where to start to try and improve it. The job just seems too big to take on. Gemma's children are two, three, and nine years of age. They frequently have bad coughs and colds and have recently been diagnosed as being asthmatic. The health visitor has noted that the eldest child is often withdrawn and lacks confidence and School have recently contacted Gemma to let her know that he has been the victim of school yard bullying. The family have to go to the doctor's surgery often, which is a long walk in the cold as they cannot afford the bus fare. Gemma has very poor self-esteem, and believes she has failed her children. She has no contact with her family, who live many miles away. She often feels weepy and depressed – that life is not worth living. She has no idea what she can do to make her life any different. Gemma owes money to a local firm who give loans with high interest rates. She borrowed the money to buy Christmas presents, but is now worried sick about paying it back. She has had various letters through the door and last week she was paid a visit by the debt collector who frightened her so much she contemplated ending it all. On top of all of this, Gemma's fridge has broken down.

The father of two of the children works on the fairground and is away many months of the year. He calls round occasionally, without warning, and stays for a few days at a time. Gemma is very fond of him, as are the children, but he is prone to mood swings, and gets sick of Gemma asking for money for the children.

Gemma feels that she needs some help, but she is scared of approaching social services in case they take the children off her. She does not know which way to turn.

ACTIVITY 2.3

The impact of poverty

Spend some time thinking about Gemma's life with her three children. If you were a social worker assessing this family's needs, how would you describe the impact of poverty upon Gemma's life and that of her children? You may wish to think about this emotionally, physically, practically and socially.

Having completed this activity, you might have recognised the feelings of hopelessness and despair that can blight people's lives when they live in poverty. It is often the *cumulative* effects of deprivation that can lead to high stress levels, feelings of strain, and utter desolation. Constant worry is common, whether this is about debt or paying bills, or whether it is about health, housing or other problems. Worrying consumes a great deal of emotional energy and can sap people's spirits and contribute to stress, anxiety and in some cases depression or other mental health problems. It is not uncommon for people who live in poverty to feel that they have failed in some way, which further contributes to poor self-esteem and feelings of worthlessness. Relationships may also deteriorate under strain, which can exacerbate stress and feelings of failure. In addition to the emotional impact of poverty, you may also have noted the lack of choices or options available to Gemma, and the fact that she felt unable to bring about any change in her circumstances. You may also have noticed the impact of the family's circumstances on the children, notably the older school age child.

Despite acknowledging the potential impact of poverty upon people's lives, it is important not to stereotype or pathologise people who are poor and to recognise that poverty affects people differently. Many people who experience poverty are able to manage their situation by showing immense strength and resourcefulness, despite extreme hardship. They are, against the odds, able to live their lives with dignity and pride. However, the impact of poverty on the lives of individuals and families is frequently so extreme that the brutal consequences of poverty can take their toll even on the most resilient.

Images of 'the poor': a moral judgement

Individuals in poverty are frequently talked about and treated without dignity or respect, which according to Novak (1997) generates irreparable psychological damage, which far outweighs the level of material poverty endured. As this quote below from a woman in poverty indicates, being poor is hard work:

> *You're more tired. I mean just the thing that being poor is so much work, your whole life. You see people going into a shop, they buy what they want and they leave. But you're there, you're having to calculate how much money you've got as you go around, you're having to look at one brand then another, and meanwhile the store detective is looking over your shoulder which is also work having to cope with that kind of scrutiny, because you're poor they expect you to take something ... There's that pressure all the time.*

(Woman talking to Beresford et al., 1999, p94)

Similarly, in Scottish research carried out by the Joseph Rowntree Foundation, the following woman talks about her experience of being poor and not being taken seriously by professionals. She explains how her GP treated her, attributing a potentially serious health condition to her not being able to cope:

> *GPs say: 'Go away, the only thing that's wrong with you is that you don't know how to cope. Now go away, I don't want to see you again'.*

(Green, 2007, p26)

Poverty then, is much more than a lack of money. It is also about how people are *treated*, how they see themselves, and about loss of dignity and feelings of powerlessness. Linked to this, is the notion that poverty also involves moral judgements.

ACTIVITY **2.4**

Think about the messages you have heard about 'poor people' from family, peers, the media, or in popular culture; list adjectives that have been used to describe people in poverty throughout history. You might also wish to think about what messages you have heard about people who claim benefits.

Collect newspaper articles related to the above (popular tabloid newspapers that frequently portray people living in poverty in a particularly negative way include the Daily Mail *and the* Daily Express*). What messages emerge from these?*

What purposes do these images and messages serve?

When undertaking the first part of the above exercise, you have probably come up with a range of terms such as 'idlers', 'rogues', 'vagabonds' and more recently, 'scroungers', 'dross', 'underclass', 'wasters', 'rough' and so on. Words like these still permeate the popular press today and in doing so they seep into the self-image of people who are portrayed as being 'different' from the rest of society. More recently, as Jones (2011) identifies, the word 'chav' has become popularised to describe people who make up the white working class in very derogatory terms. This will be discussed in more detail in the social class chapter (Chapter 8).

Popular discriminatory images of 'the poor' have shared a common theme throughout history, that poor people are somehow to blame for their state of affairs. Stereotypical images of poverty encompass a moral judgement that diverts attention from anything to do with a lack of money, and becomes a statement on the moral character of those involved. Sociologically, this is interesting as this process serves two important purposes.

- First, if poverty is reconstructed in terms of the failures and weaknesses of those who are in it, it enables attention to be shifted away from structural causes of poverty, and away from government policies which may be responsible. In short, the accountability of the state is reduced significantly.

- Second, perceptions of poverty based upon negative moral judgements may create something of a self-fulfilling prophecy for people, who begin to internalise their 'otherness' and thus become *emotionally* marginalised as well as structurally excluded.

The concept of the 'looking-glass self' is useful here. Symbolic interactionist, Charles Horton Cooley (1902) utilised this term to describe how individuals see themselves through the eyes of others, who give them feedback, which is in turn internalised and enables individuals to develop feelings about themselves, often of pride or mortification. For people who live in dire poverty, the prevailing message to emerge from popular culture is that they are lazy, irresponsible, weak and culpable for their plight. Such messages are likely to be internalised, which may lead to feelings of shame and embarrassment, psychologically excluding them from mainstream society. Dominelli (2004) utilises the helpful concept of 'othering' to explain the processes that occur when comparisons are made that judge some people as being superior to others. This creates a group who become constructed as being inferior and outside of prevailing social norms, who are distinguished as being 'undeserving' and in need of being policed. This can be clearly seen with people who claim welfare benefits. This diverse group of people has become 'othered' – benefit claimants are considered as somehow different and distinct to the rest of 'us'. The group, although actually comprising a vast range of different people with very diverse circumstances, have become homogenised in sections of the popular press, regarded as all being work shy, feck-less, hopeless, lazy individuals who 'sponge' off the rest of society. Welfare claimants are by definition the poorest people in society who are perceived as being undeserv-ing and morally culpable for their plight. Anyone who has watched an episode of *The Jeremy Kyle Show* will have seen that it is fair game to caricature this group of people and pass judgement on the intricacies of their lives, without a thought of the con-sequences, while Middle England look on as spectators of a peculiar form of 'blood sport'. Baumberg et al. (2012) recently assessed the level of 'benefit stigma' in Britain. They found a high level of social and institutional stigma experienced by people who claim benefits – that is, a pronounced sense of humiliation or shame arising from the feeling of being judged by others. The process of claiming benefits was often expe-rienced as being unpleasant and shameful, as people's business was often heard by others due to a lack of privacy. Claimants experienced the whole interaction as being deeply demeaning, feeling as though they were being looked down upon by benefits office staff:

> We're classed as being scroungers, work-shy, that kind of thing. All the negative stuff.

> (Disability benefit claimant, cited in Baumberg et al., 2012, p5)

Negative labels and derogatory images contribute to the construction of a visible and deviant group who can be easily demonised and blamed for their situation. This is important to understand within social work, because as a group, 'the poor' are highly visible and are therefore vulnerable to surveillance from health and social care profes-sionals. As agents of social control, social workers can potentially contribute to this process. Such visibility is also felt by those who live in poverty as is illustrated in the quote below:

> I am frightened of going to Social Services. Poverty is when you need help, but you are too scared of being judged as an unfit mother to ask for it. Asking for support shouldn't mean you are investigated, it shouldn't mean you lose your dignity.

> (Service user talking to ATD Fourth World, 2006)

It is imperative that social workers are aware of the power of stigmatising and dis-criminatory messages that seep into popular culture and ensure that they are prac-tising from within an anti-oppressive framework. The social work value base is an attempt to ground social work practice within a set of values and principles which counter unfair and inequitable beliefs.

ACTIVITY 2.5

Social work values

You may have noted that each time we refer to 'the poor' in this chapter, we have used inverted commas to denote the fact that this is an artificial and socially constructed group-ing. Look at the Code of ethics for membership of The College of Social Work (if you do not have one you can download this from TCSW website), paying particular emphasis to the standards that we have listed below:

Protect the rights of, promote the interests of, and empower people who use social work services and those who care for and about them.

Promote social justice and display compassion and respect in my professional practice.

Consider how you can uphold these standards in relation to service users who are in poverty. You may wish to think about:

- ways in which you can treat people as individuals rather than as a stereotype;
- how you can respect and maintain the human dignity of service users;
- how you can promote equality of opportunity for service users and carers;
- how you can guard against 'povertyism' or treating people in oppressive, stigmatising or discriminatory ways, because they are in poverty.

If you have completed the exercise above, hopefully you will have really begun to think about what it means to work ethically and uphold the social work value base. Codes of ethics and values statements must be more than words on paper and all social work students need to spend some time really thinking about how they *convey* social work values in interactions and practice. How, for example, do we convey respect to service users? How do we maintain the dignity of someone who cannot afford to feed their children, or someone who has slept in a bus shelter over night? How do we appropriately challenge disparaging remarks about a street sex worker who works to earn enough money to survive? These are tricky questions to grapple with and the most effective practitioners are those who engage with these issues carefully, to really think through how values can be more than rhetoric in social work.

It is essential that social work students develop the ability to be reflective and develop critical practice (Adams et al., 2005) to guard against discriminatory practices. As part of this it is important to adopt a sociological approach to your practice. As we have outlined in our first chapter, this attempts to move beyond individualised responses to situations faced by service users, to adopting a position which locates individuals within an understanding of wider underpinning structures. This is reflected in the QAA subject benchmark statements for social work education, which set out the knowledge, understanding and skills required to become a social worker:

> The relevance of sociological perspectives to understanding societal and structural influences on human behaviour at individual, group and community levels.

This emphasises the importance of understanding human behaviour from within a sociological perspective.

ACTIVITY 2.6

Let's return to Gemma, whom we considered in Activity 2.3 above. If you adopt a socio-logically informed approach to working with Gemma, how might your assessment of her and subsequent intervention be different from if you adopted an individualised approach? You may wish to undertake this activity with a group of other students.

By doing this exercise, you will have hopefully recognised the importance of imple-menting a sociologically informed assessment to your work with Gemma, in order to plan intervention which recognises the structural basis of some of the difficulties she is facing. This would be different from an individualised approach, which would tend to focus upon individual 'failings' or inadequacies of service users.

Sociological explanations of poverty

Competing sociological explanations for the causes of poverty are well documented. In this section, we provide a summary of some of the most influential. These fall into three categories: functionalist theories; individualistic explanations; and structural (Marxist) explanations.

ACTIVITY 2.7

Recapping key sociological theories

In Chapter 1, we outlined the key tenets of the core sociological theories to be considered in this book. As the discipline of sociology will be new to many of you, it is important that you recap and refresh the central components of each theory each time you approach a new topic in sociology. This will enable you to become comfortable with the theory base as you go along, and importantly, to situate each new topic within an understanding of underpinning theory.

Complete a 'crib list' for Marxism and symbolic interactionism. We have done functional-ism for you to assist you with this process.

Crib list: functionalism

- Structural theory.
- Macro level of explanation.
- Society is the 'whole', which has various component parts.
- Each part contributes a function which ensures the survival of the whole.
- The notion of 'consensus' (or shared norms and values) is fundamental.
- Social order is significant.
- Socialisation by family, education, wider culture.
- Key sociologists: Comte, Durkheim, Parsons, Davis and Moore.

The functions of poverty

Functionalist explanations of poverty are based around the idea that poverty serves a positive function for society. This may sound strange, as at first sight it is hard to think of any benefit at all to being in poverty. However, you should remember that functionalism is interested in large-scale (macro) structural explanations of social life. Therefore, poverty is understood in terms of the benefits it provides for *society as a whole*, rather than for the individuals in poverty. The work of Herbert J Gans (1971) is helpful here. He argues that poverty survives in part because it is useful to a number of groups in society. He suggests that poverty benefits the non-poor and also the rich and powerful, who therefore have a vested interest in maintaining poverty. According to Gans, the functions of poverty can be summarised as follows.

1. Poverty ensures that society's 'dirty work' is done
In other words, the existence of poverty ensures that there is always someone available to do physically dangerous, temporary, undignified and underpaid work; as the low wage they gain for doing it is, essentially, preferable to destitution.

2. Poverty subsidises the rich
Linked to the above point, Gans further points out that without the very low-paid in society, many industries would be unable to function as they presently do; they rely upon low-paid workers to ensure their profit and survival. Furthermore, because the poor pay a higher *proportion* of their income in taxes they directly subsidise more affluent groups.

3. Poverty directly creates jobs
Gans notes that the existence of poverty in society directly generates employment for others. He identifies a number of occupations that 'service' the poor:

> Penology would be miniscule without the poor, as would the police. Other activities and groups that flourish because of the existence of the poor are ... the sale of heroin and cheap wines and liquors, Pentecostal ministers, faith healers, prostitutes, pawn shops and the peacetime army which recruits its enlisted men mainly from among the poor.

(Gans, 1971, p21)

In addition to these occupations, Gans also identifies what he calls jobs for 'poverty warriors'. Here he is referring to the likes of social workers, social scientists and journalists, for example.

ACTIVITY 2.8

Critiquing sociological theory

There are many assumptions contained in the above quote that are rather judgemental. Can you spot them? If so, you can weave this into a critique of Gans's work. This should help you to develop skills of analysis which are vital both to the discipline of sociology and for developing professional practice in social work.

4. The social functions of poverty

Significantly, Gans suggests that the existence of poverty provides reassurance and support for the rest of society. Poverty and the presence of poor people in society provide a yardstick against which the rest of society can measure themselves. This reassures those who are not poor of their worth and reminds them that their life is worth living. In simple terms, there is always somebody else worse off, and this serves as a useful reminder to the majority of society.

5. The scapegoat function

Gans suggests that poor people in society also provide a useful scapegoat for the non-poor. He maintains that people who defend norms such as the desirability of hard work, thrift, honesty and monogamy need people who can be accused of being lazy, spendthrift, dishonest and promiscuous to justify the predominance and 'rightness' of conventional norms.

He goes on to suggest that even though there is evidence to suggest that the poor are as law abiding and moral as anyone else, they are more likely than their middle-class counterparts to be caught and punished when they participate in deviant acts. They also lack the cultural power to correct the stereotypes other people have of them. This explanation links with the 'othering' argument that was made earlier in this section. The poor are often scapegoated for all of society's ills because they are a visible group.

It should be noted that Gans offers a functional analysis to explain the continued existence of poverty. However, he is not advocating that poverty should exist, rather that it serves a number of functions for society and that affluent groups in particular benefit from its continued existence. Gans is, therefore, arriving at a similar conclusion to conflict theorists, when he concludes that:

> ... phenomena like poverty can be eliminated only when they become dysfunctional for the affluent or powerful, or when the powerless can obtain enough power to change society.

(Gans, 1971, p24)

Individualistic explanations of poverty: the focus on 'problem families'

Individualistic theories attempt to explain the existence of poverty by focusing upon the moral failings and ineptitude of those who are in it. Such explanations tend to adopt a blaming approach. These are not, however, the same as symbolic interactionism and it is important to emphasise that although they may share a focus on the 'micro' that is where the similarity ends. We have chosen to focus upon three such individualistic explanations here – the culture of poverty theory, cycle of deprivation theory and underclass theory.

1. Culture of poverty theory

This explanation for poverty was developed by Oscar Lewis in 1966, when he based his work on observations of Mexican and Puerto Rican families. Although this research is clearly dated and may seem divorced from life in Britain today, the underpinning ideas behind Lewis's work remain influential. Lewis was interested in the *lifestyle* of the poor and suggested that people are in poverty due to a set of values, which they internalise and then pass on over the generations. He referred to this as a 'design for living' and argued that people learn to accept poverty because they cannot do anything about it. According to Lewis, the poor people in his study adopted self-defeating attitudes by becoming fatalistic and resigned to the situation, which prevented them from breaking out of it. Lewis identified feelings of dependency and helplessness, with little sense of the future. He also found that family life was characterised by high levels of illegitimacy, divorce, and the predominance of women, due to high levels of male desertion. Children grew up to internalise behaviours and values, thereby perpetuating the norms and values of a 'culture of poverty'.

This theory is criticised for failing to explain the existence of poverty in the first place. Critics suggest that people in poverty are in fact no different in terms of their moral outlook from other members of society; rather it is their lack of income, and poverty, that prevent them from achieving mainstream values. The 'culture of poverty' then, is regarded as a response by the poor to the realities of their situation. Despite the obvious weaknesses of this theory, the ideas have been influential in Britain among commentators who perceive different cultural values to exist among the poor.

2. Cycle of deprivation theory

The idea of a cycle of deprivation is associated with Sir Keith Joseph, who was the Conservative Party Secretary of State for Social Services in the early 1970s. Joseph believed that it was not merely lack of income that caused poverty and that some 'problem families' had interrelated difficulties which were to a greater or lesser extent inflicted from within (cited in Denham and Garnett, 2002). Here he was referring to factors such as low intelligence, temperament and poor health. The cycle of deprivation theory holds that such chronic problems recur in the next generation, as children from poor families tend to marry into families with similar difficulties, thereby reproducing a cycle of deprivation. Such families live in inner-city areas, have poor housing, inadequate diets, poor health, do badly at school, leave without qualifications, enter poorly-paid work, bring children up in an unsatisfactory manner, are more likely to fall into delinquency and are unable or unwilling to find work. The theory is similar to the culture of poverty above as it assumes that people perpetuate their own deprivation.

The cycle of deprivation theory has also been widely criticised (Welshman, 2012). Extensive research has found that children of 'the poor' frequently break out of the so-called cycle of deprivation, which is supposed to determine and constrain their life chances. Further, the difficulties noted do not cause poverty; such problems, if in fact they exist, are likely to be a response to an unequal society which offers little chance of success. The theory falls short of addressing the root causes of poverty and fails to explain why some people get into poverty in the first place.

3. Underclass theory

This concept emerged in the 1980s and, according to Jones and Novak (1999), constitutes the return of a victim-blaming ideology of poverty with a vengeance. The most vociferous proponent of the underclass theory was Charles Murray who, in an article in the *Sunday Times* in 1989, warned of the dangers of an underclass developing in Britain, characterised by high levels of illegitimacy, crime and labour market 'dropout'. Murray argues that poverty essentially results from the behaviour of individuals:

> *When I use the term underclass, I am indeed focussing on a certain type of person defined not by his condition e.g. long term unemployed, but by his deplorable behaviour in response to that condition, e.g. unwillingness to take jobs that are available to him.*

(Murray, 1990, p68)

Murray also pointed to communities in which he claimed the family had effectively collapsed, degenerating into a 'new rabble' who would become increasingly chaotic and violent. The key danger, for Murray, was long-term dependency upon benefits and social disintegration. Lone parents were of particular concern to him in this respect, as were their children, who he believed were learning 'faulty' or dysfunctional values.

The underclass theory was extremely influential with the Conservative Party at the time, which along with a sympathetic right-wing media, contributed to the development of a moral panic around lone parents and other welfare recipients.

Criticisms of Murray's work are well rehearsed, in particular the complete disregard for structural causes of poverty and the flimsy and inaccurate nature of his 'evidence' for the existence of an underclass.

Are individualistic theories of poverty relevant to social work practice today?

Despite the obvious criticisms of individualistic explanations of poverty, they remain extremely influential. Politicians and the media continue to reinforce such interpretations, and as we have already hinted, they are having an increasingly influential role in shaping policy in the present day. For example, the Coalition's 'Troubled families' programme, a policy that we examine in greater detail in the social exclusion chapter (Chapter 3), has its roots in pathological interpretations of poverty. As we show in Chapter 3, we should not underestimate the potential of initiatives such as these to reshape and reframe debates about the direction and aims of social work practice as well as social policy.

The bedroom tax and the benefits cap, which we later discuss in the social class chapter (Chapter 8), are two other Coalition initiatives that are shaped by behavioural explanations for poverty. Justifying the government's imposition of a £26,000 cap on benefits, Jeremy Hunt, currently the Coalition's Health Minister, argued that it was not the state's responsibility to fund the 'inappropriate' family planning choices of 'shameless' individuals who assumed, irrespective of the numbers of children they had on 'welfare', that they had an automatic 'right' to state support:

The number of children you have is a choice and what we're saying is that if people are living on benefits, then they make choices but they also have to have responsibility for those choices ... it's not going to be the role of the state to finance these choices.

(BBC, 2010)

Iain Duncan Smith, the Department for Work and Pension Minister, has used much the same language to justify the Coalition's welfare reforms. Britain, he argues, is characterised by *a culture of entrenched worklessness and dependency*, which has been encouraged and fostered by a welfare system that has been *designed around the needs of the most dysfunctional and disadvantaged few*. The consequences of this were stark; *across generations and throughout communities, worklessness has become ingrained into everyday life* (Duncan Smith, 2012).

So, governments are still talking about a cycle of deprivation, or cultures of workless-ness as if they are the principal causes of poverty. Of course, this message is rein-forced on a daily basis by the tabloid press, which invariably presents welfare-related news in a negative, sensationalist way. Hence the sentiments that underpin such behavioural interpretations of poverty tend to have popular support (Cunningham and Cunningham, 2012). However, as in the past, the evidential basis for such claims is lacking. For example, a recent Joseph Rowntree Foundation-funded study drew attention to the fact that *official statistics* estimate that only 0.5 per cent of work-less families are characterised by two generations of worklessness. Moreover, despite what the researchers described as *dogged searching in localities with high rates of worklessness across decades*, they were *unable to locate any families in which there were three generations in which no-one had ever worked.* The research concluded that *politicians and policy-makers should abandon the idea of intergenerational cultures of worklessness – and, indeed, of cultures of worklessness* (Shildrick et al., 2012, p3). In our social class chapter (Chapter 8), we will examine in more detail the growing trend to demonise those in poverty and will consider the implications of this for social work practice.

Structural explanations for poverty

Structural explanations of poverty focus upon the inequalities that are endemic within the structure of society and associated political or economic factors, such as low pay, unemployment, economic recession, the demise of industry; the widen-ing gap between rich and poor; and the withdrawal of welfare services. The causes of poverty then, are located first and foremost within structural forces and not the individual.

Marxist/conflict view
This perspective critiques all individualistic arguments and maintains that poverty, like wealth, is an *inevitable* consequence of a capitalist society. Like Gans, Marxists argue that poverty benefits the ruling class, as it ensures that there is always a work-force willing to accept low wages. Similarly, the existence of unemployment and job

insecurity means that there is always a 'reserve army of labour' able and willing (or, unable to be unwilling) to take their place if they are not happy. Capitalism and the bourgeoisie therefore benefit from the existence of poverty. As Kincaid (1973) has stated, it is not simply that there are rich and poor, rather some are rich because others are poor.

For Marxists then, poverty is an intrinsic and integral feature of capitalist society, which is a direct consequence of the inequality inherent in the class system. They argue that until the bourgeoisie are overthrown by the proletariat and the capitalist system is replaced by an egalitarian socialist system, there will always be poverty, irrespective of any half-hearted attempts to alleviate it by the welfare state. How then, do Marxists explain the existence of welfare institutions including social services departments, that appear ostensibly designed to assist the poor and eradicate poverty? Jones and Novak (1999) note that it is essential for capitalism that poverty is maintained and managed, hence welfare benefits, like the rest of the welfare state, are not designed to assist people out of poverty. Rather, the welfare state has a palliative role, as it offers a partial cure for the worst effects of capitalism, ensuring at the same time that social harmony and the status quo are maintained. Social work is regarded by Marxists as an instrument of the state, which further exists to maintain the *status quo*. Social workers help people to *adjust* to their difficulties, by providing services, or a listening ear; and in doing so they ensure that structural problems become individualised, with attention shifted away from real underpinning causes. In this sense, poverty is maintained because poor people internalise their own failings; they are temporarily and partially 'soothed' by the help being provided, and any revolutionary threat arising out of discontentment is negated. Becker (1997) is critical of social workers and the state regulation they implement. He scathingly suggests:

> *Social workers have become ideologically incorporated into their employing organisation; they owe their existence and power to the power of the state, and their function is largely to maintain institutional ends. For many tens of thousands of poor families with children, contact with social services, and with social workers in particular, continues to be fraught with danger.*

(Becker, 1997, p118)

Marxists, then, clearly locate the source of poverty in the unequal nature of society; they identify the welfare system as an instrument of the state which acts to maintain gross inequalities of wealth that see some people living in dire destitution with little chance of ever really escaping from it.

Poverty: do social workers have a role to play?

> *There are good reasons why social workers should be 'willing and able' to tackle poverty and its effects. After all, poverty is associated with just about every social ill one can think of and with which social workers grapple.*

(Mantle and Beckwith, 2010, p2382)

As a profession, social work intervenes with some of the most impoverished and disadvantaged people in Britain. This is not new; social work has been linked with poverty since its birth, and the profession largely emerged out of charitable attempts to address the plight of the poor. Mantle and Beckwith (2010) advocate that *social workers should be directly involved in the relief of poverty* (p2380) and note that they have an ethical responsibility to adopt a critical perspective that conceptualises poverty as a structural problem. However, arguably social work has perhaps lost sight of its role in relation to poverty, with social workers typically *working in and around* poverty rather than working to actively combat it. According to the British Association of Social Workers (2012, p9) Code of ethics, *Social workers have a responsibility to promote social justice in relation to society generally, and in relation to the people with whom they work* and this involves challenging discrimination, recognising diversity, distributing resources fairly, challenging unjust policies and practices and *working in* solidarity *to challenge social conditions that contribute to social exclusion, stigmatization or subjugation and work towards an inclusive society*. Yet it is likely that few local authority social workers would recognise this as being part of their role, working with high caseloads in bureaucratic settings where practice is prescribed and regulated to an extent that there is a tick list for everything (except perhaps, combatting poverty).

In 1997, Becker was scathing of the profession for its lack of what he called 'poverty awareness' and suggested that social workers lacked any real insight of the issues.

> *Social workers have little understanding of the complex processes that generate and maintain poverty; they have limited insight into how their political and welfare ideologies and attitudes to poverty affect their daily practice with poor people; they have failed to place poverty on the agenda for social work theorising, education, policy and practice.*

(Becker, 1997, p114)

Although the above quote is dated, this view arguably holds resonance today, with academics such as Jones and Novak (2014) retaining the view that social workers lack any real understanding of the political and structural basis of poverty. Research by Paul Gilligan (2007) at Bradford University found that entrants to social work degrees overwhelmingly held individual explanations for problems that service users experienced. This confirms Becker's argument ten years previously that social workers are no different to others in making distinctions and judgements between different groups of the poor – between the 'deserving' and 'undeserving', between 'copers' and 'non-copers' (Becker, 1997). His view was that most social workers believe they can have little strategic impact on poverty itself and therefore that they should intervene with individuals rather than on a structural level. These ideas are interesting. Years of teaching social work students have led us to recognise that many do still want to intervene to bring about change and that they are aware of the constraints in which people live their lives. However, when students commence their placements (often those in statutory social services) they often report that their initial ideas are constrained by cultures in organisations that are mostly based upon an ideological premise that change is not possible at a structural level. Students tell us that it feels like they have a 'mountain to climb', and that they come up against barriers imposed by a dominant mode of working and a culture of defeatism. Research by other academics backs this up (see for example, Jones, 2001), but it is our view that bringing about change as a social worker is always possible, however small and however insignificant it may at first seem.

So, how can social workers fulfil their ethical obligations to combat poverty? O'Brien's work (2011) is useful here. He studied social workers in New Zealand to see if and how they translated the ethical commitment to social justice into their practice and found that there were three levels at which they could do this:

- on a *micro* level in direct practice with service users where social workers promoted the rights of people, advocated on their behalf and supported service users to address issues to effect a socially just outcome;

- on a *meso* level in terms of challenging agency policies, procedures and practices and bringing about organisational change; and finally,

- on a *macro* level, which might involve taking action at a wider political level, challenging government policies, lobbying for change, writing to ministers and aiming to effect change at a structural level.

Perhaps unsurprisingly, O'Brien found that although he was deeply impressed by the work and efforts of the social workers in his study, the most challenging and therefore less common action was at a macro level. He argues that, in order to engage effectively at that level, agencies need to ensure ongoing critical discussion of the structural issues that affect service users and that professional associations and other related bodies take the lead to develop mechanisms to engage in social change actions.

Bob Holman has long been a proponent of more radical approaches to social work practice. He has been very critical of individualised casework approaches that mask the social and political forces operating in people's lives. They do so, he believes, because focusing upon individual problems or issues in isolation tends to implicitly assume that the issues are unique to and are the fault of the individual, who needs to change to bring about a better state of affairs. Holman advocates that a casework approach denies the *collective* problems of those in poverty, preferring methods that actively aim to reduce inequality and combat poverty and oppression. In 1993, Holman suggested social workers adopt an approach of 'mutuality', facilitating collective action among those who share similar circumstances. The recognition of mutual obligations and common kinship, expressed in joint action, is key to attaining a more equitable sharing of resources and responsibilities. He argues that the role of the social services should be to support families and individuals exposed to poverty, and to prevent them reaching the point where intervention is imposed upon them. He claims that the aim should be to modify the devastating effects of social inequalities which now ruin the lives of so many (Holman, 1993, p71). To do this, *community social work* should be at the core of social services. He suggests that neighbourhood-based family centres are more valuable than approaches which aim to monitor and control families. Community-based social work has partnership, respect and empowerment at its heart and is committed to achieving change via mutual support and collective action.

Community social work has seen something of a renaissance in recent years, particularly in the voluntary sector where a plethora of agencies and projects seek to work in empowering ways to support individuals whilst also affecting change on a more macro scale.

Mantle and Beckwith (2010) strongly advocate a community-orientated social work approach, which starts with the premise that it is the community which needs to change and not the individual. The assumption is that the community itself has the capacity to solve problems and that through power sharing and a shift to collective support and empowerment, social workers can discard traditional individualistic approaches which often serve to blame service users for the circumstances they find themselves in. Mantle and Beckwith urge local approaches, which adopt community profiling to inform a structural understanding of the challenges faced by local communities and working in genuine partnership with people. They draw upon the work of Drakeford and Gregory (2008) to advocate the development of credit unions to support people in acute financial need and help them to avoid the ludicrously high interest rates on offer from payday loan sharks. Their view is that social workers have a role to play in such initiatives, mobilising collective action within poor communities.

The Social Work Action Network (SWAN) was founded by a group of academics concerned about the direction of the social work profession. Back in 2004, SWAN developed a *new manifesto for social work* (Jones et al., 2004) which identified a crisis in social work resulting from years of managerialism, a paucity of resources, and the domination of care management approaches. The manifesto highlights the fact that social workers are frustrated by 'surface' responses to deep-seated problems and note that there is a need for a new, engaged social work, committed to social justice and to challenging poverty and discrimination at a 'macro' level. The importance of collective approaches is emphasised with a redefinition of the profession in terms of its value base, rather than the functions it serves for the state. The manifesto argues that the:

> potential for social change has all but been squeezed out of social work by the drives towards marketisation and managerialism ... yet overwhelmingly it is still the case that people can enter social work not to be care managers or rationers of services or dispensers of community punishment, but rather to make a positive contribution to the lives of poor and oppressed people.

> (Jones et al., 2004, p4)

The very *role* of the social work profession is at the heart of this debate and many social workers struggle to balance their own ideological beliefs with those of their employing agency. Social workers may consider themselves to have a moral responsibility to work in partnership with service users, to at least raise the profile of those in poverty and work in an empowering way to bring about as much alleviation as possible. Whether this goes far enough, however, is an issue individual social workers must grapple with in terms of their own practice and choice of employing agency.

ACTIVITY *2.9*

Where do you stand?

In small groups, discuss the Manifesto for Social Justice and identify the key points. You can download this from **www.socialworkfuture.org/about-swan/national-organisation/ manifesto**

What do you think about the manifesto? With reference to your placement setting, how are the principles in here applicable in your agency and how can the suggestions for an alternative social work be translated into practice?

What are the potential problems and benefits of adopting such an approach?

Having read this chapter about poverty and social work, what do you think your role will be? In other words, where do you stand?

Some principles for working

Our own view is that all social workers should be actively involved in combatting poverty. This should manifest not only in *what* they do, but *how* they do it.

- First and foremost, social workers should develop a clear understanding of the structural basis of poverty, recognising that poverty arises out of unequal economic and social structures. This is not to deny individual responsibility; however, it is to acknowledge that the 'odds' are *always* stacked against those living in poverty. An appreciation of the links between disadvantage, unequal opportunities and poverty is absolutely fundamental to every aspect of practice and should be assessed in universities at the pre-qualification stage. If social workers start from the premise that poverty is somehow the personal responsibility and fault of the individual, this will permeate every single interaction they have with their service user, leading to potentially very harmful and oppressive practice. This needs to be followed up in post-qualifying training and CPD initiatives.

- Second, social workers need to understand the impact that poverty can have on people. They need to recognise and accept that poverty is the *context* in which many other issues and problems occur. Social workers need to engage with service users in ways which allow their voices to be heard, giving time to service users to explore the obvious and not so obvious impact of poverty.

- Third, in acknowledging the above two points social workers need to reflect upon how they communicate with people who are in poverty, checking out that they are acting in accordance with social work values as opposed to pre-conceived stereotypical ideas. Basic skills around communicating respect and understanding in non-patronising ways are key here and social workers should be prepared to work with people in their own surroundings.

- Fourth, social workers need to have good local knowledge of the resources around in the local area; they should familiarise themselves with knowledge about benefits, about any credit unions that exist and other services that might be of help. Service users often need practical help and social workers should be armed with knowledge about local services and resources, as well as with a working knowledge of welfare solutions.

- Fifth, social workers may need to provide the energy to work with people whose lives are blighted by poverty, to transcend the often stultifying weight of poverty. If social workers themselves approach situations believing that things cannot change, then they become part of the problem rather than part of the solution. Working with service users to help build their confidence and self-esteem is key here.

- Sixth, social workers need to be aware of and use community-based initiatives that work to tackle poverty and social exclusion – for statutory sector social workers this may be about referring on to voluntary sector projects or working in partnership with projects to involve service users and actively engage them in action that lobbies for change. In doing so, this fosters encouragement of consciousness raising and power sharing, while working to actively bring about change at local and national levels. Social workers may be involved in challenging housing departments for example, or supporting service users to appeal decisions, or empowering service users to fight for their rights where decisions have not been good ones.

- Finally, social workers need to think about their own political activities outside of work. This will vary for different people – for some, involvement in local politics is key; for others, being trustees of local organisations is another way of becoming involved. For yet others, working on national campaigns and protests, or being affiliated to campaign organisations is attractive.

Whatever the action is, our view is that something is better than nothing at all. Apathy is simply not an answer and it is not acceptable for social workers to benignly work in and around poverty. Every action, no matter how small, can make a difference.

CHAPTER SUMMARY

Poverty continues to be an enduring feature of the lives of many social work service users. It is therefore extremely important that social workers possess a sociological understanding of key debates and issues. These debates are not purely academic. Policy-makers tend to gravitate towards either behavioural or structural explanations, with those from the 'right' traditionally veering towards behavioural interpretations and those from the 'left' towards more structural interpretations. Hence sociological debates about the causes of poverty shape official responses to it and structure the framework within which social workers respond to it. In addition, the impact of poverty upon service users should not be underestimated. Social workers need to develop an understanding, not only of the material and practical consequences of poverty, but also its emotional impact upon the ability of individuals and families to cope with the associated stresses.

Peter Townsend's (1979) *Poverty in the United Kingdom.* London: Allen Lane is a classic study of poverty in which he makes a powerful case for the adoption of relative definitions. For a contrasting perspective which advocates the use of absolute definitions of poverty, see **Bartholomew, J** (2006) *The welfare state we're in.* London: Politico Publishing.

For a perspective on the experiences of children who live in poverty in Britain today, see **Ridge, T** (2011) The everyday costs of poverty in childhood: A review of qualitative research exploring the lives and experiences of low income children in the UK. *Children and Society,* volume 25, pp73–84.

Useful online resources include the Child Poverty Action Group website www.cpag.org.uk and the Joseph Rowntree Foundation website, www.jrf.org.uk.

For a discussion of poverty related to social work, see **Jones, C and Novak, T** (2014) *Poverty and inequality.* Bristol: Policy Press (forthcoming). Also, **Sheedy, M** (2013) *Power, poverty, politics and welfare.* Maidenhead: Open University Press.

Chapter 3
Social exclusion, sociology and social work

ACHIEVING A SOCIAL WORK DEGREE

This chapter will help you to develop the following capabilities from the **Professional Capabilities Framework**

- **Professionalism**
  Describe the role of a social worker.

- **Values and ethics**
  Understand the profession's ethical principles and their relevance to practice.

- **Rights, justice and economic wellbeing**
  Understand the principles of rights, justice and economic wellbeing, and their significance for social work practice.

- **Interventions and skills**
  Demonstrate the ability to engage with people in order to build compassionate and effective relationships.

It will also introduce you to the following standards as set out in the 2008 social work subject benchmark statement:

3.1.1 Social work services and service users.
3.1.4 Social work theory.
3.1.5 The nature of social work practice.

Introduction

Following on from the discussion on poverty in Chapter 2, this chapter will examine the concept of social exclusion, assessing its sociological origins and its relevance to social work. In terms of the importance of the concept to you as social work students, its relevance may seem fairly obvious, since the social work profession is responsible for delivering services to a range of 'excluded' individuals and groups. A cursory glance at the extracts from the *Subject Benchmarking Statements for Social Work* and the College of Social Work's *Professional Capabilities Framework* will serve to reinforce its significance. As the *Subject Benchmarks* state, there is a need for social work students to have an understanding of the *poverty, unemployment, migration, poor health, disablement, lack of education and other sources of disadvantage that lead to marginalisation, isolation and exclusion and their impact on the demand for social work services*. In this sense, the relevance of 'social exclusion' to you as social workers could not be made more explicit. The concept of social exclusion is, however, also interesting sociologically, because explanations as to its causes vary, as do the potential 'solutions' that have been recommended by different academics and politicians. Hence, as with many of the concepts examined in this book, 'social exclusion' has been the subject of much heated debate and disagreement, and there is no consensus as to what measures should be taken in order to tackle it. In this chapter we examine the competing interpretations of social exclusion and their implications for policy and practice. We also look at the direction of social exclusion policy in the UK, particularly in relation to the exclusion experienced by families, examining both the assumptions that underpin policy, and their sociological 'ancestry'.

Origins of the concept

The concept, social exclusion, emerged out of developments at a European Union level, but between 1997–2010, it came to permeate social policy documents and guidance across a range of government departments in the UK. The integration of 'social exclusion' into the UK social policy agenda occurred almost immediately after the 1997 general election, when the Labour government announced it was creating a Social Exclusion Unit (SEU). Riding upon a wave of optimism following its landslide election victory, the government declared that it would put the priority of tackling social exclusion at the forefront of its strategy to create a more fair, socially just society. The Social Exclusion Taskforce (SET) superseded the SEU, but its location at the heart of government in the Cabinet Office was seen as a reaffirmation of the government's commitment to combatting social exclusion. Since the election of the Coalition government in 2010, the SET has been disbanded and far fewer explicit references are made to the term 'social exclusion' in policy documents. However, the Coalition's 'social justice' strategy, like Labour's approach to social exclusion, is guided by a concern that there are *hundreds of thousands of individuals and families living profoundly troubled lives marked by multiple disadvantages* (Department for Work and Pensions, 2012, p1).

We need to begin by examining how social exclusion differs from the concept of poverty that we examined in the last chapter. The concept is essentially based on the notion that low income alone is not the only, or indeed the prime, cause of social ills such as poverty, crime, teenage pregnancy, homelessness, substance misuse and unemployment. There is, advocates of the concept argue, a need to acknowledge other causes of 'exclusion'. To quote the Labour government's SET:

> *Social exclusion is about more than income poverty. It is a short-hand term for what can happen when people or areas have a combination of linked problems, such as unemployment, discrimination, poor skills, low incomes, poor housing, high crime and family breakdown.*

(SET, 2007a)

This belief, that 'exclusion' results from factors other than income poverty, continues to be reflected in the Coalition's 'social justice' strategy. As it argues, *the focus on income over the last decades has ignored the root causes of poverty, and in doing so has allowed social problems to deepen and become entrenched* (Department for Work and Pensions, 2012, p4).

ACTIVITY **3.1**

In small groups, discuss the circumstances which can lead to some people being excluded. You may wish to think about factors which:

- *prevent some people from being successful in the job market;*
- *prevent people from being involved in their community;*
- *prevent people from accessing services;*
- *lead to some children being excluded from school;*
- *contribute to some people not exercising their right to vote;*
- *lead to some people facing harassment and being victims of hate crime.*

Try to think as widely as possible and consider a wide range of people. If you have been on a practice placement and encountered service users who were socially excluded, you may wish to focus upon the service user group you worked with and consider some of the factors that contributed to their social exclusion.

The above exercise will have helped you to think about some of the non-income based factors which can cause social exclusion. Your discussion will hopefully have focused on the impact that lack of work opportunities, prejudice and discrimination can have on the ability of certain individuals and groups to access 'inclusion'. As we show here and elsewhere (see Cunningham and Cunningham, 2012), variables such as social class, gender, race, disability, age, sexuality and even geographical location can have a profound impact upon people's life chances, constraining opportunities and shaping patterns of exclusion. In the previous chapter, we discussed how a key role of social work is to assist service users to overcome the disadvantages they experience, and in this respect, one of the main advantages of the concept of social exclusion to you as a social worker is that it can help you to understand the complex, multi-faceted factors that contribute to the problems they face. Lack of income is certainly a key variable, but so too are a range of other mediating factors.

In its most common usage, therefore, with the concept of social exclusion the emphasis moves away from material resources, particularly income, to other potential causes of exclusion. Hence, in John Pierson's (2009) summary of the main features of social exclusion, poverty/low income is just one of five key components, the others being:

- barriers to the jobs market (including discrimination);
- lack of support networks;
- the effects of living in extremely deprived communities;
- lack of access to good quality services.

Hence social exclusion is not necessarily linked to financial hardship, and although 'poverty' is clearly an important 'excluder', it is not the only one that individuals and groups face. In this sense, there is potential for a greater acknowledgement of the way other forms of exclusion can structure and shape disadvantage. When we think of social exclusion like this, as sociologists we can see its explanatory potential. For example, the discriminatory barriers that people who are disabled, black, lone parents or mental health service users face often arise irrespective of income. The societal 'inclusion' of these social groups may ultimately be impeded more by these factors than low incomes *per se.*

Despite the apparent usefulness of social exclusion as a concept, its emergence into the political mainstream has not occurred without contention. This is because there is no consensus as to what the causes of social exclusion are, or what the solutions to it should be. In the brief summary above, we referred to a range of structural problems that can contribute to exclusion. However, social exclusion is a 'slippery' concept and there are widely different interpretations as to its causes, some which point to structural factors and others to behavioural causes. Ruth Levitas (2005), a leading writer on social exclusion, has offered three dominant interpretations of the concept, each of which we outline briefly below.

Three interpretations of social exclusion

Redistributionist discourse

In explaining social exclusion, redistributionist (or redistribution) discourse places a primacy on causal factors such as low income, prejudice, discrimination, lack of opportunity to a decent education or to work, and other 'barriers' that prevent individuals and groups from participating fully in society. From this perspective, the 'socially excluded' (or certainly the bulk of the 'socially excluded') are not held responsible for their situation. Their exclusion results less from their own moral culpability or failings, and more from structural constraints that are largely beyond their control. In this respect, the concept is seen to provide an effective and more progressive alternative to the pejorative term 'underclass' that tended to dominate and shape debates about poverty and disadvantage in the 1980s and 1990s. Instead of focusing on the behaviour of disadvantaged groups, the social component of the term 'social exclusion' draws attention to the wider societal factors that create barriers to inclusion. Indeed, for some it goes much further, highlighting the relationship between the excluded and those who do the excluding. Exclusion, David Byrne (1999, p1) argues, is *something that is done by some people to other people*. When viewed in this way, not only does social exclusion offer the potential for shifting attention away from excluded people's so-called behavioural or 'handicapping characteristics', it can also lead us to focus instead on the culpability of those who are doing the excluding, whether this be employers, welfare agencies or governments.

In its most common manifestations, analyses of social exclusion written from within a redistributionist discourse stop short of calling for a radical transformation of capitalist society. It is generally believed that social exclusion can be tackled 'from within' by the removal of discriminatory barriers, by improved educational opportunity and moderate levels of income redistribution. In terms of its ideological origins, the philosophy underpinning redistributionist discourse contains elements of a concern for social justice and fairness, combined with a belief that exclusion is harmful to the social and economic fabric of society. Social exclusion, therefore, is seen as morally wrong, and as posing a threat to cohesion, efficiency and stability. Solutions focus on the need to introduce social reform to tackle the structural constraints that inhibit inclusion – for instance, economic and social inequality, prejudice and discrimination.

One of the major criticisms of redistributive discourse stems from politicians and academics on the right of the political spectrum; they argue that by overly concentrating on the supposed social and economic barriers that inhibit inclusion, the culpability of many 'problematic' individuals and families remains unacknowledged. Put simply, they argue that redistributive discourse fails to appreciate that many individuals simply choose to live a lifestyle which itself is responsible for their exclusion – some choose not to take up employment opportunities that are available; some choose to take addictive, illegal drugs; some choose to have children outside wedlock and remain dependent on welfare; and some choose to engage in disruptive antisocial behaviour. Critics, therefore, accuse redistributive discourse of misguided sentimentality, and of being too reluctant to apportion blame. This kind of criticism is linked to Levitas's second interpretation for social exclusion, moral underclass discourse.

Moral underclass discourse

Advocates of individualistic, behavioural interpretations for social problems have also sought to shape social exclusion debates. Levitas refers to this as 'moral underclass discourse'. With this interpretation, blame for exclusion is placed upon the socially excluded themselves. It is their behaviour – their lack of moral fibre, their drug addiction, their criminal behaviour, their poor parenting skills, their laziness, their unwillingness to work or to take up other opportunities offered – that determines their marginal position in society. Clearly, moral underclass discourse has much in common with the individualistic, behavioural explanations for poverty that were examined in our previous chapter. A small but significant number of 'dysfunctional' individuals and families are, it is argued, choosing to engage in anti-social, problematic modes of behaviour and in doing so are destroying their own life chances as well as the fabric of the communities within which they reside. For advocates of moral underclass discourse, the solution to social exclusion lies in coercive, targeted interventions designed to deter and control the inappropriate, 'deviant' patterns of behaviour that lie at its heart. The focus of attention (and intervention) is on a relatively small group of recalcitrant individuals, rather than wider economic and social structures.

Advocates of the moral underclass discourse also bemoan the 'morally corrupting' impact of state welfare, believing that it serves to encourage and inculcate the 'dysfunctional' patterns of behaviour that lead to social exclusion. They argue that well-meaning, but misguided welfare provision saps motivation and initiative, turning naïve, easily led sections of society into a dependent, 'cowed' clientele. The 'lure' of a council house encourages teenage girls to get pregnant; the 'promise' of a benefit income encourages idleness; and the 'coddling' of vulnerable individuals by social workers has led to a denial of the socially excluded's own agency in contributing to their circumstances. This approach is vulnerable to the same kind of criticisms marshalled against 'behavioural' interpretations for poverty in Chapter 2. In short, it stands accused of ignoring wider structural determinants of social exclusion, which are beyond the individual's control.

Social integration discourse

With this interpretation, the primary focus is on paid work and its importance as a means of ensuring effective inclusion. Although it shares some aspects of redistributionist discourse, this explanation pays far less attention to non-labour-market based causes of exclusion, such as low income and low levels of social participation, and much more emphasis is placed on the primacy of work as a means of securing 'inclusion'. Within this discourse, the terms 'social exclusion' and 'exclusion from paid work' are used interchangeably, and the panacea to exclusion is integration, or re-integration into the workplace. While there is an acknowledgement of some of the barriers that prevent access to the labour market (for instance, prejudice and discrimination), it is generally assumed that work opportunities are available and, with 'encouragement', those who are socially excluded can be enticed into taking these up.

Social exclusion, therefore, is principally construed as non-participation in the labour market and solutions are aimed at increasing work participation, through both incentives, and, crucially, in some cases, coercion. On this latter point, it is worth noting that social integration discourse, like moral underclass discourse, is concerned about the potentially dependency-inducing effects of welfare. Hence, the creation of a more 'active' welfare system, which provides greater encouragement for those who are 'inactive' to take up employment opportunities, forms an important part of any inclusion strategy. Reforming welfare, by placing more emphasis on the fulfillment of duties and obligations, will, it is hoped, help to tackle the 'lack of aspiration' that is said to contribute to exclusion. The resultant increase in employment activity will, social integrationist discourse assumes, ultimately contribute to a reduction in social exclusion.

Importantly, for advocates of social integrationist discourse, it is not only the economic status that work confers that is at the heart of its attraction. As well as providing obvious financial benefits, it also boosts self-esteem, provides participants with the opportunity to develop, socialise, build social networks, imparting a sense of dignity, self-worth and purpose. With work comes a moral and social status – a sense that one is part of and making a contribution to the economic and social well-being of society. Work, then, provides an 'integrative' function and is beneficial for all – individuals and society.

Social integrationist discourse has been criticised for failing to fully appreciate the structural barriers that prevent people from accessing work, such as a lack of employment opportunities and/or deeply embedded prejudice and discrimination. The notion that 'inclusion' can be reduced to employment activity has also been challenged:

Such an analysis ignores the possibility that paid employment per se may not, in any case, be the most appropriate answer to the problems encountered by many marginalised groups, such as people who cannot work because of, for example, disabilities, or people who have left the labour market, such as retired people.

(Barry, 1998, p7)

The suggestion that 'inclusion' can only be achieved through paid work effectively denies or negates the claim that social exclusion can or should be tackled through mechanisms other than the labour market. It can serve to legitimise the notion that being out of work and on benefits inevitably leads to poverty and social exclusion, making 'inclusion' a status to be earned through work, rather than, for example, as a potential right to be entitled to via state provision. Finally, work itself is no guarantee of 'inclusion'. More than two-thirds of 'poor' children are living in households where the parent or guardian is in work, yet their life chances continue to be harmed by the poverty that they experience (CPAG, 2013).

The three social exclusion discourses are summarised in Table 3.1.

Table 3.1   Summary of Levitas's social exclusion discourses

	Causes of social exclusion	Solutions to social exclusion
Redistributionist discourse	• Low income • Poor educational opportunity • Lack of decent work opportunities • Prejudice and discrimination • Other economic and social barriers that inhibit inclusion	• Moderate levels of income redistribution within the existing system • Higher wages • Improved welfare benefits • Improved educational opportunities • Anti-discriminatory legislation
Moral underclass discourse	• Lack of moral fibre • 'Dysfunctional', irresponsible patterns of behaviour (for example, illegitimacy, bad parenting, criminality and substance misuse) • Over-generous levels of welfare, which reward or encourage dependency and 'deviancy'	• Punitive, coercive interventions designed to deter irresponsible behaviour • Reductions in levels of welfare support, aimed at reducing dependency and forcing people to take responsibility for their own lives and situations • Stigmatisation of deviancy and reinforcement of 'appropriate' behaviour and moral values
Social integrationist discourse	• Non-participation in the labour market • Low levels of motivation and aspiration • An outdated welfare system that expects far too little in return for the rights that it confers • Prejudice and discrimination	• Encourage greater participation in the labour market • Tackle the 'lack of aspiration' that is said to contribute to exclusion • Reform welfare, so that more emphasis is placed on duties, in particular the responsibility to participate in the labour market • Anti-discriminatory legislation

ACTIVITY 3.2

Read the case study below relating to John. Using Levitas's three interpretations of social exclusion above, identify how a social work approach might be different if a moral underclass, redistribution or social integrationist approach were adopted.

John is an African-Caribbean man who is 20 years of age; he grew up in a severely deprived area with his mother, Kelly, a lone parent reliant upon benefits, and his sister, until he was 13. John was then placed in the care system as Kelly, who experienced poor mental health, felt unable to cope and expressed real concerns about her son's welfare. At the time she described John as being 'out of control', not attending school, staying out all night and getting involved in petty crime.

John spent the next five years of his life initially with many different foster carers, and eventually in a residential home. He sometimes returned home for short periods but remained 'looked after' until he was 18. He was excluded from school on numerous occasions and consequently his education was badly disrupted; he regularly smoked cannabis and became withdrawn.

When John left the care system at 18, he initially went home but felt he was a worry to his mother, Kelly, so he left and lived on various friends' sofas, sometimes sleeping rough and occasionally returning home.

John is IT literate and hoped to work in this field. After school, with the help of one of the social workers in the residential home where he lived, he applied for several jobs, but had little success. Each time he applied and was turned down, John's confidence sank further and he has never been in employment.

John is bored through the day and watches daytime TV, occasionally smoking dope. He has indicated that he is lonely and depressed and Kelly sometimes worries that he will harm himself.

There are a range of factors that moral underclass discourse might point to in interpreting John's situation. His involvement in petty crime and other forms of problematic behaviour could be put down to the lack of a positive influence and discipline of a father figure. It might also be seen in the context of the proliferation of 'liberal' criminal justice policies, which have removed the threat of deterrence and effectively absolved young criminals of responsibility for their actions. In interpreting John's unemployment, moral underclass discourse might point to the dependency-inducing effects of his mother's reliance on welfare. John, it would argue, has grown up without any work ethic, thinking he has a right to be maintained at the state's expense. Solutions would focus on the need for tough, punitive action to ensure that levels of illegitimacy and dependency, and the problems said to be associated with them, do not spiral out of control. Welfare provision must be severely curtailed and those who choose not to follow mainstream values (through, for example, having children outside wedlock, or choosing not to support themselves independently) must be made aware of the consequences of their actions.

While advocates of social integrationist discourse would not see John's mother's lone parenthood as a major issue, they too would focus on the problems associated with both Kelly and John's lack of participation in the labour market. With this perspective, work is seen to impart a sense of worth and value, acting as an integrative force, contributing to cohesion, binding people together with a shared sense of responsibility and duty. The solution to John and Kelly's 'inclusion', therefore, may lie in the introduction of a combination of supportive and coercive mechanisms, which enable and encourage them to participate in the labour market. This may involve improved childcare provision, better training opportunities and welfare reforms, designed to create a more proactive social security system which has more appropriate balance between rights and responsibilities (such as the Coalition's Work Programme).

Redistributionist discourse might point to the impact low benefit income had on Kelly's ability to cope with the stresses of everyday life. It may also emphasise the discrimination John possibly faced as both a young African-Caribbean male and a child in the care system, and how this affected his educational and employment opportunities. Redistributionist discourse would also draw attention to the unemployment that blights the neighbourhood where John was brought up and lives. In this sense, John's disruptive behaviour and, more recently, his depression and fatalistic attitude towards life, can be interpreted as an understandable response to the structural barriers that have contributed and continue to contribute to his exclusion. From this perspective, any solution must address low levels of benefit, the absence of genuine work opportunities and the prejudice and discrimination that shapes the lives of people like John.

Sociology and social exclusion

You should by now have gained an understanding of the key elements of each of the three major different interpretations of social exclusion. Before further assessing the relative influence of each of these approaches on policy and practice, it is important to consider the sociological origins of some of the ideas they contain. At first they seem to have little in common, in that they differ in their explanations for social exclusion and the solutions they advance. However, as we show below, when looked at 'sociologically' there is one key area of similarity.

Functionalism and social exclusion

While moral underclass, social integrationist and redistributionist discourses appear mutually exclusive, they do, in fact, share a common intellectual heritage, in that all three, to varying degrees, accept the *status quo* as essentially sound, and at the same time see social exclusion as posing a threat to the stability of society. In this sense, they are influenced by the functionalist tradition of sociology, and in particular the ideas of Emile Durkheim, which regards society as being held together by the integrative institutions of, for example, the labour market, the community and family. Participation in all three spheres of life is considered to be of primary importance by functionalists, with those who do not participate for whatever reason being perceived as 'dysfunctional' in some way. As outlined in Chapter 1, the central themes within Durkheimian functionalism are social order, social cohesion and solidarity, and functionalists are concerned with how these are affected by the particular conditions and pressures of modern industrial societies.

Functionalists accept that moral and social breakdown can occur within society, but they see this as being the result of temporary disturbances to the social equilibrium, which can be quickly corrected, rather than a major fault with the system itself. While differences of interest exist, and order, cohesion and solidarity are sometimes threatened, the bigger picture is one of shared values and a belief that all groups benefit if society runs smoothly. If the social order breaks down, and people or groups are perceived to present a threat to social cohesion, society needs to have adequate means of ensuring that anti-social behaviour is dealt with and conformity re-established.

In relation to our different interpretations of social exclusion above, it is clear that all three, like functionalism, are concerned with the 'disintegrative' impact of what they see as 'dysfunctional' social and economic trends. Moral underclass discourse warns of the dangers posed to society by moral failure, deviant behaviour and family breakdown, whereas social integrationist discourse focuses upon the 'disintegrative' effects of detachment from the labour market. Redistributionist discourse appears more radical than either of the other two interpretations, in that it places a much greater emphasis on wider, structural determinants of exclusion. However, as with the other two, the basic structure of society is seen as sound, fundamental reform is deemed unnecessary, and it is important for the 'greater good' for the equilibrium in society to be restored and maintained. Of course, the solutions advocated by these three discourses vary, but the main point here is that all three see social exclusion in terms of the negative impact it has upon what is seen to be an essentially 'sound', well-functioning social system. Levitas has thus described all three as conservative theories of social exclusion, in that they view current social and economic arrangements as given. Neither, for example, contemplates the solution to social exclusion as lying with a fundamental redistribution of income from rich to poor.

Marxism and social exclusion

You may have already noticed that one key sociological tradition – Marxism – is not represented in any of the three dominant interpretations of social exclusion we have discussed. As we have already seen, functionalist claims that capitalist societies are characterised by solidarity, cohesion and integration are dismissed as an illusion by Marxists, who see such societies as being defined by gross inequalities in power, wealth and privilege. For Marxists, the real world is shaped by injustice and exploitation and this inevitably generates endemic poverty, social dislocation, opposition and conflict. It is, Marxists argue, in the interest of the bourgeoisie to present this poverty, and the conflict it generates, as 'abnormal' and 'pathological', rather than an inevitable outcome of an unjust system. Herein lie the 'functions' of the social exclusion debate. According to Marxists, social exclusion discourses understate division, portray society as well functioning and cohesive, and imply that poverty and other social problems are 'aberrations', only experienced by an excluded 'minority', and are capable of 'cure':

> It [social exclusion] detracts attention from the essentially class divided character of society, and allows a view of society as basically benign to coexist with the visible reality of poverty. It does this by discursively placing the unwanted characteristics outside society.

> (Levitas, 2005, p188)

Hence, Marxists are deeply suspicious about the ascendance of the concept of social exclusion in academic and political debates. They argue that, at best, 'social exclusion' (in the form of redistributionist discourse) offers us little more by way of explanatory potential than traditional structural interpretations of poverty, which have always drawn attention to the social causes of structural disadvantage. More fundamentally, they insist that the universal embrace of the concept among political elites owes much to attempts to politically 'sanitise' debates about poverty and serve 'closure' on solutions that are based on demands for much greater income redistribution and a radical transformation of society. Thus, Piccone has described social exclusion as the *liberal snake oil prescribed for all social ills by those who uncritically assume the existing system to be fundamentally sound* (cited in Barry, 1998, p5). Levitas has also argued that the operationalisation of the concept in the UK has served a wider 'political' function in that it has detracted attention from the fundamental reforms – in particular, a wider degree of income redistribution of income from rich to poor – that are needed to tackle social exclusion:

> *The overall thrust of both policy and rhetoric has been to reduce poverty and exclusion without tackling overall inequalities in income and wealth, and without increasing either income tax or corporation tax.*

> (Levitas, 2001, p456)

In conclusion, Marxists argue that debates over social exclusion serve to obscure the unacceptable inequalities in wealth that are a feature of many advanced capitalist nations. Society is portrayed as comprising an 'included' majority and an 'excluded' minority. On the one hand, this serves to marginalise the vulnerable, often justifying coercive interventions, while on the other hand, attention is diverted away from the gross inequalities in wealth, opportunities and advantage that exist among those who are 'included'. As Levitas (2005, p7) argues, the excluded are conceptually placed 'outside' society and held morally culpable, while *the very rich are discursively absorbed into the included majority, their power and privilege slipping out of focus if not totally out of sight.* We are left with a rosy, overly homogenous view of society, one where poverty, deprivation, conflict and division are seen as marginal and pathological conditions, rather than endemic features of a fundamentally unjust system.

How can social work contribute to the demise of social exclusion?

For Marxists, social work cannot make any serious inroads into the endemic poverty that dominates the lives of service users. At best they can mitigate its impact, by providing palliative advice and services. At worst, they become agents of the state, implementing policies designed to re-moralise the poor and reintegrate them into a non-existent, harmonious Durkheimian utopia. Jones and Novak (1999) feel that, historically, this has been a key function of social work. They are, to cite one seminal Marxist social work text, *trapped in a social structure which severely delimits their power and hence their ability to initiate significant change* (Bailey and Brake, 1980, pp7–8). Chris Jones and Tony Novak (1999, p.83) feel that, historically, this has been a key function of social work:

> *For all their psycho-social rhetoric, social workers diagnosed the problems presented by clients as being rooted not in their poverty but in their flawed personalities. In many respects, their incursions into the underbelly of British society were similar to those of the missionaries of colonial Britain. There was nothing to learn from the 'natives'; social workers were the carriers of 'truth' and bringers of civilisation.*

Ultimately, Marxists argue that the solution to the social and economic problems that are a feature of capitalist societies lies in the creation of a radically different social and economic order, based upon the principles of equality and social justice. That is, of course, not to say that social workers have no role to play in working with service users to bring about positive change in their lives, or in exposing the injustices of current economic arrangements. That said, Marxists argue that poverty, discrimination and urban decay are all key features of capitalism, and their solution requires more fundamental social change than social workers themselves have the power to affect.

Nor do adherents to moral underclass discourse see the solution to social exclusion as lying with social work. Indeed, in as far as they are currently configured, social work and state welfare are seen as part of the problem. Their 'liberal' values and cosseting of vulnerable individuals has exacerbated the problems service users face, creating a dependent social service clientele. Irrespective of moral culpability, social workers, according to moral underclass discourse proponents, treat their service users as 'victims', provide excuses for their dysfunctional behaviour, and aid their attempts to eke out a livelihood on welfare. As Charles Murray (1994, p86), a leading proponent of this discourse, argues, when it comes to explanations for so-called 'disadvantage', there is *no shortage of social workers and academics prepared to make excuses to try to shield them from the consequences of their behaviour.* These notions influenced social policy reforms introduced during the 1980s and 1990s by successive Conservative governments, which sought to curtail state responsibility for welfare. From this perspective, for social work to become part of the 'solution' to social exclusion, social work education and practice will need to be radically reconfigured. As Marsland (1996, p188), another enthusiastic supporter of moral underclass discourse, insists, there would need to be a *decisive shift away from the current emphasis on rights, to education in the practical skills required to help people to help themselves.* Hence, those such as Marsland would prefer to see the development of a more judgemental form of social work practice; one that recognises that the primary causes of 'exclusion' are linked to the welfare-induced moral failings of the poor. As we will see, this approach has also informed policy and practice under the current Conservative-dominated Coalition government.

Advocates of redistributive discourse would, however, see a far more positive role for social workers in tackling social exclusion, acknowledging the potentially progressive role social workers can play in transforming the lives of service users. Social workers, for example, can help to maximise the incomes of the poor by guiding them through the intricacies of the benefit system, advising them of their rights and ensuring they receive support to which they are entitled. They can also help service users develop social networks, supporting them to access agencies and organisations that provide opportunities for further inclusion. Social workers can also act as advocates for service users, assisting them to overcome discriminatory barriers and prejudice that prevent them from accessing services and opportunities. In addition, social workers can campaign on behalf of service users, drawing the attention of policy-makers to the exclusionary impact of regressive economic and social policies. Social workers are, in short, in a position to empower service users; they can act as progressive agents of change and help reduce levels of social exclusion.

Likewise, advocates of social integrationist discourse would welcome the impact social workers can make in tackling social exclusion, though they would place much greater emphasis on the role they can play in encouraging or enabling people who are excluded to engage or re-engage with the labour market.

What direction social exclusion policy?

Within the academic literature on social exclusion in the UK, much attention has been devoted to analysing the trajectory of the previous Labour government's response to the issue. This is not surprising, given the primacy that successive Labour governments attached to the concept. Prior to losing the General Election in 2010, Labour claimed that its social exclusion strategy was a major success. However, critics argued that the potential and flexibility of the concept of social exclusion was not being realised in the Labour government's inclusion strategy. Hopes among some that Labour would embrace 'redistributionist discourse' were, they argue, dashed, and Labour's responses to social exclusion owed much more to the ideological influence of social integration, and, in particular, moral underclass discourse, than redistributive concerns. Fiona Williams argued that Labour had *managed to combine the integrationist emphasis of ... social exclusion discourse with the 'underclass notion' of neo-liberal poverty discourse, whilst moving away from the focus on inequality and redistribution* (Williams, 1998, p17).

Levitas (2001) detected a particularly strong influence of moral underclass discourse in the government's policies. She argued that Labour sought to 'marginalise' and 'individualise' social exclusion, by creating the impression that it affected only a small section of society, who were failing to take up the 'opportunities' offered to them. She noted that the SEU's (and later the SET's) initiatives were aimed at relatively small groups, whose behaviour was deemed to deviate from the prescribed norm, and who were seen to pose a threat to social and moral order. The 'poor parenting skills' of teenage mothers and lone parents were blamed for community breakdown. Young people not in education, employment or training (often referred to as NEETs) were portrayed as lazy, feckless youths who lazed around all day, engaging in idle games and petty crime. At the same time, the social exclusion experienced by much wider sections of the population, such as unemployed and disabled people, hardly registered at all within Labour's social exclusion strategy. Where these groups were discussed, they were invariably accused of failing to take up work opportunities and were held responsible for burgeoning welfare bills. Thus, interventions influenced by 'moral underclass discourse' were implemented to tackle the supposed inappropriate, 'dysfunctional' patterns of behaviour among the poor, while a 'works first' approach, influenced partly by social integrationist strategies, was introduced to drive people into employment, whatever the cost. Meanwhile, the structural causes of social exclusion – economic decline, lack of work opportunities, inadequate benefits, prejudice and discrimination – remained largely unresolved. Critics of Labour's record, therefore, argued that the 'redistributive rhetoric' that surrounded its social exclusion strategy was not matched by its interventions, the effects of which were to pathologise the excluded and blame them for their own fate and also for wider social and economic problems.

In the previous edition of this text, we analysed one of Labour's 'flagship' social exclusion strategies, which was designed to tackle 'family' exclusion, *Reaching out: an action plan on social exclusion*. Here, we update the analysis, examining the initiatives that evolved from this strategy. We also consider the trajectory of social exclusion policy under the Coalition government, assessing the extent to which it has been marked by continuity or change.

Reaching out

In September 2006, the Labour government published what it described as a key document on social exclusion, *Reaching out: an action plan on social exclusion* (SET, 2007b). In the Preface to *Reaching out*, Tony Blair reaffirmed the government's determination to tackle social exclusion, insisting that a commitment to ensuring everyone should have the opportunity to achieve their potential in life remained *at the heart of this government's mission* (p3). However, as we have already stated, the underlying philosophy of the government's social exclusion strategy was questioned. While some welcomed the report and its recommendations, for others it seemed to signal a further shift away from a redistributive approach and a movement towards behavioural, 'moral underclass' strategy.

Reaching out began by outlining the successes of the government's social exclusion strategy. However, the overarching focus of *Reaching out* was on those who, despite the government's best efforts, seemed to be *stuck in a lifetime of disadvantage* (p3). Against this background of success, the government argued, *the relative lack of progress of a small minority stands out* (p19). The 'minority' was said to consist of 2.5–3 per cent of the population, roughly 1.3 million people, though this was not made explicit in either the document itself, or in subsequent media coverage of the report's recommendations.

How did the government explain this relative lack of progress among certain sections of the community? *Reaching out* sought to draw a stark contrast between, on the one hand, the achievements of those who had embraced the 'opportunities' provided, and on the other hand, the continued deep-seated exclusion of those who had not. The message was simple: the opportunities were now there, and if individuals or families were failing to grasp them, then some more targeted, focused and coercive levels of intervention were necessary. Hence, responsibility for the chronic social exclusion experienced by the bottom 2.5–3 per cent of the population was seen to lie

largely with the socially excluded themselves. According to the report, it was a consequence of their problematic lifestyles, which resulted from *chaotic lives – such as anti-
social behaviour, criminality and poor parenting* (p74).

In language reminiscent of Keith Joseph's 'transmitted deprivation' theory (see
our chapter on poverty, Chapter 2), *Reaching out* suggested that dysfunctional
'cultural' characteristics were passed down from one generation to the next via
a cycle of deprivation (p19). In this sense, the intellectual origins of the analysis
and policy prescriptions contained in *Reaching out* did seem to have much more
in common with the moral underclass discourse than they did with the redistributive discourse. Even the rationale for intervention – that is, the reason for wanting
to tackle exclusion – focused more on the 'problems' caused by sections of community to society, than it did the need to tackle the wider societal barriers that
inhibit inclusion, such as low incomes, discrimination and barriers to the job market. The behaviour of some people, the report argued, *particularly some of the
most challenging families – causes real disruption and distress to the community
around them.* The government also outlined the financial cost of 'problem families', estimating this to be around £250,000 per year, per family (Campbell and
Temko, 2006).

Reaching out's recommendations generated a good degree of controversy when the
report was published. In short, the report outlined a plan for the early identification of future 'chaotic' and 'problematic' individuals and families, backed up by a
series of sanctions designed to force people to change their behaviour. Some of the
criticism the government faced focused on the case it made for using sanctions, such
as benefit withdrawal or even the removal of children from parents, as a means of
ensuring cooperation, and the possible dangers of removing financial support from
already vulnerable families. However, the major area of contention and controversy
centred on the age at which attempts to identify risk ought to begin. Basically,
Reaching out suggested that this process should start *before individuals are born.*

ACTIVITY **3.3**

When Reaching out *was published, the proposals were greeted by a flurry of sensationalist, but largely supportive, headlines in the tabloid press. Below is a representative selection of headlines:*

Blair's Attack on Unborn Thugs – Daily Star (1/9/06).

*ASBOs in the Womb: Blair Aims to Spot Problem Kids Before They Are Born – Mirror
(1/9/06).*

£250,000 a Time: The Cost of Problem Families – Express (4/9/06).

*What impact do you think the above headlines would have in shaping public opinion
about people who are socially excluded?*

Reaching out identified a range of 'pre-birth' and 'post-birth' 'risk factors', which, it announced, community midwives and health visitors will use to 'diagnose' an unborn child's potential for future misbehaviour and exclusion (p28). Table 3.2 shows the pre-birth risk factors highlighted in the report.

Table 3.2   'Pre-birth' risk factors

• Genetic predisposition	• Smoking in pregnancy
• Obstetric difficulties	• Neglected neighbourhood
• Prematurity/birth factors	• Low income
• Stress in pregnancy	• Poor housing
• Teenage pregnancy	

The existence of any or a combination of these pre-birth risk factors could be sufficient to trigger an initial two-year period of interventions with families. The precise nature of these interventions was not made clear, but based upon the experience of similar schemes in the United States, the government seemed to be envisaging regular checks by social workers and health professionals and compulsory involvement in programmes (again, under the threat of sanctions) designed to improve parenting, conduct and behaviour. This was subsequently confirmed when the government set out its *Think Family* agenda, the key elements of which were geared towards a series of intrusive, disciplinary-focused family intervention projects. The rationale, to cite one government-funded report, was to identify factors that place unborn children *at risk for 'life-course persistent' criminal involvement, antisocial behaviour and social exclusion* (Utting et al., 2007), and the aim was to alter what is perceived to be the families' pre-determined, 'dysfunctional' life-course.

Evidence base for the proposed intervention

While tabloid newspapers reacted favourably to this proposed clampdown on 'dysfunctional', problem families, the evidence base for such interventions was lacking. Indeed, research funded by the government itself suggested that those suffering from the most deeply rooted forms of social exclusion – that is, those targeted by *Reaching out* – were the least likely to benefit from its proposals. After considering evidence from US evaluations into similar initiatives, Utting et al. (2007, p84) found that:

> *What little evidence exists suggests that within a 'treated' population it is generally the most needy, most challenging families and young people who are least helped by these programmes. In families where parents have mental health problems, where there is substance misuse, or where there is a background of serious abuse and neglect the outcomes are often least positive.*

Another Cabinet Office-commissioned review of the literature on family-based interventions came to much the same conclusions, highlighting a number of problems that had, internationally, been associated with this kind of response to social exclusion (Morris et al., 2008). First, it had often led to the embrace of an inappropriate 'blaming' approach in policy and practice, *leading to pathologising of family members, particularly mothers* (p3). The authors suggested that this was especially the case with 'solutions' based around the sort of 'risk factors' listed in *Reaching out*, which encouraged practitioners to search for negative behaviours and traits (that otherwise may have remained unnoticed or dismissed had they manifested themselves in a different family). Second, viewing social exclusion through a 'risk focused lens' often led to an ignorance and undermining of the genuine efforts made by many socially excluded families to cope with and overcome their difficulties. *Marginalised families*, the report argued, *may themselves be demonstrating significant strengths which might go under-recognised if services focus on risk and responsibility*. Finally, where they had been introduced, family-based interventions were frequently presented by policy-makers as the *sole* panacea to the difficulties families faced, meaning that there was a failure to acknowledge and address the wider structural causes of social exclusion. As the report stated, *the current discourse across the political spectrum is almost entirely focused on the failings of parents instead of with the failure of institutions to respond to dual-earning and single-parent families* (pp21–1). The authors linked this tendency to the ideological orientation of family-focused social exclusion research and policy, much of which continued to be underpinned by 'moral underclass discourse':

> *Although [Charles] Murray's ideas have seemingly slipped from the national and academic consciousness, the themes of 'problem families' endure in policy and practice (with an emphasis on punitive measures to address family 'failings').*

> (Morris et al., 2008, p46)

In their conclusion, the authors did not deny the utility of family support work. However, for family-based interventions to succeed, there needed to be a recognition within policy and practice of the wider, societal sources of many of the problems that families faced:

> *… in many cases the kind of support that families experiencing marginalisation require is intrinsically the same as other families, including the need for adequate income, housing, formal and informal supports, engagement with schools, activities within and outside of family life, access to mainstream facilities, and so on.*

> (Morris et al., 2008, p17)

In summary then, research funded by the government itself cast serious doubt upon the appropriateness and likely success of a social exclusion strategy based mainly upon remedying 'family dysfunction'.

Reaching Out in practice: from *Think family* to *Troubled families*

Reaching out was swiftly followed by the publication of a number of documents which set out the principles and guidelines for what would become known as Labour's *Think family* approach to social exclusion. A cursory glance at the SET's *Think family* literature serves to illustrate the close ideological links between *Reaching out* and the *Think family* strategy (as, indeed, does the title of the initiative itself). While there was a tacit acknowledgment of the structural constraints that restrict opportunity, overarching emphasis was placed upon the need to tackle what was perceived to be pathological family dysfunction. It was suggested that the exclusion faced by severely marginalised families could be tackled through a range of family-focused initiatives, such as Nurse Family Partnerships and Family Intervention Projects.

Family Intervention Projects

While family intervention is clearly not a novel phenomenon within social work and social policy, Family Intervention Projects (FIPs) are a relatively new development, forming a key part of Labour's *Think family* approach to social exclusion. Delivered by a combination of local authorities and voluntary agencies, FIPS involve intensive levels of both outreach and residential-based family intervention and supervision, backed up in many cases with coercive powers to discipline families who fail to modify what is often considered to be their own 'destructive' behaviour. Sanctions, such as eviction and even the threat of removal of children from families, are seen as integral to the success of FIPS:

> The use of sanctions is an important lever for motivating families to change. Demoting tenancies or gaining possession orders suspended on the basis of compliance with the projects or, for some, the very real prospect of children being taken into care, can provide the wake up call.

(Home Office, 2010)

The location of intervention is therefore set at a family rather than a societal level, and there is an implicit assumption that families themselves are responsible for their own, and indeed their community's exclusion (Parr, 2011). In fact, Labour ministers made no attempt to disguise the behavioural assumptions that would underpin the government's FIP strategy. Announcing an expansion of FIP initiatives, the then Home Secretary, John Reed, boldly stated that, *by tackling bad parenting we are tackling child disadvantage and social exclusion* (Doward, 2006). Hilary Armstrong, the Minister for Social Exclusion, reinforced the point:

> Poor parenting can have dramatic long-term negative consequences for a child and severely limit their life-chances. It can expose children to greater risks, can contribute to the development of potentially harmful behaviour, and can reinforce inter-generational cycles of deprivation and exclusion.

(cited in M2 PressWire, 2006)

While the precise nature of FIPs does vary – some have been shown to be shaped by a more progressive, welfare-focused (redistributionist) ethos than others – the ideological inspiration for FIPS is clearly discernible. Based upon the notion that parental irresponsibility and family dysfunction are the principal causes of the UK's social exclusion problem, their intellectual origins can be found within moral underclass discourse. Another point worthy of note is, as Parton (2009) has acknowledged, the marginalisation of the social work profession from many FIP initiatives. References to the role of social workers has remained conspicuously absent from much of the related policy documentation, and many FIP practitioners are not qualified social workers. This, as we explain later, may not be an inadvertent oversight, and could be linked to Ministerial concerns that 'soft' social work values, such as the importance of non-judgemental, anti-oppressive practice, had the potential to 'dilute' the disciplinary focus of FIPs.

By 2009, FIPS were established in some 74 local authorities and around 2000 families had participated in them. Before Labour left office, it envisaged that all local authorities would embrace FIPS by 2011 and that 20,000 families would participate. As we will show below, FIPS continue to form a key part of the Coalition government's social exclusion strategy, and in December 2010 David Cameron announced that he would extend the initiative to encompass 120,000 'Troubled' families by March 2015. We have, therefore, seen something of a political consensus emerge over the solutions to family exclusion, one that is rooted largely within moral underclass discourse. However, just how effective have initiatives such as FIPs been in tackling the problems they are purported to be capable of solving?

RESEARCH ROUND-UP

FIP evaluations

As we have noted elsewhere, the assumptions underpinning FIPs, as well as their methods of intervention, have been the subject of considerable debate in academic and policy circles (see Cunningham and Cunningham, 2012). Labour ministers claimed that the projects were successful, and certainly early evaluations commissioned by the government suggested that many of the families involved in them had shown some positive outcomes, with project staff reporting significant improvements in certain kinds of behaviour. The results of these initial evaluations, however, were tentative and, as the authors of one evaluation put it, should be treated with caution (see, for example, White et al., 2008, p93). Findings, for example, tended to be based upon the subjective views of project staff, who had a vested interest in exaggerating their success. In addition, none of the earlier studies used control groups, making it impossible to assess whether the outcomes may have been the same had there been no interventions at all. In addition, the early participants in the FIP programme may have been the most motivated of eligible families, meaning that successful outcomes were more likely to be achieved.

More recently, the National Centre for Social Research has sought to assess the 'success' of FIPs by comparing the outcomes of participant families with a non-FIP control group of families with similar profiles and characteristics. The findings suggest that claims that FIPs are an unqualified success do not hold up to scrutiny. For example, although crime and anti-social behaviour among participant families appeared to diminish, no evidence was found for improved outcomes in relation to education, employment, health improvements, or indeed family functioning. In short, there was little evidence to suggest that FIPs led to reductions in poor parenting, marriage, relationship or family breakdown, domestic violence and child protection issues (Lloyd et al., 2012, p83).

(Continued)

(Continued)

However, the concerns raised around FIPs do not centre solely upon their failure to achieve the targeted outcomes. The assumptions that underpin FIPs have also been criticised, as has the wider ideological impact of such family-focused responses to social exclusion. According to Garrett (2007), there is a danger that their narrow focus upon family pathology and biological metaphors (such as generational transmission of dysfunction, and the pollution of the wider community) can act as an 'ideological smokescreen'. It can lead to the scapegoating of a small, vulnerable section of the population for problems that have wider, societal origins. The evaluation of FIPs conducted by White et al. (2008) found that many practitioners in the wider social work field expressed resistance to the FIP ethos for precisely this reason – they were uncomfortable with the enforcing or 'punitive' element of the FIP model (p34). Non-FIP practitioners also expressed concerns about a lack of qualifications and experience of FIP staff, and the emphasis that such projects placed upon the personal qualities of their staff as opposed to formal professional qualifications.

Garrett argues that we should view FIPs with caution. When interpreting the techniques and outcomes of such projects, we should be aware of how they can serve to stigmatise recipients and popularise simplified interpretations of the causes of disadvantage. From this perspective, the ideological fall-out caused by the behavioural focus of family intervention projects has the potential to impact upon all the poor, and not just those families directly affected. Newspaper headlines surrounding the FIP initiative, such as the Daily Star's Sin Bins for Scum Families *(Hughes, 2009) and the Daily Mail's* Cameron's War on Feckless Families *(Shipman and Walker, 2011), do seem to suggest that such fears are not unfounded. Moreover, there can be little doubt that the* problem family *discourses, which focus the blame for societal ills on families themselves, have re-emerged in recent years after a welcome period of absence.*

Social exclusion policy under the Coalition

The Coalition government's approach to social exclusion is epitomised in the decision it made soon after taking office to abolish the SET. This was a clear statement of political intent, as was the almost simultaneous creation of the Behavioural Insight Team (BIT) within the Cabinet Office. Also referred to as the government's 'nudge unit', the work of the BIT is based upon the premise that the aim of public policy should be to 'nudge' or 'coerce' people into changing their 'harmful' patterns of behaviour. As the foreword of one early report published by the BIT argued, *many of the biggest policy challenges we are now facing ... will only be resolved if we are successful in persuading people to change their behaviour, their lifestyles or their existing habits* (Dolan et al., 2010, p4). The ideological significance of the establishment of the BIT should not be underestimated, nor should the shift its creation was intended to signal in the Coalition's approach to problems such as social exclusion.

Of course, as we have seen, Labour's SET had, in reality, tended to eschew 'social' explanations for exclusion in favour of 'behavioural' interpretations. However, the abolition of the SET and the appointment of the BIT was doubtlessly intended to reinforce the Coalition's message that social problems had behavioural rather than structural roots. As we show in other chapters of this text, David Cameron's pre-election distancing of the Conservative Party from an orthodox 'moral underclass' approach to social ills was quickly reversed in government and, since 2010, welfare ideology, policy and practice have been subjected to a distinct authoritarian, neo-liberal 'twist'. Senior Coalition ministers, including the Prime Minister and the Chancellor, have spearheaded a concerted and, to an extent, unprecedented ideological assault on the welfare state, which has had the effect of undermining support for welfare and its recipients (Baumberg et al., 2012). This is a view that is even shared by some former ministers in the Coalition, such as Sarah Teather, the ex-Children's Minister. Since leaving office, she has described her disillusionment over the way her colleagues sought to deliberately stigmatise those on welfare for, she believes, ideological reasons. Asked whether the Coalition's approach to welfare was motivated by a desire to cut costs, or a genuine ignorance as to the structural causes of poverty, she replied, *No, I think it's more nakedly political than that* (Aitkenhead, 2013):

> *Stigmatising people on benefits is politically popular, but it isn't fair, it isn't right, and it will have long-term impacts on society that I think we will come to regret deeply. Over a period of time it will make Britain less generous, less sympathetic and less willing to cooperate. It will reduce the ability of the most vulnerable members of society to participate in that society, and make it more difficult for them to help themselves. Furthermore, it will make it more difficult for campaigners coming after.*

(Teather, cited in McCarron and Purcell, 2013, p3)

Moral underclass discourse has therefore loomed large in the Coalition's rhetoric. The message is clear; lax, overgenerous benefits have created a 'culture of entitlement', promoted fecklessness and fraud, allowing 'shirkers' to remain voluntarily idle at the expense of 'striving' taxpayers. 'Exclusion' is thus individualised. The 'social' element to 'social exclusion' is cast aside in favour of a behavioural approach, which focuses on the need to police and discipline, rather than provide support. Just to reiterate, Labour governments also allowed such interpretations to infuse its social exclusion strategy, but moral underclass discourse has permeated virtually every aspect of the Coalition's welfare agenda, justifying policy responses such as the benefits cap, bedroom tax and a tightening of disability benefits. The creation of the BIT should perhaps be seen as an attempt to provide a psycho-social, pseudo-scientific 'face' to the Coalition's neo-liberal, disciplinary 'turn' in policy.

'Troubled families', or 'troubling policy'?

David Cameron's 'Troubled families' initiative provides further evidence of a 'moral underclass' discourse influence on policy. Announced in the week following the riots that swept across the UK in August 2011, this strategy aimed to 'turn around' the lives of 120,000 families who, it was claimed, were gripped by a *culture of disruption and irresponsibility that cascades through generations*. Rejecting structural explanations for the riots, Cameron sought to locate the blame for the disorder itself with 'deviant' 'Troubled families'. However, their corrosive influence was said to stretch way beyond these one-off, spontaneous outbreaks of lawlessness. They were, he insisted, *the source of a large proportion of the problems in our society*, costing the taxpayer up to £9 billion per year. Predictably perhaps, Cameron's interpretation for the 'dysfunctional' behavioural characteristics of these families focused upon the 'morally corrupting' influence of a 'broken' welfare system. Troubled families were the victims of *an excess of unthinking, impersonal welfare*; they had *been subjected to a sort of compassionate cruelty … smothered in welfare yet never able to escape* (Cameron, 2011). A key part of Cameron's strategy for reversing this 'family dysfunction' has involved the creation of a Troubled Families Programme, now headed by Louise Casey, an outspoken, and at times controversial former advisor on anti-social behaviour to the previous Labour government. In the lifetime of the Parliament £448 million would be spent, funding intensive, 'hard headed' FIP-style interventions which would 'grip' 120,000 families, turning their lives around.

The programme has been beset by controversy since its inception. For instance, the claim that there are 120,000 'Troubled' families across the UK has not stood up to scrutiny. Indeed, the estimate appeared to originate from research undertaken by the previous Labour government, which estimated that 120,000 families were *'in trouble'* (not *'causing trouble'*). This research, published by the SET and entitled *Families at Risk*, found that these families were *suffering from* (and were not necessarily *responsible for*) a range of multiple disadvantages, including absolute and relative low income, overcrowding, parental illness and disability. As Levitas (2012) argues, senior Coalition ministers seemed to engage in a deliberate misrepresentation of this research, and in a subtle discursive 'manoeuvre', families 'with troubles' were reconceptualised and redefined as 'Troubled', or 'problematic'. As she points out, these families had indeed been identified as having 'troubles' – *physical and mental ill-health, poor housing, income poverty, material deprivation* – but the leap to presenting them as 'troublesome families' was problematic and misleading.

Despite these concerns, the Coalition has pressed ahead with this initiative, utilising the 120,000 headline figure to generate relatively crude estimates of the number of 'Troubled families' living in each local authority. Local authorities wishing to access the programme's funding (which amounts to up to £4000 per family) are required to 'populate' the targets they have been given by identifying the requisite number of 'Troubled families' in their areas, using the following criteria:

1. Families involved in crime and anti-social behaviour.

2. Families with children not in school.

3. Families with an adult on out of work benefits.

4. Families causing high costs to the public purse (Department for Communities and Local Government, 2012).

Clearly, these are *very* broad categories and, using these criteria, a identifying 'eligible' families should not be too difficult a process. For instance, in the context of a UK unemployment level of around 2.5 million people, it should be relatively easy for local authorities to identify families falling under category 3. The guidance for identifying families in category 4 – which suggests that, among others, all families containing individuals with long-term physical and mental health problems should be considered – is similarly broad, allowing local authorities considerable discretion in determining who is a 'Troubled' family. Of course, in reality, the 'troubles' experienced by the families identified may have little to do with their own culpability. While some may indeed have a history of anti-social behaviour or non-attendance at school, in the current economic context it is easy to see how worklessness may well be due to factors beyond a family's control. Likewise, is it really useful to categorise individuals experiencing long-term physical and mental health problems as 'troublesome'? This *is* an issue, because the negative rhetoric and imagery associated with this programme has, in practice, led to the widespread and popular assumption that participant families *are* problematic. The following headlines, taken from newspaper articles and web pages reporting on the 'Troubled families' programme, are representative of the media's presentation of the initiative to their readers:

- Daily Telegraph: *Blame bad parents for Britain's ills; Children are not being taught right from wrong at home* (Bingham, 2013, p1).

- MailOnline: *'Don't get pregnant, get a job': Poverty tsar says women from 'Troubled families' must go to GPs for lessons in contraception* (Chorley, 2013).

- Sunday Express: *'Shameless families' aid project helps 35,000 so far* (Buchanan, 2013).

- The Times: *Hardcore of Troubled families cost billions; Huge sums are being spent on caring and fostering children from families whose lives are marked by crime, truancy and worklessness* (Ford, 2013).

- MailOnline: *Three-year-old children spend so much time strapped into buggies or in front TV [sic] they are unable to walk, warns families' tsar* (Duell, 2013).

It is easy to see how such headlines can serve to reinforce pathological interpretations of social exclusion, and in relation to the 'Troubled families' programme specifically, can lead to the generation of stigma and hostility towards its participants. Of course, most local authorities are well are of the initiative's 'moral underclass' ideological foundations, yet despite this, by June 2012, 152 of them had shown a willingness to participate in it. They were doubtlessly encouraged to do so by the financial inducement of up to £4000 funding per family, rather than through any desire to endorse the ideological principles that underpin the initiative. At a time when local authority budgets have been severely hit by the Coalition's austerity programme, this is a valuable, alternative source of funding to them.

'Troubling' results?

How successful has the 'Troubled families' initiative been? The government claims it has been an enormous success. In her evidence to the House of Commons Local Government and Communities Select Committee in June 2013, Louise Casey claimed it had led to *amazing* results. Likewise, in September 2013, Eric Pickles, the Communities and Local Government Secretary, claimed that the *groundbreaking programme has successfully turned around the lives of ... England's toughest families* (House of Commons Hansard, 10 September, c43WS). However, at the time of writing, the data relating to the programme suggests a different scenario. If we take Birmingham as an example, none of the 1603 families that it had worked with had been 'turned around' by March 2013. Birmingham was not unique in this respect. As of January 2013, the 152 local authorities participating in the programme had identified 66,470 families and worked with 35,618 of these. However, only 1,675 (4.7 per cent) of these had been 'turned around' (DfCLG, 2013).

Of course, it may be that the 'success rate' of the 'Troubled families' programme will improve as the scheme develops. Indeed, our prediction is that the government's data will suggest that many families have been 'turned around'. However, future claims of 'success' should be viewed with some caution. First, the criteria for gauging 'improvement' are not the most rigorous. For instance, under the scheme, participation in the government's Work Programme is seen as a key 'success indicator', as is an adult moving into employment for up to 13 weeks. While movement into work is obviously a positive development, it is worth bearing in mind that this 'improvement' may have little to do with family intervention and may well have been a result of other factors, such as better job opportunities (again, there are no 'control groups' with which to compare the 'success rate' of participants on the 'Troubled families' programme). Nor, perhaps, should moving on to the government's Work Programme be constituted a success in 'turning around' the life chances of vulnerable, excluded families, given that the government's own research has found that its participants actually have a lower chance of finding work than those not enrolled on it (Public Accounts Committee, 2013). On a more general point, it is also worth noting that the incentive payments linked to 'success' may lead local authorities to ignore families whose exclusion is more entrenched and target the most motivated, easy to help families, which again will skew the programme's success rate. Finally, the government has made it clear that it is adopting a 'light touch' approach to auditing outcomes, giving local authorities (who are notoriously adept at exploiting the funding opportunities associated with schemes of this kind) opportunity to be 'creative' and exaggerate their success rates.

Just as importantly, of course, when assessing the impact of the 'Troubled families' initiative we should not underestimate its potential to tap into popular stereotypes, reinforcing negative societal perceptions of vulnerable families by portraying their exclusion as pathological. Of course, this may well be an intentional outcome of the programme, but it is not without consequences. A number of practitioner groups have warned of the dangers this poses to different categories of service users. Drugscope and Adfam (2012, p7) are concerned that the 'Troubled families' programme will serve to *reinforce the public opinion, often fuelled by the media, that there exist a number of badly behaved 'problem families' which constitute an irreversible drain on society and are categorically different from the rest of us*. They point out that the inevitable stigma that this generates could make it difficult to elicit support for meaningful, progressive practice with the kind of vulnerable individuals and groups they work with. Disability rights organisations have made much the same point. They argue that this initiative, coupled with more general rhetorical assaults upon the 'integrity' of claimants of disability benefits, has had the effect of demonising disabled people who are reliant upon welfare. Richard Hawkes, SCOPE's chief executive, has accused ministers of irresponsibly *playing directly into a media narrative about the need to weed out scroungers. Our polling*, he argued, *shows that this narrative has coincided with attitudes towards disabled people getting worse. Disabled people tell us that increasingly people don't believe that they are disabled and suddenly feel empowered to question their entitlement to support* (cited in Walker, 2012).

'Troubling' implications for social work practice?

Nor, we would argue, should we be blind to the potential of initiatives like this to change the perceptions and working practices of the social work profession itself. On this latter point, it is important to note that the introduction of the 'Troubled families' initiative has been accompanied by a rising tide of criticism of the profession, for its supposedly 'liberal', 'hand-wringing' approach towards the exclusion experienced by 'problem families'. There can be little doubt that this criticism has been orchestrated by Coalition ministers, who seem to have viewed the 'Troubled families' initiative as an opportunity to question the social work value base. For example, Eric Pickles, the Communities and Local Government Minister whose department is responsible for the 'Troubled families' programme, has sought to justify the scheme by accusing social workers of failing to challenge, and indeed promoting, an *'it's not my fault'* culture of excuses among 'problem' families. Social workers, gripped by naïve, liberal-minded political correctness have *run away from categorising, stigmatising, laying blame*, something his department's 'Troubled families' initiative would, he stated, deliberately avoid (cited in Chorley, 2012). The implication here is clear. 'Traditional' social work values, which emphasise the importance of empathy, non-judgemental and anti-oppressive practice are part of the problem, not the solution to turning these families around. Troubled families, Pickles insisted, *have got the language, they are fluent in social work*, and the social work profession needs to 'wise up' to the fact that it is being 'taken for a ride' by cunning, manipulative individuals. The Minister's comments prompted a favourable, albeit predictable reaction in the tabloid press:

> *Eric Pickles' observation ... that the welfare state's problem families were 'fluent in social work' exposed the damage that many social workers do by teaching their clients how to play the system. He confirmed the idea many of us have about social workers that they see their main duty as helping the feckless milk the welfare state for every penny, rather than weaning them off dependency.*

(Heffer, 2012)

Of course, such claims have no basis in reality, but the relentless nature of this message is beginning to resonate, particularly in the context of the reinforcement it has received due to the comments made by other senior Conservative ministers. As we discuss in other sections of the book, Michael Gove (2012), the former Education Secretary, has also accused social workers of failing in their duty to remoralise 'deviant' families. He demands that practitioners become *less indulgent* and *more assertive with dysfunctional parents* and for the care system *to expand to deal with the consequences* of problematic parenting. Social work training, he argues, has left practitioners *reluctant to directly and robustly challenge the behaviour of people whose trust they are trying to win*. Social workers have become *desensitised to the squalor they encounter and less shockable* and there is a *need to work harder to improve how the profession operates*. For those such as Gove and Pickles, part of the solution will involve a funda-mental reshaping of social work education. Gove favours *a shorter and more focused training programme*; one that will be workplace-based, stripped of critical, sociologi-cal content, and geared more towards equipping trainees with the disciplinary skills needed to force 'recalcitrant' families back onto the 'straight and narrow'. We exam-ine the ideological prerogatives that are shaping calls for the development of such a narrower, more moralistic, vocationally-focused social work curriculum elsewhere in the final chapter of this text. However, it is important to note here that these demands are not 'ideologically neutral' and are most frequently advanced by conservative com-mentators and politicians who have long sought to re-shape social work training along more disciplinary, authoritarian lines.

It is in this political context that we need to locate the 'Troubled families' initiative. Certainly, Louise Casey, the head of the 'Troubled families' programme has sought to present her teams as being the vanguard of a new, almost evangelically-driven cadre of practioners, who see the remoralisation of problem families as their raison d'etre. Repeating what is becoming an increasingly familiar theme, she argues that all too often social workers *collude with parents to find excuses for failure*. They should, she insists, learn from the work being undertaken by her practitioners: *They crack on. They get on with the job and they are quite assertive people*. In short, Casey's view is that the social work profession needs to emulate the work of her 'Troubled family' teams. They need to worry less about being *nice* and tell families the *honest truth* about the behavioural causes of their exclusion, becoming more *authoritative* and *challenging* (cited in Duggan, 2013).

What direction social exclusion policy?

Earlier in the discussion, we posed the question 'what direction social exclusion pol-icy'? If we take Labour's 'Think family' initiative and the Coalition's 'Troubled fami-lies' programme as representative strategies, then the trajectory is certainly imbued with a Durkheimian slant. First, the existing economic and social structure is seen as basically sound. If we can turn for a moment to the biological analysis favoured by functionalists, the assumption is that the 'body' as a whole is functioning perfectly well, but that there are elements within it that are malfunctioning and remedial action is needed in order to prevent further contamination. As we have seen, one of the problems with this kind of analysis is that it can lead to an underestimation of the extent of exclusion and can sometimes lend itself (as in the case of the 'Think family' and 'Troubled families' initiatives) to behavioural, moral underclass-like expla-nations for disadvantage.

It would, however, be a mistake to assume that family intervention is *necessarily* a regressive approach to dealing with social exclusion. As we stated earlier, many fam-ily intervention projects have been infused with progressive principles, and where this is the case, there is evidence of positive change and inclusive practice (Thoburn et al., 2013). As Pierson (2009) notes, as practitioners seeking to tackle social exclu-sion you may find that there is sometimes scope for *greater flexibility in practice than you might have thought*. Hence, although the intellectual origins of FIPS lie within moral underclass discourse, which focuses on disciplinary, behavioural explanations for social exclusion, in their practice social workers may continue to seek to pursue more progressive, redistributionist strategies. The point here is that although the legislative framework within which social workers operate may at times contradict and mitigate against 'redistributionist' responses to exclusion, in practice social workers are sometimes able to reconcile these contradictions, pursuing essentially progressive strategies within what is sometimes a regressive ideological and legislative climate. However, as should be evident by now, the political climate is such that the pursuit of such strategies is becoming increasingly difficult. On the one hand, the Coalition's austerity programme has starved local authorities of the funds needed to engage in meaningful, progressive practice with excluded families. On the other hand, the money that is available – such as that under the 'Troubled families' initiative – is becoming increasingly continent upon local authorities embracing behavioural interpretations for exclusion. We end the chapter with a discussion of the role social workers can play in combatting social exclusion.

Tackling social exclusion

We began this chapter by recognising that social workers are centrally involved in providing services and support to individuals and groups who are often socially excluded. In order to be able to do this effectively, it is of fundamental importance that social workers hold values that are based on a commitment to social justice; in other words, commitment to fair and equal treatment of all individuals and a fair distribution of resources.

Despite the attacks upon the social work education and practice by Coalition ministers and officials, the teaching of 'traditional' social work values continues, for the moment, to permeate social work training courses. However, for social workers who are committed to tackling social exclusion, these values must be translated into daily practice. The 'principles for working' that we outlined in our poverty chapter (Chapter 2) will help to provide you with a guide as to how you might succeed in doing this. In the current political climate, utilising those principles will obviously involve a passionate commitment to helping to make a difference to the lives of the people you work with. It will also involve resilience, as well as an ability to resist the ever-increasing political and organisational pressure to embrace behavioural, pathological solutions to disadvantage and exclusion.

As academics who have been involved in social work education for many years, we would argue that in order to intervene sensitively and professionally with individuals who are socially excluded, social workers must continue to *actively demonstrate* respect and the ability to value people from all walks of life. Actively demonstrating respect involves the social worker being warm and open, supportive and facilitative, listening carefully and allowing service users to talk freely, while facilitating a relationship that is based on honesty and trust. Coalition ministers might dismiss such an approach as 'sentimental hand wringing', but it is crucial that each service user's qualities and strengths, as well as their areas for development, are acknowledged.

As we noted earlier, one of the key problems with risk-based 'behavioural' forms of family intervention is that they frequently fail to appreciate the efforts disadvantaged families are making to cope with the difficult circumstances within which they find themselves. Nor do they often show any awareness of how the wider structural environment constrains the choices and behaviour of families. In this sense, moral underclass discourse offers us as social workers the least in terms of helping us comprehend and respond to social exclusion. Its overtly moralistic, 'blaming' explanations for exclusion, and its insistence that state welfare agencies and welfare professionals are themselves major contributory factors, affords us with little opportunity to understand the complex causes of the difficulties faced by service users, or develop positive, progressive solutions that research shows are more likely to work (Morris, 2013). Clearly, tackling social exclusion cannot be achieved solely by intervention that occurs on an interpersonal level. As Dominelli (2004) argues, commitment is needed for social workers to work in partnership with service users to intervene to make a difference at a community and structural level. She calls for needs-led universal services, rather than 'stigmatised residual services' and for an approach that works to undermine the forces of oppression.

As qualified social workers you may feel constrained by your role and organisation when faced with helping families overcome exclusion, and this is increasingly likely in the current political and economic context. However, as we argued in the previous chapter, it is vital for social workers to seek to resist these constraints to retain a commitment to change that is done so in a spirit of hope and enthusiasm. Like our 'principles for working', you will also find Pierson's (2009) work helpful in identifying achievable and practical ways of working to tackle social exclusion. As he points out, it is tempting to think that you and your colleagues can wait until someone fires the tackling social exclusion 'starting pistol' before seeking to combat exclusion. *But that is not a luxury you have. On the contrary, your role should be one of catalyst and change agent regardless* (p232). Pierson identifies core strategies for tackling social exclusion. These are:

- maximising income and welfare rights; knowing the benefits system and working to maximise the income of service users;

- working to strengthen networks, to provide emotional support and to facilitate inclusion in the community;

- building partnerships to strengthen ways of tackling exclusion, by joined-up solutions, sharing expertise and using collective muscle;

- promoting participation of service users in discussing, planning and arranging services and programmes that will affect them;

- working in the neighbourhood to help facilitate joint action and community development.

Pierson's book is a worthy and useful read for all social work students as it addresses strategies for working with different excluded groups. In terms of the three interpretations of social exclusion we outlined earlier, this kind of approach would share most in common with redistribution discourse.

CHAPTER SUMMARY

As we have seen, debates about the causes of 'social exclusion' now permeate the social policy agenda. However, popular acceptance and usage of the concept should not be allowed to disguise the real differences that exist between the explanations that have been advanced to account for social exclusion. Throughout this chapter we have drawn attention to the fact that there is no consensus as to what the causes of social exclusion are, or about what the solutions should be. It is, we have argued, a 'slippery' concept, meaning different things to different people. It is this that largely explains its appeal. For example, those on the Right can 'cash in' on the 'vogue' for social exclusion discourse, while at the same time remaining wedded to moral underclass interpretations of social problems. By contrast, those on the Left seize on the opportunity that the 'social' component of social exclusion seems to provide them to reinforce redistributive, structural explanations for social problems. We will leave you to make your own mind up as to the merits of the different discourses, but in doing so we would implore you to bear in mind the practice implications of each. At the same time, we would ask you to consider the compatibility of the competing discourses with the social work value base and their potential impact on different groups of service users. Finally, think about the reasons why you made the decision to become a social worker and consider the extent to which each of the explanations for social exclusion 'fit' with your own perceptions about what the causes of social exclusion might be.

FURTHER READING

Levitas, R (2005) *The inclusive society? Social exclusion and new labour.* Basingstoke: Palgrave Macmillan. It is in this influential book that Levitas sets out her explanations for the three different social exclusion discourses.

Jones, C and Novak, C (1999) *Poverty and the disciplinary state.* Abingdon: Routledge. This book provides a Marxist analysis of poverty, social exclusion and welfare.

Marsland, D (1996) *Welfare or welfare state? Contradictions and dilemmas in social policy.* Basingstoke: Macmillan. This book is written by a UK sociologist who offers a similar slant to Charles Murray's. Like Murray's work, it should not be read uncritically.

Pierson, J (2009) *Tackling social exclusion.* Abingdon: Routledge. This book offers an excellent read for social workers as it combines theory with clear practical approaches for tackling social exclusion.

Chapter 4
Families

A C H I E V I N G   A   S O C I A L   W O R K   D E G R E E

This chapter will help you to develop the following capabilities from the **Professional Capabilities Framework:**

- **Professionalism**
  Demonstrate the importance of professional behaviour.
  Describe the importance of personal and professional boundaries.

- **Values and ethics**
  Demonstrate awareness of own personal values and how these can impact on practice.

- **Knowledge**
  Demonstrate an initial understanding of the application of research, theory and knowledge from sociology, social policy, psychology, health and human growth and development to social work.

- **Critical reflection and analysis**
  Understand the role of reflective practice and demonstrate basic skills of reflection.

It will also introduce you to the following standards as set out in the 2008 social work subject benchmark statement:

5.1.1 Social work service, service users and carers.
5.1.2 The service delivery context.
5.1.3 Values and ethics.
5.1.4 Social work theory.
5.1.5 The nature of social work practice.

Introduction

Given the centrality of the family in social work practice, it is helpful for social workers to have an understanding of the nature of family life from within a sociological framework. This chapter analyses the variety of family forms in modern society and encourages you to think about how social work intervention may help or sometimes hinder the experiences of family members. It challenges you to reflect upon your own values and to critically consider these in light of the social work value base. Consideration of sociological theories and different feminist approaches to the family will draw upon relevant policy initiatives and the intersection with practice.

The family is one of the core social institutions in our society. The social work profession intervenes with families both in a supportive capacity and to exercise social control functions. The extent to which the family has rights to privacy from external intrusion, versus the right of the state to intervene in families to protect vulnerable citizens, is a core area of debate in social work. Sociological insights are helpful for social workers to enable them to think critically about family life. This is important so that taken-for-granted assumptions about families can be challenged and the complexities of family life understood. The precise nature of social work intervention in family life raises important philosophical questions concerning what gives social workers the *right* to intervene. Certainly this is a fundamental question and all social work students and qualified social workers need to have thought it through carefully so that they are ultimately comfortable with their role. Moreover, this is important if practice is to be grounded, legitimate and ethical.

ACTIVITY 4.1

Why do you think social workers have the right to intervene in family life?

You may have identified reasons such as the duty of the state to protect vulnerable citizens; children's rights to be safe and protected from harm; and the existence of legislation and policy. However, it is important to balance these factors with an acknowledgement of the damage that intervention can sometimes cause. As Thompson and Bates (1998) note:

> It would be naive in the extreme to fail to recognise that social work intervention is capable not only of making a positive difference to people's lives, but also doing considerable harm. The social worker has a great deal of power and such power can result in successful or unsuccessful outcomes ... intervention can have an extremely detrimental effect on individuals, families and groups. This can include: breaking up families, reducing self esteem, creating dependency, reinforcing stigma, discrimination, and oppression.

(p6)

It is also worth pointing out at this stage that social workers intervene with some families and not with others. Certain families are more visible to the gaze of the state whereas others are able to establish boundaries that keep professionals at bay. It is fair to say that social work surveillance tends to be directed at families from poorer, disadvantaged backgrounds. The disparity of state involvement with particular families and the fact that intervention can sometimes bring about more harm than good, are uncomfortable truths that social workers should be aware of and reflect upon throughout their careers. As social work intervention is premised upon decision-making of professionals, a critical approach to practice is necessary as well as an ongoing inner dialogue regarding the values that underpin decisions.

Before we proceed further with looking sociologically at the family, we want you to think more about the family and about your own experiences within families.

ACTIVITY 4.2

Make a list of the common characteristics of families. To help you do this, you might wish to reflect for a few moments on your own experiences of family life. How did your personal experiences of family life influence what appeared in your list? Working with someone you trust, share and compare your lists; what were the similarities and differences?

In this exercise, you may have come up with a list of positive characteristics such as:

- warm;
- loving;
- providing security;
- acceptable conflict;
- unconditional love;
- durable ties.

Alternatively, you may have come up with more negative characteristics, such as:

- arguments;
- violence;
- abuse;
- loss;
- bullying;
- conflict;
- separation.

Or more likely, you will have identified a combination of positive and negative characteristics. For some of you, this exercise in itself will have been a painful experience as family life can leave scars on people that go with them into their future lives. You may wish to reflect upon whether you drew up your list from experiences in your family of origin, or where applicable, from your own adult family life. Students often talk with us about their experiences of family life, some good and others not so good; one thing is clear – their experiences are incredibly diverse and varied, and they bring these into social work training with them. It is important that as student social workers you are able to think carefully about and reflect upon your personal experiences of family life, to enable you to enter the territory of family life as a professional. Failure to do so can lead to social workers being unable to separate out their own experiences and feelings from those of their service users. In the first chapter, we asked you to debunk your own life sociologically to enable you to locate yourself within society. In this chapter we will be asking you to do more of this, but specifically in relation to family life. First, we want you to begin to think about the boundaries around personal and professional life.

ACTIVITY **4.3**

Discussion exercise

Why is it important for social workers to be able to separate out their own experiences of family life from those of their service users?

To what extent are social workers' own experiences a help or a hindrance in their professional practice?

We will return to this issue later on in this chapter, but you are encouraged to give this issue some thought.

Different forms of family life

The question 'what is the family?' is frequently posed by sociologists and underlies the point that although in generic terms we talk about 'the family', in reality this can mean very many things to different people. The much-quoted popular image of 'the family' is of a typical nuclear family which consists of two married, heterosexual parents and their two children, who live together in their own home, often depicted with roses growing around the door, with a car in the drive. This is referred to by sociologists as the 'cereal packet family', as it reflects the ideal image traditionally portrayed in TV adverts. However, the reality for a large proportion of the population is a very different form of family life and the sweeping assumptions of 'normal family life' that frequently permeate popular culture are not helpful to people whose lives are so very different from the 'ideal' quoted above.

One classic definition of the family came from George Peter Murdock back in 1949:

> *The family is a social group characterised by common residence, economic cooperation and reproduction. It includes adults of both sexes, at least two of whom maintain a socially approved, sexual relationship, and one or more children, own or adopted, of the sexually cohabiting adults.*

(p1)

Murdock's formative work emerged from careful examination of 'the family' in 250 societies; he concluded that the family existed in some form in all known societies and was therefore a universal institution. Although some sociologists have refuted this claim (Oakley, 1986), Murdock's work has remained influential and his definition has been widely quoted. Notwithstanding the fact that the definition is now dated, the essence of it remains very much part of common assumptions about the average nuclear family in contemporary society. The typical nuclear 'cereal packet' family cited above reflects this norm.

ACTIVITY **4.4**

Looking carefully at Murdock s classic definition of the nuclear family, in what ways could it be critiqued for failing to reflect the reality of family life for significant numbers of the population?

In completing this exercise, you have probably identified factors that reflect trends in social life, including the following.

- *A decline in marriage* – In 2011 only 47 per cent of women in Great Britain aged between 18–49 were married, compared to 74 per cent in 1979 (ONS, 2013).

- *Increased number of divorces* – In 2012, it was estimated that 42 per cent of marriages in England and Wales would end in divorce (ONS, 2013a).

- *Cohabitation rather than marriage* – Between 1971–2011, the number of women in Great Britain aged 18–49 who were cohabiting tripled from 11 per cent to 34 per cent (ONS, 2013).

- *More births outside of marriage* – In 1961, 94 per cent of all births in England and Wales occurred within marriage or civil partnership, compared to only 53% in 2011 (ONS, 2013b).

- *Increased numbers of lone-parent families* – Between 1971 and 2011, the proportion of children living in lone-parent families in Great Britain rose from 8 per cent to 22 per cent (ONS, 2013).

- *Smaller families* – The proportion of children in Great Britain who are the only dependent child in their family has increased from 18 per cent in 1971 to 26 per cent in 2011 (ONS, 2013).

- *Increased recognition of gay or lesbian couples* – The Civil Partnership Act came into force in December 2005 and by the end of 2012 60,454 same-sex civil partnerships had been formed in the UK (ONS, 2013c). At the time of writing, same sex marriages have also recently been legalised.

- *Gay or lesbian parents* – More gay and lesbian adults are increasingly choosing to become parents, through donor insemination, surrogacy or fostering and adoption. Others have dependent children from previous relationships. In 2010, it was estimated that around 7 per cent of civil partnership couples in England and Wales had dependent children living with them (Ross et al., 2011).

- *Growth in single-person households* – In 1971, 5 per cent of adults in Great Britain were living in one-person households. By 2011 this had increased to 14 per cent (ONS, 2013).

- *Adults who live together but who choose not to have children* – In 2013, the most common family type in the UK was a married or civil partner couple family *without* dependent children (ONS, 2013).

- *Adults who live together but cannot have children* – Infertility affects one in seven couples in the UK: approximately 3.5 million people (Human Fertilisation and Embryology Authority, 2011).

- *Families who live together with other families* – Households containing two or more families are the fastest growing household type in the UK, increasing from 167,000 in 1996 to 281,000 in 2012 (ONS, 2012).

- *Extended families living under one roof* – Youth unemployment, high housing costs and population ageing are said to be leading to a growth of 'inter-generational' extended family households (AVIVA, 2012).

- *Foster families* – As of 31 March 2013, 50,900 children were being cared for in a foster placement in England alone, an increase of 16 per cent since 2009 (Department for Education, 2013d).

This exercise reveals that despite the prevalence of 'familism', (an ideology which suggests that *there is one type of family, one correct way in which individuals should live and interact together,* Gittins, 1985, p167), in reality, there is wide-ranging diversity in Britain today in terms of how people live. Indeed, taking into account all the trends outlined above, the proportion of people living in the 'traditional' family household of a couple with dependent children now constitutes a minority of the population (just 38 per cent in 2013, compared with 52 per cent in 1971) (ONS, 2013).

For social workers who work with families, it is of course essential that they are able to transcend familial ideology, which situates the typical nuclear family as being both the norm, and as being the institution that members of society aspire to. Social workers need to have a commitment to both recognising and *valuing* diversity if they are to practise in ways that are not oppressive. This is particularly pertinent if you think for a moment about the types of decisions social workers are involved in making. These potentially life-changing and sometimes devastating decisions, such as removing children from their birth families, placing children for adoption, making recommendations concerning residence and contact, for example, must be made on the basis of fair and equitable practice centred on the best needs of the child, not based on prejudiced views concerning particular family forms and lifestyles.

ACTIVITY 4.5

You may wish to complete this exercise on your own or with others in a small group. Either way, it involves a critical consideration of your value base and therefore requires complete honesty.

Taking some of the trends in family formations that you (and we) identified above, assess the potential positives and negatives of each.

Critically examine your values in relation to each of the social trends. Where have your values come from? Think about how values are influenced by the media, our families, religion and other factors.

How can social workers ensure that their practice is ethically sound?

By completing this exercise you will hopefully have considered the importance of reflecting upon your own values and practice, and the value of using others to challenge perceptions, within team discussions and supervision. It may be more helpful to think about *households* rather than families, to more accurately reflect diversity in the way that people live today. The term 'family' tends to carry with it emotional connotations which perpetuate powerful ideological ideals to aspire to, but that may not accurately reflect the reality of how people live.

Sociological approaches to the family

We will now consider a range of key sociological approaches to the family. What follows are summary explanations of some of the key writers; however, this is not intended to be exhaustive and reading will be indicated at the end of the chapter to further assist you.

Functionalist theory of the family

As we discovered in Chapter 1, functionalism is premised on the assumption that all social institutions perform an important role, both for society and its individuals. The family is regarded positively by functionalists who identify important functions that are carried out for the benefit of society as a whole.

ACTIVITY 4.6

If you have become familiar with the functionalist perspective, you should now be comfortable with the key tenets of the theory. You may wish to revisit Chapter 1 to refresh yourself with some of the core ideas.

Once you have done this, write down what you think are the functions of the family, first for society and second for the individuals within it.

Murdock's (1949) work on the family identified four positive functions that he suggested were performed by the family. These were:

- reproduction;
- sexual gratification;
- economic well-being;
- education.

Murdock's first function of reproduction may seem rather obvious as society needs to ensure the continuation of the population. Implicit in the assumption that reproduction is most effectively carried out within the institution of the family, is the notion that children are afforded the stability of being raised within the family unit. Furthermore, kinship rights and obligations of families are protected if reproduction is predominantly carried out within families and there are clear lines of heredity. This links well with Murdock's second function, that of the *sexual gratification* of adults. Murdock suggests that the nuclear family provides a socially approved structure around the fulfilment of adult sexual urges. This mitigates against adults fulfilling their desires freely which might have a negative impact – such as the spread of sexually transmitted diseases, emotional turbulence, and confusion regarding lines of heredity. Additionally, by restricting sexual activity to spouses, there is an effective barrier against the likelihood of emotional difficulties associated with incest.

Murdock's next function of *economic well-being* is also linked to the previous two functions, as he contends that providing for family members is the most effective means of 'cementing the union' between husband and wife. For Murdock, writing in 1949, there was a clear division of labour within families, whereby husbands performed the traditional hunter-gatherer role (albeit in the workplace as opposed to in the wild), and wives predominantly stayed at home to bear and nurture children and transform the product of their husbands' labour into nourishing meals. For Murdock, this is functional both for family members, and for society, as the family effectively keeps the economy strong by being a consistent unit of consumption.

Finally, Murdock identifies the function of *education* or *socialisation* as being essential for society. The family is the primary institution that teaches its members to internalise prevailing norms and values which enable them to fit into society. This point is taken up by Talcott Parsons (1951), who identifies two *basic and irreducible functions of the family*, the first being primary socialisation of children. He argues that the human personality is not born, but made; children effectively come into the world as blank slates, and it is through the socialisation process that they gradually acquire the values of society. Parsons graphically refers to the family as *'factories' which produce human personalities ... so that they [children] can truly become members of society into which they have been born* (p16). Families socialise children from the moment they are born, both formally, by explicitly teaching the rules of social life, such as manners and customs, and informally, by setting examples to children and by modelling socially desired behaviours. Parsons, however, argues that *it cannot be assumed that the human personality would remain stable in the respects which are vital to social functioning* (p16). He therefore suggests that the second irreducible function of the family is the *stabilisation of the adult personalities of the population.* By this, Parsons is referring to the role the family, and specifically the role the married couple, perform in supporting each other through daily life. Couples are expected to form durable, emotional bonds which ensure that they care for one another emotionally, which contributes to the psychological well-being of each individual. This is important in modern society in which the pressures of working life, the strain to engage in constant consumerism and competition can all have an impact upon adults. The family therefore, and in particular the marital couple, act as a buffer against such stresses by providing mutual emotional support. This is perhaps more important today, since many nuclear families live away from relatives who once traditionally fulfilled aspects of this role.

Murdock and Parsons both provide core functions that they argue the family fulfils for the well-being of society first and foremost, but also for individuals. Of course, as we have seen, the nuclear family form is not compulsory within our society. However, it is very much regarded as the norm and, as we outline below, effective pressures exist to try to support compliance to the norm. Notably, historical taboos have existed around cohabitation, having children outside of marriage, bringing up children alone, and, of course, around incest. Although, with the exception of incest, these taboos have to a greater or lesser extent broken down as society has evolved, it is clear to see how such norms permeate individual consciousness and importantly, how they form the ideas upon which social policies are crafted.

The 'disintegration' of the 'traditional' family and the rise of the 'dysfunctional' lone-parent family?

In recent years some politicians and sociologists have suggested that certain family formations – in particular lone parents – are incapable of performing key socialisation functions. Of course, the notion that lone-parent families are in some way 'inferior' to two-parent families, and are incapable of socialising their children effectively, is not new. Indeed, throughout the 1980s and 1990s, Conservative governments, backed by sympathetic newspapers such as the *Daily Mail*, condemned lone-parent families as 'dysfunctional', linking the increased incidence of lone parenthood to a range of social and economic problems. However, over the past few years such claims have re-emerged with renewed vigour, and lone parenthood – whether it be the result of divorce, relationship breakdown, or births out of wedlock – now appears to be 'under attack' from all sides. Prior to 1997, senior Labour politicians criticised Conservatives' preoccupation with 'the family', and encouraged a celebration of family diversity and difference. However, between 1997 and 2010, Labour ministers seemed equally obsessed with the family, and, in particular, with the potentially destructive impact of 'disintegration' of the traditional family. The following comments were taken from a speech made by Labour's then Work and Pensions Secretary, John Hutton.

> The family is the bedrock of the welfare state. It is the family which cares for the newborn, raises children, instils a sense of values, coaxes and encourages children to learn and thrive ... But alongside this, we cannot ignore the increasing evidence that points to the benefits for children of a stable family life with two parents living together ... For example, children from separated families are more likely to have no qualifications than those from families with two parents living together ... And not only are children in lone-parent families more likely to be living in poverty at any one point in time – but they have a consistently lower probability of moving out of poverty.

(Hutton, 2006)

Since its election in 2010, the Conservative-dominated Coalition government has continued to bemoan the decline in the 'traditional' family, linking it to a whole range of social and economic ills, such as educational disadvantage, substance misuse, unemployment, welfare dependency, childhood deprivation and even the riots in the summer of 2011. Underpinning this approach is the view that the traditional, married, two-parent family is by far the most effective means of rearing and socialising children. In the words of David Cameron (2010), *children are more likely to do well when both parents are there for them, together providing the love and the discipline.* Indeed, he goes further, arguing that it is *the poverty of the parent-child experience* generated, in particular, by 'non-traditional' families *that leads to poor child outcomes rather than poverty of a material kind.*

The notion that family breakdown is one of the most serious challenges we face as a nation has therefore been central to the Coalition's approach to welfare. Nowhere is this more evident than in its approach to child poverty, which locates a large part of the blame for children's material deprivation with the disintegration of the 'traditional' family. Indeed, the claim that parental separation and lone parenthood, rather than lack of income, lie at the heart of the UK's 'child poverty problem' forms a key part of the Coalition's Child Poverty Strategy. Children who have experienced parental separation, the Coalition's Child Poverty Strategy argues, *are more likely to have greater risk of poor outcomes in areas such as education, psychological well-being and early school leaving* (Department for Work and Pensions/Department for Education, 2011, p36). From this perspective, it is not the low incomes predominantly found within such families that lie at the root of their difficulties, rather it is the dysfunctionality associated with their 'non-traditional' family formations. Hence, attempts to tackle problems like child poverty that are based on boosting family incomes are deemed to be misguided and doomed to failure. Indeed, Coalition ministers argue that such strategies have, in the past, actually encouraged an explosion of family breakdown and lone parenthood, as teenagers and other young women have been *enticed* into lone parenthood by the prospect of lavish, morally corrupting welfare provision. This, in turn, is said to have led to greater levels of poverty, neglect and poorer outcomes for children. Instead, they suggest that solutions to problems like child poverty need to focus on strategies designed to reverse 'disintegrative' changes to family structures and reinforcing the traditional family. As Iain Duncan Smith (2012a), the Coalition minister responsible for the Child Poverty Strategy, argued, [w]hen *families are strong and stable, so are children – showing higher levels of wellbeing and more positive outcomes. But when things go wrong ... through family breakdown ... the impact on a child's later life can be devastating.* The Coalition's welfare reform agenda will, he insists, be geared towards *driving home the message that social programmes should promote family stability and avert breakdown.*

It is in such a context that we should locate the Coalition government's plans to reward marriage through tax breaks. Bizarre though this may seem, given that it will involve a redistribution of financial resources to families who are *less likely* to experience poverty, this policy constitutes a key part of the government's Child Poverty Strategy. Even the Deputy Prime Minister, Nick Clegg, expressed serious reservations about the proposal, suggesting that the money would be better spent providing support to *all* families, irrespective of their make-up. Referring to the policy as the *unmarried couple tax penalty*, Clegg accused his Conservative Cabinet colleagues of pursuing an 'unfair', misguided, ideologically motivated agenda, by seeking to *hand-pick couples through the tax system who conform to their image of how you should conduct your life* (Grice, 2013; Graham, 2014). However, at the time of writing, Conservative Coalition ministers, seem determined to press ahead with the policy, which is scheduled for implementation in April 2015. As Duncan Smith argued, [t]he *greatest thing we can do to help stabilise families and support commitment and nature is to back the most important man-made institution of marriage through a transferable tax allowance* (Chapman, 2013).

Despite differences over the controversial issue of marriage tax breaks, there does now seem to be a broad functionalist-influenced political consensus over the central role the 'traditional' family plays in securing social order and stability, and of the negative impact changing family structures have had in the UK. As we show below, this consensus is based upon somewhat shaky empirical foundations, but the assumptions that underpin it have undoubtedly resonated with the general public. For instance, the 2011–12 British Social Attitudes survey found that 56 per cent of people believe that family breakdown is one of the principal causes of childhood deprivation and poverty (National Centre for Social Research, 2012). There can be little doubt that the media's portrayal of lone parents, and, more generally, its reporting of issues relating to family breakdown, have played a part in reinforcing the notion that the 'disintegration' of the traditional family is a major cause of economic and social problems.

ACTIVITY **4.7**

While space prohibits us from devoting too much attention to the media's reinforcement of familial values, it is important you are aware of its opinion-shaping potential. We discuss the pervasive influence of the media in relation to asylum policy in Chapter 6, and what we say there is equally applicable here. In our research for this chapter, we undertook a national newspaper database search of articles relating to lone parenthood and family breakdown. The following headlines were fairly typical in terms of their negative portrayal of non-traditional families and recent family trends.

Family breakdown is now a national tragedy; Our children are the losers in the game of 'pass the partner', Daily Telegraph, *18 June 2009*

Why divorce damages teenagers every bit as much as young children, Daily Mail, *30 April 2010.*

Divorce trauma children 'earn 30% less', Daily Mail, *29 March 2011.*

Single parent shock: We have the highest rate in the world after US, Mirror, *28 April 2011.*

Divorce 'causes children to fall behind in maths', Daily Telegraph, *2 June 2011.*

A third of fraud bill on single parents, The Sun, *30 August 2011.*

I'm spending £3,200 on Christmas ... and it's paid for by my benefits: Single mum files up debt for her sons, The Sun, *6 December 2011.*

Divorce after a child turns seven could hit their GCSE results, Daily Mail, *31 January 2013.*

The single mum-of-six on benefits: The Belgravia mansion she wants you to pay for, Daily Mail, *23 March 2013.*

What divorce really does to children – in their own shattering words, Daily Mail, *5 September 2013.*

In this task, we want you to scan newspapers for a period of perhaps one month, saving all the articles on lone parenthood and family breakdown. You can either buy the newspapers yourselves or use online newspaper search engines.

> *Place the articles you have collected into two categories, positive and nega-tive (reflecting their portrayal of 'non-traditional' families and family break-down). Our powers of prediction tell us that your 'negative' category will be the larger of the two!*
>
> - *What social problems were lone parenthood, divorce and family breakdown equated to? Did you detect a functionalist influence in the language used in the articles?*
> - *Do you think the attention placed upon lone parenthood as a potential cause of the problems it is linked to disproportionate? Did you find any examples of 'distortion' or exaggerated emphasis in the articles you read? Might Stanley Cohen's moral panic the-ory (outlined in Chapter 6) be useful in helping us to understand how non-traditional families are popularly portrayed?*
> - *What other explanations might account for the economic and social problems commonly linked to lone parenthood?*

Hopefully, the above exercise will have encouraged you to think about how your views of 'the family' may have been shaped by media representations. As future social workers you will be working with many types of families, and as we have already intimated, it is essential that you are able to move beyond pejorative, deroga-tory perceptions of certain family formations.

Criticisms of functionalist views of the family

Both Murdock and Parsons have been criticised for idealising family life, with femi-nist writers among others suggesting that families can in fact be dysfunctional for some family members. This argument will be considered more fully later in this chapter but, in short, they point to the abuse and violence that some women and children experience daily as being more realistic than the happy, harmonious haven where adult personalities are stabilised and children nurtured. Other criticisms are based on the fact that the functions identified by Murdock and Parsons could in fact be performed *outside* of the institution of the family. One example of this is that children may be successfully raised in a kibbutz, a commune or within resi-dential settings (though of course each of these settings potentially brings its own challenges).

Functionalist claims that family breakdown necessarily contributes to a range of social and economic ills, threatening the well-being of society, can also be criticised with reference to other countries' experiences. For example, levels of lone parenthood, divorce and cohabitation are as high, or in some instances higher, in Scandinavian countries than they are in the UK. Scandinavian countries, however, are not character-ised by the sort of social problems that in the UK are said to be linked to the growth in 'non-traditional' families.

- In Sweden in 2012, 54.5 per cent of births were outside marriage, compared with 47.6 per cent for the UK. The respective figures for Denmark and Norway were 50.6 per cent and 54.9 per cent (Eurostat, 2013).

- The divorce rates for Sweden (2.5 per 1000 population in 2010) and Denmark (2.6 per 1000) are also higher than those in found in the UK (2.1 per 1000 population), whilst Norway's is identical to the UK's (Eurostat, 2014).

- The levels of single-parent families in Scandinavian countries are also remarkably similar to those in the UK. In 2008, 20.8 per cent of children were living with one parent, while the corresponding rates for Sweden and Denmark were 17 per cent and 17.8 per cent respectively (Eurostat, 2011).

- The percentages of families conforming to the nuclear family stereotype, containing a couple and at least one child under 18, are also considerably lower in Scandinavian countries than the UK. In 2008, 24 per cent of UK families did so, whereas the corresponding percentages for Sweden, Denmark and Finland were 22 per cent, 17 per cent, and 20 per cent. (Eurostat, 2011)

If the claims made by functionalists (and, indeed, the UK's Coalition government), were correct, then we should expect to find similar, or perhaps even higher levels of family breakdown-related problems to the UK. However, as UNICEF (2013) has shown, child poverty rates in Scandinavian nations are strikingly low, educational well-being is regarded as excellent, and children are far less likely to be engaging in risk-taking and disruptive behaviour than in the UK (UNICEF, 2013). Nor is there talk in these countries of lone parents being guilty of raising generations of 'dysfunctional' children. In fact, UNICEF concluded that these countries were characterised by the highest levels of childhood well-being in the developed world. The UK, by contrast, came towards the bottom in UNICEF's league table of child well-being.

The experiences of Scandinavian countries, therefore, provide us with evidence to counter the notion that the 'traditional' two-parent family is a crucial prerequisite for the social and economic stability of society. Although space precludes us from discussing in detail the reasons why this is the case, one of the key features shared by each of these countries is their commitment to gender equality. Extensive, subsidised in-work support (for instance, childcare, parental leave and paternity leave) is provided, enabling all parents, married and single, male and female, to balance work and family life responsibilities. Hence, Scandinavian nations have very high levels of female employment (including among lone parents), strong levels of female representation in public life, and high degrees of male participation in children's upbringing. Alongside this, there is a more general commitment to ensuring a fair, equal distribution of resources, ensuring that levels of poverty for all families remain low (Cunningham and Cunningham, 2012).

Social work, functionalism and the family

It is clear to see that the functionalist perspective holds a contemporary resonance that is the backdrop for social work practice. The family is regarded as being perhaps the most important institution in society and every effort is made to support and uphold this. A great deal of social workers' time is devoted to working in supportive ways with families to help them survive, flourish and function effectively, and to meet the needs of different family members. Indeed, if we consider some of the core pieces of legislation that underpin social work practice, you will see that the Children Act 1989, for example, is premised upon the overriding principle that in most cases children are best brought up within their family of origin. Similarly, in the NHS and Community Care Act 1990, there is a core principle that vulnerable adults are best cared for by their own families, wherever possible within their own homes. The centrality of the family in social work is clear to see, which is not surprising when one considers that ideologically, economically and politically families are deemed by all political parties to be the cornerstone of society. When things go wrong, however, and families cannot care for their own children or are unable to perform the nurturing functions to a standard deemed satisfactory by the state, social workers seek alternatives to perform the required functions of the family on behalf of the state. Two good examples of this which already mirror the birth family are of course adoptive and foster homes.

Government policy is often directed at attempting to 'correct' what it sees as dysfunctional or problem families and social workers often have a key role in implementing this. One such recent example is the 'Troubled Families' initiative that we outlined in more detail in Chapter 3. Here it is possible to see how policy is premised upon the requirement to assertively challenge and re-socialise 'dysfunctional' families that have lost their way so that they can be economically independent, stable, reproduce sensibly within the family unit and produce children who conform to mainstream norms and values. In doing so it is hoped that society as a whole will benefit.

Marxist theory of the family

Marxists are concerned with the relationship between the family and private property. Friedrich Engels' seminal work provides an important starting point for understanding Marxist views on the family. In *The origins of the family, private property and the state* (1968), Engels, influenced by the work of anthropologist Henry Morgan, adopted an evolutionary approach and suggested that the prevailing family form of any particular period was inextricably linked with the mode of production at that time. Engels cites Morgan:

> *The family ... represents an active principle. It is never stationary, but advances from a lower to a higher form as society advances from a lower to a higher condition.*

(cited in Engels, p31)

In primitive society where property ownership did not exist, Engels suggests that there was no identifiable family as such; rather a form of group marriage existed where sexually active individuals had a number of sexual partners. At this time, women were more powerful than men and society was matriarchal. Economic relations in society were based around subsistence, in other words people hunted and gathered what they needed to survive and regularly shared this among members of the local group. Over time, society became more advanced and gradually cattle and land-ownership emerged. According to the division of labour at the time, it was men who were in charge of the cattle and the instruments of labour. It follows that once property (in this case, herds of cattle and land) is seen to be owned privately, men needed to secure legitimate heirs to pass their property on to. At this stage Engels identifies a gradual shift to patriarchy and the implications for women.

> *The overthrow of mother-right was the world historical defeat of the female sex. The man seized the reins in the house also; the woman was degraded, enthralled, the slave of the man's lust, a mere instrument for breeding children.*

(p57)

For Engels then, the oppression of women is directly linked to the ownership of private property. Men needed to be absolutely sure of the legitimacy of their sons, and therefore they needed to control women's sexuality. In Engels' words:

> *In order to make certain of the wife's fidelity and therefore of the paternity of the children, she is delivered over unconditionally into the power of the husband.*

(p58)

Consequently, the monogamous family was born. Engels is clear that this family form was not based on love or sex, but rested entirely on economic foundations:

> *It is based on the supremacy of the man, the express purpose being to produce children of undisputed paternity; such paternity is demanded because these children are later to come into their father's property as his natural heirs.*

(p62)

In this way then, women effectively became the economic and sexual property of men, a direct result of the emergence of private property. With the advent of capitalism, the nuclear family came to be a central component of both its success and survival. A Marxist analysis of the family draws attention to the functions that the monogamous nuclear family performs for capitalism. In short:

- the family reflects inequalities in wider society; some family members are privileged, while others, women and children in particular, are not;

- the family passes on ideological messages to children about obedience and hard work, which prepares them for their future role as workers;

- women in particular play an important role in reproducing workers, by performing for free tasks such as cooking, cleaning, shopping, housework tasks and emotional tasks such as comforting and supporting tired workers that directly enables capitalism to continue;

- furthermore, families are the primary unit of consumption that supports capitalism commercially.

In the *Communist Manifesto*, Marx and Engels (1969) famously called for the abolition of the family, as they contended that family members were simply *articles of commerce and instruments of labour* (p70). They decried the 'bourgeois clap trap' about the family and pointed out that in reality, women are regarded as mere instruments of production. They suggested, however, that as capitalism and private property are abolished, so too would the family vanish as a matter of course.

Criticisms of Marxist theories of the family

Marxist theories of the family can be criticised for focusing exclusively upon the economic basis of family life and ignoring the powerful emotional ties that define many families. Engels' work has been refuted for being based on unreliable anthropological evidence (Haralambos et al., 2013, p111); however, as Rosalind Delmar (1977) suggests, at the very least Engels' work is pivotal in defining women's oppression *as a problem of history, rather than of biology* (cited in O'Donnell, 1992, p48). For more criticisms of Marxism, see our comments in the later section on Marxist feminism.

Social action approaches

Many of the sociological approaches to the family that we consider in this chapter are concerned with either the positive or negative side to family life. Social action perspectives, however, are less interested in the relative merits of the family and more interested in observing the smaller-scale interactions between family members. This type of approach is useful to social work because it focuses upon the meanings that underpin family activity and the processes by which relationships are negotiated in families.

As we outlined in Chapter 1, social action perspectives concentrate on the micro aspects of social life. Symbolic interactionism, for example, is interested in how individuals make sense of the social world. In relation to families, interactionists focus their attention on the minutiae of family life in order to learn about how it is experienced subjectively. As we have seen, both functionalism and Marxism place attention on the functions the family fulfils for society as a whole (functionalism) or for capitalism (Marxism). Interactionists, however, are more interested in individual experiences within families. While both of the structural theories focus upon the macro role of families in socialising children for the benefit of society, interactionists are interested in different ways of socialising children. Through the application of qualitative research, sociologists who are informed by this approach are able to elicit rich information about the micro cultures that exist within families and seek to understand how these shape individual experiences of family life. Gillies et al. (2001), for example, carried out an in-depth study into families that had a child between 16 and 18 at home to learn more about the family lives of young people. They found that a variety of experiences existed in the families they studied, but that the majority described the supportive and emotionally meaningful nature of their family lives. This contrasted with headline messages in common culture that teenage years and parent-child relationships were characterised by turbulence and stress. Many of the young people in the study emphasised agency and responsibility, negotiating their independence over time. Their parents perceived their role as continuing to steer and advise teenagers into adulthood. The authors describe the range of different approaches adopted across different families:

> Some parents emphasised their respect for the teenager's autonomy, while others felt a responsibility to ensure that appropriate decisions were made. Other parents assumed a more subtle role, seeing dictating to teenagers as counterproductive.

> (Gillies et al., 2001, p3)

Importantly, from a micro perspective, this study identifies the fact that although there are similar experiences shared across families, a range of different *meaning systems* exist with families that are more useful to understand when attempting to learn about the social world. For social workers of course, this is an important principle to inform practice; looking at the minutiae of family life helps us to gain an understanding of how individual families work and to think about the process of interaction within families. In *Beyond blame,* Reder et al. (1993) review cases where children have died within families due to abuse or neglect. They identify the need for social workers to assess the *'meaning'* of children within families, where there is a safeguarding concern about risk to the child. This is based upon findings that repeatedly show that children who have been murdered by their parents have held specific meaning or significance; for example, the child might have symbolised a previous marriage or emotional bond, if the child was not the biological child of both caregivers. More recently, the case of Daniel Pelka, who was murdered by his mother and her partner in March 2012, provides a disturbing example of how specific children can be scapegoated within families. Daniel suffered horrific pre-meditated abusive treatment that neither of his two siblings appeared to suffer, which ultimately resulted in his murder.

> It was evident that Daniel experienced a harsh degree of scapegoating and emotional abuse ... and he was often the sole subject of physical abuse and neglect, which included deliberately depriving him of food, serious physical abuse, feeding him salt and putting him in a cold bath, on one occasion ... leaving him temporarily unconscious because he had nearly drowned.
>
> (Coventry LSCB, 2013)

The Serious Case Review perhaps does not probe deeply enough into *why* Daniel was treated so differently to his siblings; however, there is learning here for social workers. First, it is important that social workers make individual assessments of children and do not make assumptions about *all* children in a family on the basis of one. Second, that different children represent different things in family systems and it is essential to tease out such subtleties in order to develop a full understanding. And finally, the psychological process of scapegoating can have very dangerous consequences indeed, that social workers and other professionals need to be aware of.

So, for social workers, a micro perspective can be useful to help us learn about the intimate functioning of families. However, as Macionis and Plummer (2012) point out, care should be taken not to miss the bigger picture in doing so. For social workers, it is helpful to understand families from a micro perspective while simultaneously locating this within an understanding of wider structural issues such as those we have considered earlier in the chapter.

Feminist theory of the family

Feminist writing has in many ways revolutionised thinking about the family by drawing attention to the more harmful aspects of family life. It is important to point out that there is no single 'feminist theory of the family'; rather, feminism is an umbrella term to describe a collection of approaches which are concerned with the oppression of women. Beyond that, the similarities end. We have chosen to focus upon some of the classic contributors to different strands of feminist thought. This is by no means exhaustive as space prevents a more detailed examination. However, we hope that you will at least be able to identify the key points of each by the end of this section and consider our suggestions for further reading.

Marxist feminism

Marxist or socialist feminism builds upon the work of Engels described previously, and this section should be read in conjunction with the relevant earlier part of the chapter. For Marxist feminists, women's oppression is a by-product of capitalism and *while a socialist revolution does not automatically liberate women, it creates the material conditions for doing so* (Smith, 2013). In other words, according to Marxist feminists, the true liberation of women is dependent first and foremost upon the overthrow of the Capitalist system. Barrett and McIntosh (1982) note that the nuclear family performs key functions for capitalism. In particular, it produces future workers who keep the system going and, at the same time, it acts as an important unit of consumption. They note that as society became more industrial-ised and there was a separation of the workplace and the home, women became identified with child-bearing and child-rearing, and importantly, the home became a much more private and personal realm.

However, Barrett and McIntosh also draw attention to the anti-social side of the fam-ily, which is significant for social workers. They argue that for women who are often confined to the home as mothers, housewives or carers, the insular nature of families can become a prison rather than a haven. This is especially so, of course, for those who experience violence within the family. In explaining domestic violence, Marxist feminists acknowledge that it is predominantly perpetrated by men on women. They see the principal cause as being the stress caused by poverty, exclusion and the pres-sure to make ends meet that is the characteristic feature of many families' lives under capitalism. Furthermore, the state-engineered dependence of women on men (institu-tionalised by the absence of affordable childcare, labour market discrimination, and low levels of income maintenance) ensures that women who do experience domestic violence find it extremely difficult to escape from abusive relationships.

Regarding women's paid employment, Barrett and McIntosh note that when women do return to work, many do a 'double shift', by retaining their prime responsibilities within the home in addition to their working life. This is because their position in the labour force is not taken seriously; it is secondary to their mother-housewife role. Women are often found in low-paid, low-status jobs, which are regarded as an exten-sion of their 'natural' female roles; they tend not to get promotions at the same rate as men and tend to be found lower down in the hierarchy.

Barrett and McIntosh argue that the family ideal is so pervasive that others who live outside this are seen as 'pale and unsatisfactory' in comparison, living in a 'cold and friendless world'. They suggest that societal norms are so engrained that many cus-toms and practices are based around families, which is exclusionary for those outside:

The cosy image of the family makes all other settings where people can mix and live together seem second best. Nurseries, children's homes, student residences, nursing homes, old people's homes, all in their different ways conjure up pictures of bleakness, deprivation ... to be resorted to only if normal family life cannot be provided.

(p77)

ACTIVITY **4.8**

Using Barrett and McIntosh's concept of the 'anti-social family', think about how this might this have relevance for some users of social work services.

You might wish to think about the emotional impact on individuals and consider how this may bring them to the attention of social work agencies.

So, what do Barrett and McIntosh suggest should be done to counter the damage they perceive to be invested in the anti-social family? Essentially, they argue for changes that will displace the family as being *the sole and privileged provider of moral and material support* (p133) and argue that these things should be more available throughout the community. In doing so, they envisage an end to women's dependence and aim for more choice around living arrangements and, importantly, for a more collective approach to caring and domesticity. They believe that a cultural and political shift should take place which cuts across the ideology of the family as the cornerstone of society, to encompass a broader range of alternatives. These would include more opportunities in the workplace for women on a more equal footing, better social security provision and a more collective approach to care, rather than seeing it as a natural (biological) duty borne by women.

Although Barrett and McIntosh's work is now dated, it has become a classic text which builds upon Engels' work and sets out a Marxist feminist position on the family. Now some 30 years on, it is worth analysing to what extent women's position has changed.

RESEARCH SUMMARY

Women in Britain today

Numerous official surveys and academic studies have sought to examine the extent to which social, economic and political life in the UK is characterised by gender inequality. All the research findings show that although women are more fairly represented in the workforce and in public life than they were in the past, they do still occupy a subordinate position to men.

In relation to the workplace, British women are less likely to be employed than men (67 per cent of women compared with 76 per cent of men in 2013), and when they are employed they tend to occupy lower-status, lower-paid positions (ONS, 2013). For example, women often work part-time, combining work with family caring responsibilities. In 2013, 42 per cent of women worked part-time, compared with only 12 per cent of men. This, together with the fact that men tend to occupy higher status occupations within particular trades and occupations, accounts for the fact that women's weekly average earnings are considerably lower than men's. This is true for all occupational categories across the UK labour market. Hence, in 2013, the weekly earnings for women employed as managers, directors or senior officials were, on average, around £169.60 less than those of men (a shortfall of £8,788 per year). The equivalent shortfall for women employed in professional occupations was around £100 (£5,200 per year), whereas for those working in caring leisure and other service occupations it was £44.90 (£2,334 per year) (ONS, 2013). These 'pay gaps' are not insubstantial, and it is easy to see how, over a working career, women could be subjected to a gender pay 'penalty' running into hundreds of thousands of pounds.

Women also tend to be employed in 'caring' services, a reflection perhaps of familial assumptions about what are 'appropriate' roles for women to perform. Thus, in 2013, women comprised 82 per cent of those employed in caring, leisure and other services, and 77 per cent of those employed in secretarial and retail work (ONS, 2013). This bias towards women working in caring professions looks set to continue in the future. For example, despite the fact that girls now outperform boys at GCSE level across all subjects, they are still being directed towards the personal service and 'caring' professions. Thus, girls constituted 97 per cent apprenticeship starts in children's care in 2008–09, 90 per cent in hairdressing and 86 per cent in health and social care (Fuller and Davey, 2010).

Regarding public life, in 2013, the Centre for Women and Democracy (CfWD) conducted an in-depth study into gender inequality in economic, social and political life. Despite some improvements, women remain grossly underrepresented across a whole range of public appointments, services and elected positions. In 2012, for example, women only constituted 22.3 per cent of all MPs in the House of Commons; 21.7 per cent of members of the House of Lords; 13.8 per cent of local authority council leaders; 22.9 per cent of local authority chief executives; 13.6 per cent of the senior judiciary; 17.6 per cent of senior police officers; and 14.2 per cent of university vice chancellors (Counting Women In Coalition, 2013).

For Marxist feminists, the outcomes we have outlined above are not a result of physiological or biological factors, nor are they a product of rational choice on the part of women. On the contrary, these differential outcomes are socially engineered. In short, for the reasons outlined above, capitalism benefits from gender segregation and hence key institutions – for instance, the education and social security systems – seek to reinforce women's domesticity. While this may sound conspiratorial, Marxist feminists are right to point out that social policy has traditionally sought to encourage and strengthen gender-specific roles. The UK's social security system has been based around the male-breadwinner model, the assumption being that women would remain in the home and be financially dependent on their husband's earnings and National Insurance contributions. In addition, as we will see in

Chapter 5, community care legislation has been based upon the notion that families are willing and able to bear the responsibility of caring for dependent relatives.

Marxist feminism has been criticised for being overly sceptical about the possibility of initiating progressive change for women without the need for revolutionary upheaval. Critics would point to the substantial gains made by the feminist movement over the past hundred years or so, which have led to a significant improvement in women's representation in political, economic and social life within capitalist nations. Arguably, the experience of Scandinavian countries, which are characterised by a high degree of gender equality, show us that women's opportunities and status can be substantially improved without the abolition of capitalism. Marxism, therefore, has been criticised for paying too little attention to the 'here and now', and how the key tenets of familial ideology can be challenged in the present to improve women's status and material well-being today. In short, Marxism has faced the charge that it has subordinated women's demands and the fight for gender equality to what it has seen as the 'real struggle' (that is, wider revolutionary change).

Radical feminism

Unlike Marxist feminism, which is based upon the premise that women's oppression stems first and foremost from capitalism, radical feminists argue that women's oppression is a direct result of patriarchy which is a universal system of male power and domination. They argue that:

> *Male supremacy is the oldest, most basic form of domination. All other forms of exploitation and oppression (racism, capitalism, imperialism etc) are extensions of male supremacy; men dominate women, a few men dominate the rest.*

> (Redstockings Manifesto, 1969, p1)

The slogan 'The personal is political' is at the heart of this perspective, denoting the idea that what happens to individual women in the home is also political because it involves wider relations of power and exploitation. The argument is that women's individual battles at home, their personal experiences of oppression and violence, in fact have an inherently political base and therefore can only be resolved through collective action.

For radical feminists such as Shulamith Firestone (1970), women's inferiority is linked to their biological sex. In *The dialectic of sex* Firestone argues that the origins of the sex class system lie in the biologically determined reproductive roles of men and women. She argues that men and women are not equally privileged, with women at the continual mercy of their biology. The natural reproductive difference between the sexes leads directly to the first division of labour which renders women dependent upon men for their physical survival. This in turn results in the domination of women by men.

However, although women's oppression has its origins in biology, Firestone argues that this does not mean it is unchangeable. Technological developments such as birth control and artificial reproduction have the potential to free women from the tyranny of their reproductive biology, so that child-rearing becomes the responsibility of society as a whole. However, she argues that oppression will not cease just because its biological determinants are overcome, as its supporting structures, such as the nuclear family, are still functioning. Thus, she argues, a feminist revolution is needed. There must be total integration of women and children into all aspects of larger society, with full sexual freedom guaranteed. The implications of this would effectively mean the destruction of the nuclear family.

Not all radical feminists subscribe to Firestone's biological explanation, but all agree that past and present societies are patriarchies, in which men have *institutionalised* their domination over women via social structures such as love, romance, marriage, motherhood, sexual intercourse, religion and the family. Radical feminists claim that violence and importantly, the *threat of violence*, play a crucial role in male systems of domination.

As noted, radical feminists argue that revolution, not reform, is needed and that institutions which foster sexist ideology must be destroyed. Men too, benefit, by being freed from the masculine binds which tie them (although radical feminists suggest, they cannot be expected to realise this as they have been warped by power psychology and the very real benefits of the current system). They argue that women need to construct alternative selves that are healthy, independent and assertive, and value themselves, rather than awaiting judgement from men.

Radical feminists have been influential in challenging established thinking about a range of social problems social workers deal with. In the sphere of child sexual abuse, for example, radical feminists have led the challenge against the 'family dysfunction' analysis of abuse, which sees sexual abuse resulting from unsatisfactory relationships within the family. This interpretation, radical feminists argue, has a strong tendency to hold the mother responsible for abuse, ignoring the culpability of the actual perpetrators – invariably men. McLeod and Saraga (1988, p40) were foremost among those who sought to locate child sex abuse within a patriarchal framework, as *one part of a spectrum of male violence against women.* In terms of its wider influence on practice, radical feminism has also played a key part in the development of a range of women-only services such as women's refuges, rape crisis centres and survivor groups.

Liberal feminism

Liberal feminists hold the view that there should be equality of opportunity for women and men. Writing in the 1960s, Betty Friedan (1963) in *The feminist mystique* identifies what she refers to as *the problem that has no name* that had blighted the lives of American women for many years:

> *It was a strange stirring, a sense of dissatisfaction ... Each suburban wife struggled with it alone. As she made the beds, shopped for groceries, matched slipcover material, ate peanut butter sandwiches with her children, chauffeured Cub Scouts and Brownies, lay beside her husband at night – she was afraid to ask even of herself the silent question – 'Is this all?'*

(p4)

Friedan's work argued that the family in its present form is oppressive to women. She maintained that as long as women are relegated to being mothers and mothers only, women would remain largely unfulfilled. Her view was that women must cut through their own psychological chains that bind them to the powerful feminine mystique, an ideology which is perpetuated by the media and popular culture, and be free to be full, equal human beings. When this is realised and women can see the binds of housework and marriage in more realistic terms, they can achieve a new life plan in which they will find creative ways to achieve their own fulfilment. Only then will the family no longer be oppressive and women can be who they want to be.

Like Marxist feminists, liberal feminists agree that women's subordination owes little to their biological or physiological differences to men. However, they do not believe that capitalism itself is the principal cause of women's oppression. For liberal feminists, the roots of women's oppression lie with the irrational prejudice, stereotyping and outdated attitudes and practices that lead to sex discrimination occurring in all spheres of life. Like Marxists, they would point to the gender bias in education, social security and community care policies, but unlike Marxists they believe that the prejudice and stereotypical attitudes inherent in these institutions and policies can be 'reformed away' through the introduction of anti-discriminatory legislation. Liberal feminists, therefore, would welcome the removal of overtly gendered children's textbooks (of the Janet and John variety, if you are as old as us!) from schools and the shift towards a non-gendered curriculum. They would also applaud the introduction of equal pay and anti-discriminatory employment law which, theoretically at least, prohibits discrimination and allows women to compete in the labour market on an equal basis to men. Likewise, liberal feminists would welcome the introduction of women-only shortlists as a means of circumventing the traditional hostility to women's involvement in politics and increasing women's representation in representative assemblies. Finally, liberal feminists are insistent that nobody benefits from gender segregation and discrimination. Women lose out on the ability to develop their talents, business loses out because it fails to harness the potential and ability of 50 per cent of the population, and men lose out because they are denied the opportunity to develop close ties with their children.

Postmodernist feminism

As we explained in Chapter 1, postmodernism rejects explanations of society that are based upon holistic theories. For postmodernism, there is no 'one truth', or 'correct' explanation for social phenomena. We saw earlier how this leads postmodernism to reject 'universal' grand narratives, such as Marxism, but postmodernism's distrust of holistic explanations also extends to what are seen as overarching strands of feminist thought. Each woman's experience is seen as unique and in interpreting each woman's situation attention needs to be paid to their own diverse identities and biographies. For example, the variables that shape the oppression experienced by a white, middle-class, married woman who is experiencing domestic violence, may be very different from those that shape the oppression of a poverty-stricken Black parent. In the case of the former, patriarchy may be the most important variable, whereas with the latter, class or race (and their interaction with possibly even more variables) may be more pertinent. The fact is, though, that without a detailed knowledge of the individual circumstances of each of these two women, it is impossible to tell which variables or identities have structured their experiences. The point, for postmodernist feminists, is that we should not 'assume' one way or the other, without detailed interrogation. With postmodernist feminism, therefore, no one source of identity – whether it be class position, gender, race or disability – is privileged, and emphasis is placed on the need to understand the way different identities determine women's experiences.

It is easy to see how the emphasis placed by postmodernism on what are sometimes referred to as 'local narratives' can perhaps be the basis for a truly emancipatory social work practice. However, as we pointed out in Chapter 1, losing sight of the wider origins of oppression, negating shared experiences and undermining the potential for collective action can result in unwittingly disempowering women.

Possibilities for a feminist approach in social work

Although feminists do not agree on the origins of women's oppression, they all recognise, albeit in different ways, that the family has been an important vehicle in perpetuating the subordination of women over the years. But what possibilities does feminism offer social workers in terms of practice with families?

First, feminist contributions to sociology and social work have enabled social workers to have a grounded awareness of gender issues. This might involve defining or even redefining the difficulties experienced by service users from a feminist perspective. The following detailed case study gives an example of how this might be done.

CASE STUDY

Ellie, a social work student, was on placement with MIND in her local area. She was allocated the case of Doreen, 45-year-old single woman who had been described by her GP as being depressed. Doreen has a 12-year-old son, Billy. The purpose of Ellie's intervention was to assess Doreen's needs and to recommend a support plan. Ellie visited Doreen on two occasions and discussed her visits with her practice educator.

Ellie's assessment of Doreen

Ellie described Doreen as weepy, depressive and fragile and as having health problems that Ellie assessed to be 'psychosomatic'.

She described how Doreen had a male visitor to the house, Tom, who initially had been very flattering of Doreen but who now came for sex. Doreen was quite frightened of Tom. Ellie felt Doreen was being weak and could not understand why she didn't just tell him he wasn't welcome any more. Ellie's view was that this situation was not good for Billy and was not consistent with acceptable mothering. Furthermore, Doreen had no control over her son, who was cheeky and stayed out too late. Ellie's view was that this was another sign of her weakness and Doreen should be reported to Children's Services.

(Continued)

(Continued)

Ellie's recommendations

Ellie felt that Doreen was depressed and should go back to the GP for antidepressants and make more effort to socialise more. Ellie decided she would contact Children's Services regarding Billy, who she felt was not being cared for properly.

Work in supervision

Ellie's practice assessor spent time with Ellie talking about gender issues. She asked her to revisit her assessment of Doreen following the discussion and to unpack some of the earlier assumptions she had made. Ellie worked hard on this and returned to supervision the following week with some further thoughts and reflections:

1. *On what basis had both she and the GP used the term 'depressed?' Ellie had now read that the term is regularly misused and could be assigned to women more than to men. Ellie wondered if perhaps Doreen was struggling with aspects of her life and needed help to address them, but that she might not after all be 'depressed'. Ellie changed her recommendation regarding Doreen seeking out antidepressants.*

2. *Ellie thought back to her visits with Doreen – she remembered that Doreen had in fact become upset on one occasion and that was when she was confiding in Ellie about Tom and how he was quite forceful. Ellie changed her assessment report where she had written that Doreen was 'weepy' and recognised that she had in fact assigned gendered characteristics quite unfairly.*

3. *Ellie thought about Doreen's interaction with her son one day she had visited; she recalled they had been laughing together about something on TV. Doreen had mentioned that the previous night Billy had stayed out past his usual time, but Billy had replied that he had lost his watch. Ellie questioned her haste to portray Doreen as a bad mother and recognised that she had been quick to pathologise her.*

4. *Ellie reconsidered Doreen's position in relation to Tom. She recognised that Doreen was lonely and had initially been pleased that Tom had shown her some affection. She also thought about how upset and fearful Doreen had been when discussing Tom. Ellie realised on reflection, that perhaps it wasn't easy for Doreen to simply tell Tom to stop coming, as she was genuinely frightened of him. Doreen needed some support with this situation.*

With her assessor, Ellie was able to revisit some of her gendered assumptions about Doreen, and question why she was assigning gendered labels to her service user. From the above scenario it is possible to see how, with supportive challenging from her practice assessor, Ellie was able to reframe her initial assessment of Doreen and begin to work in more positive ways.

An important contribution made by feminist literature has been to recognise how social work has sometimes reinforced traditional gender roles within families and contributed in some cases to women's oppression. Hanmer and Statham (1999) note the importance of social workers accepting women service users as women first and foremost, rather than as mere occupants of social roles such as wife, mother and carer. This involves valuing women and recognising their strengths and abilities as women, rather than consigning them to traditional roles and seeing them only in those terms. Linked to this is the need of social workers to understand the role that men play in family life. The complexities which underpin relationships in the home should not be oversimplified and it seems important for social workers to take time to understand individual dynamics and guard against making assumptions.

Social work has been criticised for contributing to 'mother blaming', by traditionally intervening primarily with women. Arguably, social work has consistently institutionalised mother blaming since its inception. For the most part, this stems from stubbornly pervasive notions that women, as bearers of children, are also primarily responsible for their safety and well-being. Social work intervention has traditionally been premised upon notions of good-enough parenting, but in reality this has often meant *good-enough mothering*.

> *As women are seen as responsible for the care and control of their children, when something goes wrong the mother is blamed for inadequacy and negligence.*

(Hanmer and Statham, 1999, p52)

This has resulted in social workers focusing their intervention towards women, with fathers sometimes engaging in what Milner (1993; 1996) refers to as a 'disappearing act'. She suggests that men in these instances have been able to 'disappear', by fading into the background, leaving women to answer for the well-being of their children. Milner (1996) further comments that men can be adept at using a range of strategies to resist social workers. Strategies include the intimidation of social workers, expressions of remorse, and portraying mitigating factors to effectively negate their actions. The gender dynamic in social work manifests itself in complex ways and social workers need to be aware of the implications of this.

More recently, Harry Ferguson (2011) has found that distrust continues to exist between men and social workers, with the latter on occasions fearing involvement with aggressive and abusive men.

> *It seems that as they go about their day to day work and approach the homes of services users, one of the things that most fills practitioners with anxiety and even dread is that there may be a man behind the door ... The gendered assumption that the home is a woman's responsibility and domain runs deep in the DNA of social work and child protection.*

(pp151–2)

However, according to Ferguson, the sense of 'dread' is often mutual as he suggests that men may equally fear seeing social workers and, with the help of their partners, go to great lengths to avoid meeting them at all. He notes the complexities attached to why men are kept away from social workers, including financial reasons. There are, he notes, strong incentives for the man not to be seen by 'officials' and so their names may be kept off birth certificates; they may not exist in terms of official involvement with family life and so are hidden away from sight: *Poverty stricken families who exist like this are terrified of being caught and have good reason to fear being inspected by social security officials ... in their minds, all state officials meld into one great big threat* (p153). Additionally, he suggests that socially constructed notions of some men as being 'hard', 'rough' or 'dangerous' can negate any possibility that they may also be caring or loving fathers. Sometimes men are avoided because they are perceived to be dangerous, even when they are not. Appearances such as *having tattoos, a 'hard man' persona, lifestyle, doing hard physical work or violence prone work, like being a bouncer* (p156) means that they do not fit socially conceived ideas of what it means to be a good father or partner and such personas are often deemed to be potentially threatening by professionals.

The inherent complexities of state intervention in family life and the politics of gender relations may mean that *mothers are always the focus for interventions and invariably are worked with, while men so often are not* (Ferguson 2011, p153). This can lead to extremely dangerous situations where the invisibility of a man in a household can lead to social workers making inaccurate assessments based upon partial knowledge. This was apparent in the case of Baby Peter Connelly whose mother led the authorities to believe she lived alone with Peter. As in this case, *the consequences of non-engagement with fathers can be lethal* (Ferguson, 2011, p155). It can also lead to mothers shouldering the burden of state intrusion and absorbing responsibility where things have gone wrong.

As we explained earlier when discussing radical feminism, McLeod and Saraga (1988) point out that even in cases of sexual abuse, where the perpetrator is male, women have on occasions been blamed for this too by being regarded as somehow failing in their wifely duties in relation to the sexual fulfilment of their partners, as well as in their primary duty to protect their child. Since the recognition of the institutionalised tendency of social work to intervene primarily with mothers and to regularly hold them responsible for a whole range of family failings, advocates of feminist practice have identified principles to underpin more empowering forms of intervention (see for example, Hanmer and Statham, 1999; Dominelli, 2002, 2008; Penketh, 2011). Such principles include the need to recognise the political nature of many personal troubles. In short, feminist social work reconfigures many of the difficulties experienced by female service users – abuse, sexual assault, domestic violence, low self-esteem, isolation, to name but a few – as being inherently political issues. The emphasis of intervention, therefore, shifts from pathologising individual women to assisting them to perceive and understand their particular challenges in light of wider oppressive social conditions. The aim is to empower women to be able to gradually transcend psychological factors such as the guilt and responsibility that women often feel, which in turn prevents them from moving on. We have already addressed the danger of applying stereotypical labels, and feminist social work guards against making assumptions both about women and about men. As with all good practice, it is important that social workers check things out, rather than making assumptions. This involves moving beyond powerful unconscious ideologies about the family and about gender roles, which is not always easy. Hence, it is important for workers to reflect upon practice, be open to challenge from their colleagues and managers and be prepared to challenge back where they perceive sexist practice. Social workers need to be able to recognise that, for some service users, experience of family life is at best difficult, and for some, is downright unbearable. Where this is the case, it is simply not helpful for social workers to constantly reinforce the primacy of the family, supporting damaging families to stay together come what may. As we hinted earlier, despite legislation and policy to the contrary, there is life outside the nuclear family and sometimes work with individuals which assists them to make choices will ultimately lead to a better life.

An important principle in feminist social work is to provide women with the space to talk about their lives, if they want to. This recognises the need to work in non-hierarchical ways with women to value individual experiences. Through positive communication it is possible to find positive solutions. Women are able to feel validated by sharing their experiences with others; being heard and being valued are powerful components of empowering practice. Featherstone (1999) makes an important point when she identifies the complex emotional dynamics that potentially underlie some encounters between social workers and women service users. She asks:

> *Many social workers are women, some of whom are mothers. Are they able to hear* a range of stories about mothering?

> (p50; emphasis added)

She acknowledges that social workers may sometimes find women's positions difficult to bear or hear and may themselves need support to intervene.

Women should be supported to find their own solutions and encouraged to be involved in the wider decision-making of agencies. Linking women with other women has long been a strategy of feminist groups, as this can collectively assist women to recognise the shared nature of many experiences and find collective solutions to problems that are social in nature rather than individual. By seeing women as a resource for each other, social workers can empower women to use their strengths. 'Consciousness raising' is a term associated with radical feminists, but should form part of all social workers' repertoire of skills. Often the mere process of spending time listening and gently challenging can be positive in itself, allowing women the space to make sense of their lives and value their own achievements.

However, feminist social work is not solely confined to women. Dominelli (2002) recognises that gendered power relations have implications for men too. She argues that feminist social work should be based upon egalitarian principles and recognise that power dynamics underpin relationships and personal behaviours. However, men, like women, are not a homogenous group; indeed great diversity exists among men. Dominelli identifies the need for a commitment not to impose gender stereotypes on *either* sex. This involves assisting men to find satisfaction in adopting more nurturing and egalitarian roles. Men need to take responsibility for their behaviour where appropriate and to be assisted to understand their role in oppressing others, in order that they may challenge it. Further, inclusive practice (Ferguson, 2011) requires an explicit shift in the culture of social work to transcend potentially oppressive practice.

This section has identified ways of intervening with families that are grounded in feminist thinking and which contribute to breaking down unfair practice. If you are on placement or have been on placement recently, you may wish to attempt the following exercise to further consolidate your thinking.

ACTIVITY 4.9

Thinking about a family you have worked with or are working with, identify ways in which feminist practice can assist you to work in empowering ways with families.

Being a safe practitioner

At the beginning of this chapter, we drew attention to the fact that all social work students, whether male or female, need to reflect upon their own experiences of family life in order that they can be safe practitioners. The following exercise draws attention to this.

ACTIVITY 4.10

Jim was a social work student on the BA Social Work course. He had been attracted to a career in social work because his own experiences of family life had not been easy. His father had been violent to his mother for as long as he could remember; he drank heavily and Jim could remember countless nights where he had returned home and started to push his mum around. Jim's father had always belittled him and made him feel useless; he was regularly hit as a child and Jim lived in constant fear of him. When Jim was 14, he discovered that his sister had been sexually abused by their father over a number of years. Children's Services were called in by the school and Jim's father was eventually sent to prison, where he committed suicide some months after being sentenced. From an early age, Jim had pledged to himself and his family that he would work to help others who had similar experiences to those of his family.

In the second year of his course, Jim was allocated a placement in a family support team. He was assigned the case of Mr and Mrs Baker, with the remit of working with them to see what services could be provided to assist the Bakers in caring for their 12-year-old son who had learning disabilities, and their six-year-old daughter who had begun bed-wetting and had shown some aggressive behaviour recently.

Mr Baker was a large, outgoing man, with tattoos, who used to be a biker, and Mrs Baker was a quietly spoken woman. Over time, Jim began to see qualities in Mr Baker that concerned him. He did not feel comfortable with the man and tried to visit in the afternoon when Mr Baker was at work. He began to feel concerned that the six-year-old daughter's behaviour might have arisen because she was being sexually abused by her father.

What are the potential issues of concern in this case study?

Hopefully you will have recognised the potential danger of social workers being unable to separate out their own experiences of family life from those of their service users. In this case, Jim is in real danger of projecting issues from his own childhood onto the service users with whom he is working. Jim needs to speak to his manager about this and explore possibilities such as co-working the case with another social worker. He also needs to reflect carefully upon the boundaries between his social work practice and his own life experiences. In this case, there is a real concern about whether the worker can remain objective. The reverse scenario could apply: sometimes workers who have experienced abuse in their own childhoods find abuse too painful to see, or deal with. Either way, there is a real risk of professional danger. Beckett (2003) suggests that social workers are honest and think hard about the kinds of parental behaviour they find most unforgiveable and that which they find easier to understand. Equipped with this understanding they are more able to approach their practice in a way that is professional, objective and safe.

CHAPTER SUMMARY

Early in this chapter, we acknowledged that social work can be both a help and a hindrance to families. This can depend upon a whole range of factors, not least whether intervention has been requested or imposed, upon the nature of the intervention, the dynamics between the family and the worker, the contexts that surround intervention and the process by which it is carried out. The complexities that underpin social work intervention in families are never-ending. A sociological perspective, however, can assist social workers to understand the diversity of family life in the UK, and the differential pressures that impose themselves upon families.

FURTHER READING

For an accessible introduction to feminist theories, see **Abbott, P, Wallace, C and Tyler, M** (2005) *Introduction to sociology: Feminist perspectives.* Abingdon: Routledge.

Jowitt, M and O'Loughlin, S (2013) *Social work with children and families.* London: Learning Matters at Sage, provides an overview of the principal elements of social work with children and families.

For a consideration of social work practice in child protection, which grapples with the complexities of state intervention into family life and gender dynamics, see **Ferguson, H** (2011) *Child protection practice.* London, Palgrave Macmillan.

Chapter 5
Community

ACHIEVING A SOCIAL WORK DEGREE

This chapter will help you to develop the following capabilities from the **Professional Capabilities Framework:**

- **Values and ethics**
  Understand the profession's ethical principles and their relevance to practice.

- **Diversity**
  Recognise the importance of diversity in human identity and experience, and the application of anti-discriminatory and anti-oppressive principles in social work practice.

- **Rights, justice and economic wellbeing**
  Understand the principles of rights, justice and economic wellbeing, and their significance for social work practice.

- **Knowledge**
  Demonstrate an initial understanding of the application of research, theory and knowledge from sociology, social policy, psychology, health and human growth and development to social work.

  Demonstrate an initial understanding of the legal and policy frameworks and guidance that inform and mandate social work practice.

  Demonstrate an initial understanding of the range of theories and models for social work intervention.

- **Intervention and skills**
  Demonstrate the ability to engage with people in order to build compassionate and effective relationships.

It will also introduce you to the following standards as set out in the 2008 social work subject benchmark statement:

3.1.1 Social work services and service users.
3.1.4 Social work theory.
3.1.5 The nature of social, work practice.

Introduction

Like many of the sociological concepts examined in this book, 'community' is contested and open to a variety of different meanings. Indeed, Bell and Newby identified 98 different definitions for the term (cited in Popple, 1995, p2). Certainly, the word 'community' has been used in many different ways by sociologists and politicians of competing political orientations, each of whom have sought to appropriate it to justify different policies and practices. Marjorie Mayo (1994) concludes that the word is notorious for its shiftiness, arguing that there is a case to answer whether sociologists should continue to use it at all. For others, though, it is precisely the 'shiftiness' of the concept – its ambiguity and its multiplicity of meanings – that provides the main rationale for its continuing importance to us as sociologists. As Anthony Giddens (1994) argues, *on each side of the political spectrum today we see a fear of social disintegration and a call for the revival of community* (p124). Just what is it, then, that makes the concept equally popular among academics and politicians who, ideologically, have very little in common?

ACTIVITY 5.1

Get together in a group to try and identify as many different usages of the word 'community' as you can. See if you can beat Bell and Newby's total of 98 different definitions. Here are some examples to set you on your way:

- *community care;*
- *community policing;*
- *community play area;*
- *cyber community.*

While conducting the above task, you may have thought about placing the different types of community you identified into broader categories. Below, we outline the three most common kinds of community referred to in academic literature – aesthetic communities, communities of interest and 'traditional' geographical communities. Once you have read these sections, you may want to return to this task and categorise your list of communities.

Aesthetic communities

Most of you will probably have never come across the term 'aesthetic communities' before, but according to some sociologists, such as Zygmunt Bauman (2001), they have become a key feature of modern life. Normally, when we imagine a community, we envisage a neighbourhood, a geographical area or physical space. We also tend to think of communities as permanent, long-standing entities that are steeped in stability and tradition. However, aesthetic communities are different. They are, as their title suggests, 'aesthetic': related to taste, fashion, 'the immediate' and the 'here and now'. According to Bauman, they are often built around superficial areas of identity or interest. Hence, aesthetic communities might emerge around particular fads, fashions, soap operas, television shows, movies, pop groups and celebrities within the entertainment or sports industries. In the UK, for example, all the UK's popular soap operas have their own online 'communities' or forums. In these 'community forums' fictional soap opera characters become almost 'real', to the extent that their dramatised lives and the storylines they help create become the subject of heated debate and discussion. While these kinds of idol centred communities may lack a physical entity or visibility, in some ways, like 'traditional' communities, they do provide their participants with a sense of belonging, or a 'surrogate' community. In this way, *they conjure up the experience of community without real community, the joy of comfort without being bound* (Bauman, 2001, p69).

'Spontaneous' aesthetic communities might also arise in response to one-off, often temporary events that arouse concern. For instance, residents in a particular area may come together to campaign for the provision of better leisure facilities for children. Other spontaneous campaigns may emerge in opposition to local authority proposals for a particular area. For instance, the resettlement of asylum seekers to a residential area may lead people in a particular locality to develop a campaign, or 'community' of opposition. Similar protests have occurred over fears about homeless people, mental health service users or paedophiles being resident in particular areas. Although different in some respects to idol-centred aesthetic communities, these kinds of aesthetic communities share certain common characteristics with them – they are temporary, the 'community bonds' are often one-off and short-lived, and little is expected in the way of long-term commitments or ethical responsibilities (Bauman, 2001).

In terms of the advantages of aesthetic communities, they can certainly provide those engaged in them with an 'emotional premium', a sense of belonging, worth and validation. This may even be the case with aesthetic communities based around soap operas, sports stars and football teams. It is easy to see how they may provide isolated, emotionally vulnerable people with a link to the outside world, allowing them to communicate with others about issues they feel they can relate to, and have in common. Campaigns initiated by 'spontaneous' aesthetic communities can also have a positive impact, sometimes leading to the provision of community services that would otherwise be lacking. They can also serve an educational function, providing community activists with the confidence and skills that may lead them to engaging in more substantive community work.

However, aesthetic communities are not without their shortcomings. For example, aesthetic communities - whether idol-centred or spontaneous – are more about personal fulfilment and 'personal belonging' than they are the achievement of community goals in a wider sense. In addition, 'spontaneous' aesthetic communities can sometimes cause particular problems for social workers. Ill-informed spontaneous protests against homeless people, people with substance-misuse problems, asylum seekers and suspected paedophiles can, for instance, make it very difficult for those charged with providing services to these groups to perform their roles effectively.

Communities of interest

Communities of interest are said to be comprised of people who share common characteristics, interests or identities. According to Delaney (2003), *in this view of community, people from diverse backgrounds can come together in communal activism united by a bond of common commitment and the solidarity that results* (p122). Communities of interest are more permanent than aesthetic communities, often entail a good degree of personal commitment and are frequently based around substantive and progressive goals. Unlike aesthetic communities, therefore, the focus here is not on personal fulfilment, but on the achievement of wider social transformation, such as gender equality, or the removal of prejudice or discriminatory, disabling barriers. Thus, such communities may be based on gender, ethnic grouping, disability, sexuality, occupation, or indeed any other substantive area of common interest. As we discussed in Chapter 1, it is commonly thought that the last few decades have seen a proliferation of such communities, as people have lost faith with traditional 'class-based' politics.

Most would welcome the gains made by 'communities of interest' in terms of the development of civil rights and anti-discriminatory legislation. The achievements of the feminist, anti-racist, mental health and disability rights movements, to name but four, have been hugely significant, not least in the sphere of social work theory and practice. Postmodernist sociology is particularly welcoming of the work performed by communities of interest. As we discussed in Chapter 1, it sees the emergence of new social movements as being linked to the failure of traditional politics and universal welfare provision to meet the needs of particular groups. While we would caution against an uncritical celebration of the rise of a 'politics of identity', there can be little doubt that communities of identity have increased in number, and their influence in terms of policy and practice is significant.

'Traditional' geographical communities

Sometimes also referred to as 'communities of place' or 'spatial communities', with geographical communities the principal defining characteristic is the geographical locality. While in recent years, the term 'community' has been used to denote very large spatial areas (such as the European Community, or even the 'global community'), when we think of community in a geographical sense, typically we envisage a relatively small territorial area or locality – a 'neighbourhood', consisting of an electoral ward perhaps, or an estate or a village. Those living within the 'community' obviously share geographical space but, crucially, they are also often said to share a sense of belonging, identity and loyalty to their particular areas. As Chanan and Miller (2013, p5) point out, *people encounter each other face to face, sharing amenities, shops, places of worship; they receive the same services; and some join together in social clubs, sports clubs, youth clubs, day centres and environmental campaigns*. Close geographical proximity and years of shared experience are frequently seen to have inculcated certain common values and norms. There is, therefore, a sense of permanence, of shared responsibility and duty, and mutual support. In this sense, they are different from aesthetic communities discussed above and correspond more closely to what most people think of when they hear the term 'community'. Moreover, it is these geographical communities that have provided the focus for much community development policy and practice, and it is towards an analysis of this type of community that the rest of this chapter is devoted.

There is a long history within community studies of examining small, geographical communities, much of which has sought to explore the role that close networks, ties and feelings of reciprocity have played in facilitating the development of common bonds, cohesion and stability. One of the most influential of these is *Family and kinship in east London,* written by Michael Young and Peter Willmott (1962). In this classic mid-1950s study, Young and Willmott documented the extended kinship networks and close neighbourly ties among the working-class community in London's Bethnal Green. Their investigations revealed how a complex web of reciprocal family and neighbourhood ties provided the basis for the development of community cohesion and solidarity. The key to this community spirit, they argued, was residential stability and geographical proximity of kin, which facilitated the development of mutual aid strategies. They feared that post-war slum clearance and housing relocation policies were in danger of destroying this residential stability, and in doing so shattering the community bonds that been built up through decades of shared experience and mutual support.

Young and Willmott's work is the most influential of a long line of community studies that have used geographical localities as the centre of their analysis. While the focus of these studies has been on particular geographical areas, the main intention of researchers, as with Young and Willmott, has been to examine the webs of relationship, trust and familiarity that are thought to be the mainstay of 'community life'. Such studies, and the policy recommendations that stem from them, have been influenced by a number of key assumptions:

- First, it is assumed that close-knit, cohesive communities, with a common set of bonds and values, were commonplace in the past and, moreover, that they continue to exist today in well-functioning neighbourhoods. 'Community', in this sense, is seen as a good, desirable thing and something to be celebrated and encouraged.

- Second, it is felt that the loyalty, shared values and feelings of reciprocity that have traditionally bound communities together has, in many areas, somehow degenerated or been lost, and that this is the principal cause of the economic and social ills facing particular areas. There is, to cite Taylor (2003, p17), a community deficit. Communities are *deficient in some way, whether in skills, in networks, in moral cohesion, or in responsibility.*

- Third, it is assumed that it is possible to create conditions that are conducive to the restoration of community, and, importantly, that this reinstatement of community values is the solution to the problems that certain areas face.

- Finally, it is assumed that it is possible to strengthen, or create, mechanisms which will enable those within the particular locality to themselves rebuild the ties that have been lost.

A paradise lost?
Many of these assumptions have faced criticism for offering an overly simplified, 'romanticised' view of community life in both the past and the present. However, there can be little doubt that they are largely shared by the general public and policymakers alike. For example, most people today would probably agree with the claim that community life, once the bedrock of cohesion and stability, is in decline. In one survey, nine out of ten Britons said that they felt that community life was breaking down (cited in O'Grady, 2007). An extensive online consultation into modern day

'social evils', conducted by the Joseph Rowntree Foundation (2008, p9), also confirmed the existence of widespread concerns over the impact of 'community degeneration'. Participants *identified a decline in 'the community', 'community spirit', 'social solidarity' or 'community cohesion' … People often felt that communities at the neighbourhood level have disintegrated*. In the light of such findings, the question of whether there is any less community spirit in Britain is now rarely asked – the focus instead is on *why* there is less, and the notion that community *is* in decline is invariably taken as given. If we ourselves cannot recall more civilised, interdependent and mutually supportive communities, there are countless others – newspaper editors, politicians, bishops, or even our own older relatives – who are more than happy to recount to us their recollections of a 'lost', cherished community, where law-abiding people were more prepared to come together to care and help each other. All the evidence, we are told, seems to point to a lost 'golden age' of community that today, for some reason, is far less commonplace than it was in the past. Moreover, this loss of community is perceived to lie at the heart of many of the economic and social problems that we as a nation face. Participants in the JRF 'social evils' consultation linked it to *social isolation, depression, loneliness and the fear of personal and community safety*. They also felt that the dislocation of community had contributed to a wider ideological shift. Collective commitment to community well-being had been *replaced by selfish acquisition and greed*, and now there was only *a limited desire to take a personal share of responsibility for collective problems* (p11).

At the same time, as our third assumption above indicates, many, not least leading politicians, seem to believe that it is possible to re-create or recover the community spirit and way of life that has been lost. As Bauman (2001, p3) argues, in mainstream political debates, community is held out as the kind of societal organisation which is not, regrettably, available to us at present, *but which we should dearly wish to inhabit and which we hope to repossess*. The term 'community', then, is invariably utilised by politicians to denote much more than just a geographical space; it is used to describe a time, a place or a state of being that is 'safe', that offers a haven from the dangers, trials and tribulations of what is seen an increasingly insecure, hostile and threatening world. In short, it is said to provide certain key 'functions', which help promote societal stability and harmony.

The functions of community

As we saw in our first chapter, functionalist sociology often reverts to a biological analogy when explaining how society works. Society, like the human body, is said to have certain functional prerequisites – or basic needs – which must be met if it is to work effectively. Whereas the heart, the brain, the lungs, the kidneys and so on work together to keep the body functioning healthily, institutions such as the family, education, religion and the community, do the same for society. The point is, if one of these constituent parts – for example, community – malfunctions, then the health of the whole of society is seen to be threatened and remedial, 'curative' action is necessary to prevent the spread of the 'disease'.

So, what are the functions of community? First, communities provide the 'stage' upon which shared norms and values are played out. As we saw in Chapter 1,

Durkheim used the term 'collective conscience' to refer to the totality of beliefs and sentiments, which exists to shape the behaviour of individuals such that they fit into society as a whole. The community can act as the platform for the manifestation of the collective conscience, by perpetuating systems of mutual obligation and coop-eration. If in Britain today, powerful sentiments exist around courtesy and respect, for example, this can be demonstrated very clearly in communities – examples might include pervasive but largely unspoken norms which discourage anti-social behaviour and instil in residents a sense of community pride. Although of course there are impli-cations here for individuals, it is the *patterns of relationships* and supporting norms that functionalists regard as being key; these are self-perpetuating and reinforcing as the expectations that underpin behaviour in communities create accepted behaviours, which in turn reinforce the expectations that exist, and so on.

Second and very much linked to this, communities can perform a useful and power-ful social control function when individuals fall short of shared norms and values. For instance, in an area where unacceptable behaviour occurs, such as the spraying of graffiti or substance misuse, neighbours may combine together to ring the police or address the issues themselves. In this case, the individuals involved are overtly dis-couraging anti-social behaviour by making it clear that it is not acceptable. However, for functionalists, communities may also play a more covert and silent, but very sig-nificant role in enforcing norms; for example, when members of a community take pride in their homes, gardens and communal spaces, this contributes in an unspoken way to the shared 'emotional' ownership of an area. Similarly, neighbours who auto-matically keep an eye on their neighbours' property or make it known that they are watching if vandals are hanging around (through, for instance, neighbourhood watch schemes) can contribute to implementing social control.

Third, a functionalist perspective on community would point to how communities contribute a powerful component to our social identities, which in turn assists mem-bers of society to feel that they belong to something greater than themselves. As we saw at the beginning of this chapter, belonging to a community varies considerably; for some this entails a tangible experience demonstrated by attending a community centre, participating in a local concern, chatting with others in the 'local', or 'popping in to neighbours' for a coffee. For others, our social identity may be more shaped by being part of a less tangible entity, such as an online community, or by being part of a particular interest-based community.

Fourth, communities can offer individuals support, either through organisations and agencies, or through neighbours and more localised informal support networks. An example of this can be seen more and more on our TV screens following the tragic death of a child – the local community rallies round to give support, for example by lay-ing flowers, writing messages of support, and showing solidarity with the child's family.

We can see then how for functionalism the community fulfils various roles for the well-being and cohesiveness of mainstream society. Importantly, functionalists are not so much interested in individuals here, but the way that 'community' can contribute to the smooth running of the system. Of course, functionalists are well aware of the potential dysfunctional aspects of certain communities – for example, high rates of crime, riots and gang violence – but they perceive these as warning signs of societal malfunctioning which, with appropriate interventions, are solvable. We want you to bear this point in mind when, later in this chapter, we introduce you to two different interpretations of community decline – moral underclass and redistributionist discourses. As you will see, while both offer very different explanations for community dislocation, they share a common functionalist heritage. Both, to varying degrees, view community breakdown as a 'disease' or 'malfunction' which, while temporarily disturbing to the equilibrium of society, is capable of 'cure'. Although the solutions offered by each do differ, there is a general agreement that it is possible to 'smooth over the cracks' and assist communities to function well again.

The politics of community

There does seem to be a political consensus that the trials and tribulations of modern life have led to a decline in community. David Cameron (2011a, p20), the Prime Minister, maintains that his *mission in politics is to repair ... the community breakdown that has done so much damage to people's lives – not to mention the costs that our deep social problems load on to the state*. The previous Labour government was also concerned about community. It created a Department for Communities and Local Government (DfCLG), whose aim it would be to *create strong, cohesive communities in which people feel comfortable and proud to live, with a vibrant civic culture and strong local economy* (Ruth Kelly, cited in Civil Service, 2006). The DfCLG still exists under the Coalition government. Today, it wants to *achieve more integrated communities and to create the conditions for everyone to live and work successfully alongside each other*, and believes that it is possible to *generate a strong sense of mutual commitments and obligations, promoting personal and social responsibility* (DfCLG, 2013a). Hence, as well as agreeing that community is 'in trouble', politicians also agree that it can be 'retrieved' or 'recovered'.

Gemeinschaft and Gesellschaft

Sociologically, this kind of interpretation of the concept of community is often traced back to the German sociologist Ferdinand Tönnies' seminal work, Community and society, *where he distinguished between the terms* Gemeinschaft *('community') and* Gesellschaft *('society'). Writing in 1887, Tönnies bemoaned the breakdown of kinship, order, communal ties and shared interests, which he referred to as* Gemeinschaft, *associated with the onset and progression of industrial capitalism. The family ties and small-scale, personal kinship bonds that had hitherto characterised social relationships, were, he feared, gradually being replaced by the development of a more complex, fragmented, atomistic* Gesellschaft, *where individuals pursued their own isolated self-interests. In short, as far back as 1887, Tönnies was concerned about the decline in community, its impact on wider society, and he yearned for a return to a more convivial, harmonious and better world which had been shattered by industrialisation and modern life. As the following extract shows, his work does have a*

(Continued)

> *(Continued)*
>
> *contemporary resonance, for his comparisons between a harmonious, convivial past and a fractious divided present continue to find expression in social and political debates today:*
>
>> In the Middle Ages there was unity, now there is atomization: then the hierarchy of authority was solicitous paternalism, now it is compulsory exploitation; then there was relative peace, now wars are wholesale slaughter; then there were sympathetic relationships among kinsfolk and old acquaintances, now there are strangers and aliens everywhere; then society was made up of home- and land-loving peasants, now the attitude of the businessman prevails; then man's simple needs were met by home production, now we have world trade and capitalistic production; then there was permanency of abode, now great mobility; then there were folk arts, music and handicrafts, now there is science.
>
>> *(Tönnies, 1957, p2)*

But what, exactly, do politicians today mean when they call for a restoration of 'community values'? This is an important question, because some sociologists have questioned whether the harmonious, idyllic, trouble-free 'community' that politicians and commentators often hark back to has ever really existed. They argue that notions of neighbourliness and security frequently associated with community can sometimes serve to mask the segregation, division and exclusion that are characteristic features of many localities in modern 'developed' societies. Hence, 'community' can, to cite Taylor (2003), *become a spray-on solution to cover the faultlines of economic decline and social fragmentation* (p2).

Theories of community and community breakdown

We now move on to look at different interpretations of community, and the main explanations that have been advanced for its alleged demise. In doing so, we want to make use of two theoretical approaches outlined earlier in the book, in our chapter on social exclusion (Chapter 3) – moral underclass discourse and redistributive discourse.

Moral underclass discourse and community breakdown

Those of you who have already read Chapter 3 on social exclusion will be unsurprised to discover that the moral underclass discourse locates the causes of community breakdown with the morally corrupting nature of state welfare. Well-meaning, but morally degenerative government interventions have, it is argued, created dependent, feckless 'welfare communities', and in doing so destroyed the family bonds, mutual support, self-help and voluntarism that was the mainstay and lifeblood of community life in the past. Whereas once people looked to their family, friends, neighbours and other informal community support networks for assistance, now there is an expectation that the state will unconditionally provide for any unmet needs. In this sense, the 'cushion' of the welfare state *has diminished opportunities for people to be of service to each other, impairing the quality of life and encouraging us to look outwards to the 'authorities' instead of inwards to our own strengths and skills, for solutions to shared problems* (Green, 1996, pix). As the Conservative commentator, Fraser Nelson, argues (2009) the *unreformed welfare state has wrecked what were once good areas, and the lives of the people now condemned to live in the modern-day equivalent of Blake's dark, Satanic mills.* This interpretation of community decline is epitomised in the stance taken by right-wing, neo-liberal think tanks, such as the Centre for Social Justice (CSJ). Created in 2004 by Iain Duncan Smith, now the Coalition's Conservative Minister for the Department for Work and Pensions (DfWP), the CSJ (2013) locates the blame for 'breakdown Britain' with *a complex and perverse welfare system which has trapped people by failing to reward work or support those seeking to enter the workforce.* As we will see below, this explanation for community decline has shaped the trajectory of policy under the Coalition government, most notably David Cameron's 'Big Society' agenda.

This approach sees the solution to community decline as lying not with 'top down' state-sponsored initiatives (which are thought to be the cause of the problem), but with reduced levels of welfare, the restoration of civic and community values, and the encouragement of initiatives designed to stimulate mutual support, voluntarism and community self-help. In its more orthodox manifestations, moral underclass discourse simply calls for the withdrawal of state welfare, convinced that previously recalcitrant, 'dysfunctional' people will be forced to become self-reliant, active and responsible members of their community. If such individuals were forced to bear moral and financial responsibility for their actions (for example, their idleness and promiscuity) they would, it is argued, soon conform to community norms and values. Moreover, in the absence of statutory assistance and welfare, voluntary and charitable community services, which are more attuned to the causes of community breakdown and the diverse needs of the locality, will inevitably emerge to deal with any problems that do arise. In this sense, the restoration of community will entail a return to a pre-welfare state era, which is said to have been characterised by altruism, mutual support and voluntarism (Green, 1996).

Moral underclass discourse and community policy

For an early glimpse of the policy-making impact of this kind of analysis of community, we need look no further than some of the wider social policy initiatives introduced by Conservative governments in the 1980s and the 1990s. These were designed with a view to reducing the state's responsibility for welfare, and encouraging private, or voluntary community provision. Of course, informal mechanisms of support have always been significant providers of welfare, but the ideologies of self-help and 'community care' were thereafter pursued with the utmost of political vigour.

Community care

Appeals for the introduction of 'community' welfare services do tend to elicit popular support, partly because they are portrayed as progressive alternatives to impersonal, service-led provision. This was the case in the 1980s, when successive Conservative administrations introduced a number of initiatives designed to promote 'community care'. The rhetoric that underpinned these policies implied that a desire to improve the lives of service users was at the heart of the shift. The initiatives were, it was argued, motivated by a desire to close oppressive state institutions and to deliver more humane, personalised, tailored packages of care in community settings. More services, it was intended, would be provided by the voluntary and private sectors and the family (crucially, with appropriate support), and this would lead to improvements in the standard of care and increased choice and control for service users and their relatives.

ACTIVITY **5.2**

In small groups, share your perceptions and experiences of community care. These might come from:

- *personal experiences of having a family member who is cared for in the community;*
- *placement experience of providing services;*
- *working as a carer for an agency;*
- *living close to a community-based project – for example, supported housing;*
- *media reporting on community care.*

What are the issues, advantages and challenges around this policy? Try to think of these from the perspective of service users; carers; family members; professionals; and members of the public.

Discussion

Few would disagree with the principle that in many instances it is better to provide support for people in community settings. However, when community care policies were rolled out in the 1980s and 1990s, social workers, welfare professionals and academics questioned the Conservative government's motives and expressed concern (and have continued to express concern) at the direction of community care policy. Indeed, it quickly became apparent that the government's community care strategy was driven more by concerns about costs than it was standards of care. To a government that was ideologically committed to rolling back the state and cutting public expenditure, the rhetoric of community care proved useful in its justification of the closure of large, expensive psychiatric hospitals, and its attempts to limit spending on nursing care. The introduction of a more mixed economy of care meant that a great deal of direct care provision was and continues to be provided by private-sector agencies, which raised real issues pertaining to the quality of care when profit is the key underpinning factor. The possibility that communities may have been ill-equipped to cope with the often complex needs of service users was also rarely acknowledged, and *community care became synonymous with 'care at home' and in practice relied on informal care from families [predominantly women] to look after those in need* (Pierson, 2002, p138). We do not have the space to engage in a detailed analysis of the gendered nature of community care here, but we would agree with Pierson's (2002) suggestion that much needs to be clarified before embracing the concept. As he points out, *If it is little more than another ideological device to extract unpaid, low-prestige labour out of women then it an oppressive concept in its own right* (p139).

The rhetoric of community care has continued to shape policy pronouncements in the twenty-first century. The current Coalition government, like its Labour predecessors, continues to present community care as the 'progressive' panacea to some of the worst failings of institutional care. There is, in fact, little doubt that properly funded, well-coordinated, personalised, service user-led care in the community can contribute to improvements in the lives of many people. However, where care is poorly resourced, badly coordinated and service-led, the consequences can be disastrous. In such circumstances, service users can fall through the professional net and be exposed to serious risk. A report by the Equalities and Human Rights Commission (EHRC) (2012, p7), for instance, uncovered *serious, systemic threats to the basic human rights of older people who are getting home care services*. This report found that only half of those surveyed were happy with their provision, and that for many older people, 'community care' failed to live up to its liberating rhetoric. Indeed, the inquiry's interviews with service users found a *pervasive sense of isolation for virtually all ... Almost all the older people we interviewed felt cut off from everyday life and deprived of human company, referring to 'gaol fever' and inescapable boredom* (p39). Worst still, the research found that a large number of older people receiving home care were:

- not being given enough support to eat and drink;

- experiencing financial abuse, with money being systematically stolen over sustained periods of time;

- being subjected to a chronic disregard to their privacy and dignity while being subjected to intimate tasks;

- finding their views were being ignored or treated in a patronising way, leaving them little control over the services they received;

- subjected to risks to personal security, when carers were inappropriately changed at short notice;

- experiencing physical abuse, through the use of mishandling and unnecessary physical force.

In its conclusions, EHRC (2012a) drew attention to the consequences of the systematic failure to deliver home, community care for elderly people in an adequate, dignified way. *The cumulative impact on older people can be profoundly depressing and stressful: tears, frustration, expressions of a desire to die and feelings of being stripped of self-worth and dignity – much of which was avoidable* (p4).

This investigation, like others conducted into the failings of community care for older people, documented instances of cruelty and abuse perpetrated by 'rogue' social care workers. However, the problems it uncovered stemmed mainly from a wider societal failure to adequately resource or regulate community care for older citizens, a problem that, as the King's Fund notes, has being exacerbated by the Coalition government's cuts to local authority budgets. Cash-strapped local authorities are, the King's Fund points out, forced to pass these cuts on to private sector providers of community care (who currently deliver 89 per cent of all home care hours), which inevitably leads to further reductions in the breadth and quality of provision. As the King's Fund argues, the Coalition's austerity agenda *will make it extremely difficult for councils to protect, let alone improve, investment in services that promote wellbeing and help to deflect or postpone the need for formal health and care services* (Humphries, 2013, p19).

What this example illustrates is the extent to which the progressive 'rhetoric' of community care has often borne little relation to the 'reality' of service delivery. Many users of community care services continue to receive under-funded, shoddy services with very poor standards of care, which give no consideration to their basic human right to dignity and respect. The fundamental problem is that many social care staff are still very poorly paid and inadequately trained. Older adults often find they have someone different arriving to fulfil their care needs each time, which is in itself a demeaning process. In addition to this, of course, very many carers feel unsupported and unable to cope. This is not to draw attention away from very many positive outcomes of properly resourced, well-organised community care; however, where it is poorly funded, inadequately supported and motivated by the pursuit of profit, service users' experiences of community care can be sadly lacking. Given that this is the case, it is perhaps hardly surprising that the ideological underpinnings of community care policy have been questioned, with some coming to the conclusion that it has, in practice, been used as a vehicle for promoting welfare state retrenchment.

Moral underclass discourse and social work

Moral underclass discourse sees the social work profession, as it is currently organised, as partly culpable for lower levels of civic responsibility and community decline. Social workers, it is argued, too readily embrace the notion that 'the poor' are victims of circumstance. They assume naively that the problems facing certain communities are due to external forces beyond their control, and that residents are justly entitled to support and compensation for their 'plight'. As we have seen in various chapters of this book, Conservative ministers such as Michael Gove, the former Education Secretary, and Eric Pickles are enthusiastic proponents of this interpretation of social work. The ethos underpinning the social work profession was, it is argued, not always organised in such a manner. In its earlier incarnations social work was very different, less 'indiscriminate' in its propensity to deliver welfare, and more concerned about questions of character and culpability. In advocating a model for the future, therefore, moral underclass discourse looks backwards; to the late nineteenth- and early twentieth-century work of the Charity Organisation Society (COS).

As we have discussed elsewhere, the foundation of the COS in the nineteenth century is often seen as heralding the beginning of social work in Britain (Cunningham and Cunningham, 2012). Initially organised and run on a voluntary basis, it adopted a personal casework approach, seeking to determine not just levels of need, but also levels of moral culpability. Assistance was conditional and those who were deemed 'undeserving' of support, or 'not likely to benefit' from support (a euphemism for 'undeserving'), were simply turned down, and forced to rely upon their own devices. Advocates of moral underclass discourse defend the apparent harshness of this approach:

> This was not due to hard-heartedness, as critics maintained, but to the conviction that not everybody asking for assistance was in a position to benefit from it, and that to give relief heedlessly was to make a bad situation worse ... So, for example, a man who is poor because he is addicted to drugs or alcohol will not benefit from cash handouts, as he is extremely likely to spend the funds on his addiction. (This point might seem too obvious to need making, were it not for the fact that the state welfare system today ignores it.)

(Whelan, 2001, p22)

For proponents of the moral underclass discourse, social work can *potentially* have a role in helping us recover community life, but it will entail a very different kind of prac-tice to that taught in universities today, which, according to Whelan (2001, p96), ren-ders social workers unfit to operate in the real world. Structural issues surrounding race, gender and other politically correct causes, he argues, have *assumed supreme importance, whilst the idea that social workers should help their clients to modify their habits and develop the skills necessary to participate in mainstream society seemed to have evaporated entirely.* From this perspective, then, welfare, and more specifically social work, should once again be devolved to a community level, organised primarily by the voluntary or charitable sectors, and geared towards modifying behaviour and ensuring that all are encouraged to respect community values and norms.

Redistributionist discourse and community breakdown

As outlined in Chapter 3, redistributionist discourse adopts a structural approach when explaining social problems. Not surprisingly, therefore, instead of focusing on individual culpability, redistributionist discourse draws attention to the forces that impinge on communities, which serve to undermine the development of cohesion and shared values. Hence, community breakdown is linked to factors such as eco-nomic decline, the restructuring of the labour market, the residualisation of state welfare, and changes at an ideological level. Regarding the economy and labour market, the decline of traditional manufacturing industries, such as textiles, min-ing and steel has, it is argued, torn the heart out of many communities, wiping out millions of jobs, and destroying the aspirations and dreams of younger generations. Industries that once provided employment for whole neighbourhoods or commu-nities have disappeared, leaving in their wake exclusion, hopelessness and division. Hence, the camaraderie and feelings of reciprocity that evolved from shared work-places and social experiences have been shattered not by moral breakdown, but by social and economic dislocation. These trends have adversely affected economic activity and social interaction at a community level, and small-scale enterprises – local butchers, newsagents, social clubs, pubs and grocers' shops – have closed, unable to cope with decline in demand for their goods and services. (This process has, of course, been exacerbated by the proliferation of large, multinational supermarket chains.) These local shops and leisure facilities previously provided geographical spaces where people within communities were brought together, facilitating the development of community ties and shared interests and values.

At the same time, the welfare support mechanisms which would previously have helped communities cope with such changes – for instance, welfare benefits, advisory and support services – have been withdrawn or cut, exacerbating the difficulties communities face. Meanwhile, at an ideological level, decades of neo-liberal dominance have served to foster and sustain a culture of selfishness, greed and other traits that make the development of shared community values difficult (JRF, 2008). Certainly, the ethic of competition, reward and 'just deserts' has gathered pace in the past few decades, and advocates of redistributionist discourse argue that this has impacted negatively upon community cohesion and support for the kind of collective action that is necessary to create a community ethic.

For supporters of redistributionist discourse, any solution to community decline must begin by tackling the chronic unemployment, poverty and hopelessness that have contributed to a dislocation of community. Redistributionist discourse would not deny the importance of moral underclass discourse's emphasis on community self-help, but it draws attention to two main factors that currently militate against solutions which focus primarily upon community activism.

First, there is a much wider recognition of the broader social, economic and ideological environments within which communities (and community activists) must operate. Thus, the notion that communities can themselves solve the fundamental structural problems that lie at the heart of their neighbourhoods is, they argue, naive. These problems – for instance, educational inequality, chronic unemployment, underemployment, low incomes, inadequate welfare benefits and the emergence of an individualist consumer culture – are national, or even global in nature, and while communities and community activists can mitigate their symptoms, they are powerless to deal with their origins. As Mayo (1994, p11) argues, *neither voluntary effort in general, nor community-based self-help in particular, can be expected to fill the widening gap between social needs and public provision.* Governments, therefore, need to begin by acknowledging their responsibility for ensuring that all communities benefit from, for instance, decent educational and employment opportunities and adequate incomes.

Second, and on a more practical level, poverty, unemployment, and the daily struggle to make ends meet mean that many people are *simply unable to participate* in activities designed to promote 'community cohesion'. Referring to Maslow's hierarchy of needs, Taylor (2003) argues that *there are many in marginalised communities whose main preoccupation is physical survival, so self actualisation is a long way up the hierarchy of needs* (p78). From this perspective, people can only develop the kinds of solidarity recommended by policy-makers if they have the time and resources to do so, a luxury currently lacking in many communities. Mayo (1994) agrees:

If communities are realistically to play an enhanced role in a restructured welfare state they will have to be provided with public resources to make that option viable.

(p11)

Redistributionist discourse and social work

While redistributionist discourse places much greater emphasis upon wider structural factors, as hinted above, it does also believe that social workers can play a significant role in mitigating community decline and fostering community action at a local level. Indeed, countless textbooks have been written detailing the virtues of community work and outlining the ways in which practitioners, such as social workers, can utilise their skills to help initiate progressive community change. Twelvetrees (2008) argues that community workers on deprived housing estates can help people form and organise their own autonomous representative organisations, such as tenants' associations, youth groups, play groups, senior citizens' associations and food co-operatives. They can seek to map already existing, but under-utilised 'community assets', tapping into *the agenda building and problem-solving capacities of local residents, local associations, and local institutions* (Kretzmann and McKnight, 1996, p27). While moral underclass discourse might interpret such work as 'professional busy-bodying' and representative of a 'nanny state', redistributionist discourse would emphasise its importance in empowering members of the community and encouraging them to become directly involved in improving the fabric of their own localities. This kind of work, which Twelvetrees (2008) refers to as the *community development approach,* is seen as being valuable for two reasons. First, and most obviously, it helps initiate material improvements which all members of the community stand to benefit from. Second, and just as importantly, bringing members of the community together and encouraging them to work collectively to solve some of the problems they face, helps facilitate the development of the sort of values, networks and feelings of reciprocity upon which healthy communities depend. By working together, people come to realise there really is something such as society and that they, and the communities within which they reside, stand to benefit from collectivist as opposed to selfish, individualist action.

There is, however, another important way in which redistributionist discourse feels that practitioners can facilitate the development of healthy, vibrant communities; that is, by engaging in what Twelvetrees (2008) refers to as *social planning*. By this he means working directly with policy-makers – locally, regionally, nationally and even internationally – with a view to sensitising them to the needs of particular communities, and harnessing opportunities and resources that can be used to promote community development. Supporters of redistributive discourse see this aspect of community work as crucial. Practitioners can and, it is argued, should, use their advocacy, organisational and networking skills to influence policy debates and promote a wider awareness of the structural problems that deprived communities face. They can do this in a 'consensual' way by, for instance, lobbying policy-makers and applying for grants on the community's behalf, but where necessary they should not rule out helping to organise direct political action campaigns and even protests based upon civil disobedience. That said, redistributionist discourse approaches to community tend to stop short of engaging in a wider critique of capitalism itself. It is assumed that the basic foundation of society is sound and that causes of community dislocation can be solved through gradual social reform. Table 5.1 provides a tabular summary of the two approaches to community breakdown that we have described.

Table 5.1   Summary of the approaches to community breakdown

	Causes of community breakdown	Solutions to community breakdown	Practice implications
Moral underclass discourse	• Well meaning, but morally degenerative government interventions, which reward and encourage dependency and 'deviancy', and destroy self-help and voluntarism. • Low levels of motivation and aspiration at a community level.	• Reductions in levels of welfare support, aimed at reducing dependency and forcing communities to take responsibility for their own lives and situations. • Promotion of individualism. • Encouragement of initiatives designed to stimulate mutual support, voluntarism and community self-help.	• Emphasis placed on the virtues of private, voluntary and charitable provision and practice. • Rejection of structural analysis and a focus on modifying welfare-induced dysfunctional behavioural patterns. • Practice should be geared towards inculcating appropriate norms and values, and stimulating self-help, hard work and thrift.
Redistributionist discourse	• Economic decline and unemployment. • Welfare cuts. • Poverty and inequality. • Dominance of individualistic, neo-liberal ideology.	• Substantially improved work opportunities. • Moderate levels of income redistribution. • Improved welfare benefits. • Repudiation of individualist, neo-liberal ideology. • Encourage the development of a community spirit/ethic.	• Practice underpinned by an understanding of wider structural causes of community decline. • Encouragement of community action, but with an awareness of the limitations of self-help strategies. • Promotion of strategies designed to arrest inequalities in economic and social resources.

Hopefully, this table will help you appreciate the key elements of each of the two major explanations for community decline that we have outlined. Our analysis now turns to an assessment of the relative influence of these two competing interpretations on community policy in the UK.

'Community' policy

When analysing the causes of community decline, Conservative politicians have traditionally tended to embrace moral underclass discourse, while their Labour counterparts have gravitated towards redistributionist discourse. However, in recent years the leaderships of both parties have, rhetorically at least, sought to distance themselves from what they describe as the 'extremities' of their former positions. When in government, the former Labour Prime Minister, Tony Blair, bemoaned the 'top down' state interventionist solutions to community regeneration, which had traditionally been favoured by the 'Old Left'. He claimed that under his leadership Labour would shift towards a 'middle ground', accepting, to an extent, the validity of behavioural interpretations of community decline and the need for voluntary and private sector initiatives. Likewise, prior to the General Election in 2010, David Cameron, criticised the 'Old Right' who believed that the only way of restoring 'community' was by cutting the supply of state services:

> *The fact is, we cannot arbitrarily withdraw welfare benefits for the most needy of our fellow citizens. Yes, if we did that, no doubt in 20 years' time people would have become more self-reliant – but think of the misery of those 20 years. Some people will always need help and support – and we should not imagine that government simply withdrawing from the social field will automatically and instantly cause new, independent bodies to spring up in their place.*

(Cameron, 2006)

Hence, both these leaders eschewed what they described as overly-'ideological' approaches to community development, claiming that they would seek to implement a non-ideological route between the 'extremes' of both Right and Left, or to use our typology between moral underclass discourse and redistributionist discourse. Here, we examine the influences underpinning recent community policy in more detail, assessing the extent to which it has, in practice, been guided by a more pragmatic, 'non-ideological' approach.

Community policy under Labour, 1997–2010

Influenced by the work of sociologists such as Anthony Giddens (1998), policy responses to community breakdown under Labour governments tended to combine structural and behavioural elements. Rhetorically, each was given equal prominence, but as we will see, the relative influence of structural versus behavioural explanations in shaping Labour's community development has been a matter of much debate. As with its approach to social exclusion, Labour stands accused of utilising progressive, 'redistributionist' rhetoric to disguise the 'behavioural', 'moral underclass' underpinnings of its community development policies. Hancock et al. (2012, p347), for instance, have argued that Labour relied *on the labile qualities of community to pursue its neoliberalising agenda*, which was, in reality, shaped by a desire to re-moralise and 'responsibilise' what were perceived to be 'pathological' working-class communities.

The New Deal for Communities

The New Deal for Communities (NDC) was one of Labour's flagship policies for strengthening communities. Introduced in 1998, the NDC set aside £2 billion for investment over a ten-year period in some of the country's most deprived communities. In all, 39 of some of the UK's poorest communities were to be given resources to help them tackle five key themes: poor job prospects, educational underachievement, high crime levels, poor health and poor housing and urban environments. There can be little doubt that the communities chosen were in need of investment. On average, only 42 per cent of over 16s in these

(Continued)

(Continued)

communities were in full-time work (18 per cent lower than the national average). Overall unemployment between 2001–04 stood at 8 per cent, three times the national average, and average weekly income was only £241, almost half the national average (Office of the Deputy Prime Minister, 2005, p121). The government, though, was keen to emphasise that this would not simply be a 'top down', redistributive initiative of the kind previously associated with 'Old' Labour. Too much, Tony Blair argued, has been imposed from above, when experience shows that success depends on communities themselves having the power and taking the responsibility to make things better (Social Exclusion Unit, 1998, pi). The Prime Minister's comments here hinted at a non-ideological, 'what works' approach to community development. However, the emphasis that was placed upon the need for communities themselves (and not just government) to take responsibility for improving their neighbourhoods was not ideologically neutral. Indeed, at times the government gave as much prominence to the importance of community self-help as it did to the need for wider structural improvements, such as additional resources and the provision of greater opportunities. This did seem to mark a significant break with 'Old Labour's' redistribution-ist strategies:

> Without effective self-help, it is unlikely that any other measures of commu-
> nity regeneration, however well-resourced, will provide long-term solutions
> to long-term problems ... To put the matter another way: the regeneration of
> poor neighbourhoods will take more than physical rebuilding; more than the
> improvement of local services; more even than economic opportunity.
>
> *(Home Office, 1999, p1)*

While some of the NDC initiatives had a redistributive element at their core, much of the funding was devoted to locally based 'supply side' measures, designed to stimulate and incentivise community members to solve their own problems. Hence, many of the work-lessness schemes funded by the NDC focused less on job creation and more on motivating and encouraging people to take up opportunities that were deemed to be readily avail-able. Needless to say, in the absence of genuine job creation initiatives, the impact of this approach proved to be minimal. As Crisp (2012, p248) argued, the NDC Programme made little or no contribution to observable reductions in worklessness at programme level. Likewise, in education, NDC funding was used to offer inducements for pupils to work harder, by providing financial rewards to those who pass a certain number of GCSEs, rather than to tackle the structural causes of educational disadvantage (see the education chapter (Chapter 7) for a discussion of these).

Many welcomed Labour's acknowledgement of the failure of previous community regeneration schemes, as well as its embrace of the principle that community mem-bers should be at the heart of any development strategy. Moreover, there is evidence that local organisers and participants in some NDC areas felt empowered as a result of their engagement with the programme (Crisp, 2012; Toynbee and Walker, 2011).

However, critics argue that the NDC was guilty of repeating the same mistakes of earlier regeneration initiatives, such as Community Development Programmes in the 1960s and 1970s. Space prevents us from engaging here in a detailed critical evaluation of the NDC (for this, see Wallace, 2010), but a general concern shared by many is the lack of resources that were devoted to tackling the structural causes of community decline. For example, the £2 billion allotted to the NDCs sounds like a considerable sum, but when placed in the context of the problems these 39 communities faced (and the £800 million spent on the Millennium Dome during the same period) its relative insignificance becomes clearer. As one evaluation of the NDC calculated, the £2 billion allocated to the NDC equated to less than £100 per person. Of itself, the authors concluded, *this kind of investment will not lead to major shifts for many outcomes* (Lawless et al., 2008, p116). As already hinted, others have criticised the ends to which resources were put, arguing that an inappropriate focus was placed upon 'supply-side' measures which were designed to stimulate and motivate community members to solve their own difficulties, rather than dealing with the intractable structural problems their communities faced. A more general criticism, and one that is applicable to many such micro-level community development initiatives, was that Labour ministers seemed to base their community development strategy upon a rose-tinted, outdated conception of 'community', which had long since ceased to bear any relation to reality. As each of the NDC evaluations pointed out, these were now heterogeneous, fluid, ethnically diverse, rapidly changing communities, with high population turnovers. In the light of this it was, critics argued, naïve to assume that an 'idyllic', self-supporting, 1950s-style community spirit could flourish in such surroundings, let alone solve the intractable problems these areas faced. For example, 27 per cent of the population of Newcastle's NDC area had lived there for less than a year, and the same was true of around one-fifth of London's NDCs residents. In addition, many residents who remained in these deprived areas viewed themselves as 'transient' and hence had little grounding or 'stake' in the community. In all, 42 per cent in Newcastle's NDC area had expressed a desire to relocate, as had over 50 per cent in some London boroughs. Worst still, those who did move tended to be the least 'service needy' and the ones whose 'assets', 'skills' and 'experience' were most needed to help generate community 'improvements' (Lawless et al., 2008). Indeed, one evaluation found that many community activists who had been empowered by the NDC had, once their status and skills had been enhanced via NDC funding and training, promptly moved out of their areas, never to come back (*The Times*, 6 February 2007). As Toynbee and Walker (2011, p148) argued, when discussing the experiences of Clapham Park's NDCs:

The Labour instigators of these schemes were sociologically naïve, appearing to forget the rate of churn amongst residents. Over half the people here ten years ago have gone ... People who get jobs tend to get up and go. People moving in tend to have extreme problems ... Labour was seduced by the idea of captive 'communities' that could be fixed, but in reality they are fluid, mobile and unmeasurable.

Whereas Toynbee accuses Labour ministers of naïvety, others have gone further, condemning Labour governments for embracing an overtly moral underclass agenda. For

Wallace (2010, pp2 and 9), community rhetoric and policy were the means by which the moralisation and activation of poor citizens was operationalised by Labour. While its community development policies may well have been conceived with the genuine intent of improving the lives of those in deprived communities, their neo-liberal ideological inspiration meant that they were handicapped from their very inception. The assumption that radical improvements could be wrought primarily through *transforming the individual and collective behaviour of excluded residents,* rather than tackling the exclusionary barriers that limited their life chances, meant that they were bound to fail. Crisp (2012, p233) agrees, arguing that Labour's community-based initiatives were merely *flanking strategies* that appeared progressive and benign, but were actually designed *to co-opt individuals or neighbourhood-based organisations in the service of neoliberal goals.* Ultimately, critics argue that at the root of Labour's agenda was an attempt to create a *social order in which people behaved differently rather than one in which resources are distributed differently* (Deacon, cited in Wallace, 2010, p32).

Community policy under the Coalition

The ideological trajectory of community policy under the Coalition government is less open to debate and most commentators accept that, despite Cameron's hints at the embrace of a more pragmatically-based, 'what works' approach, there is a clear neo-liberal, 'moral underclass' influence in its shape and direction. In fact, the likely route of travel was set out in a speech Cameron (2009) made before the general election, where he identified what he felt was the debilitating, and corrosive impact of the welfare state on 'community'.

> When the welfare state was created, there was an ethos, a culture to our country – of self-improvement, of mutuality, of responsibility ... But as the state continued to expand, it took away from people more and more things that they should and could be doing for themselves, their families and their neighbours. Human kindness, generosity and imagination are steadily being squeezed out by the work of the state ... There is less expectation to take responsibility, to work, to stand by the mother of your child, to achieve, to engage with your local community, to keep your neighbourhood clean, to respect other people and their property, to use your own discretion and judgement. Why? Because today the state is ever-present: either doing it for you, or telling you how to do it, or making sure you're doing it their way.

> The big government approach has spawned multiple perverse incentives that either discourage responsibility or actively encourage irresponsibility. Far too many of the people I see in my constituency surgery are, thanks to the state, financially better off if they do the wrong thing than if they do the right thing.

> But when you are paid more not to work than to work, when you are better off leaving your children than nurturing them, when our welfare system tells young girls that having children before finding the security of work and a loving relationship means a home and cash now, whereas doing the opposite means a long wait for a home and less cash later ... is it any wonder our society is broken? ... This is why we plan a complete break with the big government approach.

- *Can you identify any 'moral underclass' influences in the comments Cameron makes about the negative impact of* big government *and the welfare state?*
- *Part of Cameron's solution to the problem of what he refers to as the* broken society *involves the dismantling of* big government *and the creation of the* Big Society*. What do you think he means by* Big Society*?*

It is not too difficult to detect a moral underclass influence in Cameron's speech. His suggestions that 'big government' has inhibited initiative, and that the welfare state had destroyed self-improvement and responsibility have clear neo-liberal undertones. In addition, in accusing feckless, welfare-induced young teenage mothers of contributing to the creation of a 'broken society', Cameron draws upon one of moral underclass's most enduring and favourite 'folk devils' to reinforce his point about the morally corrupting nature of welfare. In keeping with neo-liberal critiques of the welfare state, Cameron's 'solution' to the problem of the 'broken society' is to move away from state welfare to what he refers to as the 'Big Society', where individuals and communities are responsible for securing their own economic and social well-being. Hence, communities should stop looking to the state for guidance or assistance and search 'within' for cures to their economic and social ills:

> We want to give citizens, communities and local government the power and information they need to come together, solve the problems they face and build the Britain they want. We want society – the families, networks, neighbourhoods and communities that form the fabric of so much of our everyday lives – to ... take more responsibility.

(Cameron, cited in Cabinet Office, 2010, p1)

In the period that the Coalition has been in office various initiatives have been implemented to encourage and coerce individuals and communities to take more responsibility for their own social and economic needs. On the 'encouragement' side, the Coalition has announced the appointment of 500 'senior community organisers' and 4,500 'voluntary community organisers' by 2015. *Each community organiser,* the government's guidance explains, *goes into their community and listens to residents' loves, concerns, visions and dreams and supports them to take positive action on what matters to them.* Their role is to 'inspire', to 'lead by example', and *to create a new home-grown movement of community organising for the twenty-first century, emerging directly from the strengths, concerns and hopes of all kinds of neighbourhoods across Britain.* (Community Organisers, 2013, p2)

These are clearly ambitious goals, and it is easy to see how they fit in with Cameron's 'Big Society' ethos. However, given the limited resources available, it is difficult to see how this initiative can have anything more than a minimal impact upon community regeneration. For instance, the government has provided only one year's funding of £20,000 for each of the 500 'senior community organisers', after which the posts must be self-funding, through private donations or sponsorship. No funding at all is provided for the 4,500 'non-senior community organisers' who, it is anticipated, will be part-time, voluntary workers. The temporary nature of the funding is, in part, shaped by a determination to prevent this new cadre of community workers from becoming state-funded, quasi-social workers. Likewise, the intention is to ensure that the work of community organisers will not be tainted by the influence of what ministers see as 'corrosive', social work-style, rights-based values. Indeed, the government has also openly acknowledged that this is an agenda for 'responsibilisation' rather than one geared towards providing material support and assistance to communities. Hence, in all, only £10 million has been devoted to the initiative, which amounts to just 0.5 per cent of the £2 billion Labour allocated to its NDC, which itself was widely criticised as being inadequate for dealing with the entrenched difficulties deprived communities faced. The 'self-help' philosophy underpinning the programme also is reflected in the ethos of the organisations chosen to train these new teams of community workers. The general (contestable) assumption is that 'all the assets are already out there' to restore vitality to communities, and that regeneration can be 'sparked' into life by the guiding hand of philanthropically-motivated moral entrepreneurs (Edwards, 2012).

It is probably fair to say that the bulk of the government's attempts to 'responsibilise' communities have been based less upon the principle of 'encouragement' and more on 'coercion'. At the forefront of these efforts have been the Coalition's reforms to social security, such as the benefits cap, the bedroom tax, its disability benefit reforms and its tightening of the benefits sanctioning regime. These are designed to make life on welfare 'less attractive', with a view to increasing the incentives for people and communities to support themselves rather than relying upon the state. While they follow a similar trajectory to the previous Labour government's reforms (see Wallace, 2010), they do represent a significant acceleration of pre-existing policy trends, reducing the value of social security and tightening eligibility conditions still further. In this respect, the reforms seem to have followed a typical neo-liberal, 'moral underclass' agenda. While these cuts were initially partly justified with reference to the government's deficit reduction strategy, the government has recently been forthright in reinforcing what it sees as the 'moral' case for reform, linking benefits changes to its goal of restoring a 'culture of responsibility' within 'dysfunctional' communities:

> ... *our long-term economic plan for Britain is not just about doing what we can afford, it is also about doing what is right. Nowhere is that more true than in welfare. For me the moral case for welfare reform is every bit as important as making the numbers add up: building a country where people aren't trapped in a cycle of dependency but are able to get on, stand on their own two feet and build a better life for themselves and their family.*

> (Cameron, 2014, p28)

What have been the consequences of the Coalition's attempts to restore individual and community 'responsibility', and have they helped foster the development of more 'functional', less fractious communities?

ACTIVITY 5.4

We discussed the phenomenal rise in reliance on food banks in our poverty chapter (Chapter 2), so you may want to read through that discussion again before undertaking this task. As we explained there, the numbers of individuals receiving support from food banks rose, from 129,000 in 2011/12 to more than 700,000 2012/13. Prior to the General Election in 2009–10, the Christian charity, the Trussell Trust (2014) provided food parcels to 40,898 people; in 2012/13 it assisted 346,992 people. Below, we have included two quotes which interpret the growth of food banks in very different ways. After reading the quotes, try answering the question that follows:

> Food banks are not soup kitchens, nor a sign of a society gone bad. In fact, their emergence ought to be seen as a sign of how strong Britain's social fabric is … It's the opposite of the Dickensian image conjured by the critics … It is a striking phenomenon — of the existence of charity, rather than poverty. Those who say food banks are a scandal should visit one. And when one is established in your town, don't weep and gnash your teeth. Just celebrate the fact that you live in a big-hearted society.
>
> *(Isabel Hardman (2013), assistant editor of the conservative-leaning* Spectator *magazine)*

> It is a national disgrace that this Christmas there are tens of thousands having to turn to food banks … Yet ministers view food banks as merely an expression of people's good will, a worthy charitable enterprise or the manifestation of the illusive 'big society' … Ministers should understand that it is not merely an immediate crisis for the people unable to feed themselves … By creating a generation of vulnerable people, especially children, with a poor, irregular diet, we are storing up a public health time bomb. We are starting to understand the obesity epidemic. Soon we will see an explosion in the other conditions related to poor-quality, unhealthy diets and intermittent hunger. On this government's watch, we have seen an increase in the diseases of Dickensian England: rickets, scurvy, tuberculosis and malnourishment. Just as the Edwardians discovered at the time of the Boer War, we will soon discover a generation permanently damaged by vitamin deficiency and unhealthy eating.
>
> *(Luciana Berger, 2013, Labour's spokesperson for Public Health)*

- *Should food banks – many of which are reliant upon 'community' voluntary effort for donations and functioning – be seen as a sign of 'weakened' or 'strengthened' communities?*

As evidenced by the first quote in Activity 5.4, conservative commentators have welcomed the food bank phenomenon as an example of the Big Society 'in action'. Coalition ministers share this enthusiasm. Lord De Mauley, Conservative Parliamentary Under-Secretary of State for the Department for Environment, Food and Rural Affairs, described them as *wonderful charities*, which were providing the kind vibrant, bottom up community-led response to social need that the government wants to encourage (House of Lords Hansard, 5th February 2013, c135). Responding to a Labour Opposition question, which drew attention to the 400 per cent increase in food bank usage since 2010, Tim Lansley, then Children's Minister, rejected criticism of growing food bank usage. He argued that the government *rightly appreciate the service that is being provided by food banks*, and defended the Department for Work and Pensions (DfWP) policy of food bank referral for those unable to meet their nutritional needs. David Cameron has also celebrated the growth in the food bank phenomenon, insisting that *we should recognise and welcome the work that food banks do* (Commons Hansard, 16 January 2013, c866). Of course, the government denies that there is a link between food bank use and its welfare reforms, which, as we will show in the social class chapter later, have reduced the incomes of millions of families. Michael Gove, the former Education Secretary, argues that the inability of many families to purchase food is *often the result of decisions that they have taken which mean they are not best able to manage their finances*. In other words, most food bank users have the financial means available to meet their families' nutritional needs, but are choosing to spend their income on other things. Lord Freud, Parliamentary Under-Secretary of State for the DfWP, claimed that increased usage of food banks was due to increased supply – put simply, there are now more food banks than there were previously and more people were taking advantage of the greater availability of food charity (House of Lords Hansard, 2 July 2013, c1072).

Others, however, are less sanguine when contemplating the rise in the use of food banks. Critics welcome the community 'spirit' that often underpins such initiatives, but they argue that they represent evidence of a fracturing, rather than a strengthening of communities. They deal with the symptoms of growing problems like unemployment, low wages, poverty, benefit delays, benefit sanctions and cuts and hence constitute little more than a 'sticking plaster' rather than a solution to food insecurity. They point to evidence gathered by food bank providers themselves, which suggests that the Coalition's welfare reforms, together with low wages and higher living costs, are the principal causes of increasing demand for their services (Trussell Trust, 2014). Such claims were corroborated by a government-commissioned report, which was only reluctantly released in February 2014, some seven months after it was presented to the Coalition (Lambie-Mumford et al., 2014, pviii). According to this report, the key causes of food bank usage were a *sudden reduction in household income*, such as job losses and problems associated with social security payments, *and on-going, underpinning circumstances (such as continual low household income and indebtedness) which can no longer support purchase of sufficient food to meet household needs*. No evidence was found to support the claims made by Conservative ministers that financial irresponsibility and increased supply of food aid have driven demand, which is presumably why the publication of the report was so delayed. As the report argued, *it is only after other main strategies have been employed (including changes to shopping and eating habits, cutting back on other outgoings, and turning to family and friends for help) that the most food insecure households may turn to food aid* (pxii). Moreover, the report rejected the notion that food banks should be seen as an integral, permanent solution to food insecurity. While such community-based systems of food aid *may be able to relieve the short-term symptoms of food insecurity* they are incapable of addressing *the underlying causes*. In effect, the authors of this important report were drawing attention to the fundamental shortcomings of such community-based welfare initiatives, which are powerless to address the national causes of the poverty that contribute to social problems many communities face.

Herein, critics argue, is one of the main problems with Cameron's 'Big Society' initiative. Its portrayal of self-help-based 'community action' as the panacea to economic and social ills, naïvely, or perhaps wilfully, fails to acknowledge the limitations of such action. As Chanan and Miller (2013, p11) point out, *the historical evidence for the feasibility of major change in neighbourhoods is not encouraging*. Of course, this is not to say that valuable community 'assets', 'skills' and 'experience' do not exist in many deprived communities; indeed they are often characterised by a rich tapestry of untapped talents and abilities, and clearly policy and practice should be geared toward harnessing these 'assets' for the common good. However, as we saw with Labour's NDCs, in the absence of wider attempts to reinvigorate economically depressed communities, community 'asset-based' strategies have little chance of initiating fundamental, lasting change. Hence, voluntary-run food cooperatives and food banks can help alleviate the symptoms of food insecurity, but they are largely powerless to tackle its principal causes, given that they have no control over the economic forces that shape the lives of community residents.

The historical and ideological foundations of the 'Big Society'

On a more general level, critics have questioned the historical and ideological assumptions that have informed Cameron's 'Big Society' initiative. As Corbett and Walker (2013) point out, it harks back to an idyllic, nineteenth-century Britain, where communal values, flourishing self-help, mutual aid organisations and charitable provision are assumed to have contributed to a harmonious, well-functioning, 'responsibilised' social order. According to Corbett and Walker, this is a disingenuous appeal to a *an evidence-free romanticized past;* a historical distortion, which ignores the social division and huge swathes of unmet need – poverty, squalor, chronic ill-health and physical deterioration – that were a characteristic feature of a pre-welfare state, Victorian Britain. It is, they argue, built upon a mythical, ideologically loaded vision of the past, which overlooks the failure of voluntarism and self-help to provide for the scale and variety of needs and problems generated by industrial capitalism. It also stands accused of failing to acknowledge the enormous positive contribution state welfare has made in tackling intractable economic and social problems and dramatically improving the lives of citizens. Cameron's 'utopian' vision of the 'Big Society' will, its critics fear, rapidly develop into a divisive, neo-liberal, Dickensian dystopia.

Interestingly, critics of the 'Big Society' are not confined to 'left-leaning' politicians and academics. Indeed, the very voluntary sector organisations that Cameron wishes to 'empower', and to fill the void left by the withdrawal of state welfare provision, have also expressed dismay at how their work has been seriously hampered by the Coalition's expenditure cuts. As the Civil Exchange's (2013) *Big Society Audit* pointed out, *many cuts in state funding have already fallen on the voluntary sector and dramatic falls are estimated over the next 4 years, with many organisations working with vulnerable people, often in disadvantaged areas, under serious threat*. The Civil Exchange, one of the original 'champions' of the community empowerment ethos underpinning Cameron's initiative, has now called for *a radical review of the Big Society*. The concept, it argues, is increasingly being utilised by the Coalition in a more *slippery* way, with many citizens, justifiably, regarding it merely *as a cover for cuts* (p11). The Civil Exchange also raises serious questions about the voluntary sector's capacity to cope with the level of social responsibilities contemplated by the Coalition:

> *Voluntary organisations are having to step in to provide essential services where the welfare state appears to have failed, for example through food banks. This raises questions about whether voluntary organisations should be used to provide lifeline services that should be the responsibility of the state.*

(p18)

Church leaders have also questioned Cameron's Big Society vision, with the Archbishop of Canterbury controversially describing it as a *painfully stale* concept. There was, he argued, *a widespread suspicion* that the Coalition's emphasis upon the 'Big Society' *had been done for opportunistic or money-saving reasons*. This, he argued, was not helped, *by a quiet resurgence of the seductive language of 'deserving' and 'undeserving' poor, nor by the steady pressure to increase what look like punitive responses to alleged abuses of the [welfare] system* (Williams, 2011). The perception that the Big Society is merely an elaborate ruse, designed to justify ideologically influenced cuts, also seems to be shared by the general public. A survey for *The Times*, for instance, found that 78 per cent of people agreed with the statement that *the Big Society is just an attempt by Government to put a positive spin on the damage public spending cuts are doing to local communities* (Coates, 2011). The speed and intensity of the cuts, together with the government's apparent indifference to their impact in the current economic climate, have reinforced the perception that Cameron's 'Big Society' initiative is fuelled by ideological zeal, rather than a desire to regenerate communities. These reforms have, after all, been implemented at a time when the opportunities for community members to engage in what are considered to be 'responsible' behaviours – for example, employment – are more slender than they have been for decades. As Ellison (2011, p57) argues, *the Big Society, as conceptualised by Conservative thinkers, has no place for those who, largely for reasons associated with lack of opportunity and the disadvantages resulting from their socio-economic position, find it hard to 'fit in'.*

A Marxist approach to community and community breakdown

We end the chapter with a summary of Marxist interpretations of community decline. In previous chapters we have seen how Marxists reject functionalist claims that capitalist societies are, on the whole, essentially well-functioning totalities, subject to only sporadic, relatively small-scale, 'curable' problems. In fact, the problems associated with community breakdown, such as poverty, unemployment, social division, crime and poor housing are, Marxists argue, an inevitable and intractable feature of a system based upon competition, exploitation and injustice. Moreover, these problems are far more common and endemic than any of the above approaches are prepared to acknowledge. Even redistributionist discourse, the most radical of the two approaches outlined above, seems to accept that targeted interventions, aimed at a relatively small number of communities, can help overcome social dislocation and create a more harmonious and just capitalism. In this sense, Marxists argue that the rhetoric surrounding community regeneration policy, even in its more progressive redistributionist form, can serve an ideological function, diverting our gaze from the bigger picture of social division and exclusion. It persuades us that only a small number of communities are 'malfunctioning', and that their 'sickness' is a result of abnormal, pathological and parochial factors which are capable of cure. The reality, for Marxists, is that these social and economic problems are symptomatic of a much wider malaise that lies at the heart of capitalist societies, which will only be overcome with the abolition of capitalism and the creation of a socialist society.

Marxism, social work and community

What role, then, do Marxists see for community practitioners? First, there needs to be a recognition that practice itself cannot change society or solve the multiple problems and difficulties communities face. Although practitioners can have as their aim the creation of a more fair, just society, they cannot themselves achieve the large-scale changes that are needed to effect fundamental improvements. That is not, though, to suggest they cannot perform a positive role by engaging in radical, transformatory practice. One of the problems with much community development work, Marxists argue, is that while it has made the lives of many people somewhat easier, less intolerable and unpleasant, it has not been truly transformative (Ledwith, 2011). So although it has helped alleviate some of the symptoms of the injustices that characterise capitalist societies, it has failed to draw attention to, address or challenge their root cause – the system itself. Indeed, as Craig et al. (2011, pp11–12) argue, in instances where attempts have been made to develop truly radical community development strategies, the state has intervened to either dilute their transformative potential, or to close them down. Most community development projects, they insist, have been geared towards *imbuing community activists with responsibility but neither power nor resources*, and those that have posed more fundamental questions and challenges have been *firmly ruled off limits*. Marxists therefore claim that practitioners engaged in community development work often perform a contradictory function. On the one hand, they help to mitigate the worst effects of capitalism – by effecting fractional improvements in the material circumstances of sections of the poor and providing an illusion of empowerment – yet on the other hand, they help 'prop' the system up by diffusing potential discontent, and perpetuating the myth that capitalist societies are, on the whole, characterised by solidarity, cohesion and integration. Marxists therefore insist that the work of community practitioners in capitalist societies must be shaped by an acknowledgement of wider economic and social inequality, and be driven by a desire to initiate fundamental social and economic change.

In practical terms, then, practitioners may wish to engage in propaganda and political education work, designed to stimulate a community-level awareness of the wider structures that contribute to the problems they face. Practitioners can also play a crucial organising role, assisting communities to challenge oppressive structures, through campaigns, demonstrations and sit-ins. In addition, they can help community organisations to develop links with other radical community associations and movements, with a view to increasing their collective strength. In relation to the current emphasis placed on self-help, Marxists insist that practitioners must have an awareness of the limitations of such an approach. As Ledwith (2005), a prominent advocate of transformative practice, argues:

> *If we are uncritical in our practice, we may find ourselves naively supporting policies that emphasise participation as a further erosion of rights in favour of responsibilities, rather than a process leading to social justice and equality. The end result of this would be a continued transfer of resources away from the most vulnerable communities, with an increased emphasis on local self-help as an inadequate response to the structural forces of discrimination.*

(pp19–20)

Of course, Marxists would never dismiss the potential of community empowerment *per se*, and they accept that community self-help and organisation must be part of a strategy for empowerment, harnessing the collective strength of the poor. However, they argue that the current vogue for community self-help constitutes little more than a masking defence against calls for redistribution and represents a *neo-liberal wolf dressed up as a populist sheep*:

> *Self-sufficiency, the idea that 'left to their own devices' (and their current resources) poor communities would lift themselves out from poverty just fine, makes for an attractive myth but a regressive policy.*

(Berner and Phillips, 2005, pp20 and 24)

The concern here, for those such as Ledwith (2011), is that while the rhetoric of self-help has an undeniable appeal, it places the responsibility for tackling poverty onto the very groups who are most targeted by oppressive forces, denying the reality of structural power that permeates communities and perpetuates poverty. Hence, the idea that poor communities can 'develop themselves', which, as we have shown, finds expression in much community development policy and rhetoric, is seen by Marxists as being fundamentally and dangerously flawed. It assumes, incorrectly, that communities do not need to benefit from a fundamental redistribution of resources and that the current structure of wealth and power distribution can be ignored. It also harms demands for realistic levels of funding for tackling the problems that many communities face and, overall, reinforces the view that the poor are poor because they have failed to help themselves (Berner and Phillips, 2005).

CHAPTER SUMMARY

When we wrote the first edition of this text, we concluded that the sociology of community seemed to be less fashionable than in previous years. To an extent, this remains the case today. If we cast our minds back to when we were A Level sociology students, the topic did seem to feature in most introductory sociology textbooks. Now, however, 'community' seems to have been inauspiciously removed as a substantive subject in many texts partly, no doubt, due to what we described earlier as the perceived 'shiftiness' of the concept – its ambiguity and its multiplicity of meanings. That said, the revival of the 'politics of community' has, to an extent, revitalised the sociology of community, contributing to the publication of a number of key texts, new editions and collections. This is a positive development, because as you have hopefully witnessed while reading the chapter, the concept of community lies at the heart of debates about the future of social welfare and social work policy and practice, and it is crucial that those of you who will be responsible for implementing future policy have a firm understanding of the different conceptualisations of the term. We hope that this chapter has stimulated your interest in and understanding of the topic, encouraging you to read further, and engage with the growing literature around the sociology of the community. Hopefully, those of you who do go on to engage in community work are also now in a position to give some consideration to the ideological origins of different policy initiatives, as well as their limitations.

FURTHER READING

Those of you interested in radical, transformatory community work will find Margaret Ledwith's book a useful text: **Ledwith, M** (2011) *Community development: A critical approach.* 2nd edition. Bristol: Policy Press.

The following text also provides a useful, accessible analysis of the potential of community practice and community development: **Chanan, G and Miller, C** (2013) *Rethinking community practice: Developing transformative neighbourhoods.* Bristol: Policy Press.

For a moral underclass discourse perspective on community work see: **Green, DG** (1996) *Community without politics: A market approach to welfare reform.* London: CIVITAS.

In the following influential text, Alan Twelvetrees discusses different approaches, but the book focuses mainly on the skills needed by community workers: **Twelvetrees, AC** (2008) *Community work.* Basingstoke: Macmillan/Palgrave.

For a more theoretical and critical text, see: **Popple, K** (2005) *Analysing community work: Its theory and practice.* Maidenhead: Open University Press/McGraw-Hill.

The following edited collection contains an excellent range of key sources, which chart the history of community development theory, policy and practice in the UK: **Craig, G, Mayo, M, Popple, K, Shaw, M and Taylor, M** (2011) *The community development reader: History, themes and issues.* Bristol: Policy Press.

This final book provides a very good, critical analysis of Labour's New Deal for Communities: **Wallace, A** (2010) *Remaking community? New Labour and the governance of poor neighbourhoods.* Farnham: Ashgate.

Chapter 6
Moral panics

A C H I E V I N G   A   S O C I A L   W O R K   D E G R E E

This chapter will help you to develop the following capabilities from the **Professional Capabilities Framework**

- **Values and ethics**
  Demonstrate an awareness of own personal values and how these can impact on practice.

- **Knowledge**
  Demonstrate an initial understanding of the range of theories and models for social work intervention.

- **Critical reflection and analysis**
  Understand the role of reflective practice and demonstrate basic skills of reflection.

It will also introduce you to the following standards as set out in the 2008 social work subject benchmark statement:

3.1.1 **Social work services and service users.**
3.1.3 **Values and ethics.**
3.1.4 **Social work theory.**

Introduction

Some of you may already be familiar with the term 'moral panic' as it is now commonly used to describe what are perceived to be exaggerated societal responses to particular issues or problems. In sociological and social work literature we find frequent reference to moral panics. Over recent decades moral panics are said to have emerged over issues such as youth crime, asylum and immigration, the rave scene, lone parenting and welfare fraud. As we will show, the basic premise of the concept is that the threat said to be posed by a particular issue or social group is out of all proportion to the danger actually posed. Society, it is argued, is frequently 'whipped up' into a frenzy of concern over particular issues, and this leads to inappropriately harsh policy responses. In the course of their work, social workers will quite often be working with individuals and groups who are said to be the subjects of moral panics and hence it is important to understand the concept's origins and meaning. This chapter will consider how the term 'moral panic' emerged and developed, and will discuss different relevant sociological perspectives. You will be encouraged to make sense of the ways in which individuals and groups can become labelled by the media, politicians, welfare professionals and institutions and assess how social work can, on the one hand, help generate and foster moral panics, and on the other hand, empower service users to move beyond labelling.

What is a 'moral panic'?

Societies appear to be subject, every now and then, to periods of moral panic. A condition, episode, person or group of persons emerges to become defined as a threat to social values and interests; its nature is presented in a stylised and stereotypical fashion by the mass media; the moral barricades are manned by editors, bishops, politicians and other right-thinking people.

(Cohen, 2006, p1)

The term 'moral panic' was coined by Stan Cohen to explain what he felt was the exaggerated level of media, societal and political concern generated by disturbances between 'Mods' and 'Rockers' in British seaside resorts in 1964. The catalyst was a sporadic outbreak of violence in Clacton on a wet, cold and miserable Easter Sunday in 1964. A few groups of young people with little else to do began scuffling with each other, throwing stones and engaging in other minor misdemeanours. A few windows were broken and some beach huts were vandalised. The young people began to break off into two separate groups, 'Rockers' and 'Mods'. The total estimated cost of the damage was no more than £500, yet the day after, the incidents were portrayed in most national newspapers in wildly inflated terms. The emotive language used such as 'riot', 'orgy of destruction' and 'siege' conveyed images of a besieged town being laid to waste by a rampant, lawless mob.

As a young sociologist, Cohen was fascinated by the reactions to the events as they unfolded. He identified the creation of 'folk devils', or newly created deviant groups. In this instance, these were Mods and Rockers, two groups of young people differentiated by their distinctive style of dress and musical tastes. Prior to the trouble on Easter Sunday, the differences between the two groups were not fully established, but they were later reinforced partly as a consequence of the overstated emphasis placed by the media on their distinctiveness. Cohen described how the media exaggerated, simplified and distorted the events, amplifying levels of concern to such a degree that the occurrences in Clacton assumed a national significance out of all proportion to the danger they posed. Doom-laden predictions were made about the 'threat' posed to societal norms and values by the gangs of so-called 'mindless hoodlums'. The media's sensationalist portrayal of similar events in other seaside towns in 1964 served to reinforce the perception of the mods and rockers phenomenon as a widespread evil menace that needed to be tackled. Few assumed the events were a 'transient' phenomenon, and they were presented as being representative of a general breakdown in moral values, law and order and societal well-being. As Cohen (2006) noted:

it was clear throughout that it was not only property that was being threatened, but 'all the conventions and values of life'. As the Birmingham Post *(19 May 1964) put it, drawing on Churchill's 'we will fight them on the beaches' speech: the external enemies of 1940 had been replaced on our own shores in 1964 by internal enemies who 'bring about disintegration of a nation's character'.*

(p38)

Cohen drew attention to the emotive labelling that was used to describe and demonise the participants as 'hooligans', 'thugs' and 'wild ones'. These terms became part of the prevailing mythology and were attributable to all young people wearing certain clothes and belonging to specific social groups. Cohen (2006) quoted the prosecutor at the first trial in Clacton after the events who listed the following traits of the offending youth: *no views at all on any serious subject; an inflated idea of their own importance in society; immature; irresponsible; arrogant; lacking in any regard for the law, for the officers of the law, for the comfort and safety of other persons and for the property of others* (p40). These themes were picked up by the press, who incorporated them into their headlines, which described those participating in the disturbances as *ill conditioned, odious louts, retarded, vain, young, hotblooded pay-cocks, and grubby hordes of louts and sluts.* This had the effect of further reinforcing the negative images associated with the labels, touching a chord with the general public and 'moral crusaders' who became drawn into the newly created moral panic and demanded swift measures to be implemented to counteract the 'threat'. Cohen went on to describe how politicians harnessed the moral panic around mods and rockers to justify the introduction of coercive criminal justice policies.

Since the publication of Cohen's seminal work on moral panics, sociologists have subsequently utilised the concept to describe what they see as the exaggerated levels of concern that surround certain social groups and problems. Importantly, as we will show, the subject matter of moral panics is often linked to the areas of life that social workers are involved in.

In summary then, a moral panic can be defined as a socially constructed process that occurs when there is a reaction to a social event, which produces a heightened, exaggerated sense of awareness and concern in society. As we have seen, a moral panic begins with a problem being identified; its causes are then simplified and key participants stigmatised. The media then pick up on the issue and campaign for 'something to be done'. The authorities respond, often harshly, but in many cases the media's appetite for the more lurid and inaccurate aspects of the debate remains as insatiable as ever, and its continued stereotypical reporting of the issue leads to calls for still more stringent action to be implemented.

ACTIVITY **6.1**

You may wish to do this exercise in a small group.

With reference to the above definition of a moral panic, scan the newspapers over the duration of a two-week period and try to identify any current moral panics.

- *What are the key features of these?*
- *Who are the 'folk devils'?*

- *Which groups or interests are 'manning the moral barricades'?*
- *How are the folk devils seen to challenge the moral fabric of society?*
- *What responses have there been and by whom?*
- *What solutions have been proposed to deal with the folk devils identified in your moral panic?*
- *Are there any practice implications for social workers stemming from the responses and solutions?*

You may wish to use online newspaper databases for this exercise or simply purchase a selection of different newspapers. It might be useful to collect quotations from different newspapers to compare the ways in which the issue is being presented.

In the above exercise, you were probably able to identify a range of current issues that have appeared in the media that are currently generating a great deal of concern. Many of the issues you identified may have had important implications for social work intervention. However, moral panics are not helpful for social workers, who have an obligation to adopt a measured and non-judgemental approach when working with certain popularly stigmatised groups of service users.

Moral panic: A model for understanding

Moral panics frequently seem to assume a relentless momentum, but why are moral panics so persuasive? We have developed the following model to assist with understanding the many aspects of moral panics which may help you to address this question.

The power of the media

The mass media in Britain are considered by many sociologists to be a very powerful means by which reality is constructed. It does not present the news in an 'objective' and 'neutral' way. On the contrary, the media distorts its presentation of news in a way that heightens levels of concern around certain events and phenomena. In this way, the media advance the momentum of moral panics by reporting aspects of social issues in simplistic, sensational and often inaccurate ways.

The presentation of the issue is often accompanied by powerful images and emotive language

The media are able to show visual images of issues in such a way that the audience not only hears or reads about the issue, but sees a range of persuasive and sometimes disturbing visual images. In the current world of instantly available news in a variety of mediums, the public can have access to news 24 hours a day if they wish. Further, since we wrote the first edition of this book, we have seen how the rise of social media, such as Twitter,

(Continued)

(Continued)

can amplify levels of concern, with thousands of members of the public adding their own emotive language and commentary to the issues of the day.

Moral panics are often backed by politicians who provide legitimacy to the moral panic

It is not uncommon for politicians to seek to actively feed moral panics by making statements at particularly pertinent times to reinforce and heighten levels of concern. Indeed, as we will see later, Marxists argue that politicians often seek to initiate moral panics over particular issues in order to divert attention away from structural causes of social problems.

Moral panics often feed into long-established, pre-existing fears and prejudice

The success of moral panics is often linked to the fact that their subject matter frequently taps into pre-existing public fears, striking a chord with their audience. This means that the public are often familiar with and sympathetic to the narrative as presented by the media, politicians and moral entrepreneurs. This has the effect of reinforcing existing anxieties and fears.

Moral panics are often characterised by circular, self-supporting arguments

The momentum assumed by a moral panic is often strengthened by the perpetuation of arguments and responses which are mutually reinforcing. This can derive from the impact of the initial response to the issue, which is often out of all proportion to the threat posed. Indeed, in many cases, the reaction apportions an unwarranted prominence to the 'problem group', which in turn exacerbates the perceived level of anxiety.

Moral panics are often based on a compelling mixture of myth, fact and lies

The subject matter of moral panics is regularly reported and debated in such a way that it is difficult to separate out fact from fiction. Sections of the media in Britain are well known for their over-dramatised and sensationalist reporting of certain issues and this often results in a heady combination of truth and lies. Similarly, it has been argued that politicians often distort and simplify issues, seeking to make political capital out of moral panics. The impact of this, along with all the other factors identified above, results, some suggest, in persuasive and relentless moral panics.

Asylum and moral panics

In the introduction to the third edition of *Folk devils and moral panics*, Stanley Cohen (2006) identifies current debates about asylum seekers in the UK as providing a particularly good example of the kind of hysteria that can be generated by a moral panic.

An asylum seeker is someone who is claiming that *owing to a well-founded fear of being persecuted for reasons of race, religion, nationality, membership of a particular social group, or political opinion, [he] is outside the country of his nationality, and is unable to or, owing to such fear, is unwilling to avail himself of the protection of that country* (UNHCR, 2014). Hence, asylum seekers should not be confused with economic migrants, who travel to the UK – either legitimately, or illicitly – to avail themselves of economic opportunities. Asylum seekers are seeking a 'safe haven'; a refuge from war, torture and oppression, and as signatories to the 1951 UN Convention on the status of refugees, the UK is obliged to consider their claims and provide them with protection if necessary.

According to Cohen, when discussing this issue, the media, politicians and 'moral crusaders' invariably propagate inaccuracies and simplistic stereotypical myths, focusing on the 'pull' factors which are said to entice people to Britain, rather than 'push' factors that may lead them to flee their countries of origin. Hence key influences on asylum trends such as war, conflict or persecution are disguised or dismissed and the overwhelming imagery associated with asylum seekers tends to be negative. Asylum seekers are portrayed as economic migrants or benefit tourists rather than human beings and genuine refugees. This view has contributed to policy developments which have been geared towards reducing, and in many cases removing entirely, the welfare entitlements of asylum seekers (Children's Society, 2012). These policies have had direct practice implications for social workers, who in many cases have been left to deal with the consequences of the state-enforced destitution of asylum seekers. We will now consider how the model we outlined can help us to understand the creation of a sustained and persuasive moral panic around asylum.

Power of the media

A large proportion of the British population has probably never knowingly seen an asylum seeker, yet opinion polls tell us that they are widely perceived to be an unambiguously unfavourable group. Indeed, in an October 2013 IPSOS MORI poll, the British public said that they were more concerned about immigration and asylum than they were about inflation and price rises, crime and law and order, education, the National Health Service, pensions and benefits, housing, poverty and inequality, and a host of other issues besides. The only issue to be characterised by higher levels of concern was the economy (Ipsos/Mori, 2013). Asylum seekers are therefore widely seen, to use Stanley Cohen's (2006) words, as the visual symbols of society's ills. There can be little doubt that the media have helped to construct this negative perception of asylum seekers, since it is the main portal through which people receive information about refugees. Indeed, one survey found that only 19 per cent of Britons rely on personal experience for their information on immigration and asylum (Ipsos/Mori, 2011), with the overwhelming majority relying on the media. In this respect, debates over asylum serve to highlight the sheer 'opinion-forming' power the media possess. In the absence of any direct contact with asylum seekers or refugees, it is the *sole* reference point for most people's information – it is *the* opinion former.

The presentation of the issue is often accompanied by powerful images and emotive language

In the case of the asylum debate, the repeated publication and broadcasting of images of unkempt, dishevelled asylum seekers clambering over border fences, or desperately trying to cling on to trains bound for Britain, reinforce the notion that Britain is about to be 'flooded' with a 'deluge' of 'asylum cheats'. Likewise, inaccurate media generalisations about the 'generous' levels of support provided to asylum seekers help generate and perpetuate the popularly held misconception that the assistance given to asylum seekers is 'lavish', acting as a magnet, encouraging 'bogus' asylum claims. Thus, according to dominant conceptions of the asylum debate, it is the irresistible lure of the 'honey pot' of welfare that drives asylum applications, rather than the incidence of war and political persecution. As one fairly representative headline in the *Sun* put it, *we resent the scroungers, the beggars and crooks who are prepared to cross every country in Europe to reach our generous benefit system* (cited in Cohen, 2006, pxx). With moral panics, the language used to frame debates is also important. As well as being overwhelmingly negative towards the 'folk devil' in question, like the above quote from the *Sun,* it often seeks to invoke a sense of impending doom, or disaster. In the specific case of the asylum debate, terms like 'flooded', 'deluge' and 'wave', all of which are widely used by the media and politicians to describe the 'influx' of asylum seekers, convey the image of crisis and an impending natural disaster, which must be thwarted at all costs.

RESEARCH SUMMARY

The media and asylum

The media's reporting of asylum-related news has been analysed in a number of studies, which collectively provide compelling evidence of an overwhelmingly negative bias in its coverage of the issue (Article 19, 2003; Information Centre About Asylum and Refugees (ICCR), 2004; Greenslade, 2005; Migration Observatory, 2011). These studies show, for example, how the reporting of the asylum debate is invariably characterised by an inaccurate and provocative use of language. Meaningless and derogatory terms – such as 'bogus asylum seeker' and 'asylum cheat' – are frequently used, which serve to reinforce negative, inaccurate perceptions about asylum seekers. This sensational language is then reinforced by selectively chosen images, which tend to concentrate on the stereotype of the threatening young male, with women and children rarely being seen. As the ICAR (2004) argues, tabloid newspapers are particularly notorious for this, and they often present images of asylum seekers and refugees that contain language, photographs, and graphics likely to raise feelings of fear and hostility … among their readers. Analyses of the media discourses around asylum also show how discussions of the issue focus overwhelmingly on 'numbers', while the statistics cited are frequently un-sourced, exaggerated or inadequately explained. As a consequence of this, the general public massively overestimates the numbers of asylum seekers coming to the UK. Hence, the Migration Observatory (2011) found that 62 per cent of the public believed that 'asylum' was the principal reason migrants come to the UK, whereas in reality asylum seekers account for around only 4 per cent of all migrants each year. The voices of refugees and asylum seekers themselves are also very rarely represented by the media, if at all, meaning that little or no attention is devoted to analysing the 'push' factors that force individuals and families to flee from their homelands and seek refuge in other countries. Finally, research has also documented the detrimental impact of media representations of asylum seekers on the quality of their lives. It shows, for example, that asylum seekers and refugees often feel alienated, ashamed and sometimes threatened as a result of the overwhelmingly negative media coverage. Indeed, Article 13 (2003) found that many of the asylum seekers participating in their study felt that this contributed to the prejudice, abuse or aggression they experienced from neighbours and, importantly for us, service providers. On this latter point, the Commission for Racial Equality (now subsumed into the Equalities and Human Rights Commission) told a Parliamentary Inquiry that media hostility towards asylum seekers was so prevalent it was influencing the life and death decisions being made by Home Office immigration decision-makers. The biased reporting of tabloid newspapers, *the Inquiry was informed,* influenced perceptions and engendered feelings of cynicism in immigration caseworkers which in turn affected their decision making on individual cases concerning entry and asylum *(Parliamentary Joint Committee on Human Rights, 2007, p99).*

It is not only academics that have criticised the UK media's portrayal of asylum seekers. As the following quote illustrates, the United Nations High Commissioner for Refugees has also condemned the media's portrayal of asylum seekers and refugees, calling for politicians to act to restrain the sensationalist tendencies of the press:

> In the United Kingdom, asylum seekers — and the refugees among them — have increasingly ... been turned into mere statistics by the popular press. Asylum seekers are easy to demonize. They are foreign, so an attractive target for those who are suspicious of, or actively dislike, foreigners or minorities with foreign origins. ... The Government and Parliamentarians must take all reasonable steps to ensure that asylum issues are presented in a balanced way.

> *(UNHCR, 2007, p1).*

In its latest concluding observations on the UK's adherence to the UN Convention on the Rights of the Child, the UN's Committee on the Rights of the Child (2008) also called upon the UK government to ensure more accurate, responsible reporting of asylum issues, accusing media organisations of contributing to the continued discrimination and social stigmatization experienced by asylum seeking children.

> The Committee is ... concerned at the general climate of intolerance and negative public attitudes towards [asylum seeking and refugee] children, especially adolescents, which appears to exist in the State party, including in the media, and may be often the underlying cause of further infringements of their rights.

> *(p6)*

> *(Continued)*

(Continued)

More recently, the UN Committee on the Elimination of Racial Discrimination (2011) has condemned the virulent statements in the media that are inherent within its reporting of asylum issues which may adversely affect racial harmony and increase racial discrimination. Like the UNHCR, it called upon UK governments to counter negative, inaccurate media portrayals of asylum seekers. The State party, it argued, should adopt all necessary measures to combat racist media coverage and ensure that such cases are thoroughly investigated and, where appropriate sanctions are imposed (p12).

How have UK governments reacted to calls for them to promote greater levels of 'responsibility' in reporting of asylum-related issues? Rather than challenge misconceptions, some argue that politicians have actually sought to pander to, and reinforce the negative stereotypes promoted by the media. The UNHCR, for instance, has accused politicians of simply responding to what they perceive to be the mood of their electorates, and of failing to make a concerted effort to dispel the hysteria that surrounds this issue (cited in Parliamentary Joint Committee on Human Rights, 2007, p99).

Moral panics are often backed by politicians who provide legitimacy to the moral panic

Whenever a moral panic arises, it is common to see politicians contribute to the debate, which in itself adds credence to the issue, reinforcing already heightened levels of concern. In relation to asylum and immigration, moral panics that reinforce the portrayal of the vast majority of asylum seekers as 'bogus', serve a number of 'functions' for politicians. First, they disguise Western governments' culpability in contributing to, or failing to alleviate, the 'push factors' (global poverty, famine, war, persecution and conflict) that drive asylum seekers to make the difficult decision to leave their homes and seek refuge. There is, in fact, remarkably little evidence to suggest that the 'lure' of welfare is a significant influence in driving asylum claims, while there is a direct correlation between asylum claims and persecution, war and conflict (Crawley, 2010). Second, the portrayal of asylum seekers as 'welfare tourists', 'economic migrants' or as an 'economic burden' means that the blame for unemployment, housing shortages and stretched health and education services in deprived areas is skillfully placed on the shoulders of asylum seekers rather than politicians themselves. In this way, the failure of politicians to reverse decades of economic decline is obscured, and economic and social ills are mistakenly (but, for politicians, usefully) seen to be the result of the relatively recent arrival of what in some cases is a couple of dozen asylum seekers. Finally, the overwhelmingly negative representation of asylum seekers provides justification for politicians to circumvent their legal obligation to provide support to people seeking refuge from persecution, and to restrict asylum seekers' eligibility for welfare assistance. In fact, there can be little doubt that governments in Britain – Conservative, Labour and Coalition – have drawn on negative, stereotypical images of asylum seekers to justify cutting their benefits and to deflect attention from other political issues. Politicians, in adding their weight to claims made in popular newspapers, add legitimacy to the issue for members of the public who start to see the issue as being 'real' because of contributions from 'respected' members of parliament.

Moral panics often feed into long-established, pre-existing fears and prejudice

Here in the UK, we like to think of ourselves as a tolerant society, with a long and just record of providing refuge to genuine victims of political persecution and human rights abuses. The incessant 'backlash' against asylum seekers in media commentary and political debates is often seen as a recent and justifiable reaction to an 'abuse' of our hospitality. In fact, refugees, even those fleeing Nazi Germany in the 1930s, have always been treated with suspicion, fear and hostility, being portrayed as either economic migrants or an 'alien threat' to national security (Winder, 2004). More recently, since the London bombings of 7 July 2004, asylum seekers have become linked with fears about terrorism nationally and internationally, which acts as further justification for tighter controls and vilification by certain sections of the media.

However, moral panics about asylum seekers have also tapped into a long-established fear of migrants, the origins of which can be traced back to notions of genetic, moral and intellectual superiority which have their roots in Britain's imperial history. Hence, Commonwealth migrants who came to Britain in the post-war years were greeted with hostility and abuse, and the blame for society's economic and social ills – such as poor housing and unemployment – was placed firmly on their shoulders (Winder, 2004). Fear of 'the other' therefore, is a pervading theme in British history and permeates moral panics which are linked to immigration and asylum.

Moral panics are often characterised by circular, self-supporting arguments

Hysteria about asylum seekers has developed a momentum that has in many respects become self-perpetuating. Asylum seekers are often portrayed by the media as being scroungers who come to Britain to take advantage of welfare benefits, with little acknowledgement of the fact that they are legally unable to work and are therefore required to claim benefits to survive. Similarly, the policy of dispersing asylum seekers to deprived inner-city districts, where health, education and housing resources are already stretched, serves to support the notion that asylum seekers are a burdensome drain on limited resources. In many areas this has led to an increased incidence of racist attacks and abuse, and a reinforcement of the perception that asylum seekers are the cause of community ills, shifting attention away from the underpinning structural causes of social problems.

Moral panics are often based on a compelling mixture of myth, fact and lies

If media and political commentaries are to be believed, the UK is the preferred destination of choice for 'bogus' asylum seekers. It is, we are told, easier to claim asylum in this country than any other European country, and this, together with the 'lavish' welfare support offered to asylum seekers, has contributed to a scenario whereby 'we' (far more so than any other European country) are 'inundated' with false asylum applications. The UK has, according to this interpretation of the asylum debate, become a haven for (at best) foreign scroungers, or (at worst) foreign criminals and terrorists. Is this an accurate depiction of the asylum issue or, as organisations such as the Refugee Council have argued, is it based on a confusing, yet compelling, mixture of half-truths, myths and lies?

First, Home Office statistics belie claims that we are 'inundated' with unprecedented numbers of asylum seekers, showing that asylum applications to the UK are lower than they were in the mid-1990s. Indeed, contrary to popular belief, UK asylum applications have seen a dramatic fall in recent years. Thus, in 2002, there were 84,132 applications, compared to just 23,499 in the 12 months prior to June 2013 (Home Office, 2013). Moreover, when measured in terms of applications per 1000 inhabitants, statistics show that the UK receives far fewer asylum claims than most other European countries (UNHCR, 2012). Even when assessed in numerical terms, Belgium, Sweden, Italy, Germany and France all received more applications in 2011. For example, in 2012, the UK hosted a total of 169,000 refugees and asylum seekers, compared to Germany's 589,700 (Refugee Council, 2013). Despite this, the British public continue to be convinced that 'we' are the preferred destination of choice for asylum applications, with 58 per cent believing that Britain receives a higher proportion of asylum seekers than any other European nation (Ipsos/Mori, 2011).

Second, as we have shown, asylum seekers are invariably portrayed as bogus 'welfare tourists', with little or no credence given to the possibility that they may be genuine victims of war, torture or persecution. In fact, research shows that asylum seekers coming to the UK are from nations that are characterised by some of the most horrific conflicts and human rights abuses. Indeed, as intimated above, all the evidence shows that asylum trends are correlated to the incidence of war, conflict and human rights abuses, and not the generosity of welfare payments (Crawley, 2010). This leads us to our third point, regarding welfare. While it is true that asylum seekers are often dependent on state support, this is not because they do not want to work. On the contrary, it is because UK law prohibits them from working while their claims are considered. Nor do asylum seekers get large handouts from the state. Indeed, many are made destitute as punishment for not fulfilling complex, strict eligibility criteria, and those who do receive assistance are only entitled to an amount that is lower than the normal level granted to UK citizens. A recent Children's Society (2012) report showed that many asylum seekers receive a rate of support that is less than 50 per cent of that given to UK citizens. Contrary to popular belief, therefore, asylum seekers do not jump the queue for housing, do not get routinely housed in the Ritz Hotel in London and do not receive special perks such as mobile phones, colour televisions or cars. Research suggests that the majority of asylum seekers are living on the margins of society, in dire poverty, often in housing that is unfit for human habitation (Parliamentary Joint Committee on Human Rights, 2007).

Finally, despite fears perpetuated by some sections of the media that asylum seekers are in fact hardened criminals or even terrorists in disguise, the Home Office itself has stated that there is no evidence that asylum seekers are any more likely to commit crimes than anyone else. Indeed, asylum seekers are more likely to be the victims of crime, particularly race-related crimes, a reflection, no doubt, of the suspicion and hostility generated by moral panics surrounding the asylum debate (Refugee Council, 2013).

The above model for understanding the development of moral panics will hopefully have demonstrated to you why levels of concern around asylum seekers have been so relentless. As Cohen (2006) argues, *the overall narrative is a single, virtually uninterrupted message of hostility and rejection. Moreover, successive British governments have not only led and legitimated public hostility, but spoken with a voice indistinguishable from the tabloid press* (pxix). You may wish to track the progress of this issue by keeping a watchful eye on media reporting in the future.

The problem of youth

Asylum is just one of many topics we could have considered in some detail to illustrate Cohen's ideas. In this section, we want you to apply some of the theories and concepts we have outlined above to another issue that is increasingly dominating the media and political debates – the behaviour and conduct of working-class youth.

Young people are regularly identified by sociologists as being the subjects of moral panics (Pearson, 1983; Jones, 2011). Certainly, 'youth' and youth cultures are generally presented in terms of the problems they cause for others, and in recent years, there has been a fairly persistent concern around youth crime and in particular about threats to society posed by a so-called 'new generation' of anti-social, disaffected young people. Very real fears exist about the apparent growing criminality of British young people, but some argue that these anxieties are overstated, and that reporting of the issue has taken on a momentum and energy of its own (Muncie, 1999). In this sense, 'hoodies' and 'chavs' have become latter-day folk devils, in the same way as Mods and Rockers did in the 1960s.

ACTIVITY **6.2**

Earlier, we identified a number of key factors that contribute to the creation and momentum of moral panics. In this exercise, we want you to revisit the model we introduced earlier and consider the extent to which these factors may have contributed to the development and reinforcement of moral panics about young people's behaviour. Here we list again the core components of our model for you to discuss and develop in relation to youth crime. You may wish to do this exercise in a small group, perhaps drawing from newspaper articles to assist you.

The power of the media

How influential have the media been in shaping views around youth crime or about youth in general?

(Continued)

(Continued)

The presentation of the issue is often accompanied by powerful images and emotive language

How do the emotive images and language used in the media serve to shape our opinions about young people and their behaviour?

Moral panics are often backed by politicians who provide legitimacy to the moral panic

What have politicians had to say about the issue and why?

Moral panics often feed into long-established, pre-existing fears and prejudice

Here, you might want to consider the claim that there is a long tradition of fear and hostility towards the behaviour of young people. You may wish to ask friends and family about their views on 'youth'.

Moral panics are often characterised by circular, self-supporting arguments

To what extent has the reaction to sections of 'youth' and their behaviour served to apportion an unwarranted prominence to the 'problem group', exacerbating the perceived level of anxiety?

Moral panics are often based on a compelling mixture of myth, fact and lies

Can you find any examples of ways in which the behaviour of young people has been distorted by the media?

It is important to recognise that while some young people are guilty of engaging in damaging, disruptive behaviour, this is in reality a small minority. Yet, according to those such as Muncie (1999), it is the 'anti-social', delinquent behaviour of the small minority that finds greatest exposure in media headlines. By contrast, the silent law-abiding, unremarkable majority rarely receive a mention. Why is this? According to Cohen (2006, pviii), young working-class males constitute, for newspaper editors, *one of the most enduring of suitable enemies* and hence regularly find themselves the subjects of moral panics. Thus, over the past half-century, Teddy Boys, Mods and Rockers, football hooligans, punks, muggers, joyriders, chavs and hoodies have all been portrayed as dangerous and menacing folk devils. In response, governments, wanting to be seen to be responding firmly to the threat posed by youth, have sought to introduce coercive methods of control, simultaneously feeding and reinforcing moral panics. Muncie (1999) argues that the state response to the 'problem of youth' has consistently been greater surveillance, coercion and law-and-order initiatives with a strong social control agenda.

This can clearly be seen in relation to anti-social behaviour, which, in recent years, has resulted in early intervention programmes and the use of ASBOs. Ironically, the often impossible conditions imposed by ASBOs have been regularly breached by young people, criminalising them over and above the original impact of their offence. This is an example of the circular, self-perpetuating nature of moral panics we talked about earlier. A young person may be given an ASBO for a relatively minor misdemeanour, and may then inadvertently end up breaking a condition, thereby finding themselves in court potentially facing a more serious sentence which in some cases may be custodial.

As we were writing this second edition, the Antisocial Behaviour, Crime and Policing Bill was progressing through parliament. This proposed to replace ASBOs with IPNAs or Injunctions to Prevent Nuisance and Annoyance, as part of a clampdown on unruly behaviour. However, there was a key difference – whereas ASBOs could only be granted if it was beyond reasonable doubt that a person had behaved antisocially, the proposal was for IPNAs to be granted in relation to behaviour that was *capable of causing nuisance or annoyance*. Justice (2013), the independent law reform and human rights group, criticised this criterion for being too subjective, draconian and unreasonable. In a letter to the *Observer*, Dr Maggie Atkinson, the Children's Commissioner, expressed her concern that the proposals to clampdown on so-called unruly behaviour would *'punish children over the age of 10 simply for being children'* by widening the definition of antisocial behaviour and reducing the burden of proof so sharply that the effect could be to 'outlaw everyday activities such as skateboarding or ball games' (Helm, 2013). Similarly, Jacqui Cheer, the Chief Constable of Cleveland, and Association of Chief Police Officers Lead on children and youth, expressed her concerns that society was becoming more intolerant of young people in public spaces with both the public and police too ready to label *what looks like growing up to me as antisocial behaviour* (cited in Travis, 2013). This was particularly pertinent she said, in the context of funding cuts that had led to the closure of public spaces, leaving few places for young people to meet and socialise. This was supported by Hilary Emery, Chief Executive of the National Children's Bureau who expressed her concerns about the proposed Bill.

> We are concerned that children and teenagers will get into trouble with the law just for being annoying, and it will penalise them from doing things that all children do as part of growing up – playing in the street, kicking a ball around in a public space or hanging around with their friends.
>
> (cited in Travis, 2013)

Ultimately, the strength of opposition to the introduction of IPNAs forced the government to reluctantly withdraw the measure from the Bill. While this represented a welcome, hard fought victory for children's welfare (and indeed for common sense), given the overall trajectory of UK youth justice policy in recent decades, it represented but a minor concession. The UK continues to be characterised by one of the most authoritarian youth justice systems in the world and young people continue to be portrayed by politicians and the media as archetypal folk devils.

We saw earlier how moral panics over asylum seekers could be said to serve a political 'function'. The same, it has been argued, is true over moral panics over working-class youths. Marxist sociologists, for instance, argue that by focusing attention on individual bad behaviour and pathologising groups of young people, the structural causes of the extreme social exclusion many young people experience is effectively sidelined. Thus, not only are the youth of today conveniently blamed for broader structural ills (thus absolving politicians of blame), societal attention is diverted away from real difficulties, such as homelessness and unemployment, that impinge on the lives of tens of thousands of young people. Additionally as we have seen, moral panics serve a convenient function of legitimising harsh and punitive forms of legislation.

Social work and moral panics

The connection between moral panics and the social work profession is longstanding (see for example, Franklin (1999) and Franklin and Parton (1991)). More recently, Clapton et al. (2013, p198) note that social work, and in particular, children and families social work, is *prone to periodic involvement in scares and moral panics*. They suggest that this is not new and, in fact, is built into the emergence and origins of the social work profession, which has its roots in 'moral righteousness'. Citing recent obsessions with virtual 'evil bogeymen' sitting behind their keyboards luring children into a world of online entrapment and lewdness, Clapton et al. observe that *it is perhaps no surprise that a particularly feverish child protection moral panic may be playing out in the 21st century in relation to the moral dangers posed to children and young people by their use of the internet* (p206). This is linked, they suggest, with societal concerns of 'saving children from evil' and perhaps, a wider problem of 'feckless parents who neglect to protect': *Ultimately as before, the moral guardians have to step in to fill the vacuum left by parental neglect and fight immorality* (p212).

Concerns about online abuse of children has led to the emergence of CEOP – the Child Exploitation and Online Protection Centre – a multi-agency grouping of child protection specialists and online experts who *patrol the highways and byways of the internet with its panic buttons that will call for child rescue* (p212). Interestingly, Clapton et al. link this moral panic to the scramble for resources that is now central among voluntary sector and statutory agencies. Here, they make an important point about how professional groups can play a pivotal role in creating and sustaining moral panics. As Goode and Ben-Yehuda (1994) have previously argued, welfare professions – including social work – have a vested interest in encouraging heightened levels of anxiety around issues of concern to them. This is because, they suggest, in doing so the status of their profession and the resources attached to it are enhanced. In relation to child protection, Clapton et al. are scathing of the myriad of systems and processes embedded within Safeguarding teams that *have little or no effect on the welfare and lives of children and families*. While alarmist and dramatic panics over issues like online safety of children may benefit organisations like CEOP, they can serve to divert attention from real issues such as the negative consequences of child poverty, ill health and access to education. These are structural factors which do not routinely generate panic or national alarm but which have devastating consequences for children's welfare, arguably on a much greater scale than online exploitation of children.

> *Focussing on identifying and hunting down demons, real or imaginary, at the expense of any more critical or structural understanding of social work as an agent of social change and social justice, strips out the 'social' from social work.*

(Clapton et al., 2013, p213)

This is interesting when we think about the concept of safeguarding. We tend to think of it in relation to forms of child abuse – physical abuse, sexual abuse, neglect, sexual exploitation and so on. Yet by focusing disproportionately upon factors where the perpetrator is either a parent, carer or a shadowy stranger, attention is focused away from the harm caused by problems like child poverty. We have made this point elsewhere (see Cunningham and Cunningham 2012), arguing that the skewed focus upon abuse and neglect, and more recently on online dangers means that other narratives such as those which emphasise the damaging impact of poverty are 'crowded out'. Of course, ongoing moral panics over children's welfare that focus excessively upon 'online bogeymen', or parents and their 'failings' serve a political function, directing attention away from the pervasiveness of child poverty, the harm it creates and the failure of the state to address it. Arguably, the failure to tackle poor material conditions that have such a devastating impact upon children's lives poses a greater risk to their well-being than many of the folk devils identified in the popular press.

Sociological considerations of 'moral panic'

As in previous chapters, we now wish to interrogate the concept of moral panic from different theoretical standpoints. Perhaps the most relevant position to begin with is labelling theory, which is central in terms of understanding the processes by which moral panics come to exist.

Labelling theory

Labelling theory remains as pertinent to social work today as it was when it was first developed. Rooted in symbolic interactionism, the concept was introduced in 1938 by Tannenbaum, but it is frequently associated with the work of Howard Becker in the 1960s. To develop the concept, Becker (1963) used the example of a brawl involving young people. He describes a scene in a low-income area of town where a fight breaks out between gangs of young people. Neighbours might be alarmed, the police called and arrests made, with the individuals concerned finding themselves in court facing breach of the peace charges. Alternatively in the present day, they might find themselves subject to an ASBO. Becker's argument is that a similar brawl that breaks out between middle-class youths in a more affluent area of town is likely to have a very different outcome. Neighbours might come out of their houses and diffuse the situation or break up the fight, assuming the acts to be 'youthful high spirits'. The police may not be called at all, but if they were called, Becker suggests that they would be more likely to have a polite but firm word and move things on. No sign of an ASBO here! Importantly, Becker's point is that although the *acts* may be the same, the *interpretation* of them, the response to them and the context in which they occur, are not.

Becker uses the term 'labelling' to make the point that *Deviant behaviour is behaviour that people so label* (p9); in other words, there is no such thing as a deviant act *per se*, it is only when it becomes interpreted and labelled as such that it takes on the properties of being deviant.

Labelling then, refers to a process whereby sometimes evocative labels are applied to individuals, often by powerful agents of social control such as the police, the legal system, medical professions or social workers. The labels applied often evoke powerful imagery or stereotypes, so for example, the labels 'asylum seeker', 'mentally ill' or 'yob' may evoke a range of different images and assumptions. In relation to moral panics, the concept of labelling is important, as the 'actors' in the moral panic are usually given a range of powerful labels. For example, as we have seen, asylum seekers are frequently labelled as being 'scroungers', 'criminals', 'bogus', 'irresponsible' by the media and politicians. People with mental health problems are sometimes labelled in sections of the media as being 'dangerous', 'violent' or 'evil'. It is labels such as these that can feed into media and political hysteria concerning a particular group.

It is vitally important of course, that such damaging, dehumanising and discriminatory labels do not impinge upon social work practice. Social workers are bound by moral and ethical codes of practice to protect vulnerable service users and to ensure the integrity of the profession. However, social work does not take place in a vacuum and social workers are of course functioning members of society who are bombarded with the same images from the media as anyone else. It is therefore essential that social workers reflect upon and understand the ways in which labelling and resultant stereotypes can impact upon practice. Furthermore, social workers as potentially powerful agents of the state, also play a part in *assigning* labels to individuals with whom they work.

ACTIVITY 6.3

Jason is a 12-year-old boy who has come to the attention of the local Youth Intervention Project (YIP). As a student social worker on placement with the YIP you have been given Jason to work with in a preventative way. On your first visit to Jason, he is sitting hunched up wearing a dark hoodie, with the hood over his head. You find engaging in conversation with him difficult. He seems unresponsive, preoccupied and uninterested in taking up any of the opportunities you suggest. You return to the office after half an hour feeling that you have been unable to engage effectively with Jason, and when discussing him with your supervisor, you describe him as sullen, difficult, uncommunicative and uncooperative.

> *Your supervisor fails to challenge you and you continue to work with Jason based upon the impressions gained in your first assessment of him. Jason recently committed a minor act of vandalism in the grounds of the local park one night. He has been referred to the multi-agency panel which considers low-level offending. You attend the panel and share your views on Jason as being difficult, unwilling to engage and possibly a high risk to the community in terms of future offending.*
>
> *However, it may be that if you had approached Jason differently at the very beginning (or indeed, if your supervisor had challenged some of your early perceptions), you would have discovered that Jason's reaction to you was based upon a fear of authority, a scepticism resulting from the allocation to him of yet another social worker, and a general state of withdrawal linked to being bullied by some older pupils at school. However, as a student social worker, your opinion of Jason could be assimilated by the other professionals around the table who might unquestioningly take on board your views.*
>
> *What are the dangers of Jason being assigned a deviant label in a multi-agency panel meeting of this kind?*

In this instance, Jason has been assigned a label which may well stick with him for a long time. There is always a danger that professionals, who undoubtedly possess a great deal of power, can create a 'dominant view' of a particular service user, such that all future behaviour by the service user is interpreted in this light, serving to confirm the original judgement about that person. In such instances, the service user may be powerless to challenge this view. The worst-case scenario here would arise if Jason internalised the views of the professionals around him and came to see himself as delinquent or deviant in some way, and began to act accordingly. This would be an example of a self-fulfilling prophecy.

The concept of the self-fulfilling prophecy is central to labelling theory and is used to describe the process whereby individuals who are labelled *internalise* the characteristics of the label assigned to them and start acting according to its defining features. In other words, they begin to see themselves in the light of the label applied. Lemert (1972) refers to this as a *symbolic reorganisation of the self*. It can therefore be understood how powerful agents of social control, including social workers, who are fundamentally involved in the assigning of labels, can actually be seen to *contribute* to stereotypes and in some cases, to criminal or deviant behaviour occurring.

Becker (1963) notes that once an individual has been successfully labelled in a particular way, this can often become their 'master status', which comes to define them, over and above all other statuses. So, once a person has been labelled a 'criminal' for example, this then becomes the dominant means by which others see them, as opposed to other labels the person might have as well, such as son, father, artist, student and so on. The 'master status' becomes in effect the *defining status*, and brings with it a range of other images and characteristics often associated with the label.

ACTIVITY 6.4

Labelling

To some extent, we are all labelled at various times throughout our lives. Working with someone you trust, take some time out to think about labels you may have been given throughout your life. Some examples might include 'disabled'; lone parent; unemployed; victim of domestic violence; youth offender; mentally ill.

How did the labels come to be assigned to you? What was the impact of these? What assumptions were assigned to the label?

If you are on or have been on a placement in your social work degree, think about the ways in which service users you have worked with have been labelled and the potential impact of these labels. How can social workers challenge these labels and work in a more empowering way?

Labelling theory is useful in the study of moral panics as it enables us to think about the processes by which moral panics might be constructed. It is also helpful for social workers who need to understand the ways in which individuals come to be assigned identities which can ultimately shape their lives.

Labelling theory has, however, been criticised for being deterministic, in that it assumes that a person who has been labelled has no ability to reject that label, and has no option other than to commit further acts of deviancy. In this sense, the labelling process can be cited as an 'excuse' for future deviancy. Who is to say, for example, that it is the label of 'deviant' that has encouraged a young person to engage in further criminal acts? It may be that they would have chosen to engage in that behaviour anyway. Furthermore, it is possible that the initial labelling may have had a positive effect, reducing rather than amplifying deviance. From a different perspective, Marxists have also criticised labelling theory, arguing that while it recognises class differences in the ways in which labels are assigned, it stops short of a more sustained, structural analysis. It fails to acknowledge, for instance, the unequal distribution of power in society, or the fact that the solution to the problems identified by labelling theorists involves a far greater level of structural reform than they are prepared to contemplate. In response to this criticism, symbolic interactionists defend the validity of micro-level analysis which is concerned with small-scale interactions and the processes by which meanings are applied.

Functionalist perspective

As we discovered in Chapter 1, the concept of value consensus is central to functionalism. As moral panics are usually based upon issues that potentially disrupt value consensus or seek to threaten the *status quo*, functionalists are likely to take the view that ultimately, a moral panic has the effect of separating out 'folk devils' from the rest of society, uniting the majority of society in order to clarify shared norms and values in the face of the threat. In effect, the storm caused in the wake of the moral panic will ultimately result in a celebration of the 'majority view', reaffirming and re-establishing the moral equilibrium. Although Durkheim did not specifically use the term moral panic, his writings on crime enable us to develop a Durkheimian perspective on 'moral panics'. Durkheim's view was that crime was both inevitable and functional (Durkheim, 1982, first published, 1895); it was functional because it enabled society to change and develop, and because, importantly, it provided the means by which shared norms and values could be clarified. In drawing attention to rules that have been broken, a line is drawn between 'normal' and the 'deviant' members of society, ensuring punishment or vilification of the latter and providing clarification for the former regarding what is and what is not acceptable conduct. Applied to moral panics then, this Durkheimian interpretation could be extended to argue that moral panics provide a vehicle by which the folk devils or 'outsiders', such as young criminals or asylum seekers, are highlighted because of the threat they pose to shared norms and values. The reaction to the threat is the stigmatisation of the offending individuals and society stamping down hard through legislation and policy to ensure that the moral consensus remains intact.

Functionalist theories of the media are concerned with ways in which the media contributes to the well-being and maintenance of society. The media serves different functions to this end; in particular, it transmits social norms and values, and performs a key role in terms of socialisation, ensuring that children and adults alike are shaped by society's values, norms and cultural fabric. In relation to moral panics then, the media can draw attention very powerfully to folk devils at times of anxiety, to ensure that moral boundaries are drawn around deviant norms or behaviours. The overall effect is that although a warning siren may be sounded regarding the specific aspect of dysfunction, importantly the overall consensus is preserved. This can be seen clearly in relation to moral panics that arise around aspects of youth culture. In the 1970s, a new subculture began to emerge in the form of the punk movement, when mostly working-class young people began to hang around in groups wearing bondage trousers, ripped clothes, safety pins and bin-liners, and having brightly coloured, often spiky, unconventional hair. The overwhelming message from the punk movement was discordant and anti-establishment, with a groundswell of anger against the monarchy, the political establishment of the day and the police. This, some have suggested, was related to high unemployment and the ensuing economic disadvantage and social alienation felt by many young people. However, despite protracted media hype concerning the anarchistic drive of the punk movement, eventually it found itself at least partly incorporated by the establishment, as 'designer' punk clothes were advertised on the pages of *Vogue* magazine and commercial enterprises sought to institutionalise the movement by mass reproduction of certain aspects of it. In effect, by popularising punk, or as Dick Hebdidge (1979) suggests by the process of *incorporation,* the punk movement became 'safe', and ceased to be a threat to shared norms and values. Nevertheless, a warning siren had been sounded that all was not well, giving those in power the opportunity to respond. Thus it can be seen that the media here, along with other aspects of society, actively overcame the threat to collective values. The panic generated by the punk movement was effectively 'managed' and attention shifted away from the underpinning issues which had perhaps led to the emergence of the movement that was so opposed to conventional norms.

Functionalists then, see a positive role for moral panics, as they provide the means by which attention is drawn initially to any threat to the value consensus, enabling society to respond so that shared social norms can be reaffirmed and celebrated.

There are weaknesses however with this perspective. First, we can question whether moral panics, in reality, act as a 'warning siren' for society. While our example of the punk movement seems to provide evidence to support this notion, there are numerous instances where the warning sirens have simply been ignored. Moreover, they have heralded the beginning of a process whereby 'folk devils' are stigmatised and pathologised, arguably for reasons other than the reinforcement of 'shared norms and values'. As we show below, for Marxists the vilification of 'hoodies', asylum seekers and the like is motivated less by a desire to reinforce a 'shared value consensus', and more by a wish to promote ruling-class culture, values and ideals. Indeed, for Marxists, the very notion that there exists a 'shared value consensus' is contentious and open to debate.

A Marxist perspective

As we have seen above, functionalists argue that there are positive benefits to moral panics occurring in society. Marxists also suggest that moral panics serve a purpose; however, their interpretation differs in one important respect. Rather than suggesting that moral panics are useful to the whole of society, Marxists believe that they serve positive functions for the powerful ruling classes. As suggested above, moral panics serve to shift attention away from underlying structural causes of society's socioeconomic problems, laying the blame instead on visible, scapegoated 'deviant' individuals or groups. This has the effect of *individualising* the causes of socio-economic ills, which leads to solutions based upon modifying 'deviant' *behaviour*, rather than addressing deep-seated structural inequalities. In the example of asylum that we used at the beginning of this chapter, a Marxist perspective would focus upon ways in which asylum seekers are blamed, for example, for housing inadequacies, unemployment and racial tensions. Solutions, therefore, are directed at deterring and stigmatising asylum seekers rather than addressing the chronic underfunding of public services and mitigating the inequalities that are a feature of capitalist societies. Similarly, 'hoodies' or other young people are pathologised and blamed for urban decline and the breakdown of law and order, with little attention given to the chronic poverty and economic decline which shapes the lives of those living in deprived communities. In our social class chapter (Chapter 8), we show how the social construction and demonisation of the 'chav' has served a similar purpose (Jones, 2011).

In explaining the emergence and reinforcement of moral panics, Marxists, like functionalists, are particularly interested in the role played by the mass media. However, whereas for functionalists the media acts as a positive 'moral guardian' of societal values, for Marxists it is a conservative guardian of ruling-class interests (Badgikian, 2004; Chomsky and Herman, 2002). Marxists regard the media as an important component of the superstructure, which, as shown in Chapter 1, is seen to promote and transmit ruling-class culture, values and ideals in an uncritical way to the masses. There is no single authoritative Marxist interpretation of the mass media in capitalist societies, but one influential explanation has emerged, based on Antonio Gramsci's (1971) concept of 'hegemony'. Basically, according to Gramsci the ruling classes in any society cannot rule for any period of time simply through coercion alone, and a subtler means of gaining the consent of the masses is required. Hegemony, therefore, refers to means by which the ruling class obtains the consent of subordinate groups to their own domination, by imposing an appealing world view, or 'common sense'. 'Hegemonic status' is achieved when the ruling class has successfully managed to represent its own values and ideals as those of society as a whole, and created a terrain favourable to resolving economic and social problems in a way that is conducive to its interests (Gramsci, 1971). The media is, for Marxists, one of the crucial mechanisms by which this process is accomplished. It uncritically transmits messages that serve to uphold prevailing ruling-class ideologies, thus ensuring that the consent of the masses for their own domination is manufactured and maintained (Chomsky and Herman, 2002). To a certain extent, this process may be 'unconscious' – the ruling class may not directly control the media, but the pervasive, all-encompassing nature of ruling-class values means that events and issues are unconsciously and instinctively reported in a way that reproduces and reinforces the ideals of dominant groups. In this sense, the importance of the media lies not just in its transmission of moral panics, but also in its reproduction and sustenance of dominant values. In some other respects, though, the media's bias is more deliberate. For example, key sections of the media are often owned by powerful individuals or corporations who themselves have a strong desire to preserve the *status quo* (Badgikian, 2004). Hence, national newspaper proprietors and commercial broadcasters, most of whom are likely to be averse to paying 'punitive' rates of taxation to fund decent public services, are more than happy to promote cheaper, 'individualised', 'behavioural' solutions to social problems.

Irrespective of the causes of the media's 'bias', in relation to moral panics, Marxists suggest that media representations of certain events do undoubtedly distort and simplify, providing inaccurate, yet persuasive interpretations of issues that attract attention away fundamental problems inherent in capitalist societies. In this way, the structural causes of unemployment, poverty, urban decay, crime and a host of other social problems are 'individualised'. 'Folk devils' are identified, stigmatised and blamed for situations which in reality are the result of more deep-rooted social problems. For Marxists then, the extent of the media's opinion-forming potential should not be underestimated. As we intimated in our asylum example, for many people it is their only 'portal' through which to view certain issues. It can provide an immensely powerful means of shaping the belief systems of its audience such that the messages inherent within particular moral panics become engrained in the consciousness of the nation. In this way, claims such as 'all asylum seekers are bogus', or 'the care of mentally ill people in the community poses a "grave threat" to society', or 'the welfare system is "rife" with abuse', or 'youths who wear hooded tops are hooligans', all become established, unquestioned facts, rather than debatable assertions.

Like the other theoretical approaches outlined above, Marxist analyses of moral panics have also faced criticisms. First, Marxist explanations, though powerful, are, some argue, just that – explanations. The logic of Marxism, its detractors argue, seems to suggest that as long as capitalism exists and the ruling classes continue to profit from the obscuration and division generated by moral panics, then groups will continue to be labelled, stigmatised and subjected to punitive forms of control. The 'solution', then, for Marxists, lies in the abolition of capitalism and the creation of a more fair society, based upon the principles of equality and egalitarianism. However, while it is fine for Marxist academics to theorise about the need for, and the prospects of, a radical transformation from capitalism to socialism, what happens in the meantime? Do stigmatised asylum seekers, mental health service users, marginalised young people and other subjects of moral panics have to await the 'triumph of the proletariat' before their plight is addressed? This is an interesting critique, but as we saw in Chapter 1, the claim that Marxism fails to offer any readily accessible or deliverable solutions for 'the here and now' is one that Marxists strenuously refute. In their defence, Marxists argue that such claims are based on a simplistic and dogmatic interpretation of Marxist thought. Certainly, few Marxists today would dismiss the need to engage in immediate political action to mitigate inequalities within capitalist societies. Indeed, many of those involved in the radical social work movement, or its more recent manifestation the Social Work Action Network, are Marxists, and they campaign vigorously for an immediate end to the stigmatisation and oppression of vulnerable groups.

Marxist approaches have also been targeted by those generally critical of the overall concept of moral panics. For some, such as Norman Dennis and George Erdos (2005), the 'moral panic' concept is itself a 'social construction', 'invented' by biased, left-wing academics who use it, wrongly, to deny the culpability of certain 'deviant' groups for moral and social breakdown, and to inappropriately apportion blame for social problems on the shoulders of political and economic elites. We examine this critique in further detail below. In its total dismissal of the moral panic concept it does, to a certain extent, represent a criticism of all the theoretical approaches we have examined, but the sort of critique adopted by Dennis and Erdos is most often directed at 'left-wing' academics and politicians.

ACTIVITY **6.5**

Returning to the moral panic you selected in Activity 6.1, apply first a functionalist and then a Marxist perspective to it, to develop two contrasting arguments. When concentrating on the functionalist perspective, you might wish to think about which aspects of value consensus are under threat by the moral panic and what responses there were. When looking at Marxism, you may want to consider what functions the moral panic serves for the ruling class.

How do your two analyses differ?

Moral panics or genuine fears?

Having provided you with a detailed and perhaps persuasive overview of the moral panics, we will now end by looking at an alternative approach to the concept advanced by Dennis and Erdos (2005). These authors argue that the concept is fundamentally flawed. A key feature of moral panic arguments, they insist, is the notion that it is the politically powerful, or the ruling class, who are said to exaggerate concerns about particular issues, in an attempt to 'scapegoat' certain groups, and divert attention away from their own culpability in creating or failing to alleviate social problems. Using data from various surveys on crime and anti-social behaviour, Dennis and Erdos argue that it is, in fact, those living in poor, deprived areas that report the highest levels of anxiety about crime, disorderly behaviour and moral breakdown. On crime specifically, they argue that data *shows that if or to the extent that the fear of crime is exaggerated, it is the poor who do the exaggerating, not the rich.* This, they insist, contradicts one of the main arguments in theories based on the moral panic concept.

However, their more fundamental point is that this fear of crime and other social problems among the poor is not based upon media-induced 'naivety' or 'irrationality'. On the contrary, worry about social problems in these areas is associated with the actual incidence of social problems. Dennis and Erdos castigate those such as Cohen for, in effect, accusing decent, honest working people in deprived communities of 'conjuring up', or 'imagining' the high levels of crime and the lack of respect for common values that they are forced to endure on a daily basis. If only the 'liberal intelligentsia' (that is, left-wing academics, media commentators and politicians) lived in the residential areas affected by these genuine social ills, they might be forced to reappraise their own 'fantastical' denials of growing levels of moral breakdown. From this perspective, therefore, the 'moral panic' concept, which as we have seen purports to expose common myths and misconceptions, is itself rejected as a delusion. In its representation of genuine fears about endemic social problems *as a defect of the aged, the timid and the ill informed,* it is guilty of incorrectly dismissing people's very real anxieties about their security, their homes and their livelihoods (Dennis and Erdos, 2005, p57).

> *The error and folly have not lain, therefore, with a benighted public that has succumbed to unrealistic fears of crime, or has been stampeded into a moral panic by a sensationalist gutter press. The error and folly has lain with ideologically driven academics, and the broadsheet, radio and television journalists who depend on their 'findings'.*
>
> (Dennis and Erdos, 2005, p67)

Moreover, and paradoxically, Dennis and Erdos argue that the moral panic concept can serve a political function, in that it allows politicians to claim that popular anxieties about crime, immigration, drug use, and a whole range of other social ills, are 'disproportionate'. In this respect, they suggest, the left-wing liberal intelligentsia may have scored an 'own goal'. In their haste to 'bash' the politically powerful, they have inadvertently provided ruling elites with a 'get-out' concept, which allows them to dismiss people's concerns as unwarranted, and claim a higher degree of success for their policies on, for instance, 'law and order', 'community cohesion' and 'asylum' than is actually the case.

The arguments presented by Dennis and Erdos certainly provide an interesting alternative to the ideas presented above. However, it is worth noting a few points of caution. First, as the authors themselves acknowledge, much of the statistical evidence for their arguments is based on surveys examining people's perceptions of moral breakdown, vulnerability and crime, rather than their actual incidence. The problem here, as most sociologists would acknowledge, is that perceptions about the threat posed by groups such as 'hoodies', 'muggers' or, to cite another of our earlier examples, asylum seekers, are often exaggerated or inflated, partly as a result of inaccurate, sensationalist media and political commentaries. Dennis and Erdos would no doubt dismiss such suggestions as 'misguided paternalism', but as our asylum example showed, the media's influence in shaping our perception of certain problems and groups, and inflating the prominence of particular issues, cannot be denied. Second, while Dennis and Erdos accuse advocates of moral panics of constituting a left-wing intelligentsia, they say little about their own ideological dispositions. In fact, both authors have written extensively for CIVITAS, a right-wing think tank, and both have long bemoaned the impact of what they see as deteriorating moral values, 'liberal' criminal justice policies, and 'corrupting state welfare' on levels of permissiveness, responsibility and lawlessness. In short, Dennis and Erdos are not without their own 'ideological baggage'.

CHAPTER SUMMARY

This chapter has examined different theoretical debates relevant to moral panics and assessed the importance of the concept to you as students of social work. The exercises we included to support the analysis should have helped you appreciate the importance of being aware of the origins of some of your own views and prejudices. As we have stressed, much of what we know and think about certain issues and social groups stems not from direct experience, but from powerful images presented in the media and by politicians, many of which are inaccurate and based on popular stereotypes and myths. We hope that reading this chapter will encourage you to think critically about the negative way certain groups are presented and the need for you as practitioners to challenge your own value base.

FURTHER READING

Pearson, G (1983) *Hooligan: A history of respectable fears.* Basingstoke: Macmillan. This classic book argues that moral panics are not a new phenomenon, by examining historical societal reactions to 'hooliganism'.

Goode, E and Ben-Yehuda, N (1994) *Moral panics: The social construction of deviance.* Oxford: Blackwell. This text will provide you with an excellent introduction to the concept.

Finally, we would recommend you read Cohen's original text. It provides a fascinating clearly written, accessible insight into the evolution of his ideas: **Cohen, S** (2006) *Folk devils and moral panics.* 3rd edition. Abingdon: Routledge.

Chapter 7
Education

A C H I E V I N G   A   S O C I A L   W O R K   D E G R E E

This chapter will help you to develop the following capabilities from the **Professional Capabilities Framework**

- **Diversity**
  Recognise the importance of diversity in human identity and experience, and the application of anti-discriminatory and anti-oppressive principles in social work practice.

- **Rights, justice and economic wellbeing**
  Understand the principles of rights, justice and economic wellbeing, and their significance to social work practice.

- **Knowledge**
  Demonstrate an initial understanding of the application of research, theory and knowledge from sociology, social policy, psychology, health and human growth and development to social work.

It will also introduce you to the following standards as set out in the 2008 social work subject benchmark statement:

3.1.1 Social work services and service users.
3.1.4 Social work theory.

Introduction

As two individuals who have worked in education for a long time, we are passionate about education and learning. As sociologists, however, we are also very aware of the subtle nuances inherent in the system that can significantly impact upon individuals and their future prospects. There are, without doubt, clear links between child poverty, low educational attainment and reduced life chances, and social workers often find themselves working with socially excluded and marginalised individuals who have struggled within the education system, the impact of which can be long standing. Social work students need to have an understanding of the education system for a number of reasons. First, an understanding of differential educational opportunity helps to contextualise why some people have limited chances in life and why they may experience social disadvantage. Second, social workers work closely with schools and need to understand something of the cultures and processes that characterise education and the ways in which education regulates and shapes children and young people. Third, social workers may work with children who have poor attendance or have been excluded from school.

An understanding of the system is fundamental to be able to work with service users in ways that are not inherently oppressive or judgemental. Finally, in working with young people who are not in education, employment or training, it is helpful for social workers to appreciate broader contexts and political drivers around education.

Education then, holds particular relevance for social workers working within children and families settings and within the education welfare sector. The topic frequently resonates with students who have themselves experienced the idiosyncrasies of the education system. As you progress through this chapter, we would like you to reflect upon your own experiences in the education system and consider how factors such as the messages you received from teachers or from home, shaped your experience.

This chapter will seek to understand some of the core sociological theories of education and will then consider educational achievement and disadvantage.

The functionalist theory of education

For functionalists, the education system provides an important means by which individuals are linked with society. It does this formally, by educating individuals to understand what they are a part of, and informally, by teaching them about society's values and beliefs. The teaching of history for example, ensures that individuals *see they are part of something larger than themselves* (Haralambos and Holborn, 2013, p663), and in doing so, education *exercises an influence upon individuals which is usually irresistible* (Durkheim, 1972, p204).

In common with the approach outlined in previous chapters, functionalists are interested in the positive functions the education system performs for the benefit of society and its relationship with other institutions such as the economy and the family. First, Durkheim (1972) identified the function of secondary socialisation. The social learning that takes place in schools supplements primary socialisation which occurs within families. Socialisation is the process by which children learn about appropriate societal norms and values. Schools do this in a range of different ways: overtly through the taught curriculum, or more subtly via what has been referred to as a 'hidden curriculum'. By the latter we mean the other, less obvious ways that schools seek to inculcate in children's minds and consciousness the values, skills and modes of behaviour which are deemed important and necessary for society. For example, 'home school' agreements, which are a statutory requirement for state schools, oblige children and parents to 'sign up' and conform to a host of punctuality, attendance, behavioural and disciplinary requirements, all of which are designed to instil a respect for functionally 'appropriate' values and norms (Department for Education, 2013). In addition to this, many schools use a points system to reward appropriate behaviour and to punish that which is deemed to fall outside acceptable bounds. For Durkheim (1972) the social training of the next generation is necessary to ensure conformity and the acceptance of dominant values so that children learn to fit into mainstream society:

> Society can survive only if there exists among its members a sufficient degree of homogeneity; education perpetuates and reinforces this homogeneity.

(p203)

More generally, the culture of the school environment teaches children the importance of norms such as good manners, timekeeping, a positive attitude, the importance of discipline and respect for authority. Children learn about discipline from their very first day in school – they may be asked for example, to sit quietly, crossed legged on the carpet with their finger on their lips and told to listen to the teacher. Any child that digresses from this becomes aware very quickly of the consequences and disapproval incurred. The combination of social disapproval and other informal mechanisms as well as more formal systems of punishment and control soon come to be understood by children as a normal part of school life. The majority of pupils conform, but those who do not are dealt with, often in very visible ways. Observing other pupils being told off by the teacher, sent to the head teacher's office, kept in at playtime or break, given a detention or even being excluded serves as a means by which other pupils are kept in check. In this way, the education system also performs a social control function. Importantly, children are learning about deference to authority and the importance of obedience, which ultimately prepares them for their future lives in the workforce where they are required to be deferential and disciplined workers capable of taking orders and respecting authority.

The education system ensures that appropriate training is given to society's future workers, so that all constituent parts function effectively. This function of the education system demonstrates the fit between the education system and the economy. For society to operate smoothly and efficiently, it is necessary to have an appropriately skilled workforce to fulfil the requirements of the economy. As children get older, they are encouraged to think about their future careers and embark upon educational training to this end. This function can be most sharply understood when there is a shortage of a certain type of worker, needed to keep both society and the economy ticking over – indeed, a good example of precisely this can be found with the social work profession in recent years. Over the past decade or so, the government identified a chronic shortage of appropriately skilled social workers and so the response was the introduction of the new social work degree crafted alongside a huge recruitment campaign which sought to increase the numbers of trained social workers. In order to achieve this aim, the government reduced the minimum age for qualifying social workers to allow and facilitate school leavers at 18 to begin to train (the argument was that preventing 18 year olds from training meant that they tended to embark on alternative careers and were then 'lost' to the profession). Additionally, universities were encouraged to raise their numbers for social work training courses significantly and introduced 'incentive' bursaries. This trend is perhaps in the process of being reversed, as political changes have shifted the roles and tasks previously carried out by qualified social workers onto unqualified workers. A cap has also been imposed upon bursaries and the numbers of students entering social work education look set to reduce. In this way you can see the fit between the education system and society, and how each part functions to support the overall functioning of the whole.

Linked to the above, Davis and Moore (1945) identify a further function of education – that of role allocation. This is the argument that for society to function efficiently, it must ensure that all roles needed to keep the economy ticking over are filled. It would obviously not be good for society if all pupils trained to be social workers!

Similarly, if insufficient pupils wanted to be doctors or physiotherapists or bus drivers, then of course society would have significant unmet need. Clearly, the extent to which children 'choose' to be what they ultimately end up becoming is a matter of great debate and as we hinted in Chapter 1, for very many members of society, their choices are constrained choices. However, for functionalists such as Durkheim, and Davis and Moore, the education system performs a significant task in allocating roles to individuals by sorting pupils according to talent and ability. In *Some principles of stratification*, Davis and Moore argue that stratification (or the hierarchical division of society into layers) is necessary for societies who must place and motivate individuals in the social structure. They note that some positions are: *inherently more agreeable than others ... some require special talents or training and some are functionally more important than others* (p24). This latter point is interesting, as it raises questions about which jobs are more 'functionally important'.

ACTIVITY **7.1**

In small groups, look at the list of jobs below and try to rank them according to which are most functionally important. Another way of doing this exercise is to hold a 'balloon debate'. If you choose to complete the exercise this way, you will each need to take one of the roles outlined below and mount a convincing argument as to why your role should stay in a sinking balloon. The idea is that the group needs to decide the order each role should be thrown out of the balloon in order to save the other individuals.

> *Town planner*
> *Public toilet cleaner*
> *Social worker*
> *Sewerage worker*
> *Premiership footballer*
> *Estate agent*
> *Nurse*
> *Doctor*
> *Refuse disposal worker*
> *Waiter*
> *Care worker*
> *Lawyer*
> *Brain surgeon*
> *IT expert*
> *Plumber*
> *Car assembly line worker*
> *Postman*
> *University lecturer*

How did you come to your decisions?

Was there any disagreement among you?

The chances are that you had some difficulty deciding upon the relative extent to which roles were functionally important (or not). Furthermore, the way that society rewards different roles does not necessarily give an indication of functional importance. We only have to compare the wages of a premiership footballer with those of a refuse disposal worker to sharply consider this argument. As football fans ourselves, we are not suggesting that footballers are not important (clearly our Saturday afternoons would never be the same without football!); however, what we are saying is that if we consider which role is more important for the smooth running and maintenance of society, clearly the refuse disposal worker is far more critical than the footballer, even though the wages of the former are in no way comparable to those of the latter. Notwithstanding these criticisms, Davis and Moore were clear in their argument that society needed to attach different rewards to different positions and that the existence of differential rewards would ensure that the most talented individuals in society would be motivated to train to fulfil the most important positions. They pointed to the sacrifice that individuals who remain in education are required to make in order to allow them to fulfil their dreams. Unlike their peers who can begin earning much sooner, those staying on must defer their rewards until such time they have finished their training.

According to functionalists, the education system is the institution in which individuals compete to find their natural place in society. By the formal system of examinations, and to an extent via more informal systems that we talked about earlier, individuals are sifted and sorted so that they find their 'natural' place within a stratified society. The most talented and skilled individuals are motivated by the rewards attached, to train for longer and harder to fulfil the most functionally important roles. The reverse argument then, must also be true for functionalists – the least skilled and talented individuals who do not do so well within the education system will find their way into less well-paid roles. Functionalists argue that this system is inherently fair because all individuals have the same opportunities to do well. Their belief is that the education system is a 'meritocracy' or a system which allows pupils to achieve success proportionate to their talents and abilities, as opposed to one in which social class or wealth is the controlling factor.

Davis and Moore's ideas have been criticised by sociologists who identify a range of shortcomings with their argument. In particular, Melvin M Tumin (1953) questioned the very notion of 'functional importance' by suggesting that for any social system to survive, all social roles are equally important to maintain the status quo. Furthermore, he questioned Davis and Moore's assertion that only a limited number of individuals in society have the talents that can be trained into skills. Tumin argues that there may well be very many individuals who have talents, but various obstacles exist which prevent the conversion of talent to qualifications. Obstacles might include differential access to education at every level, subtle processes within the education system that motivate some but dissuade others and the ability of some professions to restrict access. We will consider some of the barriers within the education system later on in this chapter, but for now it is sufficient to identify factors such as negative labelling of some pupils based on class, race or gender and the power of teachers to potentially shape a pupil's educational career by the messages they give and the influence they can wield.

Moreover, Tumin is very critical of the idea that those who stay in the education system are undergoing some kind of sacrifice. He notes that the cost of training is often borne by parents who themselves have had privileged positions; and that any loss of earnings in the early years is more than made up within the first ten years when trained professionals finally enter the labour market in significantly higher-paid roles than their contemporaries who left school earlier. Tumin further identifies the 'psychic and spiritual rewards' and the opportunities for self-development that those who go on to university enjoy: *There is ... access to leisure and freedom of a kind not likely to be experienced by the persons already at work* (p390).

Marxists such as Bowles and Gintis are also critical of Davis and Moore's ideas, arguing that the education system merely perpetuates existing inequalities. These ideas will be considered later on in this chapter.

A level playing field?

In this section, we examine further the functionalist claim that the education system acts as a meritocracy. Certainly, at first glance the evidence may seem to support functionalist assumptions. For example, in the UK, formal secondary education is available to all children and young people, irrespective of their social class background. It is free, compulsory and relatively well resourced, and in state-funded schools (the vast majority of all schools), it is delivered through a national curriculum. This, theoretically, ensures that all children receive the same standard and level of education. It is therefore perhaps reasonable to assume that the UK's education system mitigates the impact of different family backgrounds and social class on educational experience and attainment. In short, common sense would suggest that a free, standardised education, delivered through a national curriculum to all, should provide children from disadvantaged backgrounds with a route out of poverty and social exclusion. After all, if all children have the same levels of opportunity, then surely the quality of their educational experiences, and their qualifications at the end of their school careers, will have been determined by the amount of effort they have put in to their schooling?

In this meritocratic interpretation of education, academic outcomes are seen to mirror intelligence plus 'merit' or effort, reflecting the work and commitment pupils are prepared to put into their schooling. Pupils start their school careers, it is assumed, with a 'level playing field' and if they are prepared to work hard, they will succeed academically. Conversely, if they fail to apply themselves, or choose not to attend school or to misbehave, then at best, they will fail academically, and at worst, they may be excluded from school. From this perspective then, all children start with the same chances and they get out of education what they put in. If we accept this interpretation of education as valid, we can perhaps see how education has the potential to 'flatten out' class differences and equalise educational opportunities and ultimately life chances. It can perform an intrinsically progressive function, providing disadvantaged children with the same opportunities to succeed academically as more advantaged children. As the famous US educational philosopher, John Dewey wrote, *it is the office of the school environment to see to it that each individual gets an opportunity to escape from the limitations of the social group in which he was born, and come into contact with a broader environment* (cited in Bowles and Gintis, 1976, p21). Tony Blair, the UK's former prime minister, saw the role of education in precisely these terms. Education, he argued, had the potential to create a 'true meritocracy', and his aim was to provide a system that enabled *the full potential of every individual to be liberated* (cited in Webster, 2001).

As well as guaranteeing 'just deserts', an education system based upon meritocratic principles also ensures that intelligence, aptitude and effort are rewarded, and that those who 'succeed' in education, and subsequently in their professional lives, are the most talented.

However, the notion that the education system acts as a meritocracy has generated much criticism. In the following exercise we would like you to use your analytical skills and draw up a critique of the concept.

ACTIVITY 7.2

Thinking carefully about the education system, in what ways can you criticise the principle that it is truly meritocratic?

You will hopefully have identified the fact that not all children begin school at the same, equal, starting line, and therefore it is unlikely that education can ever truly provide an equal platform for children to enter the 'race' on an equal footing. Some children clearly have considerably more privileged home lives that positively impact upon their school experiences. As Ball (2010) argues, affluent families are able to fund extracurricular activities and 'buy in' opportunity-enhancing resources and services, such as educational software and toys, supplementary learning materials and, increasingly, private tuition. Conversely, some children have difficult experiences at home that can negatively impact upon them in school. Other 'home-related' factors can include the physical environment, such as the space a child has or does not have to study. Some children, for example will have their own room, with a desk, a computer, internet access, very many books, and other 'mod cons' which make the home environment conducive to studying. Conversely, other children may share a room with several others, they may live in a chaotic, noisy environment, or they will not have a computer or internet access. Lack of internet access is immediately disadvantaging for children, as much homework is increasingly based around this resource, leaving those without it unable to utilise the same range and quality of educational material as their peers. Internet access has certainly improved since we wrote the first edition of this book – from around 65 per cent of households in 2008 to almost 80 per cent in 2012, but many children still cannot use this crucial resource uninterrupted at home. Data from the government's 2013 Family Expenditure Survey shows that 446,000 children live in households without a PC, and 486,000 in households without internet access. As might be expected, it is the poorest children who are most disadvantaged and more than half (57 per cent) of the poorest ten per cent of households with children do not own a computer (compared to only one per cent of the richest ten per cent) (eLearning Foundation, 2013). What this illustrates is that children from disadvantaged backgrounds are sometimes denied the same opportunities that children from more affluent backgrounds take for granted.

Other factors within school can mean that some children are held back while others are pushed forwards; children may be labelled in particular ways by teachers which can result in self-fulfilling prophecies, an issue we will consider later in this chapter. The micro culture within schools tends to be very middle class, and this can sometimes be alien to working-class children. This manifests in terms of the language codes used by teachers (see for example the ground-breaking work done by Basil Bernstein in 1971 around elaborated and restricted codes); the value systems of teachers; and the cultural gulf between the home lives of some children and the expectations within schools. Furthermore, there may be factors linked to the school itself – some schools have been identified as 'failing schools' while others excel at targets and are awarded specialist status. It is possible that where schools are publicly labelled as 'failing', the children will to an extent internalise this deep in their subconscious and understandably see themselves as failing too. We will return to many of these factors later on in this chapter in more detail, but it is pertinent to note that any concept of the education system truly being a meritocracy or a level playing field where children who work hard and achieve their potential will be rewarded is significantly flawed. The data we present in the next section serves to illustrate the extent to which this is the case. As we will see, if the aim of education is to flatten out social class differences then it has been proven to be a spectacular failure.

Educational achievement and disadvantage

All the available research shows us that children from disadvantaged backgrounds tend to perform less well at school, and gain fewer qualifications than those from more advantaged backgrounds. As Raffo et al. (2007) argue:

> Put simply, the poorer a child's family is, the less well they are likely to do in the education system ... Far from offering a route out of poverty, education simply seems to confirm existing social hierarchies.

(p1)

Moreover, social class differences in attainment rates seem to hold true throughout an individual's educational career. The receipt of free school meals is often seen as an indicator of disadvantage, since eligibility is based upon parents' entitlement to means-tested income support. How, then, do the educational attainment rates of children receiving free school meals compare with those who do not? In the UK, the data consistently show that children who receive free school meals are far less likely to achieve five A*–C grade GCSEs (including Maths and English) than those who do not receive free school meals. In 2012/13, only 37.9 per cent of children in receipt of free school meals did so, whereas the equivalent figure for non-free school meal children was 64.6 per cent (Department for Education, 2014). However, under-attainment at GCSE level is not just a phenomenon affecting children who are entitled to free school meals. Indeed, research shows a clear correlation between income and attainment, with GCSE success rates increasing with parental income. Put simply, the higher the parental income is, the better the GCSE attainment rate is. As the government's Social Mobility and Child Poverty Commission (2013, p178) argues, *for children in the UK, how well they do at school is strongly correlated with what their parents do for a living, how well qualified they are and how much they earn:*

Table 7.1   Percentage of children attaining five GCSEs A*–C, by parental income

Income quintile	Five GCSEs A*–C	Five GCSEs A*–C, including Maths and English
Children from the poorest 20% of households	33.2	21.4
Children from the second quintile of households	46.4	33.6
Children from the third quintile of households	59.3	46.4
Children from the fourth quintile of households	70.6	57.9
Children from the richest 20% of households	84	74.3

Source: Chowdrey, Crawford and Goodman, 2010

Similar social class inequalities in attainment are evident among much younger age cohorts of pupils, as illustrated by Table 7.2.

Table 7.2   Average test score at Key Stage 2

Income quintile	Average test score rank at aged 7	Average test score rank at aged 11
Children from the poorest 20% of households	41	42
Children from the second quintile of households	48	50
Children from the third quintile of households	54	56
Children from the fourth quintile of households	59	63
Children from the richest 20% of households	73	73

Source: Gregg and Washbook, 2010

Social class differences in educational attainment continue into higher education. For example, in 2010/11, only 20 per cent of young people who were eligible for free school meals participated in higher education at aged 19, compared with 38 per cent of non-school meal children (Department for Business Innovation and Skills, 2013).

Social class is not the only variable that seems to influence educational attainment, and ethnicity is also a significant variable. As Table 7.3 illustrates, the picture here is mixed. Children from certain minority ethnic group backgrounds now tend to perform better than their white equivalents, whereas children from other minority ethnic groups fare less well.

Alarmingly, children in care are among the worst performing of all children in England, with only 13.7 per cent of them achieving 5 or more A*–C grades (including Maths and English) at GCSE level, compared to 58 per cent of non-looked-after children.

Table 7.3 *Attainment of five or more A*–C GCSEs (including Maths and English) by ethnic group in England, 2012/13*

Ethnicity	Per cent obtaining five or more A*–Cs
All pupils	60
Chinese	78
Indian	75
White	60
Black African	60
Bangladeshi	53
Pakistani	55
Black Caribbean	52
Gypsy/Roma	12

Source: Department for Education, 2014

These low levels of education at secondary school have a knock-on effect in terms of post-secondary school outcomes and progression. Thus, in 2011 roughly one-third of care leavers were not in education employment or training (NEET) at 19, compared to 14 per cent of non-care leavers. Likewise, whereas 40 per cent of all 19 year olds were at university in 2011, only 6 per cent care leavers were (just 390) (National Care Advisory Service, 2013).

ACTIVITY 7.3

In this task we want you to consider the sort of factors which may have contributed to the low levels of educational attainment among looked-after children. In doing so, we want you to critically engage with the functionalist claim that all children start their schooling with a 'level playing field', and that educational success is simply a reflection of merit and effort alone. What variables, for example, may detrimentally affect the educational potential of looked-after children?

While undertaking this task you may have identified a number of factors that impact detrimentally on the educational opportunities available to looked-after children. Research, for example, has shown that looked-after children are far less likely than their peers to go to higher-performing schools, so geographical residence may be a factor. The disruption caused to looked-after children's education by multiple placements is also significant. For instance, 11 per cent of looked-after children in the year ending March 2012 had been subjected to three or more placements in the previous 12 months. Worse still, 660 children had experienced between six and nine different placements and 240 children had experienced more than ten (Department for Education, 2013a). We must put this in the context of research findings which suggest that on average pupils who move schools during Key Stage 4 attain 75 points lower at GCSE – equivalent to between one and two grades in every subject

(Department for Education and Science, 2007, p69). The impact of this level of place-ment activity cannot but have a detrimental impact upon the educational opportu-nities of looked-after children, something which is corroborated by Department for Education data, as shown in Table 7.4.

Table 7.4   *Educational attainment for looked-after children at Key Stage 4, by placement stability*

Number of placements experienced in the year	Percentage achieving 5+ A*-C GCSE grades
One placement	43
Two placements	29
Three placements	19
More than three	13

Source: Department for Education, 2013b

Furthermore, these children are likely to be experiencing varying amounts of emotional distress associated with the very reasons why they are being looked after in the public care system. For children who are separated from their birth families, coping with psy-chological anguish, and dealing with a range of personal and social problems, there is little wonder that they fall short of average educational achievement. In addition to this, of course, the environments of care homes themselves are often rarely condu-cive to educational study and attainment, and they frequently lack books, educational materials and appropriate study areas (Liabo et al., 2013).

Not only are looked-after children less likely to achieve better qualifications, they are also more likely to be excluded from school. Indeed, the school exclusion rate among looked-after children is very high – they are also more than twice as likely as other pupils to be permanently excluded from school, and nearly three times as likely to have a fixed term exclusion (Department for Education, 2013). Clearly being excluded from school compounds existing disadvantage, something that governments are clearly aware of. For instance, the previous Labour government issued guidance which insisted that *every practicable means should be tried to maintain the [looked-after] child in school* (Department for Children, Schools and Families, 2010, p22). Despite the existence of such guidance, rates of exclusions of looked-after children have remained consistently higher than those of other sections of the school population.

School exclusions and ethnicity

Here we will concentrate briefly on the issue of school exclusions and the experiences of minority ethnic group children, an issue that has rightly generated a good deal of controversy in recent years. The controversy stems from statistics which show us that black pupils are three times more likely to be excluded from school than their white counterparts. The Social Exclusion Unit's (1998a) Report, *Truancy and school exclusion,* pointed out that 16 per cent of excluded children are from minority ethnic group backgrounds, a much higher percentage than would be expected statistically. More recent statistics suggest that this trend has become even more pronounced and 24.6 per cent of all permanently excluded children in 2011/12 were from minority ethnic backgrounds. The permanent exclusion rates of Traveller of Irish Heritage and Gypsy/Roma pupils were over four times those of the average for all pupils, while permanent exclusion rates for black Caribbean pupils were almost three times higher than those for white pupils (Department for Education, 2013c). Maggie Atkinson, England's Children's Commissioner, has called upon policy makers to take immediate action to tackle a problem that she describes as a *scandal*:

> *One stark figure should make us all want to confront this scandal. In 2009–10, if you were a Black African-Caribbean boy with special needs and eligible for free school meals you were 168 times more likely to be permanently excluded from a state-funded school than a White girl without special needs from a middle class family.*

> (Children's Commissioner for England, 2012, p9)

ACTIVITY 7.4

In this exercise we would like you to consider some of the factors that might account for the different ethnic rates of school exclusion outlined above.

Some of your explanations may have focused on cultural factors. For example, it has been suggested that black Caribbean pupils may experience considerable levels of peer pressure to adopt the norms associated with urban street culture. This culture, it is argued, places a primacy on unruly behaviour and non-compliance with authority, including school authorities. From this perspective, higher levels of school exclusions among black Caribbean pupils are a reflection of their rejection of mainstream school values, and their attempts to look 'cool' in front of their peers. *What we now see in schools*, argues one commentator, *is children undermined by poor parenting, peer group pressure and an inability to be responsible for their own behaviour. They are not subjects of institutional racism* (Sewell, 2010, p33). Needless to say, there are problems with this kind of interpretation. In particular it stands accused of failing to acknowledge potential structural determinants of school exclusion, in particular racism.

An alternative explanation then is that pupils from black and minority ethnic group backgrounds are treated differently from their white peers by teachers and the school authorities. Certainly, this is the perception of black pupils who have themselves been excluded from school. As Ofsted suggests:

> *many Black pupils who find themselves subject to disciplinary procedures perceive themselves to have been unfairly treated ... Black pupils were more likely to be excluded for what was defined by schools as 'challenging*

behaviour'. The length of fixed-term exclusions varied considerably in the same school between Black and white pupils for what are described as the same or similar incidents.

(cited in Wright et al., 2005, p3)

Wright et al. (2005) interviewed a number of black excluded pupils, and they found that nearly half of those excluded believed that racism or racial stereotyping had played a part in their exclusion from school. Similar concerns were raised during the Children's Commissioner for England's (2012) recent investigation into school exclusions. This found that concerns about racism go well beyond children themselves; *young people of Black Caribbean heritage, or of mixed Black Caribbean and White heritage, are still many times more likely than others to be excluded, and there is still a widespread perception amongst parents and community leaders, put to this Inquiry in different parts of England, that the causes lie in practices, routines and expectations in schools* (p94).

Is there any justification for such claims? In the case of some schools, higher rates of exclusion among black pupils are undoubtedly the result of what the Children's Commissioner for England (2013a, p39) refers to as unacceptable directly, or indirectly discriminatory practices. For example, evidence submitted to its Inquiry found examples of *exclusion of children for hairstyles that are overwhelmingly worn by Black boys (for example, corn rows). It is simply unacceptable*, the report argued, *that any of this is allowed to happen*. Other research has drawn attention to the fact that in schools where exclusions are most commonly occurring, the teaching staff tended not to be representative of the ethnicity of the pupil population. While this may not necessarily be a problem, studies suggest that in some instances this 'imbalance' is accompanied by the existence of inaccurate, stereotypical and indeed racist assumptions about the behaviour of children from different ethnic backgrounds. For example, in a DfES-funded study on school exclusions, the head teacher in one such large comprehensive school, with 75 per cent of pupils from minority ethnic backgrounds, complained about the challenge he and his staff faced from *West Indian boys [who] tend to be loud and aggressive* (Parsons et al., 2004, p66). Evidence submitted to the recent Children's Commissioner's (2013a) Inquiry also concluded that the failure of teachers to appreciate cultural differences among pupils contributed to higher exclusion rates for some. In making decisions about discipline and exclusion, many schools, it was found, *take little or no account, in diverse communities, of linguistic, cultural or ethnic differences in, for example, intergenerational respect and how it is to be shown by children in ways that are not always the same as they are in White English society* (p39).

In fact, research suggests that pupils from minority ethnic group backgrounds who are excluded are less likely than white excluded children to have had prior behavioural problems, attendance issues, or be classified as having special needs difficulties. In addition, they are less likely to be classed as having low educational attainment and are far less likely to be excluded for reasons of ongoing, persistent misconduct. Indeed, in 2009/10, only 16.3 per cent of black pupils received fixed period exclusions for this reason, compared to 25.4 per cent of their white counterparts. Likewise, black

185

pupils are far less likely to be excluded for verbally abusing teachers. Statistics do, though, suggest that black and mixed-heritage pupils are far more likely than other groups to be excluded for one-off violent offences (32.1 per cent of all those receiving fixed period exclusions compared with 22.6 per cent of excluded white pupils in 2009/10) (Department for Education, 2010). The reasons for this are not clear, but one suggestion is that teachers and the school authorities, influenced by stereotypical views on the 'aggressiveness' of black youth (such as those held by the head teacher mentioned above), are less tolerant of relatively isolated bouts of bad behaviour when committed by black children. Inaccurate assumptions about the educational potential and behaviour of black pupils have been well documented within the sociology of education, and there is plenty of evidence to suggest that black children are sometimes inappropriately labelled as challenging, aggressive and as troublemakers, and that their behaviour is interpreted in the light of the label (Wright et al., 2005). This was the conclusion of a study sponsored by the Department for Children, Schools and Families into the educational experiences of pupils from minority ethnic group backgrounds (Strand, 2007, p99). It endorsed the interpretation favoured by a secret high-level official report into differential ethnic rates of school exclusions, which was leaked to the *Independent* in December 2006. The author of the report, Peter Wanless, Director of School Performance and Reform at the DfES, argued that the exclusions gap was *caused by largely unwitting, but systematic, racial discrimination in the application of disciplinary and exclusions policies.* Black pupils, he argued, were disproportionately denied mainstream education and the life chances that go with it:

> *It is argued that unintentional racism stems from long-standing social conditioning involving negative images of black people, particularly black men, which stereotype them as threatening. Such conditioning is reinforced by the media portrayal of black 'street culture'. It encourages school staff to expect black pupils to be worse behaved and to perceive a greater level of threat.*

> (cited in Griggs, 2006, p8)

Wanless also rejected 'cultural' explanations for different rates of exclusion, stating that there was a comparatively weak basis for arguing that street culture has a more persuasive influence on black young people than it has on other young people (p8). In summary then, much of the available evidence points to the likelihood that the higher rates of exclusion experienced by black pupils results from institutional racism, much of which may be the result of inadvertent, unconscious discriminatory practices on the part of teachers. This was one of the key conclusions of the Children's Commissioner for England's (2013a) investigation into school exclusions, which, worryingly, found that a large proportion of teachers themselves feel ill-prepared from their training to teach and manage diverse pupil populations. All trainee teachers, it concluded, should be trained to understand the importance of the need to appreciate cultural differences commonly found in UK schools, and to be cognisant of these, not only when teaching, but also when framing and implementing school disciplinary procedures.

Sociological explanations for educational inequality

The evidence we have presented so far leads us to question the notion that true equality of educational opportunity exists in the UK. As we have seen, educational experiences and outcomes vary between social classes and ethnic groups. In the following section, we look at sociological explanations which purport to account for these unequal outcomes. We begin with the symbolic interactionist perspective, because it follows on from the preceding discussion on labelling and school exclusion.

The role of the school: symbolic interactionist perspective

Symbolic interactionists are interested in the micro processes of communication within schools that can contribute to the relative success or failure of individual pupils. Drawing upon Howard Becker's work on labelling that we considered in the moral panic chapter, it is possible to see how teachers can potentially assign labels to pupils in their class, which has a powerful impact upon them and can lead to their education and subsequent career being shaped in particular ways. One of the earliest experiments carried out in 1968 by Rosenthal and Jacobsen demonstrates this well. They conducted IQ tests on school children at the beginning of the school year before the teachers had had an opportunity to form an opinion about their pupils. Without looking at the actual results, the researchers grouped children into so-called ability groups, telling teachers that a certain number of pupils had above-average ability and could be expected to 'spurt'. They then returned to the school some months later and retested the pupils. They compared both sets of test results and to their astonishment found that the pupils who had randomly been selected to be in the 'above average', 'spurters' group had improved their actual IQ scores significantly. Rosenthal and Jacobsen concluded that there must have been something in the way that the teachers interacted with the so-called 'star' pupils that contributed to their success. Although this study can be criticised on many fronts, not least because of the ethical issues around carrying out such a study, it does give us an indication of how potentially powerful teachers can be in shaping the attitudes and abilities of pupils, possibly by giving them additional attention, responding more positively to them, or pushing them to a higher level. Conversely, other pupils may be labelled as failures, be provided with less encouragement and be more likely to be perceived and treated as troublemakers. The expectations that teachers have can influence pupils, who may internalise these and act accordingly. This is called a self-fulfilling prophecy.

Research carried out by Stephen Waterhouse (2004) also found that teachers construct conceptions of pupils' identities over time, as they form impressions of them. This entailed categorising or labelling children in relation to the social boundaries of the school and largely involved categories of 'normal' and 'deviant' pupils. Waterhouse found that 'deviant' pupils were of great concern to teachers and occupied a significant amount of time; by contrast, the 'normal' pupils were to some extent invisible in comparison. Furthermore, he found that once children were categorised as 'deviant' or 'normal' there was a tendency to interpret other behaviours in light of the master label assigned:

*Once the dominant category of 'normal' or 'deviant' was adopted by
the teacher, it then became the pivotal identity for interpreting other
[behaviours] – even in those episodes of classroom life in which the child was
apparently not demonstrating behaviour typical of the dominant 'deviant or
'normal type .*

(p74)

Waterhouse notes how one of the teachers in his study predicted the future behaviour of a pupil: *Today he's been good. But I think this afternoon he'll probably be naughty because he has to stay in because the dinner ladies can't control him* (p75). It is clear from this research that teachers are involved in categorising and labelling pupils as part of their core business of assessment and relating to their pupils. Although Waterhouse's research did not set out to measure the impact of labelling on specific pupils, he did identify the positive outcomes associated in two schools that had adopted new initiatives with the aim of reducing pupil exclusions. The schools in question adopted a range of measures that had a clear emphasis upon inclusion, and in doing so, both schools significantly reduced the numbers of school exclusions. Measures included an incorporative ethos and a culture in which the pupils were seen as being entitled to be there and entitled to support. There was a focus upon positive interactions with the pupils by teachers and the senior management; and high-profile 'crowd control' whereby a visible presence signalled *strong behavioural expectations, and at the same time creating spontaneous opportunities for informal, supportive and generally positive interactions with pupils* (p80). If such measures are regarded as constituting a form of institutional labelling of pupils, by consciously reconstructing the pupils as being positive members of the school community, it is possible to see how self-fulfilling prophecies were occurring here both for the pupils and the staff. Indeed, the number of pupils to be excluded in both schools decreased significantly.

If we accept as a general point that it is likely that teachers label and categorise pupils according to their educational ability and their social attributes, the impact of this is significant upon large numbers of children. Of course, for some pupils the impact will be positive, but for others it will be negative and may contribute to poor outcomes for some children. The labelling of children linked to their social class background, their gender, race, disability or other factors (such as their status as a looked-after child, for example) can substantially impact upon their educational experiences and outcomes. Indeed, our own students are usually very aware of the subtle but powerful labelling that they themselves have experienced and the impact it has had upon them.

However, in addition to the largely unconscious labelling that may be done by individual teachers, children are also labelled more formally by being streamed into ability groups. However subtly or otherwise this process is carried out, children are usually aware that they are in the 'top group for maths' or the 'bottom group for English' and such *institutionalised labelling* may also play a part in how children perceive their own ability. In some areas of the UK, there are systems of selective education where children can enter an 11+ examination which they need to 'pass' in order to go to a selective grammar school. The impact of such a system can be far reaching for some pupils, who can perceive themselves as 'failures' if they do not pass the test. Such institutionalised labelling can have a significant social impact upon geographical areas, where there is a two-tiered system perceived to be in operation, with great stigma or pride attached to which school a child attends. However, there are a range of difficulties associated with the IQ test that is the highly sought-after passport to grammar school; rather than genuinely testing intelligence, the 11+ may actually test the ability of the child to do the test. It is argued that middle-class pupils are at an advantage here as their parents are more likely to be able to pay for a private tutor to assist their child and/or purchase (expensive) test papers to practise with. There are other criticisms of the 11+ system, not least the immense stress that it can put children (and their parents) under. Furthermore, the two-tier system can simultaneously disadvantage some children while advantaging others.

Genetically determined intelligence?

A radically different explanation for unequal educational outcomes shifts the focus away from schools and teachers and onto what are perceived to be pupils' innate abilities or inabilities. According to this interpretation, children from disadvantaged backgrounds, or from different ethnic groups, are simply genetically less intelligent than their better-off, or white counterparts. Hence, intelligence is seen as an inherited trait, determined by genetic rather than cultural, structural and environmental factors. In 1969, the American educational psychologist Arthur Jensen (1969) published a deeply controversial paper which implied that racial differences in educational attainment had a genetic origin. In this paper, which was based on IQ data, he argued that compensatory educational initiatives which were aimed at raising the relatively low levels of educational attainment among black children in the US were effectively a waste of time and resources. Their educational underachievement, he argued, had little to do with environmental influences, such as labelling, poverty and poor educational opportunities, and more to do with their genetically inherited low levels of cognitive ability. Jensen explained social class differences in education in much the same way, and, more recently has hinted at genetic explanations for a range of social ills, and not just educational failure. Many social behaviour problems, he states, *including dropping out of school, chronic welfare status, illegitimacy, child neglect, poverty, accident proneness, delinquency, and crime, are negatively correlated with ... IQ independently of social class of origin* (Jensen, 1999).

Jensen's ideas provided the basis for Charles Murray and Richard J Herrnstein's (1994) controversial book, *The bell curve,* which sought to re-emphasise the links between genetics and intelligence. These are the main points made in the book.

- Intelligence is significantly (between 40 and 80 per cent) genetically determined and can be measured objectively through the use of IQ data.

- Social class differences in educational attainment and 'success' are largely genetically determined. Those who rise to the top of American society are there because they happen to be the most intelligent, and not through patronage or privilege. Likewise, those at the bottom are so placed because of their lack of intelligence, and not the absence of sufficient opportunities to succeed.

- Social problems such as illegitimacy, crime and unemployment are linked to genetically determined differences in intelligence.

- Social policies designed to improve educational attainment among children of the lower classes, such as the Head Start initiative in the United States, are doomed to failure.

- Racial differences in intelligence and educational attainment are largely inherited. (This was probably the most controversial of Murray and Herrnstein's findings.)

It is now more than 20 years since Murray and Hernstein's book was published, but as one recent analysis of its impact points out, *it is difficult to overestimate the impact of the Bell Curve* (Nisbett, 2013). The largely uncritical response that it received in the popular press in both the US and the UK meant that many of its deeply controversial conclusions were represented as uncontestable 'facts', helping to shape public and professional attitudes towards the causes of educational disadvantage:

> *The conclusions that many people drew from the book were that IQ tests are an accurate and largely sufficient measure of intelligence, that IQ is primarily genetically controlled, that IQ is little influenced by environmental factors, that racial differences in IQ are likely due at least in part, and perhaps in large part, to genetics, and that educational and other interventions have little impact on IQ and little effect on racial differences in IQ.*

(Nisbett, 2013, p10)

Not surprisingly, many criticisms have been made of *The bell curve.* For example, studies which show social class and ethnic differences in educational attainment to be due to cultural factors, environmental effects, biases built into the tests themselves, or a combination of all of these, are either side-stepped by the authors, completely ignored or inappropriately dismissed. In addition, evidence highlighting the positive effects of compensatory forms of schooling, which are designed to mitigate the educationally detrimental impact of poverty and disadvantage, are also cast aside. There is, in fact, a good deal of evidence to indicate that targeted interventions, aimed at stimulating the intelligence of children from deprived backgrounds, and providing them with packages of educational support, can have huge impact in terms of improving educational performance. Why then do Murray and Herrnstein persist in pushing the case for genetic interpretations of intelligence? According to Alexander Alland (2004) and Nisbett (2013), they are driven by their own preconceived ideological opposition to state-funded welfare programmes, including public education. As we have seen in other chapters in this book, Murray has always been a vociferous opponent of state welfare for the poor, and if, through the use of dubious genetic arguments, he is able to show it to be ineffective, then his arguments against progressive welfare interventions are given greater credence. As Nisbett (2013, p10) points out, *The Bell Curve encouraged skepticism about the ability of public policy initiatives to have much impact on IQ or IQ-related outcomes.*

We would, therefore, caution against letting our guard down against the inherently problematic assumptions that stem from explanations of educational underachievement that are based on the ideas of those such as Jensen, Murray and Herrnstein. The flaws associated with IQ data are many and varied and we should not take IQ data as 'given'. IQ tests are notoriously fallible and are certainly not neutral – indeed, it is important to realise that they are socially constructed, and the questions asked can be designed and framed in such a way as to secure any outcome the author desires. IQ data has in the past been used to justify a whole range of deeply problematic theories, which, in their 'milder' forms, have been used to justify racist practices, and in their more extreme forms, have been used to justify the extermination of whole races. It is no coincidence that references to Jensen's and Murray and Herrnstein's work can be found in the publicity literature of various racist and white supremacist organisations, from the British National Party and English Defence League in the UK to the Ku Klux Klan in the US.

Poor upbringings and parental shortfall

Other explanations for the educational 'failure' of working-class and black children focus on what are perceived to be their poor upbringings, and the failure of their parents or carers to support and nurture their talents. These kinds of explanations can be divided into two broad 'camps', according to the degree of sympathy or blame they apportion to the parents and carers.

A 'blaming' approach

A less than sympathetic interpretation of parental failure to fully support children can be found within what we have referred to elsewhere in the book as 'moral underclass discourse'. A view that has traditionally been shared by politicians and academics on the political 'right' is that there exists an underclass of problematic families who are incapable of socialising their children effectively. While advocates of this approach do sometimes point to genetic influences, their main focus is on the immaturity, low intelligence, and dysfunctional behavioural characteristics of certain parents. Again, while we can sometimes find a hint of genetics in these explanations, on the whole these, and other dysfunctional traits, are said to have been encouraged by well-meaning but harmful welfare interventions, which reinforce rather than modify the 'deviant' behaviour of morally degenerate parents. These parents, it is argued, are simply unable to provide their children with the stable environment, intellectual stimulation and appropriate role models that are necessary to inculcate a desire for learning and educational success. Moreover, their lack of ambition and aspiration is passed on to succeeding generations, and children unconsciously absorb their parents' fatalistic outlooks on life. The Conservative politician and former Education Minister, Keith Joseph, was an early advocate of this theory. A high and rising proportion of children, he argued in 1974, were being born to mothers least fitted to bring children into the world. Many of the parents, he insisted, were of low intelligence, and most of them of low educational attainment. They were unlikely to be able to give children the stable and emotional background they needed, and if they were allowed to procreate unchecked they would continue to *produce problem children, the future unmarried mothers, delinquents, denizens of our borstals, subnormal educational establishments, prisons, hostels for drifters.* Joseph argued that those calling for more educational resources and preventative work with disadvantaged children were missing the point. The nation's 'stock' was being diluted by high birth rates among poor families and parents of low intelligence, and the solution, he insisted, lay in a massive expansion of birth control among the lower classes (Clark, 1974, p1). Not surprisingly, Joseph's comments excited a great deal of controversy at the time, and indeed are said to have dented his political ambitions. However, these ideas remain influential today.

Charles Murray is one of a number of academics on the 'right' to embrace this kind of approach. He too draws attention to increased birth rates among what he sees as certain 'dysfunctional' sections of the poor and he also dismisses the notion that targeting additional educational resources at children of the 'underclass' can significantly improve their education opportunities or life chances:

> *Experience gives no confidence that social services can counteract the effects of bad family environment. On the contrary, research is filled with studies showing how intractable these environments seem to be. Less charitably, some observers, of whom I am one, think a case can be made that activist social policy exacerbates the problems it seeks to ameliorate.*

> (Murray, 1998, p43)

More recently, in a report entitled, 'Requires Improvement', the right-wing Centre for Social Justice (CSJ, 2013a), the think tank set up by the Coalition's Conservative Work and Pensions Minister Iain Duncan Smith, also sought to reinforce 'behavioural' interpretations for educational disadvantage. Educational failure, the report argued, was less to do with a lack of opportunity, or discrimination, and more a result of poor, inadequate parenting, which had palpably failed to provide many children with the aspiration and skills they needed to progress academically. *The CSJ*, the report begins, *has been told of children entering the age of school at four who:*

- *Commonly act as though they are 12 to 18 months old;*
- *Are unable to socialize having had no practice at being sociable;*
- *Are still in nappies and not toilet trained;*
- *Do not know their names and are unable to speak.* (p13)

Little empirical evidence was advanced to support the report's assertions, or its conclusions. Rather, a subtle and liberal usage was made of largely unattributed, carefully selected anecdotal examples, all of which reinforced interpretations that focused upon parental pathology. Despite having little evidential basis, the report's 'findings' were extensively and sympathetically reported in right-wing tabloid newspapers. The assertions that children were arriving at school in 'nappies', not knowing their names and unable to speak were given particularly widespread publicity. Even the supposedly ideologically neutral BBC was 'hooked' by the 'bait' offered by the CSJ. Its uncritical presentation of the report's findings was indistinguishable from that of the conservative press. *Children from the poorest homes*, it declared, *risk becoming an educational underclass, starting school in nappies and behaving like toddlers* (Coughlan, 2013). The BBC extensively cited passages from the report, including the head teacher responsible for the 'nappies' comments, without making any attempt to question the validity of the CSJ's assertions, or to offer an alternative perspective:

A head teacher told the researchers: 'In the last three years we have had to toilet-train children who came to school in nappies at age five. Parents ask me how we managed to do it. Many of them just can't be bothered, they think it's our responsibility to do it for them'.

(Coughlan, 2013)

As might be expected with a neo-liberal think tank, the CSJ also identified profligate welfare as one of the key causes of educational disadvantage. Hence, its report also highlighted the views of other, equally carefully chosen head teachers, who believed the welfare state had corroded levels of parental and pupil motivation:

Families where generations of parents have been on benefits have created dependency and a lack of aspiration and ambition for what education can deliver. Many of the families I see don't value what education can offer. Instead, there is a culture of 'easy money' – where the parents look first to avenues like benefits, compensation claims, engaging in illegal activity and the informal economy.

(CSJ, 2013a, p39)

'Moral underclass discourse' permeated sections other sections of the CSJ report, and the usual neo-liberal 'folk devils' – in particular, family breakdown and lone parents – were also held responsible for educational inequality. Family breakdown, we were told, had *a monumental impact on children's success at school* and *lies at the root of almost all exclusions*. Meanwhile, lone parents *just don't have enough time to invest in their [children's] education … and educational attainment often falls by the wayside*.

As we have already explained, there was no real evidential basis for the claims made by the CSJ. The 'nappies' comment, for instance, had been made by one, anonymous, probably carefully selected head teacher, whose views are doubtlessly at variance with the vast majority of his peers. As one commentator argued at the time, *it's hard to see the purpose of its inclusion, except to make a kind of atmospheric point that there are parents out there, not like you and me, who live like savages* (Williams, 2013). The best we can say about this interpretation for educational disadvantage is that the emphasis moves away from genetics towards an approach which acknowledges cultural influences on educational attainment. However, when it comes to providing solutions to educational inequalities, it is almost as pessimistic in outlook as genetic interpretations for educational disadvantage.

A more sympathetic approach to understanding parental 'failure'

Not all explanations for educational inequality which focus on a perceived 'parental deficit' are quite as blaming as the perspective outlined above. A more sympathetic version acknowledges the difficult circumstances that mitigate against parental involvement in education. It accepts the fact that many parents themselves may lack the educational and cognitive skills needed to shape their children's learning careers and stimulate their interest in education. This approach also appreciates that many low-income parents feel that they are too busy coping with the day-to-day stresses of making ends meet to show any meaningful involvement in their children's education

193

(Cauce et al., 2003; Ball, 2010). There is also an acknowledgment of the way parents' own negative experiences of education can feed into the dynamics of family life, negatively impacting on their children's chances at school (Gregg and Washbook, 2010; Chowdrey et al., 2010). Based upon their own lack of opportunities and negative experiences, it is hardly surprising that parents themselves see little value in educational attainment, and this too will impact detrimentally on the encouragement and support they give their children. They are also likely to show less interest in the range of educational 'choices' available to their children, and be content to see them attend the local 'sink' school.

There are links here to Oscar Lewis's 'culture of poverty' thesis discussed in Chapter 2, which sees negative traits – fatalism, lack of motivation and inability to defer gratification – being learned by successive generations of working-class children as a response to their position in society. From this perspective, any 'solution' must seek to change the outlooks and perceptions of working-class parents. It must encourage them to show a greater interest in their children's education, to motivate them, and to provide them with the nurturing, encouragement and support needed to guarantee educational success. In short, what this perspective argues is that what we need to do is make working-class parents more like middle-class parents. Sharon Gewirtz (2001) has outlined some of the assumptions upon which this interpretation of educational inequality is based:

- Middle-class parents are far better at assessing and engaging with the range of options available to parents in the educational marketplace. They know more about the pros and cons of different of schools in their areas, and hence are more able to make informed choices about the quality and types of schools that their children attend. They are, therefore, more 'tuned in' to the 'choice agenda' in education and better equipped to discriminate between good and bad schools.

- Middle-class parents are more effective at monitoring what schools provide to their children, and intervening when they feel it necessary to rectify what they see as being problematic. They know what to expect from schools in terms of, for example, volume of homework and feedback on their child's progress, and are more prepared to intervene if they feel something is wrong.

- Middle-class parents possess more 'cultural capital' than their working-class counterparts. This concept was introduced by Pierre Bourdieu (1973) to refer to the social skills, language skills, interests and attributes that middle-class parents confer upon their children that help them to succeed in the education system (see the next chapter for a more in depth discussion of 'cultural capital'). It is argued that such parents are in a much better position to show a much greater level of interest in their children's education, encouraging and incentivising them, helping with homework and taking them on educational trips of interest. They are less fatalistic and more likely to instil in their children a desire and love for learning.

There can be little doubt that many of these assumptions underpin much official thinking around education policy and educational disadvantage. For example, there now exists a plethora of information – either online or in leaflet form – aimed at informing working-class parents of the different 'choices' available to them, encouraging them to engage more effectively in the educational marketplace. Governments – both the current government and its predecessor – have also sought to encourage working-class parents to take a more active role in monitoring what their children's schools do. The introduction of home/school agreements, which set out what parents can expect from schools, was partly designed to this end. Likewise, great efforts are being made to persuade working-class parents to spend more time helping their children with school work. Finally, ministers also determined to change what they see as the negative cultural traits possessed by many working-class families, which operate against their children's educational opportunities. As David Laws, the Liberal Democrat Schools Minister in the Coalition government stated, *I think that many of the problems with low attainment in school are due to factors that are outside the school gate: parental support or lack of support, parental aspirations, poverty in the home environment, poor housing, lack of experience of life*. He argued that tackling these *low aspirations and tolerance of failure* was *a challenge for all governments* (cited in Adams, 2014).

At first glance, all these kind of comments, and the initiatives that stem from them, seem eminently reasonable. Surely, all parents should have an understanding of the different choices available in terms of their children's schooling? In addition, all parents should show an interest in their children's schools, be prepared to nurture a desire for learning, and assist their children with homework. However, this strategy does have its critics. In particular, it is accused of ignoring the structural constraints that shape educational opportunity and disadvantage.

Structural explanations for educational inequality

With each of the above two 'parental deficit' interpretations, the focus is, to a lesser or greater degree, on the essentially negative personal and cultural attributes of children and families themselves, which are said to predispose them to problematic behaviour and/or lower levels of educational attainment. Other explanations for educational disadvantage focus on the structure of the education system itself – its hierarchical nature, the quality of schooling in disadvantaged areas, and the failure to address geographical inequalities in the distribution of educational resources.

The previous and current governments certainly locate at least part of the blame for educational disadvantage within the education system, and a number of reforms have sought to improve the educational experience of disadvantaged children. Under Labour administrations, we saw the introduction of its Sure Start initiative, an expansion of nursery education, reductions in class sizes, educational action zones, the building schools for the future programme, the introduction of learning mentors in schools, the development of numeracy and literacy strategies, and the introduction of citizenship education (Whitty, 2008). The Coalition government's 'pupil premium', which is intended to provide additional funding and support to disadvantaged school children, is also geared towards tackling some of the structural causes of educational inequality. However, some argue that a disproportionate amount of emphasis has been placed upon what we referred to above as the 'parental deficit' and too little on wider structural factors. In short, advocates of structural explanations for educational inequality accuse governments of:

- reinforcing negative imagery of poor working-class families, strengthening the view that educational inequality is the fault of parents rather than a lack of opportunity;

- neglecting the impact poverty, stress and ill-health have on parents' ability to devote time to assisting their child's education;

- engaging in an uncritical celebration of the ideologies of 'choice' and 'competition' in education.

The latter criticism relates to the way governments, both Labour and Coalition, have seemingly uncritically accepted the rhetoric of choice, competition and the market in education. As Whitty (2008) acknowledges, *there have been significant continuities between Conservative and New Labour policies in terms of the drive for an essentially market based education system.*This has led, as we saw above, to the development of initiatives designed to educate working-class parents about the range of choices available to their children. It is assumed that this will help counter the deficit in knowledge that working-class parents face, thus equalising their children's opportunities of enrolling at 'good' schools. However, critics argue that this strategy is misconceived, and indeed misleading, arguing that *the evidence to support the case that diversity and choice are the key to higher standards remains weak and highly contested* (Whitty, 2008, p176). As Whitty (2001) states, *education reforms couched in the rhetoric of choice, difference and diversity often turn out to be sophisticated ways of reproducing existing hierarchies of class and race* (p289). From this perspective, instead of teaching working-class parents how to identify 'good' and 'bad' schools, ministers should be directing their efforts at ensuring that all schools provide an excellent quality of educational experience. In other words, there should not be a hierarchy of schools to choose from at all – rather, all schools should be equally good. This was the key principle underpinning the drive towards comprehensive education in the 1960s and 1970s, but in recent years it has been undermined by a plethora of initiatives designed to encourage choice, competition, specialisation and a hierarchy of schools. Hence, under Labour we saw the creation of 'Academy' schools, an initiative that the Coalition government has embraced and expanded. Further competition and choice has been added since 2010, with the introduction of the Coalition's Free Schools programme. These developments are not without their critics. As Gewirtz (2001) notes, with hierarchies comes competition, and in any competition for educational resources, the odds are severely stacked against working-class families. First, the worst resourced and underperforming schools tend to be located in working-class areas, and unlike middle-class families, working-class families are unable to relocate to better catchment areas. The Sutton Trust estimates that parents wanting to re-locate to a house near a 'top' state primary school in 2012 would have had to pay a £91,000 premium for the privilege of doing so, a sum which is clearly beyond the means of many families. The equivalent premium for a 'top' secondary school would be £77,000 (Francis and Hutchings, 2013). Second, it is naïve to assume that the cultural capital possessed by middle-class families, which enables them to engage more effectively in their children's education, can be mimicked overnight. Clearly, this is something that the Coalition's Liberal Democrat School's Minister, David Laws, believed is possible, when he stated that he wanted to encourage the proliferation of more *pushy, sharp-elbowed* parents, who would use all the resources at their disposal to improve their children's educational opportunities (Adams, 2014). However, even if such a re-socialisation strategy could be moderately successful, this, in itself, would not be sufficient. As Gewirtz (2001) points out:

> ... *however successful the government is in reconstructing working-class parents in the image of the ideal-typical middle-class parent, not everyone can be 'successful' or achieve 'excellence' because there are only a limited number of schools or jobs that are deemed to be 'excellent'. So long as hierarchies of schools and jobs exist, the middle classes will always find ways of getting the best out of the system, of ensuring that their cultural capital is more valuable than that of any working-class competitors.*

(p10)

Ball (2010, p158) concurs with this analysis. The ability to choose the best schools and to provide guidance about the best curricular routes and qualifications *rely on social, cultural and economic capitals that are unevenly distributed across the population*. This 'work of learning', which, in some respects, is equally important in shaping educational opportunity and outcomes as schooling itself, entails time, knowledge, demands, navigational skills and costs that can only consistently and realistically be borne by more affluent sections of the population.

RESEARCH SUMMARY

Middle-class colonisation of educational opportunity?

Are academics right to suggest that the elite sectors of public education have been colonised by the better-off? Certainly, there are significant social class differences in secondary school enrolment, with working-class children severely underrepresented in the 'best' schools. In 2005, for example, a Sutton Trust Report showed that only 3 per cent of children in what are considered to be the top 200 state schools were in receipt of free school meals, compared with a national secondary school average of 14.3 per cent. The report found that children who attended the highest performing schools were from significantly more affluent backgrounds than the population as a whole, implying that middle-class parents do indeed manage to 'colonise' the better publicly funded secondary schools:

> *The intake of the top 200 schools is significantly more affluent than both the school population as a whole and the local areas in which they are sited. Or, to look at it another way, poorer children are much less likely to benefit from a top quality state education than their better-off peers, even if a leading maintained school is on their doorstep.*

(Sutton Trust, 2005, p8)

A more recent analysis by the Sutton Trust (2013) confirms the continued existence of the patterns of inequality that it identified in 2005. Thus, in 2012 only 6.4 per cent of children

(Continued)

(Continued)

in the top 200 performing state schools were entitled to free school meals, compared with a national secondary school average of 16.5 per cent. The scope of this most recent inquiry was extended to 500 top performing schools, but the results were much the same, with free school meal children significantly under-represented. In all, only 7.6 of children in the top 500 schools were entitled to free school meals, and a mere 53 of these schools had what could be considered to be a representative sample of such children.

Why is this the case? As well as more obvious factors, such as the geographical location of the 'best' schools in affluent areas (which is the case), the fact that middle-class parents can in some respects 'pay' for their children's education by being able to afford to buy houses in areas where the 'best' schools are is significant. So too is the point that middle-class parents are more aware of the 'choices' available to them. In addition, many of these schools subject applicants to entrance tests or examinations which, as hinted at earlier, disadvantage working-class pupils. For instance, many of the country's top secondary schools are grammar schools, each of which selects their pupils by means of what is known as the 11+ test. As we have already explained, while these tests are described as 'neutral', 'objective' tests of intellect and ability, there is no such thing as a neutral test of intelligence. The history of the sociology of education is rife with research which shows that more affluent middle-class parents are able, with the aid of their cultural and financial capital, to coach their children to pass the 11+. They can, as we previously indicated, also draw on their own cultural capital, they are in a better position to purchase practice papers (which are not cheap), and perhaps most of all, they are able to pay for private tuition for their children. In summary then, the research findings suggest that greater marketisation, diversity, competition and choice in secondary education have disproportionately benefited more privileged children. As Whitty (2008, p177) argues, there is no doubt that advantaged schools and advantaged parents have been able to seek each other out, *meaning, according to Reay (2012, p7),* that the working class have largely ended up with the 'choices' that the middle class do not want to make.

It is worth noting that these inequalities at secondary school level are mirrored in the higher education sector, with working-class children underrepresented at the top 'traditional' universities. For instance, children with professional/managerial parents are three times more likely to enter a high status, Russell Group University than those with working-class parents (Jerrim, 2013). By definition, this means that access to students from lower social class backgrounds is limited and they tend to find themselves excluded from such institutions. Hence, despite the fact that 32.3 per cent of young higher education first degree entrants in 2012/13 were from skilled manual, partly-skilled and unskilled backgrounds, only 11.7 per cent of Cambridge University's entrants and 9.6 per cent of Oxford University's entrants were. The equivalent percentages for the other pre-1992 'traditional' universities were not much higher; 12.5 per cent at the University of Durham; 15.8 per cent at the University of Exeter; 16.8 per cent at the University of Bath and 19.5 per cent at the University of Warwick. By contrast, the percentage of such students found in post-1992 universities and higher education colleges was much higher; for instance, they constituted 54.4 per cent of entrants at the University of Greenwich and 51.2 per cent at London Metropolitan University (Higher Education Statistics Agency, 2013). In short, what

> *this data shows is that there is very little chance that children of working-class parents will attend Oxford or Cambridge, and only slightly less limited chance of them attending a prestigious Russell Group institution. Moreover, as the Sutton Trust argues research shows that this phenomenon cannot be explained by academic ability alone, and there are significant numbers of working class children who, even though they have the academic ability to attend … enter a non-selective institution instead* (Jerrim, 2013, p8).

In the light of the findings highlighted above, it has been argued that any genuine widening of educational opportunity will involve a dismantling of the hierarchies that structure schooling in the UK. One solution that has been suggested for enhancing opportunity in secondary education is a system of 'fair banding' of pupils. Under this system all pupils in a given area are tested by ability. However, rather than using the data to cream off the most able pupils (as with the grammar system), banding is used to ensure that all schools have a more balanced, mixed ability range of pupils. While this reduces the element of parental 'choice' in school allocation, according to the Sutton Trust, it is the most effective means of enhancing opportunity and ensuring that a wider mix of children (in terms of ability and social class) are able to attend popular schools. In part, this is because it effectively eradicates one of the key causes of the middle-class 'colonisation' of the best secondary schools: that is, the ability of more affluent families to purchase houses in 'good' catchment areas. Although it will not negate the other opportunity-enhancing 'privileges' that coming from a higher income family confers, it will, the Sutton Trust argue, contribute to more equal educational outcomes. Banding is currently permitted, but in 2012/13 only four per cent of secondary schools (121, in all) used it to allocate places. Moreover, in 2010, the Coalition's new School Admissions Code withdrew the previous Labour government's endorsement of banding as 'good practice', so there is little official encouragement to expand this system of allocation (Noden et al., 2014).

Marxist approaches to education

Marxists seek to understand the education system within its wider social context. In their much-cited book *Schooling in capitalist America,* published in 1976, Samuel Bowles and Herbert Gintis provided a detailed Marxist critique of education systems in capitalist societies. They began by seeking to demolish the 'meritocratic myth', which implies that education is an 'objective competition' that provides all children with the opportunity to 'make it'. Education in capitalist societies, they argued, was never intended to be, and indeed never had been, a vehicle for creating a fairer, equal, socially just society. This, they insisted, was borne out by data on social mobility, which showed that despite the expansion of educational resources and 'opportunity' in the US, social mobility was just as low as in the past. Meanwhile, income inequality and poverty remained endemic, and indeed had increased rather than decreased. Education, they concluded, could not therefore be seen as an engine of opportunity or social improvement. In short, the likelihood of working-class children improving their economic and social status and avoiding poverty in the future was just as low when they wrote their book as it had ever been.

Ralph Miliband (1975) agrees with Bowles and Gintis, arguing that one of the principle functions of schooling is to maintain rather than reduce existing social class distinctions and patterns of inequality. *In most cases*, he argues, *working class children attend schools which are ... 'custodial institutions', where they wait the time when school-leaving regulations allow them to assume the role for which their class circumstances destined them from birth, namely that of hewers of wood and drawers of water* (p40). Of course, Marxists do not deny that the education of some, indeed many working-class children, sometimes enables them to be socially mobile. However, ultimately, what 'opportunities' that do arise are linked to the changing demands of capital and business rather than a desire to promote social mobility. Modern capitalist economies need a relatively well-educated, technically efficient workforce, and education systems provide this function – in short, they ensure that employers have a pool of workers with sufficient knowledge to carry out the tasks required of them. Hence, although educational expansion has occurred, and as we saw in our research summary above, many working-class children do now attend universities, this has not proven to be an engine of social mobility and nor is it likely to in the future. Working-class students are largely confined to 'proletarian' universities, denied access to those high prestige institutions that provide recruits for the 'command posts' of society. Writing in 1969, Miliband (1975, p41) insisted that *as higher education spreads, so does an old distinction between the institutions which provide it assume a new importance,* in terms of the role of universities in the promotion and maintenance of existing patterns of privilege. In the light of the findings of our research summary above, as well as the comments we made earlier in the book about the narrow recruitment pool to 'elite' economic, political and societal roles, Miliband's comments can perhaps be viewed as somewhat prescient.

The maintenance of class divisions is not the only role said to be performed by education. It is seen to fulfil other crucially important 'disciplinary' functions. Hence, Bowles and Gintis argue that one of the key aims of education is to nurture the attitudes and behaviour required for participation in the labour force. Here, they are referring to the inculcation of discipline, the work ethic and other personality traits conducive to preparing young people psychologically for work. Schools, they point out, *foster types of personal development compatible with the relationships of dominance and subordinacy in the economic sphere* (p11). Or, put another way, they teach children (future workers) to be docile, to submit to authority, to accept instructions unquestioningly and to accept their station in life as given. To cite a more recent Marxist analysis, education plays a crucial role *in conditioning and institutionalizing children not only for exploitation at work but toward an acceptance of their future life conditions and expectations* (Greaves et al., 2007). This interpretation sounds very similar to functionalist views of education that we outlined earlier, and in some respects it is. There is, of course, one fundamental difference. Whereas functionalists see the functions of education as being desirable and good for the whole of society, Marxists see in them a more sinister element. Education, they argue, is one of the crucial means by which bourgeois values are transmitted. It promotes 'false consciousness' and serves to perpetuate an inherently unjust system – capitalism.

Of course, Marxists such as Bowles and Gintis do not envisage that educational practitioners, whether teachers or lecturers, are aware of the functions they provide for capitalism. On the contrary, these functions have become 'institutionalised' into their professional training and practice over a period of more than a century, and hence are performed in an almost unconscious, 'natural' way. Teachers, lecturers and other educational practitioners may themselves be unaware of the constraints within which they operate, or the extent to which the curricula they teach and codes of practice they follow have become increasingly uncritical, and narrowly focused on ensuring children and young people conform to the needs of capitalism. In recent years, Marxists have pointed to developments in UK education policy, such as the introduction of the National Curriculum as being symptomatic of attempts to severely circumscribe what is taught in schools (Kumar, 2012). In relation to school curricula, however, it is as interesting to think about what is not taught as what is taught. The absence of sociology in the National Curriculum, for example, means that the majority of children will leave school without the insights that a sociological imagination can give them. And while citizenship has now been added as a compulsory subject at secondary schools, some have argued that this too is motivated more by a desire to control than to promote a critical understanding of the world.

Marxist analyses of education do sound very pessimistic. Marxists do, though, have a vision – an optimistic vision which envisages the creation of an equal, socially-just society, where education is not subordinated to the needs of the economy. It will, however, involve the overthrow of capitalism:

> [W]e believe that the key to [education] reform is the democratisation of economic relationships: social ownership, democratic and participatory control of the production process by workers, equal sharing of necessary labour by all, and progressive equalisation of incomes and destruction of hierarchial relationships. This is, of course, socialism.

> (Bowles and Gintis, 1976, p14)

Marxism and education: an evaluation?

In a sense, it is difficult to disagree with certain elements of Marxist analyses of education. Indeed, it could perhaps be said that Marxists are at least partly guilty of stating the obvious. For example, if recent speeches by senior UK politicians are anything to go by, the shape of secondary education is clearly linked to the imperatives of the market and the economy. While Tony Blair and his successors, Gordon Brown and David Cameron, may extol the 'meritocratic virtues' of education, neither would deny that their education policies have been geared towards improving economic growth and the country's ability to compete internationally. Indeed, educational policy documents are full of references to the importance of education to the UK's levels of economic performance. So while Marxists are correct to highlight the intrinsic economic functions that education performs, this is neither a particularly novel insight, nor one which leading politicians would deny.

Marxist comments on the failure of educational policy to deliver a true 'meritocracy' are perhaps more useful. Regarding the higher education sector, a Marxist analysis might also help us understand relatively recent changes to higher education student funding, particularly the drive to force students to fund their own studies. Marxists are not alone in suggesting that this has been influenced by a desire to 'divert' students away from theoretical, critical subjects (such as sociology), towards more business-orientated disciplines.

For example, the increase in tuition fees and the abolition of the maintenance grant, means that average student debt on graduation could be as high as £53,400 for those starting their courses in 2012 (BBC, 2011). This, of course, must be paid off, and it seems logical that potential undergraduates may now think twice about enrolling on a socially critical course which, while intrinsically rewarding and interesting, may not appear to carry the same vocational weight with employers as a skill-focused, or business-related subject.

Perhaps the most illuminating aspect of the Marxist view of education, however, lies in the recognition that the education system maintains, perpetuates and legitimates inequality. An understanding of this seems important to assist us to achieve more realistic understanding of inequality in our society.

CHAPTER SUMMARY

This chapter has encouraged you to synthesise your knowledge and experience of the education system with sociological theory and to think about the educational experiences of disadvantaged groups and how these can impact upon the rest of their lives. The chapter has considered how factors within and outside the school can contribute to and in some instances determine children's educational experiences, achievement and life chances, and encouraged you to move beyond pathological explanations that focus solely on parental and individual failure. If as social workers we are aiming to significantly improve the lives of the children and understand the contributory factors to the life paths of the adults we work with, it is fundamental that we move beyond a blaming approach, and acknowledge the wider structural causes of unequal educational experiences and outcomes. In the next chapter, we revisit some of the arguments about education, locating these within a broader analysis of class.

FURTHER READING

Those of you interested in trends in school exclusions will find the Office of the Children's Commissioner's two inquiries into the issue useful. You can access the publications generated by the inquiries here: www.childrenscommissioner.gov.uk/info/schoolexclusions

The following Centre for Social Justice report offers a neo-liberal, 'moral underclass' interpretation for what it refers to as *educational failure*: Centre for Social Justice (2013) *Requires improvement: The causes of educational failure*. www.centreforsocialjustice.org.uk/UserStorage/pdf/Pdf%20reports/requires.pdf

If you are interested in learning more about the Marxist interpretation of the education system, you might wish to look at the seminal work, **Bowles, S and Gintis, H** (1976) *Schooling in capitalist America*. Abingdon: Routledge and Kegan Paul. For a more recent Marxist analysis, see: **Kumar, R (ed.)** (2012) *Education and the reproduction of capital: Neo-liberal knowledge and counterstrategies*. Basingstoke: Palgrave Macmillan.

The following Sutton Trust report examines the impact parental income can have upon educational opportunity: **Francis, B and Hutchings, M** (2013) *Parent power? Using money and information to boost children's chances of educational success*. London: Sutton Trust.

Chapter 8

Social class

A C H I E V I N G   A   S O C I A L   W O R K   D E G R E E

This chapter will help you to develop the following capabilities from the **Professional Capabilities Framework:**

- **Professionalism**
  Demonstrate the importance of professional behaviour.
  Describe the importance of personal and professional boundaries.

- **Values and ethics**
  Demonstrate awareness of own personal values and how these can impact on practice.

- **Diversity**
  Recognise the importance of diversity in human identity and experience, and the application of anti-discriminatory and anti-oppressive principles in social work practice.

- **Rights, justice and economic wellbeing**
  Understand the principles of rights, justice and economic wellbeing, and their significance to social work practice.

- **Knowledge**
  Demonstrate an initial understanding of the application of research, theory and knowledge from sociology, social policy, psychology, health and human growth and development to social work.

- **Critical reflection and analysis**
  Understand the role of reflective practice and demonstrate basic skills of reflection.

It will also introduce you to the following standards as set out in the 2008 social work subject benchmark statement:

5.1.1 Social work service, service users and carers.
5.1.2 The service delivery context.
5.1.3 Values and ethics.
5.1.4 Social work theory.
5.1.5 The nature of social work practice.

Introduction

A number of factors have influenced our decision to include a new chapter devoted entirely to social class in the second edition of this textbook. Perhaps of most importance, is our perception that there has been a renewed and sustained attack on sections of the working class, one that we cannot afford to ignore. The attack is multi-pronged – it is simultaneously ideological, political and fiscal. We have witnessed this

assault in social policies that disadvantage service users and other sections of the working class, and we have seen it embedded, subtly and not so subtly, in ideological messages that permeate political debates, the media and popular culture. As we have stated
in previous chapters, social class inequalities are the backdrop against which many service users live their lives and poverty and disadvantage are the *context* for many other
social issues faced. For social workers to ignore this is tantamount to a doctor ignoring the intricacies of the human body. Martin Narey (2014), an adviser to the Coalition
government on social work training, has recently called for social work to re-think the
'politics of social work teaching' in favour of an approach that focuses upon the 'practicalities of the job' rather than upon the effects of an 'unequal society'. However, we
argue vociferously that an understanding of inequality and social class is absolutely fundamental in social work. We are not suggesting, of course, that social workers do not
need to understand the practicalities of the job and develop skills to be able to intervene
in very complex situations. But this must not be at the expense of understanding the
impact of inequality – quite simply, social workers need both. We will pick up the political debates about the politics of social work teaching, with emphasis upon the Narey
report, in the concluding chapter. Here, we will examine ways in which the working class
have become 'demonised' in Britain over recent decades and consider the implications
of this for social work practice. However, we begin with an examination of what social
class is and seek to understand the 'class landscape' in the UK today.

What is social class?

Social class has a significant impact upon all our lives and, importantly, upon the lives
of social work service users. There are vast inequalities in wealth between the richest
and poorest in our society, with Britain ranking among one of the most unequal societies in the western world. Only Portugal and the USA are more unequal than Britain
(Wilkinson and Pickett, 2010; Roberts 2011). In 2014, The Equality Trust reported that
*the richest 100 people have as much wealth as the poorest 30% of all households – or
around 18,900,000 people* (p1). This is a staggering statistic. Moreover, for the past
four decades the gap between the richest and the rest has become progressively wider
(Dorling, 2012). Put simply, the very rich are getting richer at the expense of the rest.
An Oxfam report '*A Tale of two Britains*', published in March 2014, noted that, *the
five richest families in the UK are wealthier than the bottom 20 per cent of the entire
population*. In other words, just five households possessed more wealth than 12.6 million people (Oxfam, 2014, p1). The report shows how families are increasingly reliant
upon food banks and struggling to make ends meet as living costs continue to rise,
while at the same time *the highest earners in the UK have had the biggest tax cuts of
any country in the world* (p1). The scale of inequality has profound effects which we
will consider later in this chapter, not just for the poorest in society, but for all. Such
extremes are possible because we live in a class-divided society.

But what exactly is social class? At its simplest, social class is a grouping of people that
share similar characteristics. Most definitions of class use *occupation* and associated
income as the key defining characteristic. However, as we shall see, class encompasses
so much more than income alone.

ACTIVITY **8.1**

In small groups, try to define what social class is and what aspects of our lives it influences.

What social class are you? How have you come to this judgement?

We are guessing that when you began to think carefully about this, agreeing upon a clear definition of social class was not as easy as you might first have thought. When considering how social class affects our lives, you may have identified factors such as the amount of income or wealth we have; our job and prospects; beliefs and values; voting behaviour, the type of housing we live in and where we live; leisure patterns; experiences of the education system; health and well-being; 'taste'; the way we talk and use language; the amount of power or influence we have; consumption patterns; the people we mix with, and many other aspects. Quite simply, as you will see from this exercise, social class shapes virtually every aspect of our lives. There are both subjective and objective components of social class and people often struggle to define their own class position clearly. For example, you may work in a 'middle-class occupation' and live in a middle-class area of town, but have few savings, enjoy a pint before the match on a Saturday and hold views and beliefs more commonly associated with the working class. Whenever we ask our students to consider which social class they are in, it is always interesting to hear the debate. They usually begin by confidently articulating which class they think they belong to, but as discussions progress they become less certain as they consider the varying components of class identity. Social class is therefore a slippery and complex concept. To what extent, for example, is social class defined by our current role or occupation versus that of our parents? Is social class confirmed by our savings, our mortgage size, where we shop, or our choice of holiday? Or is social class defined by our childhood experiences, where our parents shop, or our political leanings or opinions on certain matters?

Space prevents us from providing a detailed analysis here of the various class schemas that exist (see Roberts, 2011 for a useful summary). It is accurate to say, however, that social class is a contested concept and that there has never been agreement over the precise nature of the class system. Traditionally, three main class groupings have been identified, the upper, middle and working classes, however this is far from straightforward. More recently, the *Great British Class Survey* in 2013 identified seven classes in the UK, not three (Savage et al., 2013). We have detailed these in the box below. This survey differs from its predecessors because rather than trying to differentiate social class according to occupational groups, the sociologists involved, Mike Savage and his colleagues, opted for a more multi-dimensional schema including measures such as *social* and *cultural* capital as well as economic capital. They argued that social class and its associated identities extend *beyond* the income a person has; put simply, *Class used to be about how much you earned ... Now it's about how you spend your money at the weekend* (Wallop, cited in BBC 2013) and whose company you spend it in! Influenced by the work of sociologist Pierre Bourdieu (1984), Savage et al. utilised the concepts of social, cultural and economic capital to locate class positions. They argued that *it is possible to draw fine-grained distinctions between people with different stocks of each of the three capitals, to provide a much more complex model of social class than is currently used* (p223).

- *Social capital* refers to the connections and contacts a person has within their social networks and the advantages or otherwise this may confer upon them.

- *Cultural capital* involves the ability to engage with and appreciate aspects of culture that enable those who have it to do well in the education system and society in general – we will examine this in more detail below.

- Finally, *economic capital* refers to income and accumulated wealth.

When considering social class based upon each of these three forms of capital – economic, social and cultural, it is possible to develop a fuller understanding that incorporates a complex range of factors that shape people's lives and, importantly, that confer different amounts of privilege or disadvantage.

So, the *Great British Class Survey* of 2013 asked 161,000 respondents about a range of factors. As you would expect, this included questions about their income and occupation, the price, nature and location of their properties (owned, mortgaged, rented, etc.), and their savings. However, the survey also asked people about who they knew socially. Respondents were asked if, for example, they socialised with electricians, nurses, university lecturers, cleaners, teachers, lorry drivers, shop assistants and solicitors. They were also asked about leisure activities and hobbies – did they for example go to the opera, listen to jazz, use Facebook or Twitter, go to the gym, do arts and crafts, listen to hip hop or rap, socialise at home, watch sport or go to gigs? Savage et al. distinguished between what they referred to as 'highbrow' culture and 'emerging' culture. Highbrow cultural capital might involve engagement with classical music, visiting stately homes and art galleries, eating at Michelin-starred restaurants and visiting the theatre. Emerging cultural capital on the other hand included playing and watching sport, going to gigs, enjoying rock music or rap and spending time with friends or social networking.

The survey concluded that *seven* discernible social classes existed in Britain today. These can be summarised as follows:

The Great British Class Survey's seven classes

1. *Elite* – Very high economic capital (especially savings), high social capital, very high highbrow cultural capital. *This is the most privileged group in the UK (the mean household income is 89K) and might include those with substantial inherited wealth, as well as those in roles such as chief executives, barristers, judges and financial managers. This group has remarkably high savings and they live in expensive homes. The top location for the elite might be South Buckinghamshire, Surrey and the City of London. This group are very wealthy and are set apart*

from the rest, on the basis of their economic advantage. Individuals in the elite class are likely to have graduated from prestigious universities and have often been to private schools. This group makes up about 6 per cent of the population.

2. **Established middle class** – High economic capital, high status social contacts, high highbrow and emerging cultural capital. *This comfortably off group scores highly on all three measures, but they lack the marked wealth of the elite. Their mean household income is around 47K a year. This group is much larger than the elite and tend to be professionals or managers. The established middle class are also likely to be graduates, who have many strong social connections and are highly culturally engaged, both with 'highbrow' and 'emerging' social culture. This group comprises around 25 per cent of the population.*

3. **Technical middle class** – High economic capital, very high status social contacts, but relatively few contacts reported, moderate cultural capital. *This is a small, distinctive, relatively isolated, quite prosperous group, with good incomes (a mean of £37K a year) and high savings, who live in expensive houses in the South East. However despite their assets, this group score low for social and cultural capital. They have few social contacts, albeit of a relatively high status, and tend to socialise within their own limited social circle. Their cultural capital is also limited and they may be 'culturally apathetic'. Some members of this group (but not all) have been to university and tend to be concentrated around scientifically or technically orientated people who have used their skills to gain reasonably secure and well-rewarded work. This group accounts for around 6 per cent of the population.*

4. **New affluent workers** – Moderately good economic capital, moderately poor mean score of social contacts, though high range, moderate highbrow and emerging cultural capital. *This group (around 15 per cent of the population) are typically young (often male), with medium levels of economic capital – a moderate income (a mean of £29K a year), reasonable house value and a small amount of savings. People in this group had a high number of social contacts of moderate status and are culturally engaged but more with 'emerging' than 'highbrow' culture. Few have been to university (and those that have tend to have attended newer universities) and achieved their roles outside of conventional education systems. People in this group tend to come from working-class backgrounds.*

5. **Traditional working class** – Moderately poor economic capital, though with reasonable house price, few social contacts, low highbrow and emerging cultural capital. *This group score low on all forms of capital, and although they have a moderately low income (mean of £13K a year) and little in the way of savings, they tend to own their own homes. Few have been to university and they tend to be concentrated in occupations that might be considered 'typically working class' (for example, lorry drivers, cleaners, electricians). Their range of social contacts is restricted and they are not culturally engaged, scoring low on both 'highbrow' and 'emerging' culture. This group now comprises around 14 per cent of the population and are at the older end of the age scale.*

(Continued)

(Continued)

6. ***Emergent service workers*** – Moderately poor economic capital, though with reasonable household income, moderate social contacts, high emerging (but low highbrow) cultural capital. *This group are typically young with only a modest income (a mean of £21K a year) and few savings. They are likely to rent. They may not have been to university, however they score highly on emerging cultural capital with high levels of engagement with music, sport and internet activities, though they score less well on highbrow capital. This class also has a significant number of social contacts, though they are moderate in their status scores. Service sector work is common, such as bar work, chefs, call centre workers and other insecure occupations. Those that have been to university tend to have studied the arts and humanities. The group is predominantly urban, and consitutes around 19 per cent of the population. They are labelled 'emergent' to recognise that they are young with high levels of emergent cultural capital. They tend to live in places like Manchester, Liverpool and Brighton.*

7. ***Precariat*** – Poor economic capital, and the lowest scores on every other criterion. *This group, approximately 15 per cent of the population, are the poorest class (with mean incomes of £8K a year). They are unlikely to have savings and usually live in rented accommodation, in old industrial areas such as Stoke-on-Trent or Newcastle-under-Lyme. They may be unemployed or on temporary contracts, concentrated in occupations such as care workers, cleaners and cashiers. This group tend to be relatively isolated with a small range of contacts, who are of low social status. They also score poorly on both emerging and highbrow culture and live insecure, precarious lives.*

Adapted from Savage et al., 2013.

We have only been able to summarise the findings of the Great British Class survey here, but at the end of this chapter we will signpost you to a useful journal article which gives a more detailed consideration of its key findings. It is clear that the seven classes identified above are more nuanced than those in previous schemas, and recognise social and cultural factors which subtly differentiate the groupings that are broader than income alone. Professor Fiona Devine, one of the sociologists involved in the study, points out that there is still a clearly discernible top and bottom of British society, with a very wealthy elite group at the apex and a group of very poor people at the bottom. However, she draws attention as well to the more 'stretched out' middle groups that are perhaps less well defined and more diverse than in the past:

> *There's a much more fuzzy area between the traditional working class and traditional middle class. There's the emergent workers and the new affluent workers who are different groups of people who won't necessarily see themselves as working or middle class.*

(Devine, cited in Jones, 2013)

This lack of a clear demarcation reflects in part a change to the economic and occupational complexion of Britain. Since the 1970s, the decline in Britain's traditional manufacturing industries such as coal mining, fishing, steel and ship building has been significant and although Britain is still engaged in manufacturing, it now accounts for a much smaller number of jobs than it once did (Roberts, 2011). Arguably, the decline of manufacturing signalled the demise of the 'traditional working class', leading to important changes in the constitution of social class in Britain. As the number of manufacturing jobs diminished, so too did traditional communities that had been based around industry. In many mining towns for example, it was normal for successive generations of men of working age to work down the pit. Their shared experiences and those of their wives and families led to a strong sense of common identity, solidarity, mutual reliance and friendship. A strong sense of collectivity with durable ties between its members permeated typical mining communities (Massey, 2012). As the mines closed, however, people began to move away in a bid to find work. This tore apart traditional communities, leaving gaping voids and extreme deprivation in their wake. Many of the ex-mining communities today, for example, are characterised by a range of social problems, such as unemployment and substance misuse (Parker, 2005; Chesshyre, 2010). The long-term impact of the decline in manufacturing therefore, was not purely economic. As communities became more fragmented, traditional identities also became disjointed and life, quite simply, changed forever.

Industrial change inevitably brings in its wake new and different kinds of employment and as manufacturing has declined, Britain has seen a vast growth in the service sector – or jobs that 'service' society. This includes roles such as shop assistants, shelf stockers, cleaners, waitresses, customer service advisers, administrators, fast-food operators, or as Roberts (2011) puts it *anything you can't drop on your foot* (p65). Additionally we have seen a growth in jobs based around technology and information. Many who might once have been employed in manual jobs are now employed in non-manual or white collar roles. The working class then, has changed. It undoubtedly still exists as we have seen, but developments in social and economic life mean that the traditional working class has shrunk in number and new sections of the working class have been created (Savage et al., 2013). Given the changes we have seen, it is no surprise as Devine puts it, that a 'fuzziness' exists between the traditional working and middle classes.

Interestingly, a combination of factors such as economic change, improved living standards for many, greater accessibility of foreign travel and the decline of class-based politics has led to the prevailing belief among some that, as John Prescott mooted in 1997, 'we are all middle class now'. In fact, there may be a reticence among the population to self-identify as 'working class' partly because of the negative connotations the term carries and partly because of the dissonance between the perception that the working class are people who live 'up north' in dowdy terraced houses, work the nightshift in dirty, noisy factories and go to Blackpool for their holidays, and the reality of people's lives. In fact what is happening here, we suggest, is a subjective process of 'self-embourgeoisement' or a subconscious identification with an amorphous 'middle class', which, although it has no real basis in reality, serves to negate any political consciousness relating to the *objective* class position of the people concerned. The fragmentation of the traditional working class poses interesting debates around their relative power as a group and we will turn to this later in this chapter.

ACTIVITY *8.2*

Now we would like you to take the social class test by going to the following link:

www.bbc.co.uk/news/magazine-22000973

Once you have your result, consider how if at all, this differs from the outcome of your discussion in Activity 8.1.

Does it accurately reflect how you see your own social class position?

Hopefully, you will now have an understanding of the different components of social class and begun to think about how the class system in Britain is structured.

Sociology and class analysis

Social class has always been central to the student of sociology. As Roberts (2011, p11) notes, this is because *class matters*; it makes *a difference in most areas of people's lives*. Job opportunities, incomes, educational attainment, leisure opportunities and health status, are just some aspects of our lives that are influenced by our social class backgrounds. Our education chapter vividly illustrated the links between educational attainment and social class. In relation to health, as we show below, numerous social investigations have shown a correlation between social class background and health status. In this sense, social class really is a matter of 'life and death'. Hence, the energy that sociologists devote to defining and analysing class relationships is not motivated simply by a desire to categorise people into identifiable groups. On the contrary, their interest in the class system stems from a desire to understand the social, economic, political and ideological forces that:

- determine people's location in the class structure;
- influence movements within the class structure, and enhance or impede opportunities for social mobility;
- shape the social and economic advantages and disadvantages that are associated with particular class positions;
- influence societal attitudes towards the legitimacy of the existing class structure.

Marx, Weber and class

Many of sociology's founding fathers – Karl Marx and Max Weber, for example – saw 'class' as being crucial in their attempts to understand how society functioned and systems of subordination and opportunity were maintained. *The history of all hith-erto existing society is the history of class struggles*, wrote Marx and Engels (1969, p40). In their classic 1848 *Manifesto of the Communist Party*, they sought to high-light how capitalist production had driven a process whereby society was *more and more splitting into two great hostile camps, two great classes directly fac-ing each other: Bourgeoisie and Proletariat* (p411). As we explained in Chapter 1, Marx devoted his whole life to exposing the mechanisms by which the ruling class (the bourgeoisie) ruthlessly exploited the working class (the proletariat). For Marx, the bourgeoisies' ownership and control of the means of production provided the basis of their 'class power'. This economic power brought them vast riches and privi-leges, but also political power, which they used, equally ruthlessly, to maintain their dominant status as a class. By contrast, the working class were condemned to a life-time of alienation, exploitation and 'wage slavery', and this would remain the case as long as capitalism existed. More recent Marxist analyses of class are, of course, more nuanced, noting the existence of more complex class divisions than the 'two-class' schema, originally identified by Marx. For instance, in the 1980s and 1990s, Erik Olin Wright developed a more complex schema which ultimately identified 12 classes, and acknowledged the relevance of educational qualifications and job characteristics in shaping class status (Roberts, 2011). However, ownership and control of capital remains central to Marxist analyses of class.

'Class' also figures prominently in Max Weber's work, and as with Marx, Weber saw ownership and control over economic resources as being one of the key, central determinants of privilege. In his 1964 book, *Theory of social and economic organisa-tion*, he talked of the *primary significance of a positively privileged economic class*, which is able to use its economic power to pursue its material interests (p427). However, there was a subtle difference between Weber's and Marx's analysis of class. For Weber, social divisions, inequalities and hierarchies were not determined *solely* by property relations – that is, whether people owned or controlled the means of production. Ownership and control was an important source of power for some, but others were able to use other market-based life chances to further their interests and maintain their privileges. Weber developed the concept of 'social closure' to explain how social groups throughout the class structure are able to maintain their economic and social positions – their 'status' – through a variety of exclusionary practices. For instance, Frank Parkin (1979), a neo-Weberian, has drawn attention to the way professional groups are able to use 'credentialism' to maintain their privileged mar-ket status. Their control of strict entry criteria into their professions allows them to monopolise high status occupations, thereby enhancing their economic position. The privileges that they derive from utilising these forms of 'social closure' are not prop-erty based, but they are real, tangible privileges nonetheless. In a similar way, as we show later in this chapter, more affluent parents are able to utilise their market-based privileges – for example, their higher incomes and social and professional ties – to enhance their children's educational opportunities, using their economic and cultural capital to guarantee their children's educational success.

While there are clear differences between Marxist and Weberian analyses of class in capitalist societies, there is, as the Marxist Erik Olin Wright argues, now a good degree of commonality. As he argues, posing *Marx and Weber as polar opposites is a bit misleading*, since both agree that *what people have imposes constraints on what they can do to get what they want*. The sentiments expressed in this final point underpin much of the analysis we adopt in this chapter. Social class, we argue, *really does matter*; while not the sole determinant of life chances, it plays a crucial part in shaping economic and social resources and opportunities.

We now turn to consider in more detail the impact that social class has on our lives, and importantly, upon the lives of social work service users.

Life chances – the impact of social class

The term 'life chances' is used by sociologists to refer to the statistical chance of attaining relative outcomes and successes in life, according to various measures such as income levels, educational success, health outcomes and housing. Life chances are significantly affected by the social class you are born into and, as already intimated, this involves not just matters of life, but also of death. As Roberts (2011) notes:

> There are serious consequences. Compared with children of top professionals, the children of unskilled workers are 50 per cent more likely to die in infancy. As adults, the unskilled group are roughly twice as likely to die before reaching retirement age, and ten times more likely to have no natural teeth. Residents in Britain's most prosperous neighbourhoods can expect to live disability free into their 70's, whereas in Britain's most deprived neighbourhoods disability-free life typically ends when people are in their 50's.

(p1)

Despite the fact that Britain is a welfare state that purports to care for all its citizens from cradle to grave, inequalities in health are not new and are well documented. The Black report (1980), the Acheson report (1998) and Marmott review (2010) all confirmed a clear relationship between mortality, morbidity and social class. The same is true of mental illness, with all forms of psychiatric disorder consistently found to be more common among lower socio-economic groups (Murali and Oyebode, 2004). Hence Wilkinson and Pickett (2010) found consistently higher levels of mental illness among countries with higher levels of inequality. It is not surprising that emotional well-being is so closely linked with economic disadvantage. Stressful living conditions, the impact of poverty upon mood, higher levels of anxiety, family and relationship break-up and related problems mean that poverty can be both a determinant and a consequence of poor mental health (Murali and Oyebode, 2004). Poor quality housing and fuel poverty are also related variables which have been demonstrably linked to both poor mental and physical health (Marmott Review Team, 2011).

In addition to health, life and death, we know that social class impacts directly upon life chances in relation to education, as we discussed in the previous chapter. Here, suffice it to say that children who are recipients of free school meals (an indicator of poverty) are less than half as likely to achieve five good GCSEs including English and maths and are less likely to go to university, stay there and be socially mobile

(Department for Education, 2014). They are also more likely to have special educational needs, been in the care system and attended the lowest performing schools in deprived areas (Perry and Francis, 2010). Children who are born into elite groups are highly likely to stay there, as advantage is perpetuated in every aspect of life. Roberts (2011) identifies that while only 7 per cent of children are educated in Britain's independent (public) schools, they account for around 50 per cent of Oxbridge graduates. It is these same children that go on to gain high ranking and high earning positions – 70 per cent of high court judges for example are privately educated; 68 per cent of barristers are; 62 per cent of Lords and 54 per cent of CEOs (Sutton Trust, 2009), enabling them to pass on advantage to their own children who become the next generation of public school entrants and Oxbridge graduates. Conversely, a study commissioned by Save the Children found that it is possible to predict GSCE results of children who are born poor in Britain by the age of seven. Chief Executive, Justin Forsyth, said:

> Many children starting school … already have the odds stacked against them. These children of the recession, born during the global financial crisis into a world of slow growth, stagnant wages and increasing living costs, where communities are feeling the effects of austerity, need our help more than ever. The cost of failing is a young child without a fair chance in life however hard they try.

(cited in Ramesh, 2013)

In *The spirit level*, Wilkinson and Pickett (2010) compare income inequalities between and within societies, concluding that countries with high levels of income inequality have considerably worse records on virtually *all* economic and social indicators. They provide a compelling analysis of the data, drawing upon a range of variables such as life expectancy, infant mortality, physical and mental health, crime, social mobility, child well-being, high school dropout, drug use, teen pregnancies, maths and literacy scores, homicide, imprisonment, obesity, trust and involvement in the community. Wilkinson and Pickett conclude that the larger the gap in income within any given society, the worse that society will perform on each of these indicators. Moreover, all groups in society – not just those at the very bottom – are affected by the resulting low levels of health and social well-being. So while the biggest impact is upon those at the poorer end of society, even those at the top do less well across all measures. Wilkinson and Pickett note the immense costs of inequality, both individually and for society as a whole. They point to the psycho-social effects of inequality for all members of society, noting the damaging dynamics of *superiority and inferiority*, of being *valued and devalued*. In recognising that inequality is a powerful social divider, they argue that the quality of social relations in unequal societies deteriorates so that *mistrust* in society is high and feelings of security low. The costs of dealing with the fall out of such high levels of inequality are immeasurably high when one considers the public money spent on addressing the associated health and social problems. The argument for working towards a more equal society is compelling. Putting aside material costs, *Greater equality matters because under it more people are treated as being fully human* (Dorling, 2012, p39).

ACTIVITY **8.3**

Reflection point

What does Danny Dorling (2012) mean when he says Greater equality matters because under it more people are treated as being fully human?

Taking Wilkinson and Pickett's (2010) measures of mistrust and insecurity, how might these manifest among members of society?

We hope that you will have thought about the implications of being treated inhumanely and considered how oppressive and brutalising life can be for people who lack power. Additionally, you will hopefully have considered how mistrust can lead to prejudice, an inability to empathise, hostility and in some cases aggression. To some extent these are philosophical debates, however, they are highly relevant to social workers who have at the heart of their profession an ethical commitment to social justice. We have seen how life chances are unequally distributed and it is likely that as social workers you will be working with people whose outcomes in life have been poor because of the social position they occupy. It is therefore imperative that for social workers who are committed to promoting social justice, respecting the dignity of every human being we come across, actively challenging injustice and working with service users to raise self-esteem and access opportunities is at the centre of daily practice.

Social mobility

The class system is not a fixed, legal or religious entity, and it is possible to move up or down the social scale. Inter-generational social mobility is measured by comparing the income and social class of members of society with that of their parents (Deputy Prime Minister's Office, 2013). The Social Mobility and Child Poverty Commission (2013), established by the Coalition, found that although social mobility rose in the middle of the last century, it flat lined towards the end and was in danger of stagnating altogether in the first part of this century. It rather gloomily reported that *only one in eight children from low-income homes goes on to achieve a high income as an adult. The association between incomes of fathers and sons, a key measure of social mobility, is twice as strong in the UK as in Finland, Australia and Canada* (p10). For Wilkinson and Pickett (2010) this is no surprise. They argue that the low level of social mobility in Britain is a direct result of the particularly high levels of inequality found there. Conversely, they note that societies with much lower levels of income inequality such as Denmark, Sweden, Finland and Norway, have much higher levels of social mobility. The Social Mobility and Child Poverty Commission (2013) identified several key factors necessary for improving social mobility. These included addressing child poverty, investing in early years provision and developing high quality childcare, improving schools and closing the gap in attainment, providing high quality careers advice, addressing youth unemployment, tackling income inequality, improving access to higher education and opening up the professions. Space prevents us from addressing all of these factors in detail; however, it is clear that a life cycle approach to enhancing social mobility and achieving more equal outcomes requires sustained commitment and resources.

Perhaps the most significant potential enabler of social mobility is the education system. In the previous chapter on education, we introduced you to the concept of 'meritocracy', or *IQ plus effort = merit*. This is the idea that the education system provides *equality of opportunity* and that achievement is based upon ability or merit rather than upon the social position ascribed at birth. As we suggested, however, equality of opportunity in education is more myth than reality. Children do not begin their educational careers equally at the same starting line. Some children enter the education system from very disadvantaged backgrounds and others come from privileged homes, meaning that children's experiences *within* the education system are far from equal. Nevertheless, education is the mechanism by which social mobility is deemed possible, or as Wilkinson and Pickett (2010, p161) put it, the *main engine of social mobility in modern democracies*. It is perhaps for this reason that more affluent parents – for instance, those categorised as being located in social classes 1–3 in the British Class Survey – are able to exercise a good deal of 'soft power' (Toynbee and Walker, 2011) when it comes to securing their children's educational success. While all parents want the best for their children, more affluent parents are more likely to possess the economic, social and cultural capital needed to secure the school of their choice for their children. This enables them to employ a range of strategies, including moving house to areas where the best schools are, attending church services to secure a place in a coveted church school, paying privately for a tutor to ensure their child passes an entrance exam, or purchasing education privately. Francis and Hutchings (2013) contend that far from enhancing social mobility, the education system tends to replicate inequality and at times exacerbates it. More affluent parents have an advantage at every stage of their child's education by virtue of the fact that they have attended university themselves, gained an understanding of the system, and are able to negotiate their way through it as a result, enabling them to secure consistently good outcomes for their children. They discovered that such parents were able to confidently help their children with school and college work, speak assuredly to teachers, feel their views were valued and influence the school by becoming a governor or joining the Parent–Teachers Association. Furthermore, more affluent parents used their networks or social capital to secure other advantages, such as accessing suitable work experience for their children. Additionally, their high levels of economic capital enabled them to purchase enrichment activities such as drama or music classes after school that broadened experience and importantly furnished children with their own cultural capital to succeed in life. In short, more affluent parents are able to boost their children's chances of success not just because they have the economic means to do so, but also because they possess a knowledge of and a familiarity with the system. Hence, while equality of opportunity exists on paper for all children, in reality it is an illusion, with some parents adept at using their economic, cultural and social capital to reproduce and secure future privilege for their offspring. In this way advantage is perpetuated so that children from more affluent backgrounds do consistently better in the education system than children from lower socio-economic groups:

Middle class and upper class people have the right accents, know how to behave in 'polite society', know that education can enhance their advantages. They pass all of this on to their children, so that they in turn will succeed in school and work, make good marriages, find high-paying jobs etc. This is how elites become established and maintain their elite status.

(Wilkinson and Pickett, 2010, p163)

Deep-rooted elitism at the top of British society has inevitably resulted in limited social mobility and, as we saw earlier, top positions continue to be filled by those born into elite classes.

Wilkinson and Pickett argue that people use *markers of distinction and class, their 'good taste' to maintain their position*, and *discrimination and downward prejudice to prevent others from improving their status* (p164). They note that despite notions of equality of opportunity, 'matters of taste and class' are powerful mechanisms by which some people can exercise superiority and which serve to keep other people in their place, *stopping them from believing they can better their position and sapping their confidence if they try* (p164). Conversely, the purchase of private education for example, promotes confidence and a sense of superiority that serves as a powerful subjective mechanism to enable upward social mobility. Dorling (2012) is scathing of this:

One of the worse effects of private schooling is that it can imbue an unhealthy sense of superiority among those affluent children who have been deprived of the opportunity to mix with others. Often they receive high examination marks, which is hardly surprising, as that is mostly what their parents have paid for ... They think of their private schools as a better education, but if it teaches them to look down on other people, it cannot be.

(Dorling, 2012, p31)

Like it or not, the outcomes of private education and 'purchased superiority' are clear to see as just four private schools and one college continue to see more of their students entering Oxbridge than the combined efforts of 2,000 state schools and colleges (Independent Reviewer on Social Mobility and Child Poverty, 2012). It seems fair to conclude that while Britain is so fundamentally unequal, any attempt at promoting social mobility will only ever achieve marginal and insignificant outcomes.

In addition to institutionalised barriers to social mobility, there are more insidious and pervasive barriers that are more difficult to quantify. Earlier in this chapter, we referred to Bourdieu's concept of *cultural capital* when we were interrogating the differing components of social class. We now return to examine this in more detail, considering how cultural capital can be a powerful means of preserving elitism and advantage. We will then go on to look at the antithesis of cultural capital and consider ways that working-class culture has been constituted as being inherently distasteful and morally worthless.

Cultural capital – the subtle transfer of privilege

The concept of cultural capital first emerged from Pierre Bourdieu in the 1970s and refers to the possession of knowledge of dominant culture, or factors that help individuals succeed in the education system and in society. This includes experiences, knowledge and familiarity with the dominant culture and the ability to 'handle oneself' in company by being able to converse fluently about the arts, literature, music and travel. Cultural capital is transmitted by fluent use of language and other social skills and is closely associated with social class. For Bourdieu, cultural capital is passed on in middle and upper class homes via the socialisation process and is directly related to success in the education system. This, he suggests, is because the education system is based almost entirely upon dominant mainstream culture and children who possess cultural capital are well versed in knowing the 'code' to be able to crack the peculiarities of both formal and informal structures, as well as the pervading culture of the system. Recently, we attended a university open day with our son who hopes to study politics at university next year. The university in question had invited existing students along to talk to prospective students and it was clear that those chosen were rich in cultural capital – they were able to talk fluently, with confidence, to a room full of parents and students about the course, the attractions of university life, about literature and societies external to the course, about their travels internationally, their dissertations, and their hopes and dreams for the future. The students were well spoken, articulate and had clearly enjoyed many privileges throughout their lives. As the day progressed we were not surprised to hear that many had been to private boarding school, had travelled widely and were conversant with highbrow culture. These students were clearly comfortable in their environment, well able to converse intellectually with their university lecturers and peers. Bourdieu's view was that students like this are much more comfortable in the education system because of the cultural capital they take with them when they enter. By contrast, working-class children lack cultural capital and therefore are likely to feel 'out of place' or lacking in some way. He suggests that such students may go to great lengths to try and disguise this.

ACTIVITY *8.4*

In small groups, come up with a list of examples of how middle-class parents are able to pass on cultural capital to their offspring. You may have some examples from your own lives, or if you come from a more working-class background, think about some examples that children growing up around you may have had.

Can you think of any instances where the possession of cultural capital would have been useful? Or, can you think of examples of where others have demonstrated their cultural capital?

You may have mentioned examples in childhood of trips to the opera or theatre, having piano lessons, classical music being played and discussed routinely in the home, educational leisure events, trips to museums or National Trust properties and holidays in settings that broaden horizons and experiences. One of our colleagues talks about how her parents insisted upon her pursuing piano lessons to Grade 6 so that she had something to write about on her UCAS personal statement! We have a memory of taking our son to the opera at Verona in a beautiful Roman amphitheatre when he was 12, only for him to proclaim at the interval that he would rather sit through a month of triple maths than experience another half of Madame Butterfly!

The possession of cultural capital is key to the social class system because it can contribute to the acquisition of both economic and social capital, acting as a kind of *passport* to circles of privilege. Making one's cultural capital known can be advantageous, because it bestows status and is likely to lead to acceptance and recognition. Individuals who are deficient in cultural capital, on the other hand, may be excluded or socially ignored. The process of exclusion may be enforced via social closure as the privileged tighten the invisible border controls around their social class. Alternatively, individuals without cultural capital may exclude themselves, by dropping out of their university course or opting out of social circles, because they feel out of place or 'lacking'. Members of the middle and upper classes learn to demonstrate and express their social superiority and 'good taste' in the way they converse, move and present themselves, all of which serves them well.

The concept of 'taste' has become interesting to sociologists because of the social processes involved in deciding what 'good taste' is. The social construction of taste is perhaps best illustrated by a recent example involving actress Danniella Westbrook and the Burberry fashion brand. Westbrook had been castigated by the media as being a 'celebrity chav' – someone who was 'rough around the edges' who had achieved success, but whom had reverted to type when her cocaine habit was exposed and she subsequently had to have her nose rebuilt by plastic surgery. Westbrook was regularly castigated in the media and regarded as lacking in taste. Burberry, branding itself on its website as *a luxury brand with a distinctive British sensibility*, was traditionally associated with middle and upper classes who wore its iconic chequered brand as a mark of good taste and money. Interestingly the brand suffered immensely when Danniella was snapped by the British paparazzi decked out in Burberry, symbolising a ruinous collision of taste:

> *Unfortunately, Burberry became too ubiquitous for comfort, and soon the distinctive house check was adopted as a badge of honour for the newly emerging chav generation. The day that former soap star Danniella Westbrook and her daughter stepped out head to toe in Burberry sounded the death knell for the company's credibility. It had to change, and it had to change fast.*

(Jones, 2008)

Understanding the concept of cultural capital is important when learning about social class as it enables us to understand the more subtle ways that people can be excluded and ways in which privilege can be perpetuated and maintained. In the next section, we move on to look further at the concept of 'taste', particularly where it is applied to the working class and consider ways in which the working class have become systematically demonised in Britain. While this is not a new phenomenon, recent attacks have been particularly vicious and it is important that social workers stop and take stock of this.

The demonisation of the working class

As we suggested in the introduction to this chapter, we have recently witnessed a renewed and sustained attack against sections of the working class and, in particular, against those whose lives are blighted by poverty. This has developed into a kind of 'classist prejudice', whereby stereotyped labels and sweeping generalisations against the poorest in our society have become commonplace, in the media, in society in general and in popular culture.

As Clarke (2013, p325) contends, *images of violent, intoxicated young men in hooded tops loitering in groups at street corners and irresponsible single mothers in tracksuits watching soap operas all day in council flats provide a simple, fictive explanation for inequality, that [simultaneously] enables its extension*. Social workers, as we have commented before, do not live in a vacuum. They are not immune to the powerful messages about 'chavs', 'welfare scroungers', and people on benefits. Social workers too will tune into programmes such as *Benefits Street* that has recently been on Channel 4 and see the pejorative populist headlines on tabloid billboards as they pass. Social workers will also watch television programmes that depict stereotypical images of the working class, such as *Little Britain* and its portrayal of Vicky Pollard, and the characters of Wayne and Waynetta Slob in *Harry Enfield and Chums*. However, social workers and social work students must be able to critically reflect upon what they see and not be seduced by such pervasive messages. One of our first year students said to us recently that before she studied the social justice module at university on her social work degree, she had believed everything she read in the *Daily Mail* and held unspoken values that were very negative towards people on benefits. She went on to say that the module had challenged her views and that she was now able to see things differently. This very honest, thoughtful and intelligent student recognised that if she had not been prepared to challenge her own 'common sense' thinking, she could potentially have entered the social work profession with those views and made decisions about people's lives grounded upon harsh judgements – which blamed service users for their lives and homes *not being like her own*. She was able to recognise the dangers of unknowingly applying caricatured stereotypes to an entire social class of people based upon the extreme or the comedic, and the risk of judging them all as being similar to now infamous people like Mick Philpott and Karen Matthews, or characters such as Wayne and Waynetta Slob or Vicky Pollard. Given the disdain that underpins clichéd views of the working class, there is a real danger that service users could potentially become figures of ridicule in social work teams, configured as a breed of feckless, lazy, inadequate, incapable, dangerous, harmful parents who engage in extreme acts like burning down their own house and killing their children to avenge a former partner, or faking their own daughter's abduction to gain publicity and financial gain.

Whilst the demonisation of the working class is not new (see our discussion below), what is significant for us to understand and reflect upon, is its renewed acceleration in recent years. It is worth pausing for a few minutes to think about how popular culture has contributed to this.

ACTIVITY **8.5**

For this activity you may wish to dig out your Christmas DVDs or access YouTube and watch a few clips of Vicky Pollard in Little Britain *and Wayne and Waynetta Slob in* Harry Enfield and Chums.

Additionally, if you have not done so already, try and access a few episodes of Benefits Street *that was shown on Channel 4 in January 2014.*

Either alone or in small groups, think about the subtle and not so subtle messages contained in these popular TV sketches and documentaries.

You will probably have identified common themes such as the comedy characters being portrayed as being vulgar in their clothing, their mannerisms and their approach to life. Wayne and Waynetta Slob first appeared on our TV screens in the 1990s on the popular comedy sketch show *Harry Enfield and Chums*. Viewers were treated to a series of sketches portraying Wayne and Waynetta Slob as two filthy, smelly, greasy haired, overweight, chain smoking characters who lived together in a dirty and chaotic house together with their children. They were presented as being crude, lacking in intelligence and importantly, lacking in *taste* and moral decency. In one sketch Waynetta, in her customary dirty purple velour tracksuit, tells Wayne that she thinks they should split up because it is 'unnatural' being together after ten years. She goes on to bemoan that she's the *only mum on the estate with a live-in partner. Other mums on the estate look at me like I'm a bit of a tit ... I'm 26 years old Wayne, I'm not getting any younger – I should be a single mother by now ... It's embarrassing for the kids, they get teased by the others, 'you've got a daddy, you've got a daddy'*. Later in the same sketch, Waynetta laments the lack of a 'brown baby' like all the other mums on the estate. She informs Wayne that it was time he had lots of different kids by now by lots of different women who he does not see (BBC, 1994). The sketch is loaded with exaggerated stereotypes portrayed in a deliberately simplistic way that pokes fun at the lifestyles of an entire social class. It is also fairly typical of its genre. Through comedy and other forms of popular culture, ridiculing and castigating disadvantaged people becomes institutionalised as being 'ok'. It is broadcast in the living rooms of the nation and everyone laughs together at the grotesqueness of the 'tardy' lifestyle and morals of working-class families. As ever, popular culture is a powerful means of transmitting subtle messages about different groups in society. The message is clear – people like *that* (as opposed to people like *us*) inhabit a different culture to that of the decent major-ity. They subscribe to inferior values, make lifestyle choices that disregard common decency and are beneath the rest of us.

Those of you who watched *Benefits Street* recently will have identified similar themes with one crucial difference – that is, that the 'characters' on this were in fact real peo-ple living in poverty in an area of Birmingham. There has been a barrage of criticism levelled at the producers of this programme, not least because the participants were misled into believing that they were taking part in a documentary about community spirit. One of the women in the programme, known as 'White Dee' expressed her dis-belief when she saw what was to be aired to a *Guardian* journalist:

> We couldn't believe what we were watching. We went mad. People growing drugs, smoking drugs, shoplifting. That is not what our street is about. Half the people they showed don't even live in our street. We knew from that second that we were well and truly screwed over by them.

> (cited in Aitkenhead, 2014)

In fact the programme makers had one aim, and that was to reveal the extremities of the lives of benefit claimants to an eager watching public. In the manner of typi-cal tabloid journalism, devoid of any grounded ethical conscience, the programme presented a partial and distorted view of daily life on benefits, portraying the extreme and exceptional as being normal and typical, fuelling existing resentment to those in receipt of welfare. The reaction on social media was predictably depressing, with numerous disrespectful comments being made, such as the ones below that appeared on the Facebook newsfeed:

> Their situations are real ... Their crap parenting and poor behaviour choices and crap all over their houses is real ... You don't have to be rich to have some self-respect, send your kids to nursery so they can speak properly and tidy up!

> Thick people moaning about having no money ... Yet they all smoke. Get a flippin job!!

> It gets better ... The muppet is a father of two yet he's spending his day down by the canal practising his skids on his bike ... No wonder his kids are on the at-risk register.

> They are all as bad as each other, they make me sick. What losers!

Whether through comedy portrayal, documentaries or newspaper reporting, exam-ples like those considered here clearly demonstrate the media's power to shape pub-lic opinion. The 'othering' of welfare recipients – the process by which certain groups are constructed as being somehow distinct and different to the mainstream popu-lation, to the 'rest of us' – is not new. It reinforces the perception that significant sections of the working class engage in behaviour that is an offence to decency and threatens the moral fabric of society, living on taxpayers' money and openly flouting the norms and values of society.

From residuum to 'troubled families': the social construction of a 'deviant' section of the population.

Attempts to scapegoat and stigmatise sections of the poor, in order to blame them for their plight and to justify the introduction of coercive, stringent welfare policies, are not particularly novel. As Macnicol (1987, p296) argues, The concept of an intergenerational underclass displaying a high concentration of social problems – remaining outwith the boundaries of citizenship, alienated from cultural norms and stubbornly impervious to the normal incentives of the market, social work intervention or state welfare – has been reconstructed periodically over at least the past one hundred years. *The 'label' attached to this 'deviant' section of the poor may have changed, but there are striking continuities in the terminology and imagery that has been used. In the late nineteenth and early twentieth centuries, for example, social commentators condemned the 'degenerate', 'intergenerational', 'fecklessness' of what they referred to as the 'residuum'. Needless to say, this 'demonisation' was based upon a mixture of misconceptions, myths and downright lies, but it nonetheless maintained a pervasive grip on policy and practice. State social policy and embryonic social work, in the form of the COS, enthusiastically and uncritically embraced this conception of the poor, using it as justification for forms of policy and practice that were geared towards disciplining and re-moralising, rather than helping to alleviate the structural causes of the difficulties many faced (Cunningham and Cunningham, 2012). It was notable that the so-called 'residuum' disappeared during the First World War, when opportunities to work or contribute to the war effort were provided to all citizens. As Stedman Jones argues,* the residuum never existed, except as phantom army called up by late Victorian and Edwardian social science to legitimise its practice *(cited in Welshman, 2013, p17).*

However, with the return of mass unemployment after 1918 we saw a resurgence of attempts to conceptualise the poor as 'depraved', 'idle' and 'morally deficient'. The 'residuum' became the 'social problem group'. The label may have changed, but the 'social problem group' were said to share the same behavioural and psychological flaws possessed by their predecessors. In reality, the claims that were made had no empirical, sociological basis. It was as obvious to contemporaries then as it is to economic and social historians today that the unemployment, poverty and chronic ill-health experienced by large sections of the population were due to structural factors that were beyond their control. However, as is often the case today, conservative commentators, academics and politicians alleged that 'welfare' was encouraging 'deviancy' among the 'social problem group', including unemployment, criminality and alcoholism. This welfare-influenced 'dysfunctionality' was the target of stringent social policy interventions, such as the household means test and the genuinely seeking work test, as well as social work interventions that were aimed at 'reforming' the poor. Worse still, a genetic, hereditary causation was also attached to the behaviour of the 'social problem group', and calls were made for this class of 'degenerates' to be gradually eliminated through a process of compulsory sterilisation of the 'unfit'. Indeed, for a time, eugenic explanations for social problems attracted sizeable and influential support, again despite having no evidential basis (Searle, 1979).

Conservative commentators, in particular, found the suggestion that unemployment and poverty were the result of hereditary defects rather than economic and social ones very appealing, mainly because it pointed towards 'solutions' that left the existing unequal distribution of wealth and privilege unchanged (Macnicol, 1987). Ultimately, Hitler's embrace of eugenics to justify systematic torture, murder and genocide discredited genetic interpretations for social problems in the UK. However, the spectre of the 'social problem group' continued to haunt the political classes throughout the inter-war years, reinforcing and justifying policy and practice responses that blamed vulnerable individuals and families for their difficulties. Of course, as with the 'residuum', the so-called 'social problem group' miraculously disappeared soon after the outbreak of the Second World War when, once again, opportunities were provided for citizens to either work or contribute to the war effort in other ways.

One might have imagined that the speed with which the 'social problem group' melted away between 1939–45 would have finally laid to rest the notion that there existed an 'unemployable', 'helpless', 'lumpen' mass of people, unwilling to, or incapable of acting responsibly. However, in the 1950s, the 'social problem group' was reconceptualised into the guise of the 'problem family' (Cunningham and Cunningham, 2012). In the 1980s, it became the 'underclass' (see our poverty chapter) and more recently it has transformed into the 'troubled family' (which we examined in the social exclusion chapter). Like the BBC's fictional Time Lord, Dr Who, negative conceptions of the poor have shown a remarkable capacity to regenerate, re-emerging in a different guise, but always returning to fight the same old 'alien hordes'! However, as we have shown elsewhere in this text, the 'demons' invoked by proponents of pathological interpretations of social and economic ills have no more basis in reality than Dr Who's fictional adversaries, the Daleks and Cybermen. The existence of a sizeable, 'residuum' of the population, which can be defined according to its alleged inter-generationally transmitted, welfare-induced deviant patterns of behaviour is, as Welshman (2013) argues, a conceptually flawed, carefully assembled, ideological construct. It is largely a myth, albeit one with a long and undistinguished pedigree, *which has historically been propagated by* those who wish to constrain the redistributive potential of state welfare (Macnicol, 1987, p316). That is, of course, not to deny the importance of this ideological construct in shaping and reinforcing negative attitudes towards the poor. Indeed, new technologies, more sophisticated, subtle methods of media communication, and the emergence of sensationalist popular culture, mean that the virulence, ferocity and intensity of the 'message' it seeks to disseminate is perhaps unprecedented.

This process of categorising an 'undeserving' section of the population is powerful because it seeks to make what is first and foremost an economic divide into a social and psychological schism so great and so divisive that it is virtually unassailable. The social commentator Owen Jones has been a passionate opponent of the right-wing media and politicians that have sought to demonise the working class. Recently, in the face of accelerated attacks on welfare recipients, Jones has found himself at the forefront of attempts to counter the backlash that has occurred, following the widespread media and political publicity given to several high profile cases.

In 2012 the Philpott case generated a great deal of media attention when six children died in a house fire in Derby. It soon transpired that, far from being a tragic accident, the children's father, Mick Philpott, had deliberately started the fire in an ill-conceived attempt to frame his ex-partner with whom he was embroiled in a custody battle. Philpott had already courted controversy by appearing on *The Jeremy Kyle show* in 2007 to talk about his life on benefits with two live-in-lovers and 15 children. This was quickly followed by an appearance on a TV documentary *Ann Widdecombe Versus The Benefit Culture*, where it was revealed that Philpott was in receipt of thousands of pounds each year in benefits, with his children being described as 'meal tickets'. The deaths of six children in a house fire was distressing on many different levels but when it was revealed how and why the children died, the tragedy became even more unimaginable. The reporting of the case was sociologically interesting. Not surprisingly, certain sections of the media seized on the opportunity to present Philpott's children as victims of a 'reckless' and 'wasteful' welfare state and their tragic deaths quickly became conflated with the family being recipients of benefits – the tragedy came to be seen as a direct product of 'welfare Britain'. As might be expected, the *Daily Mail* led the attack with headlines such as:

> **Michael Philpott is a perfect parable for our age: His story shows the pervasiveness of evil born out of welfare dependency** – *Daily Mail*, 2 April 2013

> **Vile product of Welfare UK: Man who bred 17 babies by five women to milk benefits system is guilty of killing six of them** – *Daily Mail*, 3 April 2013

Interestingly, the case made by the *Daily Mail* was supported by the Chancellor George Osborne who, on a visit to Derby, reinforced the link between the deaths of six children and the welfare state, saying that the case posed questions about the influence of benefits on people's behaviour. He told the BBC:

> *Mick Philpott is responsible for these crimes that have shocked the nation. The courts are responsible for sentencing, but I think there is a question for government and for society about the welfare state and the taxpayers who pay for the welfare state, subsidising lifestyles like that. I think that debate needs to be had.*

> (cited in Tapsfield, 2013)

Osborne's comments were backed by the Prime Minister David Cameron, who added that although Philpott was responsible for his crimes, that we should ask some wider questions about the welfare system and related lifestyle choices. While welcomed by the right-wing press, these comments provoked a furious backlash from critics angry at the potential political point scoring from ministers and their attempts to link the deaths of six children to the receipt of welfare. Writing in the *Independent*, Owen Jones (2013) cautioned: *The truth is that the Philpotts say nothing about anyone, except for themselves, just as the serial murderer GP Harold Shipman said nothing about middle-class professionals. There are, and have always been, a small minority of individuals capable of breathtaking cruelty. The Philpott case relates in no way to people on benefits in this country.* Even some readers of the *Daily Mail*, a group who are presumably desensitised to the toxicity of the paper's anti-welfare stance, expressed their anger. Nissim (2013) cites the following readers' comments:

'Regardless of the parent's behaviour, it is morally repugnant to use the deaths of those poor children to make a political point. Anyone jumping on this bandwagon should be ashamed', wrote one reader.

'Irresponsible and inflammatory sensationalist headlines', wrote another. 'To assume that this evil act is a product of a broken welfare state is deeply offensive to people who, through no fault of their own, rely upon the state for their survival'.

The Philpott case is a classic example of how the extreme and the repugnant are used to contribute to an increasingly powerful and pervasive case that purports to show how welfare benefits damage the moral fabric of society. The Philpott case sparked a particularly explicit attack, but the Shannon Matthews case in 2008 was perhaps more subtle. Shannon was the nine-year-old girl from Dewsbury Moor who was kidnapped and drugged by her mother and an accomplice in a misguided attempt to benefit financially from the publicity and claim reward money offered for her disappearance. In much the same way that the Philpott case linked the behaviour of Mick Philpott with so called 'Benefits Britain', the same was true in much of the reporting around the Shannon Matthews case:

> The case of Karen Matthews, convicted of kidnapping her own daughter in order to claim a reward, has again pulled back the curtain to allow us a glimpse of this netherworld of taxpayer-funded fecklessness.
>
> Matthews did not live in poverty, though she did not have much money. She drank heavily, smoked 60 cigarettes a day and received benefit payments of almost £300 a week, which went up every time she had another child.
>
> A report by social services said she was unable to put the interests of her children above her own. This is real impoverishment – not a meaningless income target set by the Government, but the creation of perverse incentives for people to spend an entire lifetime wedded to a belief that the rest of society will continue to subsidise their idleness.

(*Telegraph*, 2008)

In his book *Chavs: The demonization of the working class*, Jones sets out a persuasive case for demonstrating how poor people in Britain have been demonised, via the creation of the identity 'chav'. Jones (2011) devotes his first chapter to '*The strange case of Shannon Matthews*' and notes how attention was paid to Karen Matthews' looks and lifestyle even before it was known that she was behind her daughter's disappearance. Jones compares this with the attention paid to the Madeleine McCann case, contrasting the well-groomed, photogenic, medical professionals with the dour, greasy-haired, chain smoking mother of Shannon, as well as the backdrop of the upmarket white-washed Praia da Luz resort, compared to the Northern, impoverished, council estate in Dewsbury. Importantly, Jones notes how the stark social class differences came to define each case. In relation to Shannon Matthews, there was an intense focus upon how many children Karen Matthews had by different fathers, how many benefits were claimed, the state of the house, and the lifestyle not just of Karen

Matthews and her partner Craig Meehan (who incidentally was in full-time employment) but also of the other residents of Dewsbury Moor. When the truth about the case was discovered, Jones argues that the media relentlessly pursued their campaign of class hatred and prejudice that would have generated outrage if the same had been true of other marginalised groups: *It was as though everyone in the country from a similar background was crammed into the dock alongside her* (p20). Jones cites numerous examples of media hatred, penned by journalists who themselves had come from well-to-do middle-class backgrounds. But the Shannon Matthews case exemplified a growing and prolific trend in using the media to construct and reinforce the 'chav' caricature. The purpose of this is clear, says Jones:

> Demonising the less well-off makes it easier to justify an unprecedented and growing level of social inequality. After all, to admit that some people are poorer than others because of the social justice inherent in our society would require government action. Claiming that people are largely responsible for their circumstances facilitates the opposite conclusion.

(p37)

ACTIVITY 8.6

The social construction of the 'Chav'

If you have not done so already, we strongly recommend that you read Chapter 1 of Owen Jones' book Chavs *(and if possible, at some stage, the whole book).*

In small groups with other students, discuss the following:

- *What media representation do you remember from Madeleine McCann and Shannon Matthews's disappearance? What social class stereotypes do these media images play into?*
- *To what extent do you think there is a negative image of some sections of the working-class people sometimes referred to as 'Chavs' or as the 'underclass'? Reflect upon why it is important for social workers to be mindful of stereotypical messages.*
- *Using your sociological knowledge, how would Marxists explain the 'demonisation of the working class'?*

As we have seen, the process of caricaturing and ridiculing people who live their lives in poverty exaggerates and focuses upon their failings to such an extent that attention is shifted away from the economic circumstances that create and maintain poverty within what is a highly unequal society. The 'othering' process is influential because it serves to separate out 'chavs' and other similarly scapegoated disadvantaged groups from the rest of 'decent' society, suggesting that other than a dangerous residuum at the bottom of society, 'we are all middle class now'. For Marxists, this process of systematic division and fragmentation of the working class serves the purpose of weakening collective bargaining power, rendering the working class powerless and ultimately maintaining an unequal system. It also conveniently diverts the attention of citizens away from the real causes of economic and social problems, including the recent global economic crisis (Jones, 2012). However, it is not only Marxists who have expressed concern at the 'demonisation' of the working class. The Fabian Society has also called for class discrimination to be taken seriously, in the same way that other forms of discrimination are, and call for the word 'chav' to be banned. It suggests that *it is deeply offensive to a largely voiceless group and – especially when used in normal middle-class conversation or on national TV – it betrays a deep and revealing level of class hatred* (Hampson and Olchawski, 2008).

The policy attack on the working class

Following the election of the Coalition we saw the introduction of an unparalleled programme of welfare reforms, designed to reduce the support available to individuals and families. As Toynbee and Walker (2012, p47) argue, the resulting cuts to the budgets of 'poor' households were *without historical or international precedence*. In part, ministers sought to justify its reforms with reference to the perilous state of the country's finances and the need to make 'prudent' cuts. However, as we explain below, powerful moral and ideological justifications were also advanced to support these measures. Appealing to the longstanding prejudices against welfare recipients that we have just described, ministers presented their welfare programme as an attempt to clamp down on welfare-induced 'fecklessness' and 'irresponsibility'. We discuss one of the Coalition government's more controversial welfare reforms below, the bedroom tax.

The bedroom tax

The spare room subsidy, or bedroom tax, allows the government to reduce Housing Benefit for social housing tenants of working age who have more bedrooms than they are deemed to require. The reduction rates are 14 per cent of eligible rent for 'under-occupying' one bedroom and 25 per cent for two or more bedrooms. In terms of the bedroom tax's rationale, the government claimed it would 'nudge' tenants in 'unnecessarily' large housing to move into smaller accommodation, freeing up bigger properties for those who genuinely need them. It was also intended to stimulate those who wished to remain in 'over-size' homes to enter work, or increase the hours they work, generating funds themselves that they need to pay for their 'unnecessarily' large accommodation, rather than relying on the taxpayer. *For too long*, Ian Duncan Smith (2014) argued, *we have been content to subsidise people on housing benefit living in homes in the UK which had a million spare bedrooms*. 'Fairness' was also cited as a reason for the reform. It simply was not 'fair', Duncan Smith argued, that Housing Benefit recipients with spare bedrooms should be *taking money from taxpayers*, many of whom themselves were facing housing difficulties. The bedroom tax would initiate *striking cultural change ... ending the something for nothing entitlement and returning fairness to the system*. Hence, we saw an attempt to reinforce a distinction and division between 'shirkers' and 'strivers'. In this sense, like other Coalition welfare reforms, the bedroom tax was also ideologically driven, designed to restore independence and self-sufficiency among welfare recipients.

Indeed, David Cameron claimed that it was part of the Coalition's *moral mission* to bring *new hope and responsibility* to those *trapped in a cycle of dependency.* It was *about giving new purpose, new opportunity, new hope – and yes, new responsibility to people who had previously been written off with no chance* (Bingham and Dominiczak, 2014, p1).

Perhaps not surprisingly, there is little evidence to suggest that the bedroom tax has infused those households affected with a sense of *hope* and *opportunity*. In fact, it has caused considerable hardship for countless individuals and families. Many find themselves stuck 'between a rock and a hard place', punished for having a spare bedroom, but unable to move because smaller houses are not available. In its evidence to a House of Work and Pensions Committee (2014) Inquiry into the Coalition's welfare reforms, the West London Housing Partnership pointed out that, because of the unavailability of smaller properties, only 234 of its 4000 households affected by the bedroom tax had been able to downsize. As they argued, *the majority will be stuck for many years being penalised for something they cannot swiftly change* (p24). The Work and Pensions Committee received a wealth of evidence from other social housing providers, drawing attention to the perversity of punishing poor, powerless, vulnerable households, for circumstances over which they had no control.

Indeed, it is perhaps ironic that a measure which was justified on the grounds of 'fairness' seems to have hit the most vulnerable the hardest. For instance, estimates suggest that between 60–70 per cent of affected households in England and 80 per cent in Scotland contain somebody with a disability (Work and Pensions Committee, 2014). Unsurprisingly, organisations representing disabled people expressed incredulity at the inflexibility and harshness of the regulations. For example, carers providing care for their disabled partners are not exempt from the bedroom tax, meaning that they are forced to share a room with their partners, even in instances where their partner's condition, or the equipment they need, will mitigate against this. Those who 'choose' to remain in their 'oversize' homes have their Housing Benefit reduced accordingly, causing considerable hardship. Carers UK (2013) estimated that 75 per cent of affected households that it represents had, as a result of the reductions in benefits, cut back on heating and food, and many others had accrued debt and rent arrears. *Not only is this illogical,* it argued, *but it is causing huge distress amongst families who are often already struggling with the mental and physical pressures of caring, ill-health and disability.*

Disabled people living in accommodation that has (at some cost), been adapted to meet their specific needs are not exempted from the bedroom tax either. Indeed, more than 100,000 such disabled households are now faced with the dilemma of being forced to either pay the bedroom tax, or move to accommodation which may not be suitable. One housing association giving evidence to the Work and Pensions Committee pointed out that many of its disabled tenants who were *willing and able to move might still be compelled to wait up to 10 years for a suitably accessible property, meaning affected tenants could be forced into a situation where they would need to fund the extra housing costs themselves for up to 10 years* (p26). In its evidence, the National Housing Federation (2013) drew attention to the quandary many disabled households now face. *Many*, it pointed out, *will have to choose between making up the shortfall in their rent which would reduce their weekly household budget, and moving to a less suitable property which would put limitations on going about their daily lives.* Arguably, this is not only dehumanising, but is also discriminatory and oppressive.

Nor is there any evidence to suggest that the bedroom tax has achieved the government's intended objectives – a shift to smaller accommodation; cuts in public expenditure, and greater levels of 'responsibilisation'. On the question of 'downsizing', we now know that the Coalition was well aware of the shortage of smaller homes and the problems that this would cause prior to the bedroom tax's implementation (Department for Work and Pensions, 2012a). It pressed ahead with the bedroom tax regardless, in the full knowledge that relocation was not an option for the majority of affected households. Regarding costs, evidence given to the Work and Pensions Committee suggested that the additional costs accrued due to the 'fallout' surrounding the bedroom tax – as a result, for instance, of rent arrears, increases in homelessness, funding debt advice and support, or having to fit new aids and adaptions to the new homes of disabled people forced to move – may well outweigh the savings. There are of course additional psychological and emotional costs to many individuals and families. The conclusions of the Work and Pensions Committee's Inquiry into the Coalition's reforms were damning, describing the bedroom tax as a *blunt instrument* that needed to be reformed:

> *In many areas there is insufficient smaller social housing stock to which affected tenants can move, meaning that they remain in housing deemed to be too large and pay the SSSC [bedroom tax]. This is likely to be causing financial hardship to a significant number of households … Where a household is under-occupying but there is no suitable, reasonable alternative available, the … reduction in benefit should not be applied.*

> (p24)

The bedroom tax even attracted the approbation of the United Nations (2013). Its special rapporteur for housing, Raquel Rolnik, a Brazilian, undertook an inquiry into the UK's compliance with international human rights standards on adequate housing between August and September 2013. Her views on the bedroom tax mirrored those of the Work and Pensions Committee:

> *In the face of hard choices, between food, heating or paying the rent, many testimonies to the Special Rapporteur placed a strong value on staying in and saving a home. Some mothers in their 50s talked about their homes as the place they had raised their children and lived their lives. Many felt targeted and forced to give up their neighbourhoods, their careers and their safety net. While in principle the policy does not force people to move, the reality of people's experience, many of whom are working people with no income to spare, left no doubt in the Special Rapporteur's mind that many have no other option, which has left them in tremendous despair.*

> (p13)

In her conclusions and recommendations, she stated that, *the removal of the spare-room subsidy should be suspended immediately and be fully re-evaluated in light of the evidence of its negative impacts on the right to adequate housing and general well-being of many vulnerable individuals and households* (United Nations, 2013, p20).

Predictably, ministers responded by rejecting all criticisms of the bedroom tax. For example, Iain Duncan Smith described the United Nation's special rapporteur's conclusions as *utterly ridiculous*, while the Coalition's Housing Minister, Kris Hopkins, dismissed her report as a piece of *misleading Marxist diatribe*. As might be expected, the right-wing tabloid press duly entered the fray on the side of ministers. *How dare this idiot preach at Britain on human rights*, railed Leo McKinstry (2014) in the *Express*. Meanwhile, the *Mail Online* followed the lead of its print equivalent in describing Rolnik as a 'Brazil nut', placing a particularly unflattering picture of her alongside a portrait of Karl Marx (Chapman, 2014). As Toynbee and Walker argue, this kind of response – from ministers and the press – should be seen for what it really is; a concerted ideological campaign, led by leading Coalition politicians and their allies in the right-wing media, to undermine support for welfare. The 'feckless poor' (and those that support them) have constituted the convenient 'folk devils', providing the ideological justification for this assault. However, for those such as Jones (2012), the true objective of this neo-liberal 'project' is far more ambitious than its stated desire to simply punish the welfare-induced 'irresponsibility' of a minority. On the contrary, the ideological onslaught against the poor has provided the 'cloak', or 'ideological smokescreen', that has disguised what, in reality, is an attempt to engineer a much more fundamental reversal of the post-war welfare settlement. As Jones (2012) argues, *taking away support from the disabled, the unemployed and the working poor is not straightforward* and *can only be achieved by a campaign of demonization*. The success of this project can perhaps be gauged by the support for Coalition's bedroom tax, which, like many of the Coalition's social security reforms, goes well beyond punishing the so-called 'undeserving'. On the contrary, these reforms constitute part of a much broader project of 'responsibilisation', one that has implications for *all* welfare recipients, including those who have hitherto been considered 'deserving' of help and support.

Class and social work: some conclusions

In this chapter, we have sought to demonstrate that an understanding of social class is a central concern of social work. We have identified reasons why social class is so critical by considering the impact of differential life chances. We have also outlined how the working class has become progressively demonised socially, culturally and economically. Strier et al. (2012, p407) argue that *social class is an unavoidable variable for understanding the interaction between social workers and clients* because of two inter-related variables. First, the profession's ethical commitment to addressing inequalities and injustices in society is crucial. Second, social work professionals are, by definition, middle class and therefore this is something they must be cognisant of when working with service users. Strier et al. acknowledge that social class is a complex concept and one that is intertwined with oppression; they identify class prejudice as 'classism' and argue that class bias affects individuals' self-concepts, their relationships with others and self-esteem. A detailed analysis of 50 core social work textbooks between 2000 and 2010 led them to conclude that social class is largely absent from core social work curricula. They call for social work education to *confront future professionals with the complexity of the concept* (p416) by devoting more attention to *the understanding of class as a major social process*. Part of this, according to Strier and his colleagues, is for social work students to be aware of their own class prejudices and assumptions so that they develop a consciousness regarding the complex ways that class potentially shapes their interactions with service users.

As we commented earlier, social workers are not immune from the subtle and not so subtle messages embedded in popular culture and there is a danger that unless social work education focuses explicitly and unashamedly upon social class, students may unconsciously internalise and act upon cultural stereotypes about welfare recipients who may also be social work service users. Social workers, themselves middle class, do need to be mindful of not attributing *deficit* to *difference*. The importance of conceptualising the experiences and lack of opportunities that underpin the lives of many social work service users from within a structural paradigm as opposed to a personal deficit model is of key importance if social workers are going to be 'part of the solution' as opposed to being 'part of the problem'. We have tried to demonstrate how emotions of 'disgust' and contempt have been systematically linked to sections of the working class in such pervasive ways that it has become part of the 'wallpaper of common sense' – the backdrop that we rarely notice or reflect upon and unswervingly fail to examine in more critical terms. The implications of this for social workers are that there is a persistent danger that judgements and decisions are made based upon popular myths and misconceptions rather than objective assessment.

Back in the 1970s, in their seminal text *Radical social work*, Bailey and Brake (1975) argued that the centrality of social class must not be ignored and advocated for a radical social work that was essentially about *understanding the position of the oppressed in the context of the social and economic structures in which they live* (p9). They made an impassioned plea for social workers and social work students to reflect upon the issues raised and their hope was that the recipients of social work would themselves *oppose stigma and stereotyping, and resist all authoritarian attempts by the state to undermine their dignity* (p12). Radical social work was premised upon Marxist analyses of the class position of social work clients and advocated the view that social workers needed to join the struggle of the oppressed to bring about structural change. This would inevitably involve opposing authority and becoming politically active by taking part in union activity (Mayo, 1977) and raising the interests of the oppressed, as well as resisting pathologising practice such as casework in favour of community action-based approaches.

The Professional Capabilities Framework or PCF that was introduced in 2012 by The College of Social Work as part of the reforms to social work education, identifies 'Rights, justice and economic wellbeing' as one of its nine domains. We discuss the contested politics around this in our final concluding chapter. For us, however, this was a meaningful step forward in reaffirming a commitment to social justice as being at the heart of social work education and practice. We welcome the clear and explicit focus for social workers throughout their career upon economic wellbeing and applaud the recognition of social class inequalities and their associated impact.

ACTIVITY 8.7

Rights, justice and economic wellbeing

In small groups, we would like you to come up with a definition of social justice – what does it mean?

Once you have done this, reflect upon how social workers can demonstrate their commitment to social justice in practice, across a range of practice settings. To do this, if you are on placement, you might wish to ask your practice assessor or social workers in the team, how they meet this element of the PCF in their daily work.

You may have struggled to agree upon a definition of social justice as it can have many different components to it. We did a simple internet trawl and found different elements such as 'fairness in society', 'the promotion of human rights', 'mutual obligation', 'redistribution where life chances are not equally distributed', 'respecting the dignity of every human being', 'equal access to opportunity', 'a just share in the benefits of society'. We like the following definition which suggests that social justice is a:

framework of political objectives, pursued through social, economic, environmental and political policies, based on an acceptance of difference and diversity, and informed by values concerned with;

- *achieving fairness, equality of outcomes and treatment;*

- *recognising the dignity and equal worth and encouraging the self-esteem of all;*

- *the meeting of basic needs;*

- *reducing inequalities in wealth, income and life chances; and*

- *the participation of all, including the most disadvantaged.*

(Craig, 2002, pp71–2)

This is quite long and contains several elements. However, if we attempt to break it down, we can see that it has both a *structural* and an *individual* component – structural because it acknowledges the need for macro, political action by governments to address economic and social change, and individual because it involves subjective qualities such as dignity, self-esteem and feelings of equal worth. For social workers both of these components are important. It is necessary for social workers to challenge structures and work with service users to contest discriminatory policies, such as the bedroom tax. It is also important for them to take action to challenge stigmatising messages, pursue political goals and represent interests. Social workers must also ensure that every micro involvement with service users aims to *communicate* respect, build up self-esteem and convey positive regard. By working in partnership with service users to help them find sustainable solutions and actively challenging both prejudice and oppression, social workers can work to achieve social justice in their daily work. To do this, they must first comprehend the complexities and dynamics of social class. Understanding social class, we would argue, is a central and unavoidable aspect of social work training – central to the ethical basis of the profession and unavoidable because of the pervasive inequalities and their consequences that blight the lives of many users of social work services.

CHAPTER SUMMARY

In this chapter, we have sought to emphasise the importance of social class in relation to social work practice. The chapter has considered how social class can shape people's lives and significantly impact upon their health, their educational opportunities and determine their life outcomes. We have encouraged social work students to reflect upon recent attempts to pathologise certain sections of the working class and have argued that recent attempts to demonise them should be seen in the context of the Coalition government's welfare reform strategy which has impacted particularly harshly upon already vulnerable groups. The reinforcement of pervasive negative attitudes conveniently undermines support for those affected while at the same time providing justification for punitive welfare cuts. It is critical that social work students have a careful understanding of social class and are able to practise in the spirit of critical awareness and social justice.

FURTHER READING

For a comprehensive consideration of social class, including a summary of different class schemas, theoretical perspectives on class and an understanding of social mobility, **Ken Roberts'** (2011) *Class in contemporary Britain,* is an excellent rounded resource (2nd edition. Basingstoke: Palgrave Macmillan).

To read more detail about the Great British Class Survey, we would direct you to the journal article that presents the findings of the study: **Savage, M, Devine, F, Cunningham, N, Taylor, M, Li, Y, Hjellbrekke, J, Le Roux, B, Friedman, S and Miles, A** (2013) A new model of social class? Findings from the BBC's Great British Class Survey experiment. *Sociology,* 47 (2) 219–50.

For a discussion of the demonisation of the working class, we would direct you to **Owen Jones's** book (2011) *Chavs: The demonization of the working class.* London: Verso.

John Welshman's book provides an excellent summary of how negative conceptions of the poor have historically influenced policy and practice: **Welshman, J** (2013) *Underclass: A history of the excluded since 1880.* 2nd edition. London: Bloomsbury.

Chapter 9

Looking back, looking forwards: The relevance of sociology for social work

Introduction

Social work is an immensely complex and difficult undertaking. When things go wrong in social work, the profession finds itself at the forefront of adversarial media glare with depreciatory questions asked about why social workers are seemingly not up to the task. Attention inevitably turns to social work education and its apparent failings. Since we wrote the first edition of this book, social work education has been reviewed and reformed and, frustratingly, given that the ink is barely dry on the last set of reforms, reviewed again. At the time of writing, we await to see what will emerge from the two most recent reviews – *Making the education of social workers consistently effective,* the report of Sir Martin Narey (2014) and *Revisioning social work education: an independent review,* carried out by David Croisdale-Appleby (2014). It is clear that the relationship between sociology and social work remains a source of disquiet for the present government and particularly for former Education Secretary Michael Gove who recently castigated social work education for apparently encouraging students to regard social work service users as being 'victims of social injustice'. We examine what some have described as his 'thoroughly toxic' views (Smith, 2013) below in more detail.

The final chapter of this book assesses the historical relevance of sociology for social work, demonstrating a longstanding and somewhat troublesome relationship between the two. Notwithstanding this, however, we hope to convince you of the need to locate your practice within a structural understanding of society and to defend the ethical basis of the profession which rightly has at its heart, a commitment to social justice and promotion of the human rights of the people it serves.

The uncomfortable intertwining of sociology and social work

There is a longstanding relationship between sociology and social work. As far back as 1903, Charity Organisation Society (COS) workers and volunteers were encouraged to study sociology by those responsible for creating the newly formed London School of

Economics (LSE) (Jones, 1983). The assumption was that in order for social workers to intervene effectively, they needed to be equipped with relevant sociological knowledge about the nature of society to underpin their practice. As we pointed out in the introduction to this book, the LSE's initial efforts to educate its social work students about the structural causes of social problems were not greeted with universal enthusiasm. This is perhaps hardly surprising, since the core emphasis of the COS was to reform the character of the poor in order to maintain the cohesiveness and well-being of society. Poverty was largely seen by the COS as a morally culpable condition and its interventions were directed at modifying deviant behaviour (rather than providing welfare), and cajoling the poor back on to the 'straight and narrow'. Hence the COS's vision of social work training was very different from that envisaged by sociologists. For the COS, social work training should fulfil a conservative function, inoculating volunteers and workers from potential 'contamination' which might result from developing an undue empathy with those with whom they worked. In his informative work on the history of social work education, Chris Jones (1996) notes that concern has always existed about the potential of sociology to taint social workers, and that the 'contaminating' influence of sociology was concerning for some in the early days of the COS:

> The concern to prevent social workers from being either radicalised or demoralised by their daily experience of contact and involvement with some of the most deprived and impoverished sections of society was a driving force in the creation and development of formal social work education at the beginning of the twentieth century. This notion that a carefully constructed education programme rather than an apprenticeship training regime was essential if field workers were to cope with the pressures of the job and be immunised from disillusionment or even radical contamination.
>
> (Jones, 1996, pp191–2)

In the introduction we explained how, from 1912 onwards, the moralistic philosophy of the COS faced a concerted challenge. Compelling evidence linking social and economic ills to wider structural problems served to undermine the COS's attempts to explain problems like poverty, unemployment and squalor in terms of individual and family pathology. At the same time, the COS's grip on social work training was weakened by ideological shifts that occurred within social work academia itself. Around this time, Clement Attlee, TH Marshall and RH Tawney represented a 'new generation' of social work academics who saw it as their role to inject a greater political and sociological dimension into social work education. Hence, we gradually began to see attempts to articulate a different vision for social work training, one that grounded it in an understanding of the extent to which social injustice shaped the lives of the people that social workers engaged with (Attlee, 1920). That said, it would be some time before the wider social work academic community would fully embrace the 'structural' perspectives offered by sociology. Certainly, the overtly moralistic stance advocated by the COS became less widespread, but variants of it continued to shape social work training and practice (Cunningham and Cunningham, 2012).

According to Jones, such concerns remained prevalent within mainstream state social work training at least until the mid-1970s. There was fear that an overly sociological perspective would spawn radical social workers who would ultimately be a threat to the establishment, by exposing unequal power relations and empowering service users in ways that could potentially threaten the *status quo*. Social workers, as agents of the state, needed to be 'safe', thus the content of the social work training curriculum at the time, and indeed ever since, has been carefully constructed. At times, notably in the 1950s and 1960s, sociology was virtually absent from the social work curriculum. The domination of a psychological perspective marginalised the discipline of sociology, with an emphasis on the individual and casework; and an underpinning need to endorse the prevailing social order by assisting individuals who had fallen by the wayside to come back into mainstream society. Emphasis was placed on the need to resocialise deviant individuals, rather than bringing about change in the nature of society. As Jones (1996) argues, the inclusion of any sociology in the social work curriculum at that time tended to be predicated upon functionalism and a perceived need to understand dysfunctional families. Critical or conflict perspectives were virtually absent from the curriculum. Jones (2011, p30) recalls his own experiences of social work education in the late 1960s:

> *I remember all the professional lecturers promulgate views of poverty as though they were manifestations of pathological personalities and inadequate mothering; of how the well-functioning family with the mother at the hearth was the ideal and how clients were both devious and childlike. It was really so much stuff and nonsense and a million light years away from what we were discovering about class inequalities and the reproduction of poverty and disadvantage under capitalism.*

In the 1970s, however, the emerging radical social work movement found a voice, with a resurgence of sociological insights which sought to explain the role of capitalism and the welfare state, and how these were related to the poverty that characterised many service users' lives. The emergence of the radical social work movement coincided with *the creation of the polytechnics, followed by the growth of state social work ... [with] many of the new social science graduates drawn into and attracted by social work careers* (Jones, 1996, p199). Social work began to be perceived as being a potentially radical activity, as social science graduates entered the profession, taking up positions of community workers, and began to align themselves with service users in the pursuit of social justice. There was a subtle shift in emphasis away from service users being regarded as ill-fitting, poorly socialised, social misfits, to a perspective which began to see society as being in need of radical change. However, according to Jones, the insights gleaned from the social sciences began to be perceived as being dangerous once more by employers and agencies. The Central Council for Education and Training of Social Workers (CCETSW), the then governing body for social work, noted at the time that employers were pressing for better practical training and a need for social workers to understand the rules and regulations of the organisations they worked for. In their annual report in 1975, CCETSW noted a concern amongst employers about the nature of social work training and its potential to 'radicalise' newly qualified practitioners. It argued that the *education they receive makes them difficult employees, more concerned to change the 'system' than to get on with the job* (cited in Jones, 1996, p203).

It is interesting to note that the employers of the era clearly did not regard changing the system to be part of the job. This raised questions regarding the very role and remit of the social work profession and whether social workers were merely agents of the state employed to implement social control agendas, or whether they also had a role in actively bringing about social change. Employers were concerned once more that social workers were being radicalised by the social science content that they were being taught in their training, and worse, that they were ill-equipped to undertake the task in hand. This coincided with the well-publicised death of Maria Colwell, the inquiry of which criticised social workers for failing to protect the little girl who should have been under their auspices.

In the 1980s and 1990s, the backlash against social workers being educated in the social sciences continued to gather pace, and the Diploma in Social Work (DipSw), the social work qualification of the time, contained only social science teaching that was directly relevant to practice (Jones, 1996). Jones identifies what he refers to as the 'employer takeover', which began in the 1970s and continued to gain sway thereafter, pressurising CCETSW to ensure that social work courses were 'fit for purpose', with a clear shift away from producing qualifying workers who *thought*, to workers who *did*. There occurred a movement away from a form of social work education that interrogated, analysed and inspected, to training which could not *be bothered with ... questions of deep structure* (Webb, 1996, p182). The competence-based 'can do' curriculum was born and sociology and critical social policy were sidelined once more. Howe (1996) traces the concomitant shift away from 'depth' in social work, to 'surface'; a preoccupation with service provision and the performance of tasks and a move away from deeper work and attempts to understand the individual and the structure in which they are located. Jones identifies these shifts as a purge of all things intellectual, with an embracing of what he calls 'anti-intellectualism' and hostility to the social sciences:

> Universities are sneered at as being ivory towers far removed from the pressures of everyday life; theorisation is deemed as escape, or even a symptom of a cold and uncaring personality; what is demanded of state welfare workers is obedience and loyalty, not thought... Consequently, subjects which were once in the core of the curriculum have been virtually stripped out.

> (Jones, 1996, pp205–6)

However, many social work academics consistently resisted attempts to obliterate sociology and continued to urge a sociological presence on curriculum. Indeed, the QAA benchmarks for social work training that accompanied the development of the new social work degree that was to replace the DipSw identified the importance of:

> Sociological perspectives to understanding societal and structural influences on human behaviour at individual, group and community levels

> Social science theories explaining group and organisational behaviour, adaptation and change.

Nevertheless, there was still a latent concern to keep social workers 'safe' when the new BA (Hons) in Social Work was under development in 2003. The 'steer' from the Department of Health at this time was certainly very much away from critical, theoretical 'isms' and 'ologies' towards a curriculum that would be more skills and practice focused. Any theory that was taught must, the minister responsible for overseeing implementation of the new degree argued, be geared to strengthening practice skills:

> It is no help to service users and their carers if their social worker understands the theory but does not use that understanding to inform and support their practice. That is why I have made it clear that the training requirements should prepare students for the reality of becoming a social worker and that on qualification a person can apply their skills and knowledge to the intervention and support that vulnerable service users need and deserve.

(Smith, 2002, p5)

The General Social Care Council that took over from CCETSW in 2001 soon published its code of practice for social care workers (GSCC, 2002). All social workers and social work students were required to sign up to the code and abide by it, both within and outside of work. Although this was intended to communicate the standards required of social care workers, it was also widely interpreted to be the defining document that encapsulated the ethical base of the profession. The GSCC code barely mentioned any commitment to or recognition of social justice and was arguably, more a list of skills and standards to adhere to, than a clear value base. The closest the GSCC code got to acknowledging social justice was in identifying the need to promote equal opportunities for service users and carers and respecting diversity. This was in stark contrast to the much more strongly worded statement in the British Association of Social Work's (BASW) code of ethics that was first published in 1975 and updated in 2002, which articulated that:

> Social workers have a duty to bring to the attention of those in power and the general public, and where appropriate challenge ways in which the policies or activities of government, organisations or society create or contribute to structural disadvantage hardship and suffering, or militate against their relief.

(BASW, 2012, p3)

The BASW code dedicates an entire section to discussing social justice, which includes:

- fair and equitable distribution of resources to meet basic human needs;
- fair access to public services and benefits;
- recognition of the rights and duties of individuals, families, groups and communities;
- equal treatment and protection under the law;
- social development and environmental management in the interests of future human welfare;
- and importantly, in the pursuit of social justice: identifying, seeking to alleviate and advocating strategies for overcoming structural disadvantage (p3).

With the clear omission from the GSCC code of conduct of any discussion of social justice or structural disadvantage, it did seem that social work had once again fallen prey to influences which sought to de-radicalise the profession. Nonetheless, the social work benchmarks remained which allowed universities to include social science content in the social work degree and continue to educate students about the impact of disadvantage and its clear relationship with many of the issues faced by social work service users.

In 2009, the Social Work Task Force, established by the Department of Health and the Department for Children, Schools and Families following the death of baby Peter Connelly, published its long awaited report *Building a safe and confident future*. This proposed a programme of national reform that would significantly raise the quality of social work practice (Social Work Task Force, 2009). Central to this was improving the quality of social work education and training. Additionally the report recommended the development of an assessed and supported year in employment (ASYE) following qualification, the introduction of new standards, enhancing the leadership and management of social workers and a commitment to continuous professional development. Alongside this was recognition of the need to raise the public profile of the social work profession and to give social work a voice. These changes saw the end of the General Social Care Council (GSCC) and the beginning of The College of Social Work (CSW), the new voice of the profession. Social Work education became regulated by a separate body from 1 August 2012 – the Health and Care Professions Council (HCPC) with all social work programmes in England being required to undergo approval events to demonstrate how qualifying social workers would meet the new Standards of Proficiency, or SOPS. The HCPC SOPS were developed separately from The College of Social Work's Professional Capabilities Framework or PCF (originally devised by the Social Work Reform Board) to set out expectations of social workers at *all* stages of their career. However, work was done, arguably rather clumsily, to map the standards of proficiency with the expectations set out in the nine domains of the Professional Capabilities Framework.

The Professional Capabilities Framework was largely welcomed by social work practitioners and academics alike. Its aim was to provide an overarching professional standards framework that set out the capabilities needed by social workers from entry to the profession onwards. The emphasis was upon developing a holistic understanding and the nine domains of the PCF were designed to be interdependent and comprehensive. It was pleasing to see that embedded within the domains of the PCF was a recognition that social workers needed to understand the positioning of service users in relation to the social structure. This was evident particularly in the domain 'Rights, justice and economic wellbeing' which recognises that social work is premised upon principles of social justice and acknowledges the social worker's role in understanding the impact of oppression, inequality and poverty. The promotion of the rights of service users was at the heart of this domain, signalling an ethical commitment to anti-oppressive practice. Additionally, the 'Diversity' domain recognises the multi-dimensional nature of diversity and that *as a consequence of difference, a person's life experience may include oppression, marginalisation and alienation* (CSW, 2012). Further, embedded within the 'Knowledge' domain is recognition that social workers need a comprehensive understanding of theory and knowledge from sociology and social policy, among other theoretical disciplines. Similarly the HCPC Standards of Proficiency for social workers requires qualifying social workers to *be able to reflect on and take account of the impact of inequality, disadvantage and discrimination on those who use social work services and their communities* and *be able to work with others to promote social justice, equality and inclusion* (HCPC, 2012). Moreover, The College of Social Work's code of ethics (2013) and the HCPC Standards of conduct, performance and ethics (2012) contain consistent messages. It would seem therefore, that going forward following the work of the Social Work Reform Board in 2009, the social work profession was once again resting upon solid foundations, with a commitment to promoting social justice at its heart. This was a rare celebratory moment that unfortunately did not last long. The change of government in 2010 brought with it a wholly different ideological approach and one that is at odds with the social work profession. This was made clear when Michael Gove, at that time the Secretary of State for Education, made a speech to the NSPCC in 2013. After acknowledging that his own life was transformed by the skills of social workers who had placed him for adoption, he told the audience:

> In too many cases, social work training involves idealistic students being told that the individuals with whom they will work have been disempowered by society. They will be encouraged to see these individuals as victims of social injustice whose fate is overwhelmingly decreed by the economic forces and inherent inequalities which scar our society. This analysis is, sadly, as widespread as it is pernicious. It robs individuals of the power of agency and breaks the link between an individual's actions and the consequences.

(Gove, 2013)

Although Gove was able to recognise that social workers *have to weigh very delicate technical, psychological, social and moral questions in their minds as they work with these families*, he was scathing of what he called 'theories of society' predominating over an understanding of child development. As much of social work academia sighed in frustration at yet another ideological attack on both the profession and its service users, dozens of high profile Professors of Social Work criticised Gove's speech in an open letter to the *Guardian*:

> It's difficult to escape the conclusion ... that Gove's praise amounts to little more than a cover for attacking the social science and ethical basis of the profession. He suggests, for example, that 'idealistic students' are being encouraged to see service users as having been 'disempowered by society' and as 'victims of social injustice'. In fact, the promotion of agency, self-determination and independent living continue to be at the heart of social work education and social work practice, not least in relation to current personalisation agendas. Social work is an evidence-based profession, however. When highly respected research studies such as Wilkinson and Pickett's The Spirit Level *show the extent to which inequality contributes to social problems – and when even a former Conservative prime minister laments the lack of social mobility in the UK – then social workers*

need to recognise this in their practice. The alternative is the kind of victim-blaming and scapegoating of poor and disabled people that too often characterises current government attacks on people on benefits.

(Professors of Social Work, 2013)

Gove's message was alarmingly clear and the writing was on the wall for the forthcoming review of social work education commissioned by Gove and conducted by Martin Narey. The report, *Making the education of social workers consistently effective*, published in January 2014, focused mainly on social work with children and families. Narey harangued what he referred to as 'the politics of social work teaching' for focusing excessively on anti-oppressive practice and portraying those who received social work support as being *necessarily victims* (p11). Narey conceded that he was not ignoring *the reality that many families in which parenting is inadequate struggle with disadvantage, poverty and social isolation. He also acknowledged* that *those at the bottom of an unequal society face day to day challenges, including coping with cramped living conditions, limited income and often grinding debt, which can significantly undermine their ability to cope and to provide children with the safety and security with which they thrive* (p11). However, he went on to state that many other parents managed to bring up their children without abusing them and that it was imperative that social work educators did not *seek to persuade students that poor parenting or neglect are necessarily consequences of disadvantage* (p11). What Narey failed to grasp here is that social work educators do not seek to inculcate their students with a mantra that completely denies personal responsibility and presents poor parents as being puppets of a heartless society who have no option but to neglect their children. Rather, social work educators need their students to understand one simple fact – and that is that we live in a deeply divided society that advantages some and disadvantages others, and that disadvantage and poverty are the *context* in which many service users live their lives. If students do not understand this simple fact, then they may compound the difficulties experienced by those whose lives are disadvantaged. Understanding the *context* in which service users lead their lives and appreciating the impact of this does not simultaneously mean that social workers are 'soft' on poor parenting and unable to perceive the child in the scenario. Narey is correct when he asserts *sometimes, parents and other carers neglect and harm children.* He is misguided however, when he goes on to say *in such circumstances, viewing those parents as victims, seeking to treat them non oppressively, empowering them or working in partnership with them can divert the practitioner's focus from where it should be: on the child.* What is he suggesting? That in order to focus on the child social workers should behave oppressively in authoritarian ways and actively seek to disempower parents? This is a ludicrous outcome of Narey's argument and it is as dangerous as it is misguided. A more balanced approach is needed. Social workers must of course focus upon the child first and foremost, but this does not mean that social workers cannot practice in accordance with the principles of social justice. To fail to do so would potentially be in breach of the human rights act:

We do not teach social work students that service users are passive victims of social forces. What we teach them are the knowledge and skills to work

> *within the values of human rights and social justice to enable people to take control of their lives, rather than being ruled by factors outside of their control.*

> (Baldwin, 2013, p22)

Hot on the heels of the Narey report, David Croisdale-Appleby published his report *Revisioning Social Work Education: an independent review* in February 2014. This had been commissioned by Norman Lamb, Minister of State for Care and Support at the Department of Health and was believed to have more of a focus on the education of social workers working with adults. On the whole, Croisdale-Appleby's report was a welcomed antidote to the Narey report with Croisdale-Appleby acknowledging the complex nature of work that social workers do on a daily basis:

> *The evidence I have seen, both of itself and in comparison with the other professions with which I am familiar … leads me to the view that social work education is an extraordinarily complex subject because it draws upon a wide range of other academic disciplines, and synthesises from those disciplines its own chosen set of beliefs, precepts, ideologies, doctrines and authority. As a profession, social work requires its practitioners to understand intricate and often seemingly impenetrable behaviours and situations.*

> (p15)

In recognition of the complexities entailed, Croisdale-Appleby argued that social work required education *in which both theory-informing-practice and practice-informing-theory are inexorably linked* (p15). He identified what he termed the three components of social work – social worker as *practitioner*, social worker as *professional* and, significantly, social worker as *social scientist*. Croisdale-Appleby is to be congratulated for accepting the theoretical underpinning of the social work profession, particularly in the current climate, and for endorsing what he later refers to as a profession that knows *why* rather than merely knowing *how*. It is perhaps unfortunate that Croisdale-Appleby backed fast track 'elite' routes into the profession, albeit with some cursory notes of caution around them. Many within the social work profession have expressed caution about the development of fast track routes. One of the major concerns with 'elite routes' such as 'Frontline' that was introduced in 2012 for childcare social workers, is that they effectively reduce social work education to 'on the job' training. Frontline candidates receive just a five-week summer school and 12 months' training on the job. How can anyone, irrespective of how bright they are, really get to grips with the complexities of social work theory, legislation and policy, let alone have time to reflect upon it and upon their own strengths and weaknesses within five weeks? Moreover, a narrow focus upon childcare means that Frontline social workers will not benefit from broader education across the life course and may be unable to appreciate factors such as the impact of mental health upon parenting for example, or understand families that have an older adult with dementia living with them. In real life, social work cannot take place in neatly defined 'service user group' boxes. There is a danger that childcare-only social workers may end up being process driven, 'tick box' workers who lack a holistic understanding of the complexities of the families that they come into contact with. If it was not such a dangerous and inherently distressing prospect, it would be laughable. However, fast track routes look set to continue. It is disappointing that The College of Social Work did not vociferously oppose them on behalf of the service users whose interests it seeks to promote.

An understanding of social class, poverty and inequality must remain at the heart of social work education. If social workers do not have an appreciation of the way that inequality impacts upon people's lives and opportunities, they would be, like Narey, at best misguided, at worst unsafe professionals who have the ability to damage people's lives. One of the roles and remits of social workers is to help bring about change – change on a structural level, but also on a personal level. If social workers do not have at their heart a commitment to anti-oppressive practice, how can they ever seek to work in empowering ways with service users to assist them to change? We strongly defend the right of social work educators to teach anti-oppressive practice – it is what social work is about. It is what puts the 'social' into social work. The Coalition government is deeply uncomfortable with this because, heaven forbid, if social workers are educated to think and understand oppression, inequality and dis-advantage, they might see flaws in some policies that they have to work within.

Locating your practice

Throughout this book, we have encouraged you to situate or locate your practice with service users within an understanding of the social structures that underpin their experiences, by encouraging you to develop a sociological imagination. The aim of this is to discourage an overly negative and blaming focus upon individuals' prob-lems and to encourage understanding and analysis of the factors beyond the con-trol of individuals that shape and constrain their experiences. So, we have asked you to think about how the unequal structural of society can mean that some people's lives are characterised by poverty, disadvantage and oppression. We have asked you to deconstruct some of your taken-for-granted assumptions about your own lives, the lives of your service users and the nature of society at large. We remain passionately convinced of the relevance of sociology for social workers and urge you to keep your sociological imagination alive. Early on in this book, we encouraged you to develop awareness of the endemic poverty that underpins the lives of very many service users and the related consequences of living in poverty for long periods. We have asked you to think about the nature of social exclusion and, related to this, to try to under-stand the way that moral panics can be engineered by the media and politicians to shift attention away from the structural source of many problems that excluded individuals face. We spent time thinking about families and powerful ideologies that exist, deeply embedded within our culture, that provide us with messages about how we should live. We also acknowledged that for very many of our service users, the reality of their family life falls far short of these ideals. We then looked at the nuances of the education system and recognised how factors within and outside the system can contribute to educational 'failure', which can compound existing disadvantage. We have considered the social class system in Britain and identified ways in which class directly impacts upon life chances. We have detailed ways in which sections of the working class have become demonised and regarded with cultural disgust by many sections of our society. For service users, these issues are live and real and without a sociological analysis to assist social workers to make sense of the complexity of the challenges they face, social workers can only intervene at best on the 'surface' and are in danger of pathologising service users, further adding to their oppression.

Social workers need to possess skills to assist them to analyse the vast amounts of information they gather about service users, in order to intervene effectively. A sociological perspective will assist them in this quest. A sociological approach to social work is consistent with the value base of the profession. An awareness of the structural constraints that underpin all our lives can assist social workers to work in ways that are empowering and help social workers to be aware of their own potential power to contribute to the oppression of those we work with. A sociological approach to social work complements anti-oppressive practice and supports and strengthens critical practice, as it sets out the theoretical basis for understanding oppression and disadvantage. A sociological approach sits side by side with critical practice in advocating conscious and collective action to bring about social change. In this book we have introduced you to different sociological approaches, some of which you will accept and others of which you will reject. However, notwithstanding the differences and relative merits of each, we hope that you have been able to analyse the differing approaches to develop a clear idea of what each has to offer. We hope that you will be able to use some of the ideas in this book to help you to make sense of your practice from a sociological point of view, with the aim of intervening in ways that are truly empowering and make a difference to people's lives.

References

Abbott, P, Wallace, C and Tyler, M (2005) *Introduction to sociology: Feminist perspectives.* Abingdon: Routledge.

Adams, R (2014) Schools minister praises pushy parents and complains of 'low aspirations'. *GuardianOnline*, 26 February 2014. www.theguardian.com/politics/2014/feb/26/schools-minister-pushy-parents-uk-low-aspirations

Adams, R, Dominelli, L and Payne, M (2005) *Social work futures.* Basingstoke: Palgrave.

Aitkenhead, D (2013) The Saturday interview: Sarah's war. *Guardian*, 13 July 2013.

Aitkenhead, D (2014) Deidre Kelly, AKA White Dee: 'I would never watch a show called benefits street'. *Guardian*, 7 March 2014.

Alland, A (2004) *Race in mind: Race, IQ and other racisms.* Basingstoke: Palgrave Macmillan.

Article 19 (2003) *What's the story? Results from research into media coverage of refugees and asylum seekers in the UK.* London: Article 19. www.article19.org/pdfs/publications/refugees-what-s-the-story-.pdf

ATD Fourth World (2006) *Empowering families.* www.atd-uk.org/ukprogrammes/denise.htm.

Attlee, CR (1920) *The social worker.* London: G Bell and Sons.

AVIVA (2012) The AVIVA family finances report, August 2012. www.aviva.com/data/media-uploads/news/File/RDhub_reports/Family%20Finances%20Report%2022%20August%202012.pdf

Badgikian, BH (2004) *The new media monopoly.* Boston: Beacon Press.

Bailey, R. and Brake, M. (eds) (1975) *Radical social work.* London: Edward Arnold.

Bailey, R and Brake, M (1980) *Radical social work and practice.* London: Edward Arnold.

Baldwin, M (2013) Blame and pathologies the victims of social forces – they are worth more like that. In Social Work Action Network (2013) *In defence of social work: Why Michael Gove is wrong.* London: SWAN.

Ball, S (2010) New class inequalities in education: Why education policy may be looking in the wrong place! Education policy, civil society and social class. *International Journal of Sociology and Social Policy*, Vol 30 (3/4), 155–66.

Barrett, M and Mcintosh, M (1982) The *anti-social family.* London: NLB.

Barry, M (1998) Social exclusion and social work: An introduction. In Barry, M and Hallett, C (eds) *Social exclusion and social work.* Dorset: Russell House Publishing.

Bartholomew, J (2006) *The welfare state we're in.* London: Politico Publishing.

Bauman, Z (2001) *Community: Seeking safety in an insecure world.* Cambridge: Polity Press.

Baumberg, B, Bell, K, and Gaffney, D (2012) *Benefits stigma in Britain.* Kent: University of Kent.

BBC (1994) *Harry Enfield and chums* www.myvideo.de/watch/8046177/Harry_Enfield_and_chums_The_slobs_Brown_baby_Wayne_Waynetta_in_The_ten_year_itch

BBC (2010) State 'should not finance' big families on benefits. BBC News Online. 7 October 2010 www.bbc.co.uk/news/uk-politics-11490294

BBC (2011*) Average UK student debts could hit £53,000.* 12 August 2011. www.bbc.co.uk/news/education-14488312

BBC (2013) Class calculator: Can I have no job or money and still be middle class. 4 April 2013. www.bbc.co.uk/news/magazine-21953364

Becker, H (1963) *Outsiders.* New York: The Free Press.

Becker, S (1997) Responding to poverty: The politics of cash and care. Harlow: Longman.

Beckett, C (2003) *Child protection: An introduction.* London: Sage.

Beresford, P, Green, D, Lister, R and Woodward, K (1999) *Poverty first hand: Poor people speak for themselves.* London: CPAG.

Berger, L (2013) We must not normalise food banks: Their proliferation is a mark of shame on this country. *Independent,* 18 December 2013.

Berger, P (1963) *Invitation to sociology.* London: Penguin Books.

Berner, E and Phillips, B (2005) Left to their own devices? Community self-help between alternative development and neo-liberalism. *Community Development Journal,* 40 (1), 17–29.

Bernstein, B (1971) *Class codes and control, volume 1: Theoretical studies towards a sociology of language.* Abingdon: Routledge and Kegan Paul.

Bingham, J (2013) *Blame bad parents for Britain's ills; Children are not being taught right from wrong at home. The Daily Telegraph,* 15 October 2013.

Bingham, J and Dominiczak, P (2014) Benefit cuts give people hope. *The Daily Telegraph,* 19 February 2014.

Blood, I (2010) *Older people with high support needs: How can we empower them to enjoy a better life.* York: Joseph Rowntree Foundation.

Bossley, S (1987) School sociology attacked over 'anti-business bids'. *Guardian,* 13 July 1987.

Bottomore, TB (1963) *Karl Marx - early writings.* London: Watts and Co.

Bourdieu, P (1973) Cultural reproduction and social reproduction. In Brown, R (ed.) *Knowledge, education and cultural change.* London: Tavistock.

Bourdieu, P (1984) *Distinction: A social critique of the judgment of taste.* London: Routledge and Kegan Paul.

Bowles, S and Gintis, H (1976) *Schooling in capitalist America: Educational reform and the contradictions of economic life.* Abingdon: Routledge and Kegan Paul.

Brindle, D (1996) How Whitehall kept poverty off the agenda. *Guardian,* 31 December 1996.

British Association of Social Workers (2012) *The code of ethics for social work.* Birmingham: BASW.

Buchanan, K (2013) 'Shameless families' aid project helps 35,000 so far. *Sunday Express,* 12 May 2013.

Byrne, D (1999) *Social exclusion.* Buckingham: Open University Press.

Cabinet Office (2010) Building the big society. www.cabinetoffice.gov.uk/sites/default/files/resources/building-big-society_0.pdf

Callinicos, A (1989) *Against postmodernism: A Marxist critique.* Cambridge: Polity Press.

Cameron, D (2006) Chamberlain lecture on communities. Balsall Heath, Birmingham, 14 July 2006. www.cforum.org.uk/blog/wp-content/uploads/2006/07/DavidCameronChamberlain lecture.doc

Cameron, D (2009) *The Big Society. Hugo Young Speech,* 10 November 2009. www.conservatives.com/News/Speeches/2009/11/David_Cameron_The_Big_Society.aspx

Cameron, D (2010) *Supporting parents.* Speech, 11 January 2010. www.conservatives.com/News/Speeches/2010/01/David_Cameron_Supporting_parents.aspx

Cameron, D (2011) Troubled families speech, 15 December 2011. www.gov.uk/government/speeches/troubled-families-speech

Cameron, D (2011a) How we will release the grip of state control. *The Daily Telegraph,* 21 February 2011.

Cameron, D (2014) Why the Archbishop is wrong about welfare. *The Daily Telegraph,* 19 February 2014.

Campbell, D and Temko, N (2006) £250,000: the cost of care for every problem family: No 10 backs new 'mentors' scheme to break cycle of dependency and crime. *Observer,* 3 September 2006, p14.

Carers UK (2013) *Written evidence to the Work and Pensions Committee inquiry: Support for housing costs in the reformed welfare system.* http://data.parliament.uk/writtenevidence/WrittenEvidence.svc/EvidenceHtml/2592

Cauce, A, Stewart, A, Rodriguez, M, Cochrane, B and Ginzler, J (2003) Overcoming the odds? Adolescent development in the context of urban poverty. In Luthar, S (ed.) *Resilience and vulnerability: Adaptation in the context of childhood adversities.* Cambridge: Cambridge University Press.

Centre for Social Justice (2013) Economic dependency and worklessness. www.centreforsocialjustice.org.uk/policy/pathways-to-poverty/economic-dependency-and-worklessness

Centre for Social Justice (2013a) *Requires improvement: The causes of educational failure.* www.centreforsocialjustice.org.uk/UserStorage/pdf/Pdf%20reports/requires.pdf

Chanan, G and Miller, C (2013) *Rethinking community practice: Developing transformative neighbourhoods.* Bristol: Policy Press.

Chapman, J (2013) We must back marriage: Iain Duncan Smith announces plan to 'stabilise families and support commitment. *Mail Online,* 1 October 2013. www.dailymail.co.uk/news/article-2440819/Marriage-tax-allowance-announced-Ian-Duncan-Smith.html

Chapman, J (2014) A Marxist diatribe: Ministers fury as 'Brazil nut' UN inspector who lectured Britain publishes report condemning our housing benefit. *MailOnline,* 3 February 2014. www.dailymail.co.uk/news/article-2551114/Ministers-condemn-UN-inspector-reveals-report-slamming-Governments-housing-welfare-policies.html

Chesshyre, R (2010) 'Return to Easington': How one community is coming to terms with life after mining'. *Independent,* 16 July 2010.

Child Poverty Action Group (2013) Child poverty facts and figures. www.cpag.org.uk/child-poverty-facts-and-figures

Children's Commissioner for England (2012) *They never give up on you: Office of the Children's Commissioner school exclusion inquiry.* London: OCC.

Children's Commissioner for England (2013) Measuring child poverty: A Consultation on better measures for child poverty. London: OCC.

Children's Commissioner for England (2013a) They go the extra mile: Reducing inequality in school exclusions. London: OCC.

Children's Commissioners for the UK (2011) UK children's commissioners midterm report to the UK state party on the UN Convention on the Rights of the Child. www.childrenscommissioner.gov.uk/content/publications/content_542

Children's Society (2012) *Highlighting the gap between asylum support and mainstream benefits.* London: The Children's Society.

Children's Society (2013) *Through young eyes.* London: The Children's Society.

Chomsky, N and Herman, ES (2002) *Manufacturing consent: The political economy of the mass media.* New York: Pantheon Books.

Chorley, M (2012) Eric Pickles: The man who wants to bring back blame. *Independent,* 10 June 2012.

Chorley, M (2013) 'Don't get pregnant, get a job': Poverty tsar says women from 'Troubled families' must go to GPs for lessons in contraception. *MailOnline,* 11 September 2013. www.dailymail.co.uk/news/article-2416842/Louise-Casey-poverty-tsar-says-women-troubled-families-contraception-lessons.html

Chowdrey, H, Crawford, C and Goodman, A (2010) Outcomes in the secondary school years: Evidence from the longitudinal study of young people. In Goodman, A and Gregg, P (eds) *Poorer children's educational attainment: How important are attitudes and behaviour.* York: JRF.

Civil Exchange (2013) The big society audit. www.civilexchange.org.uk/wp-content/uploads/2013/12/THE-BIG-SOCIETY-AUDIT-2013webversion.pdf

Civil Service (2006) *Capability review of communities and local government.* London: HMSO.

Clapton, G, Cree, V and Smith, M (2013) Moral panics, claims-making and child protection in the UK. *British Journal of Social Work,* Vol 33 (4) 803–12.

Clark, G (1974) Sir Keith Joseph denies bid for Tory leadership as critics amount attack. *Times,* 21 October 1974.

Clarke, B (2013) In pursuit of the working class. *Cultural Studies Review,* Vol 19 (2) 324–34.

Coates, S (2011) Voters see Cameron's plan as a ruse to disguise cuts. *The Times,* 8 February 2011.

Cohen, S (2006) *Folk devils and moral panics.* 3rd edition. Abingdon: Routledge.

College of Social Work (2012) *Domains within the PCF.* London: CSW.

College of Social Work (2013) *Code of Ethics.* London: CSW.

Community Organisers (2013) Organising jobs: Nurturing an independent labour market. www.cocollaborative.org.uk/sites/default/files/Community%20Organisers%20Employers%20booklet.pdf

Comte, A (1974) *The positive philosophy.* New York: AMS Press.

Cooley, CH (1902) Human nature and the social order. New York: Scribner's.

Cooper, N and Dumpleton, S (2013) *Walking the breadline: The scandal of food poverty in 21st century Britain.* Manchester: Church action on poverty/Oxfam.

Cooper, K and Stewart, K (2013) *Does money affect children's outcomes?* York: Joseph Rowntree Foundation.

Corbett, S and Walker, A (2013) The big society: Rediscovery of 'the social' or rhetorical fig-leaf for neo-liberalism? *Critical Social Policy,* Vol 33 (451) 451–72.

Coughlan, S (2013) Children 'already two years behind when they start school'. *BBC,* 3 September 2013. www.bbc.co.uk/news/education-23931080

Counting Women In Coalition (2013) *Sex and power, 2013: Who runs Britain?* Leeds: Centre for Women and Democracy.

Coventry LSCB (2013) *Final overview report of serious case review re Daniel Pelka.* Coventry: Coventry Safeguarding Children Board.

CPAG (2013) The UK poverty line www.cpag.org.uk/content/uk-poverty-line

Craig, G (2002) Poverty, social work and social justice. *British Journal of Social Work*, Vol 32 (2) 669–82.

Craig, G, Mayo, M, Popple, K, Shaw, M and Taylor, M (2011) *The community development reader: History, themes and issues*. Bristol: Policy Press.

Crawley, H (2010) *Chance or choice: Understanding why asylum seekers come to the UK*. London: Swansea University/Refugee Council.

Cribb, J, Joyce, R and Phillip, D (2012) *Living standards, poverty and inequality in the UK*. York: Joseph Rowntree Foundation.

Crisp, R (2012) Conceptualising local approaches to tackling worklessness: The new deal for communities programme as neoliberal 'flanking strategy'? *Space and Polity*, Vol. 16 (2) 233–51.

Croisdale-Appleby, D (2014) *Re-visioning social work education: An independent review*. London: Department for Health.

Cunningham, S. and Cunningham, J (2012) *Social policy and social work*. London: Learning Matters at Sage.

Cunningham, S and Lavalette, M (2014) Children's rights or employers' rights? The destigmatisation of child labour. In Wagg, S and Pilcher, J (2014) *Thatcher's grandchildren*. London: Palgrave.

Davies, A, Friedman, D, Grimes, R and Taylor, B (2013) *Experiences and effects of the benefits cap in Haringey*. London: Chartered Institute for Housing.

Davis, K and Moore, WE (1945) Some principles of stratification. *American Sociological Review*, 24, 242–9.

Delaney, G (2003) *Community*. Abingdon: Routledge.

Denham, A and Garnett, M (2002) From the cycle of enrichment to the cycle of deprivation. *Benefits*, 35 (10) 3.

Dennis, N and Erdos, G (2005) *Cultures and crimes: Policing in four nations*. London: CIVITAS.

Department for Business Innovation and Skills (2013) *Widening participation in higher education*. HMSO: London.

Department for Children, Schools and Families (2010) *Promoting the educational achievement of looked after children*. DfCSF: London.

Department for Communities and Local Government (2012) *Working with troubled families: A guide to evidence and good practice*. www.gov.uk/government/publications/working-with-troubled-families-a-guide-to-evidence-and-good-practice

Department for Communities and Local Government (2013) *Troubled families: Progress information at March 2013 and families turned round at January 2013*. www.gov.uk/government/publications/troubled-families-progress-information-at-march-2013-and-families-turned-round-at-january-2013

Department for Communities and Local Government (2013a) *Bringing people together in strong and united communities*. www.gov.uk/government/policies/bringing-people-together-in-strong-united-communities

Department for Education and Science (2007) *Care Matters: Time for change*. Cm 7137. London: HMSO.

Department for Education (2013) *Home school agreements: Guidance for local authorities and governing bodies*. HMSO: London.

Department for Education (2013a) *Outcomes for children looked after by local authorities in England, as of 31 March 2013.* London: Department for Education.

Department for Education (2013b) *Data pack: Improving permanence for looked after children.* London: Department for Education.

Department for Education (2013c) *Number of permanent exclusions by ethnic group and gender, England 2011/12.* London: Department for Education.

Department for Education (2013d) *Children looked after in England, including adoption.* London: Department for Education.

Department for Education (2014) *GCSE and equivalent attainment by pupil characteristics in England, 2012/13.* London: Department for Education.

Department for Work and Pensions (2011) *A new approach to child poverty: Tackling the causes of disadvantage and transforming families' lives.* London: HMSO.

Department for Work and Pensions/Department for Education (2011) *A new approach to child poverty: Tackling the causes of disadvantage and transforming families' lives.* Cm8061. London: HMSO.

Department for Work and Pensions (2012) *Social justice: Transforming lives.* Cm8314. London: HMSO.

Department for Work and Pensions (2012a) *Impact assessment: Housing benefit – under-occupation of social housing.* www.gov.uk/government/uploads/system/uploads/attachment_data/file/214329/social-sector-housing-under-occupation-wr2011-ia.pdf

Deputy Prime Minister's Office (2013) *Improving social mobility to create a fairer society.* London: Office of Deputy Prime Minister.

Dolan, P, Hallsworth, M, Halpern, D, King, D and Vlaev, I (2010) *Mindspace: Influencing behaviour through public policy.* London: Cabinet Office.

Dominelli, L (2002) *Anti-oppressive social work theory and practice.* Basingstoke: Palgrave Macmillan.

Dominelli, L (2004) *Social work, theory and practice for a changing profession.* Cambridge: Polity Press.

Dominelli, L (2008) *Anti-racist social work,* 3rd edition. Basingstoke: Palgrave Macmillan.

Dorling, D (2011) *Injustice: Why social inequality persists.* Bristol: Policy Press.

Dorling, D (2012) *The no nonsense guide to equality.* Oxford: New Internationalist.

Doward, J (2006) 'Nanny state' clash on parent classes. *Observer,* 19 November 2006.

Drakeford, M and Gregory, L (2008) Anti-poverty practice and the changing world of credit unions: New tools for social workers. *Practice,* 20 (3) 141–50.

Drakeford, M and Gregory, L (2008) Avoiding sub-prime lenders: Credit unions and their diversification in Wales. *Research Policy and Planning,* 26 (2) 123–34.

Drugscope and Adfam (2012) The troubled families agenda: What does it all mean? www.adfam.org.uk/docs/adfam_drugscope_troubledfamilies.pdf

Duell, M (2013) Three-year-old children spend so much time strapped into buggies or in front TV they are unable to walk, warns families' tsar. *Mail Online,* 3 February 2013. www.dailymail.co.uk/news/article-2272704/Some-year-old-children-spend-time-TV-strapped-buggies.html

Duggan, E (2013) Get tougher! Social workers cannot collude with parents to find excuses for failure. *Independent,* 3 July 2013.

Duncan Smith, I (2012) *Reforming welfare, transforming lives.* Speech, 25 October 2012.

Duncan Smith, I (2012a) *Social justice: Transforming lives.* Speech, 31 October 2012. www.gov.uk/government/speeches/the-govknow-conference-social-justice-transforming-lives

Duncan Smith, I (2014) *A welfare state fit for the 21st century.* Speech, 23 January 2014. www.gov.uk/government/speeches/a-welfare-state-fit-for-the-21st-century

Durkheim, E (1972) *Selected writings.* Cambridge: Cambridge University Press.

Durkheim, E (1982) *The rules of sociological method.* New York: The Free Press.

Eagleton. T (2011) *Why Marx was right.* London: Yale University Press.

Edwards, G (2012) What does the Big Society mean on the ground? BBC News, 7 March 2012. www.bbc.co.uk/news/uk-politics-17260353

eLearning Foundation (2013) *Family spending survey, 2013.* www.e-learningfoundation.com/Websites/elearningfoundation/images/Word%20Documents/family_spending_survey_2013.doc

Ellison, N (2011) The Conservative party and the big society. In C. Holden, M. Kilkey and G. Ramia (eds) *Social policy review 23.* Bristol: The Policy Press.

Engels, F (1968) *The origins of the family, private property and the state.* Moscow: Progress Publishers.

Equalities and Human Rights Commission (2012) *Close to home: An inquiry into older people and human rights at home.* London: EHRC.

Equalities and Human Rights Commission (2012a) *Close to home: An inquiry into older people and human rights at home: Executive Summary.* London: EHRC

Eurostat (2013) *Live births outside marriage.* http://epp.eurostat.ec.europa.eu/tgm/table.do?tab=table&plugin=1&language=en&pcode=tps00018

Eurostat (2014) *Marriage and divorce statistics.* http://epp.eurostat.ec.europa.eu/statistics_explained/extensions/EurostatPDFGenerator/getfile.php?file=86.169.21.79_1389278619_10.pdf

Eurostat (2011) *Population and social conditions: Statistics in focus.* http://epp.eurostat.ec.europa.eu/cache/ITY_OFFPUB/KS-SF-11-052/EN/KS-SF-11-052-EN.PDF

Featherstone, B (1999) Taking mothering seriously: The implications for child protection. *Child and Family Social Work,* 4, 43–53.

Ferguson, I, Lavalette, M and Mooney, G (2002) *Rethinking welfare: A critical perspective.* London: Sage.

Ferguson, H (2011) *Child Protection Practice.* London: Palgrave Macmillan.

Field, F (2010) *The foundation years: Preventing poor children from becoming poor adults.* London: HM Government.

Firestone, S (1970) *The dialectic of sex.* London: The Women's Press.

Ford, R (2013) Hardcore of troubled families cost billions: Huge sums are being spent on caring and fostering children from families whose lives are marked by crime, truancy and worklessness. *The Times,* 3 March 2013.

Francis, B and Hutchings, M (2013) *Parent power? Using money and information to boost children's chances of educational success.* London: Sutton Trust.

Franklin, B (1999) *Social Policy, media and misrepresentation.* Florence, KY, USA: Routledge.

Franklin, B and Parton, N (1991) *Social work, the media and public relations: A framework for analysis.* London: Routledge.

Friedan, B (1963) *The feminist mystique.* New York: Dell.

Fuller, N and Davey, G (2010) *Equality groups and apprenticeship: Report conducted for the Equality and Human Rights Commission's triennial review.* Southampton: University of Southampton.

Equality Trust (2014) *The cost of inequality.* www.equalitytrust.org.uk/sites/default/files/The%20Cost%20of%20Inequality%20%20-%20full%20report.pdf

Gans, HJ (1971) The uses of poverty, the poor pay all. *Social Policy,* July/August 1971, 20–4.

Garrett, PM (2007) 'Sinbin solutions': The 'pioneer' projects for 'problem families' and the forgetfulness of social policy research. *Critical Social Policy,* 27 (2), 203-30.

General Social Care Council (2002) *Code of practice.* London: GSCC.

Gewirtz, S (2001) Cloning the Blairs: New Labour's programme for the re-socialization of working-class parents. *Journal of Education Policy,* 16 (4) (July 1, 2001) 365–78.

Giddens, A (1994) *Beyond left and right: The future of radical politics.* Cambridge: Polity Press.

Giddens, A (1998) *The third way.* Cambridge: Polity Press.

Giddens, A (2013) *Sociology.* 7th edition. Cambridge: Polity Press.

Gillies, V, Ribbens McCarthy, J and Holland, J (2001) *The family lives of young people.* York: JRF.

Gilligan, P (2007) Well motivated reformists or nascent radicals: How do applicants to the degree in social work see social problems and their origins and solutions? *British Journal Social Work,* 37 (4) 735–60.

Gittins, D (1985) *The family in question.* Basingstoke: Macmillan Press.

Goode, E and Ben-Yehuda, N (1994) *Moral panics: The social construction of deviance.* Oxford: Blackwell.

Gordon, D, Mack, J, Lansley, S, Main, G, Nandy, S, Patsios, D and Pomati, M (2013) *The impoverishment of the UK.* London: PSE.

Gove, M (2012) *The failure of child protection and the need for a fresh start.* Speech, 16 November 2012. www.gov.uk/government/speeches/the-failure-of-child-protection-and-the-need-for-a-fresh-start

Gove, M (2013) *Getting it right for children in need.* Speech to the NSPCC, 12 November 2013.

Graham, G (2013) Clegg presses Tories to give up 'pet' tax breaks. *The Daily Telegraph,* 7 July 2013.

Gramsci, A (1971) *Selections from the prison notebooks.* London: Lawrence and Wishart.

Greaves, MN, Hill, D and Maisuria, A (2007) Embourgeoisment, immiseration, commodification: Marxism revisited, a critique of education in capitalist systems. *Journal for Critical Education Policy Studies,* Vol 5 (1). Online edition.

Green, DG (1996) *Community without politics: A market approach to welfare reform.* London: CIVITAS.

Green, M (2007) *Voices of people experiencing poverty in Scotland.* York: Joseph Rowntree Foundation.

Greenslade, R (2005) *Seeking scapegoats: The coverage of asylum in the UK press.* London: IPPR.

Gregg, P and Washbook, E (2010) From birth through primary school: Evidence from the Avon longitudinal study of parents and children. In Goodman, A and Gregg, P (eds) *Poorer children's educational attainment: How important are attitudes and behaviour.* York: JRF.

Grice, A (2013) Nick Clegg attacks Tories over Europe and marriage tax breaks. *Independent,* 1 July 2013.

Hampson, T and Olchawski, J (2008) Ban the word 'chav': It is deeply offensive to a largely voiceless group and betrays a revealing level of class hatred. *Guardian*, 15 July 2008.

Hancock, L, Mooney, G and Neal, S (2012) Crisis social policy and the resilience of the concept of community. *Critical Social Policy*, 32 (3) 343–64.

Hanmer, J and Statham, D (1999) *Women and social work.* 2nd edition. Basingstoke: Palgrave Macmillan.

Haralambos, M. and Holborn, M (2013) Sociology, themes and perspectives. 8th edition. London: Collins.

Hardman, I (2013) Why it's wrong to be ashamed of Britain's food banks. *Spectator*, 29 June 2013.

Health and Care Professions Council (2012) *Social workers in England: Standards of proficiency.* London: HCPC.

Hebdidge, D (1979) *Subculture: The meaning of style.* London: Methuen.

Heffer, S (2012) What the Victorians could teach today's social workers about Mr Pickles' problem families. *Daily Mail*, 12 June 2012.

Helm, T (2006) Cameron invites Polly Toynbee to join Conservative conference. *Telegraph*, 25 November 2006.

Helm, T (2013) New ASBOS will 'punish children for being children'. *Observer*, 13 October 2013.

Higher Education Statistics Agency (2013) *Young full-time first degree entrants by state school marker, NS-SEC marker (excluding 2008/09) and low participation marker.* www.hesa.ac.uk/dox/performanceIndicators/1213_J62I/t1a_1213.xlsx

Hirsch, D (2009) *Ending child poverty in a changing economy.* York: JRF

Hirsch, D (2013) *An estimate of the cost of poverty in 2013.* London: CPAG.

Holman, B (1993) *A new deal for social welfare.* Oxford: Lion Books.

Home Office (1999) *Report of the policy action team on community self-help.* London: Home Office. www.asylumsupport.info/publications/homeoffice/acu/selfhelp.pdf

Home Office (2010) What is a family intervention project? http://webarchive.nationalarchives.gov.uk/20100405140447/asb.homeoffice.gov.uk/members/article.aspx?id=8678

Home Office (2013) *Statistical news release: Immigration statistics, April-June 2013.* London: Home Office.

Hooper, CA, Gorin, S, Cabral, C and Dyson, C (2007) 'Poverty and 'place': Does locality make a difference?' *Poverty*, 128 (Autumn), 7–10.

House of Commons Hansard, various dates.

House of Commons Work and Pensions Committee (2014) Support for housing costs in the reformed welfare system. HC 720. London: HMSO. www.publications.parliament.uk/pa/cm201314/cmselect/cmworpen/720/720.pdf

House of Lords Hansard, various dates.

Howe, D (1996) Surface and depth in social work practice. In Parton, N (ed.) *Social work, social theory and social change.* Abingdon: Routledge.

Hughes, S (2009) Sin bins for scum families. *Daily Star*, 23 July 2009.

Human Fertilisation and Embryology Authority (2011) Fertility treatment in 2011: Trends and figures. www.hfea.gov.uk/docs/HFEA_Fertility_Trends_and_Figures_2011_-_Annual_Register_Report.pdf

Humphries, R (2013) *Paying for social care: Beyond Dilnot.* London: Kings Fund.

Hutton, J (2006) *Supporting families: The role of welfare.* Speech to the Clapham Park project. 15 December 2006.

Independent Reviewer on Social Mobility and Child Poverty (2012) *University challenge: How higher education can enhance social mobility.* London: HMSO.

Information Centre About Asylum and Refugees (2004) *Media image, community impact.* London: ICAR. www.icar.org.uk/micifullreport.pdf

Ipsos/Mori (2011) *Does immigration matter?* www.ipsos-mori.com/Assets/Docs/News/IpsosMORI_ImmigrationFeb2011.pdf

IPSOS MORI (2013) *Issues facing Britain, October 2013.* www.ipsos-mori.com/researchpublications/researcharchive/3288/EconomistIpsos-MORI-October-2013-Issues-Index.aspx

Ismail, S, Thorlby, R and Holder, H (2014) *Focus on social care for older people: Reductions in adult social services for older people in England.* London: Health Foundation and Nuffield Trust.

Jensen, A (1969) How much can we boost IQ and scholastic achievement? *Harvard Education Review,* 39, 1–123.

Jensen, AR (1999) The G factor: the science of mental ability, Intelligence G Factor. *Psycoloquy,* 10 (23) http://psycprints.ecs.soton.ac.uk/archive/00000658/

Jerrim, J (2013) *Family background and access to 'high status' universities.* London: Sutton Trust.

Jones, C (1983) *State, social work and the working class.* London: Routledge.

Jones, C (1996) Anti-intellectualism and the peculiarities of British social work education. In Parton, N (ed.) *Social work, social theory and social change.* Abingdon: Routledge.

Jones, C (2001) Voices from the frontline: State social workers and New Labour. *British Journal Social Work,* 31, 547–62.

Jones, C (2011) The best and worst of times: Reflections on the impact of radicalism on British social work education in the 1970s. In Lavalette, M (2011) *Radical social work today: Social work at the crossroads.* Bristol: Policy Press.

Jones, C, Ferguson, I, Lavalette, M and Penketh, L (2004) *Social work and social justice: A manifesto for a new engaged practice.* Liverpool University. www.liv.ac.uk/sspsw/

Jones, C and Novak, T (1999) *Poverty, welfare and the disciplinary state.* Abingdon: Routledge.

Jones C and Novak, T (2014) *Poverty and inequality.* London: Policy Press

Jones, L (2008) The luxury brand with a chequered past. MailOnline, 2 June 2008. www.dailymail.co.uk/femail/article-1023460/Burberrys-shaken-chav-image-fashionistas-favourite-more.html

Jones, O (2011) *Chavs: The demonization of the working class.* London: Verso.

Jones, O (2012) The hatred of those on benefits is dangerously put of control. *Independent Online,* 18 May 2012. www.independent.co.uk/voices/commentators/owen-jones-hatred-of-those-on-benefits-is-dangerously-out-of-control-7763793.html

Jones, O (2013) Philpott verdict: Blame the man, not his class. *Independent,* 2 April 2013.

Jones, S (2013) Great British class survey finds seven social classes in the UK. *Guardian,* 3 April 2013.

Joseph Rowntree Foundation (1995) *Inquiry into income and wealth: Volumes 1 and 2.* York: Joseph Rowntree Foundation.

Joseph Rowntree Foundation (2008) *What are today's social evils? The results of a web consultation.* York: JRF.

Jowitt, M and O'Loughlin, S (2013) *Social work with children and families,* 3rd edition. London: Learning Matters/Sage.

Justice (2013) Lords debate anti-social behavior bill. 28 October 2013 www.justice.org.uk/news.php/107/lords-debate-anti-social-behaviour-bill

Kenny, M (2003) Social workers please, not social engineers! *Daily Mail,* 29 January 2003.

Kincaid, JC (1973) *Poverty and equality in Britain: A study of social security and taxation.* London: Penguin.

Kretzmann, J and McKnight, JP (1996) Asset-based community development. *National Civic Review,* Vol. 85 (4) 23–9.

Kumar, R (2012) *Education and the reproduction of capital: Neo-liberal knowledge and counterstrategies.* Basingstoke: Palgrave Macmillan.

Lambie-Mumford, H, Crossley, D, Jensen, E, Verbeke, M and Dowler, E (2014) *Household security in the UK: A review of food aid.* Warwick: University of Warwick/Food Ethics Council/DEFRA.

Lancashire Evening Post (2007) Blast for homeless gym, 4 May 2007.

Lansley, S (2013) *Poverty minus a pound: How the poverty consensus unravelled.* London: CPAG.

Lavalette, M (ed.) (2011) *Radical social work today.* Bristol: Policy Press.

Lawless, P, Dickinson, S, Fordham, G, Fuller, C, Meegan, R and Wells, P (2008) *Challenges, interventions and change: An overview of neighbourhood renewal in six new deals for communities areas.* London: Department for Communities and Local Government.

Ledwith, M (2005) *Community development: A critical approach.* Bristol: The Policy Press.

Ledwith, M (2011) *Community development: A critical approach.* 2nd edition. Bristol: The Policy Press.

Lemert, EM (1972) *Human deviance, social problems, and social control.* 2nd edition. Englewood Cliffs, NJ: Prentice-Hall.

Levitas, R (2001) Against work: A utopian incursion into social policy. *Critical Social Policy,* 21 (4) 449–65.

Levitas, R (2005) *The inclusive society? Social exclusion and New Labour.* Basingstoke: Palgrave Macmillan.

Levitas, R (2012) *There may be trouble ahead: What we know about those 120,000 'troubled' families.* London: PSE.

Lewis, O (1966) *La vida: A Puerto Rican family in the culture of poverty.* New York: Random House.

Liabo, K, Kerry, G and Mulcahy, D (2013) A systematic review of interventions to support looked-after children in school. *Child and Family Social Work,* 18 (3) 341–53.

Lloyd, C, Wollny, I, White, C, Gowland, S and Purdon, S (2012) *Monitoring and evaluation of family intervention services and projects between February 2007 and March 2011.* London: Department for Education.

Lyotard, JF (1984) *The postmodern condition: A report of knowledge.* Manchester: Manchester University Press.

M2 PressWire (2006) UK government: Supporting parents, strengthening communities. 21 November.

Macionis, JJ and Plummer, K (2012) *Sociology: A global introduction.* Harlow: Prentice-Hall.

Macnicol, J (1987) In pursuit of the underclass. *Journal of Social Policy,* 16 (3) 293–318.

Manchester Guardian (1904) Mr Bryce on sociology, 20 April 1904.

Manchester Guardian (1922) Sociology and the sciences, 10 October 1922.

Mantle, G and Beckwith, D (2010) Poverty and social work. *British Journal of Social Work,* 40, 2380–97.

Marmott Review Team (2011) *Fair society, healthy lives: The Marmott review.* London: Marmott Review.

Marsland, D (1996) *Welfare or welfare state? Contradictions and dilemmas in social policy.* Basingstoke: Macmillan.

Marx, K and Engels, F (1969) *Manifesto of the Communist Party.* Moscow: Progress Publishers.

Massey, T (2012) *Digging Deep: The ups and downs of a 1960s Yorkshire mining community.* Teesdale: Mosaic.

Mayo, M (ed.) (1977) *Women in the community.* London: Routledge and Kegan Paul.

Mayo, M (1994) *Communities and caring: The mixed economy of welfare.* Basingstoke: Macmillan.

McCarron, A and Purcell, L (2013) *The blame game must stop: Challenging the stigmatisation of people experiencing poverty.* Church Action on Poverty. www.church-poverty.org.uk/stigma/report/blamegamereport

McKinstry, L (2014) How dare this idiot preach at Britain on human rights? *Express,* 12 September 2014.

McLeod, M and Saraga, E (1988) Challenging the orthodoxy: Towards a feminist theory and practice. *Feminist Review,* 28, 16–55.

Mead, GH (1934) *Mind, self and society.* Chicago, IL: University of Chicago Press.

Migration Observatory (2011) *Thinking behind the numbers: Understanding public opinion on immigration in Britain.* Oxford: Migration Observatory.

Miliband, R (1975) *The state in capitalist society.* London: Quartet.

Mills, C Wright (1959) *The sociological imagination.* London: Penguin Books.

Milner, J (1993) A disappearing act: The differing career paths of fathers and mothers in child protection investigations. *Critical Social Policy,* 38, Autumn, 1993.

Milner, J (1996) Men's resistance to social workers. In Fawcett, B, Featherstone, B, Hearn, J and Toft, C (eds) *Violence and gender relations.* London: Sage.

Mind (2011) *Still in the red: Update on debt and mental health.* London: Mind.

Morris, K, Hughes, N, Clarke, H, Tew, J, Mason, P, Galvani, S, Lewis, A and Loveless, L (2008) *Think family: A literature review of whole family approaches.* London: Cabinet Office.

Morris, K (2013) Troubled families: Vulnerable families' experiences of multiple service use. *Child and Family Social Work,* (18) 198–206.

Muncie, J (1999) *Youth and crime: A critical introduction.* London: Sage.

Murali, V and Oyebode, F (2004) Poverty, social justice and mental health. *Advances in Psychiatric Treatment,* 10, 216–24.

Murdock, P (1949) *Social structure.* New York: Macmillan.

Murray, C (1990) *The emerging British underclass.* London: IEA.

Murray, C (1994) *The crisis deepens.* London: IEA.

Murray, C and Herrnstein, RJ (1994) *The bell curve.* London: Scribner.

Murray, C (1998) *Income Inequality and IQ.* Washington, DC: American Enterprise Institute. www.aei.org/docLib/20040302_book443.pdf

Narey, M (2014) *Making the education of social workers consistently effective.* London: Department for Education.

National Care Advisory Service (2013) Written evidence submitted to the House of Commons education select committee, 22 January 2013. www.publications.parliament.uk/pa/cm201213/cmselect/cmeduc/632/632vw46.htm

National Centre for Social Research (2012) *British social attitudes*, 28. London: Sage.

National Housing Federation (2013) *Written evidence to the Work and Pensions Committee inquiry: Support for housing costs in the reformed welfare system.* http://data.parliament.uk/writtenevidence/WrittenEvidence.svc/EvidenceHtml/2469

Nelson, F (2009) The tragedy of welfare ghettoes. *The Spectator*, 6 February 2009. http://blogs.spectator.co.uk/coffeehouse/2009/02/the-tragedy-ofwelfare-ghettoes/

Nisbett, RE (2013) Schooling makes you smarter: What teachers need to know about IQ. *American Educator*, Spring. https://www.aft.org/pdfs/americaneducator/spring2013/Nisbett.pdf

Nissim, M (2013) 'Daily Mail' Mick Philpott 'welfare UK' front page sparks outrage. Digital Spy, 3 April 2013. www.digitalspy.co.uk/media/news/a470224/daily-mail-mick-philpott-welfare-uk-front-page-sparks-outrage.html#~oB1H3FmIDU73oT

Noden, P, West, A and Hind, A (2014) *Banding and ballots.* London: Sutton Trust.

Novak, T (1997) Poverty and the underclass. In Lavalette, M and Pratt, A (eds) *Social policy: a conceptual and theoretical introduction.* London: Sage.

Oakley, A (1986) *Subject women: A powerful analysis of women's experience in society today.* London: Fontana.

O'Brien, M (2011) Social justice alive and well (partly) in social work practice. *International Social Work*, 54 (2) 174–90.

O'Donnell, M (1992) *A new introduction to sociology.* 3rd edition. Cheltenham: Thomas Nelson and sons Ltd.

Office for National Statistics (2012) Families and households, 2012. www.ons.gov.uk/ons/dcp171778_284823.pdf

Office for National Statistics (2013) General Lifestyle Survey, 2011. www.ons.gov.uk/ons/rel/ghs/general-lifestyle-survey/2011/index.html

Office for National Statistics (2013a) What percentage of marriages end in divorce? Press release, 9 February. www.ons.gov.uk/ons/rel/vsob1/divorces-in-england-and-wales/2011/sty-what-percentage-of-marriages-end-in-divorce.html

Office for National Statistics (2013b) Live births in England and Wales by characteristics of mother, 2011. www.ons.gov.uk/ons/dcp171778_296157.pdf

Office for National Statistics (2013c) Civil partnerships in the UK, 2012. www.ons.gov.uk/ons/dcp171778_329457.pdf

Office of the Deputy Prime Minister (2005) *New Deal for Communities: An Interim Evaluation.* 121, www.neighbourhood.gov.uk/displaypagedoc.asp?id=1625

O'Grady, S (2007) Britain's breakdown in traditional values. *Express,* 16 April 2007.

Oxfam (2014) *A tale of two Britains.* http://oxfamilibrary.openrepository.com/oxfam/bitstream/10546/314152/1/mb-a-tale-of-two-britains-inequality-uk-170314-en.pdf

Parker, S (2005) *Mentor UK coastal and ex mining areas project: A review of literature.* York: York University.

Parliamentary Joint Committee on Human Rights (2007) *The treatment of asylum seekers: Volume 1.* London: HMSO.

Parr, S (2011) Family policy and the governance of anti-social behaviour in the UK: Women's experiences of intensive family support. *Journal of Social Policy,* 40 (4) 717–37.

Parsons, C, Godfrey, R, Annan, G, Cornwall, J, Dussart, M, Hepburn, S, Howlett, K and Wennerstrom, V (2004) *Minority ethnic exclusions and the Race Relations (Amendment) Act 2000.* London: HMSO DfES.

Parsons, T (1951) The *social system.* Abingdon: Routledge and Kegan Paul.

Parton, N (2009) From Seebohm to think family: Reflection on 40 years of policy change of statutory children's social work in England. *Child Family and Social Work,* 14, 68–78.

Pearson, G (1983) *Hooligan: A history of respectable fears.* Basingstoke: Macmillan.

Penketh, L (2011) Social work and women's oppression today. In Lavelette, M (2011) *Radical social work today: Social work at the crossroads.* Bristol: Policy Press.

Perry, E and Francis, B (2010) *The social class gap for educational achievement: A review of the literature.* London: RSA.

Pierson, J (2002) *Tackling social exclusion.* London: Routledge.

Pierson, J (2009) *Tackling social exclusion,* 2nd edition. London: Routledge.

Pople, L, Rodrigues, L and Royston, S (2013) *Through young eyes.* London: Children's Society.

Popple, K (1995) *Analysing community work: Its theory and practice.* Buckingham: Open University Press.

Professors of Social Work (2013) Gove's wrong choices over call for social work reform. *Guardian* (correspondence), 13 November 2013.

Public Accounts Committee (2013) Department for Work and Pensions: Work programme outcome statistics. London: HMSO.

Quality Assurance Agency for Higher Education (2000) *Subject benchmark statements, social work.* http://www.qaa.ac.uk/Publications/InformationAndGuidance/Documents/socialwork08.pdf

Raffo, C, Dyson, R, Gunter, H, Hall, D, Jones, L and Kalambouka, A (2007) *Education and poverty: A critical review of theory, policy and practice.* York: JRF.

Ramesh, R (2013) Poor children's life chances are decided in primary school, report finds. *Guardian,* 8 October 2013.

Reay, D (2012) *What would a socially just education system look like?* London: Centre for Labour and Social Studies.

Reder, P, Duncan, S and Gray, M (1993) *Beyond blame: Child abuse tragedies revisited.* Abingdon: Routledge.

Redstockings Manifesto (1969) http://fsweb.berry.edu/academic/hass/csnider/berry/hum200/redstockings.htm

Refugee Council (2013) The UK's role in the international refugee protection system. www.refugeecouncil.org.uk/assets/0002/9706/Sep_2013_The_UK_s_Role_in_the_international_refugee_protection_system.pdf

Ridge, T (2011) The everyday costs of poverty in childhood: A review of qualitative research exploring the lives and experiences of low-income children in the UK. *Children and Society*, 25, 73–84.

Ritzer, G (2010) *Sociological theory*. 8th edition. Maidenhead: McGraw-Hill.

Roberts, K (2011) *Class in contemporary Britain*. 2nd edition. Basingstoke: Palgrave Macmillan.

Ross, H, Gask, K and Berrington, A (2011) Civil partnerships five years on. *Population Trends* (ONS), 145, Autumn.

Rosenthal, R and Jacobson, L (1968) *Pygmalion in the classroom*. New York: Holt, Rinehart and Winston.

Savage, M, Devine, F, Cunningham, N, Taylor, M, Li, Y, Hjellbrekke, J, Le Roux, B, Friedmaan, S and Miles, A (2013) A new model of social class? Findings from the BBC's great British class survey experiment. *Sociology*, 47 (2) 219–50.

Scruton, R (1985) Who will cure this social disease? Sociology. *The Times*, 8 October 1985.

Searle, GR (1979) Eugenics and politics in Britain in the 1930s. *Annals of Science*, 36 (2) 159–69.

Sewell, T (2010) Masterclass in victimhood. *Prospect*, 1 October, 33–4.

Sheedy, M (2013) *Power, poverty, politics and welfare*. Maidenhead: Open University Press.

Shildrick, T, MacDonald, R, Furlong, A, Roden, J and Crow, R (2012) *Are 'cultures of worklessness' passed down the generations?* York: Joseph Rowntree Foundation.

Shipman, T and Walker, K (2011) Cameron war on feckless families. *Daily Mail*, 16 August 2011.

Smale, G, Tuson, G and Statham, D (2000) *Social work and social problems*. Basingstoke: Palgrave.

Smith, A (2013) Teach first or business first? In Social Work Action Network (2013) *In defence of social work: Why Michael Gove is wrong*. London: SWAN.

Smith, J (2002) Speech by the Minister of State for Health to the Joint Social Work Education Conference, 11 July 2002. www.swap.ac.uk/docs/gov/minister.rtf

Smith, S (2013) Marxism, feminism and women's liberation. SocialistWorker.Org, 31 January 2013. http://socialistworker.org/2013/01/31/marxism-feminism-and-womens-liberation

Social Exclusion Taskforce (2007a) *Context for social exclusion work*. Cabinet Office: London.

Social Exclusion Taskforce (2007b) *Reaching out: Progress on social exclusion*. Cabinet Office: London.

Social Exclusion Unit (1998) *Bringing Britain together: A national strategy for neighbourhood renewal*. London: SEU.

Social Exclusion Unit (1998a) *Truancy and school exclusion*. London: HMSO.

Social Exclusion Unit (2004b) *Mental health and social exclusion*. London: Social Exclusion Unit.

Social Mobility and Child Poverty Commission (2013) *State of the nation in 2013: Social mobility and child poverty in Great Britain*. London: HMSO.

Social Work Taskforce (2009) *Building a safe and confident future*. London: Department for Children, Schools and Families.

Strand, S (2007) *Minority ethnic pupils in the longitudinal study of young people in England.* London: HMSO.

Strier, R, Feldman, G and Shdaimah, C (2012) The construction of social class in social work education: A study of introductory textbooks. *Journal of teaching in social work,* 32: 406–20.

Sutton Trust (2005) *Rates of eligibility for free school meals at the top state schools.* London: Sutton Trust.

Sutton Trust (2009) *The educational backgrounds of leading lawyers, journalists, vice chancellors, politicians, medics and chief executives.* London: Sutton Trust.

Sutton Trust (2013) *Selective comprehensives: The social composition of top comprehensive schools.* www.suttontrust.com/our-work/research/download/219

Szasz, T (1972) The *myth of mental illness.* London: Paladin Grafton.

Szasz, T (1973) The *second sin.* New York: Anchor/Doubleday.

Tapsfield, J (2013) David Cameron backs George Osborne in Philpott welfare row. *Independent,* 5 April 2013.

Taylor, M (2003) *Public policy in the community.* Basingstoke: Palgrave Macmillan.

The Daily Telegraph (2008) Editorial: Karen Matthews and the underclass thrive on Labour's welfare state. 6 December 2008.

The Times: various dates.

Thoburn, J, Cooper, N, Brandon, M and Connolly, S (2013) The place of 'think family' approaches in child and family social work: Messages from a process evaluation of an English pathfinder service. *Children and Youth Services Review,* (35) 228–36.

Thompson, N and Bates, J (1998) Avoiding dangerous practice. *Care: The Journal of Practice and Development,* 6 (4).

Tönnies, F (1957) *Community and society (Gemeinschaft und Gesellschaft).* East Lansing, MI: The Michigan State University Press.

Townsend, P (1979) *Poverty in the United Kingdom.* London: Allen Lane.

Toynbee, P and Walker, D (2011) *The verdict: Did Labour change Britain.* London: Granta.

Toynbee, P and Walker, D (2012) *Dogma and disarray: Cameron at half-time.* London: Granta Books.

Travis, A (2013) 'Growing up' behaviour too often labelled anti-social, says police chief. *Guardian,* 11 November 2013.

Trussell Trust (2014) *The Trussell Trust's UK Foodbank Network.* www.trusselltrust.org/resources/documents/Press/TrussellTrustFoodbanksMay2013Small.pdf

Tumin, M (1953) Some principles of stratification: A critical analysis. *American Sociological Review,* 18 (4) 387–94.

Twelvetrees, AC (2008) *Community work.* Basingstoke: Palgrave.

United Nations (2013) *Report of the Special Rapporteur on adequate housing as a component of the right to an adequate standard of living, and on the right to non-discrimination in this context.* www.ohchr.org/EN/HRBodies/HRC/RegularSessions/Session25/Documents/A_HRC_25_54_Add.2_ENG.DOC

UN Committee on the Elimination of Racial Discrimination (2011) *Consideration of reports submitted by state parties (UK): Concluding observations.* http://daccess-dds-ny.un.org/doc/UNDOC/GEN/G11/454/89/PDF/G1145489.pdf?OpenElement

UN Committee on the Rights of the Child (2008) *Consideration of reports submitted by state parties (UK): Concluding observations.* www2.ohchr.org/english/bodies/crc/docs/AdvanceVersions/CRC.C.GBR. CO.4.pdf

UNHCR (2007) *Memorandum from the UNHCR to the Joint Parliamentary Committee on Human Rights.* www.publications.parliament.uk/pa/jt200607/jtselect/jtrights/81/81we83.htm

UNHCR (2012) *Global Trends, 2011.* www.unhcr.org/4fd6f87f9.html

UNHCR (2014) *The facts about asylum in the UK.* www.unhcr.org.uk/about-us/the-uk-and-asylum. html

UNICEF (2000) *A league table of child poverty in rich nations.* Florence: UNICEF.

UNICEF (2005) *Child poverty in rich countries.* Florence: UNICEF.

UNICEF (2007) *An overview of child welfare in rich countries.* www.unicef.org/media/files/ ChildPovertyReport.pdf

UNICEF (2012) *Measuring child poverty: New league tables of child poverty in the world's richest countries.* Florence: UNICEF.

UNICEF (2013) *Child well-being in rich countries: A comparative overview.* Florence: UNICEF.

Utting, D, Monteiro, H and Ghate, D (2007) *Interventions for children at risk of developing anti-social personality disorder.* London: Policy Research Bureau.

Walker, P (2012) Anti-disabled abuse fuelled by benefits cuts. *Guardian,* 6 February 2012.

Wallace, A (2010) *Remaking community? New Labour and the governance of poor neighbourhoods.* Farnham: Ashgate.

Waterhouse, S (2004) Deviant and non-deviant identities in the classroom: Patrolling the boundaries of the normal social world. *European Journal of Special Needs Education,* 19 (1) 69–84.

Webb, D (1996) Regulation for radicals: The state, CCETSW and the academy. In Parton, N (ed.) *Social work, social theory and social change.* Abingdon: Routledge.

Weber, M (1964) *Theory of Social and Economic Organisation.* New York: The Free Press.

Webster, P (2001) Blair sets 2003 Euro deadline. *The Times,* 8 February 2001.

Welshman, J (2012) *From transmitted deprivation to social exclusion: Policy, poverty and parenting.* Bristol: Policy Press.

Welshman, J (2013) *Underclass: A history of the excluded since 1880,* 2nd edition. London: Bloomsbury.

Whelan, R (2001) *Helping the poor: Friendly visiting, dole charities and dole queues.* London: CIVITAS.

White, C, Warrener, M, Reeves, A and La Valle, I (2008) *Family intervention projects: An evaluation of their design, evaluation and early outcomes.* London: National Centre for Social Research.

Whittam, G (2012) *Child Poverty in 2012: It shouldn't happen here.* Manchester: Save the Children.

Whitty, G (2001) Education, social class and social exclusion. *Journal of Education Policy,* 16 (4) (1 July), 287–95.

Whitty, G (2008) Twenty years of progress? English education policy 1988 to the present. *Educational Management Administration and Leadership,* 36 (2) 165–84.

Wilkinson, R and Pickett, K (2010) *The spirit level: Why equality is better for everyone.* London: Penguin.

Williams, F (1992) Somewhere over the rainbow: Universality and diversity in social policy. *Social Policy Review* (4), 1992.

Williams, F (1998) Agency and structure revisited: Rethinking poverty and social exclusion. In Barry, M and Hallett, C (eds) *Social exclusion and social work.* Dorset: Russell House Publishing.

Williams, R (2011) We are being committed to radical, long-term policies for which no one voted. *New Statesman*, 9 June.

Williams, Z (2013) The early year's educational underclass is a handy moralisers' myth. *Guardian*, 4 September 2013.

Winder, R (2004) *Bloody foreigners: The story of immigration to Britain.* London: Little, Brown.

Wright, C, Standen, J, German, G and Patel, T (2005) *School exclusion and transition into adulthood in African-Caribbean communities.* York: JRF.

Young, M and Willmott, P (1962) *Family and kinship in East London.* London: Penguin.

Appendix 1

Professional Capabilities Framework

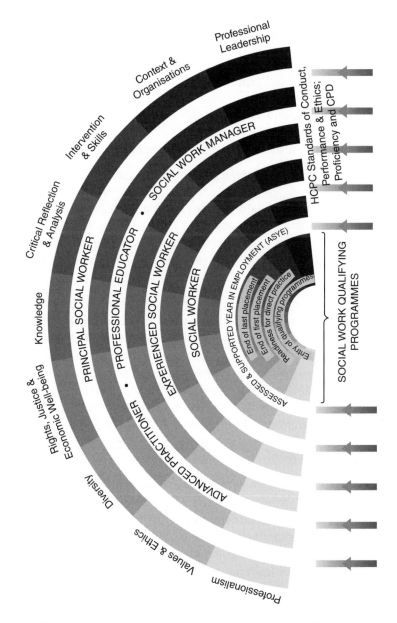

Professional Capabilities Framework diagram reproduced with permission of The College of Social Work.

Appendix 2
Subject benchmark for social work

3 Nature and extent of social work

3.1 This subject benchmark statement covers social work as an applied academic subject at honours level. It sets out expectations concerning:

- the subject knowledge, understanding and skills of an honours graduate in social work
- the teaching, learning and assessment methods employed in their education
- the standards expected of them at the point of graduation.

3.2 Legislation establishing regulatory bodies in social work and introducing statutory registration of social workers was passed across the UK from 2000 onwards. These acts also recognise the terms 'social work' and/or 'social worker' as protected titles. Anyone using the title 'social worker' is required to be registered with the relevant care council.

3.3 Professional social work qualifications in the UK are linked to a specific level of academic achievement and may be attained through undergraduate or postgraduate study. Convergence of academic and professional awards established an undergraduate honours degree as the minimum required qualification for social workers. The curriculum design and assessment of academic work and practice within the respective social work degrees is determined by the specific requirements in England, Scotland, Wales and Northern Ireland. The NOS and the subject benchmark statement for social work inform these requirements. The *Codes of Practice for Social Care Workers and Employers* should also shape the curriculum. This statement covers only honours degrees that constitute a professional qualification in social work.

3.4 This subject benchmark statement informs descriptions of professional competence for registration by identifying the required academic level and the range of subject matter necessary for an undergraduate degree. The process of establishing undergraduate degree programmes in social work should only be undertaken in partnership with other stakeholders including regulatory bodies, employers, professional bodies, providers of practice-learning, service users and carers, and those who work within social work and social care.

3.5 Honours degree programmes in social work may be studied in full-time, part-time, open and distance-learning, work-based, and post-experience modes.

Irrespective of learning mode, all honours degree programmes covered by this statement must include structured opportunities for supervised or directed practice in relevant and appropriate practice-learning settings.

3.6 In addressing the content and standards of honours degrees, this statement takes account of European and international contexts of social work, including the Bologna Process and the desirability of the mutual recognition of social work qualifications within the European sector of the International Federation of Social Workers.

3.7 Contemporary social work increasingly takes place in an inter-agency context, and social workers work collaboratively with others towards interdisciplinary and cross-professional objectives. Honours degree programmes as qualifying awards are required to help equip students with accurate knowledge about the respective responsibilities of social welfare agencies, including those in the public, voluntary/ independent and private sectors, and acquire skills in effective collaborative practice.

3.8 To facilitate broad access to honours degree programmes in social work, holders of sub-degree and vocational qualifications (normally in social care) may be offered entry with advanced standing by means of approved procedures for the recognition of prior (experiential) learning. Honours degree programmes must, however, ensure that all such arrangements enable students to achieve fully the standards required by the relevant care council. Advanced standing is not available in respect of the practice learning requirements in the degree.

3.9 The term 'service user' is used in this statement to cover the wide and diverse set of individuals, groups and organisations who are involved in, or who benefit from, the contribution of social work to the well-being of society. This group will include some that are involuntary or unwilling recipients of social work services. The term 'carer' is used in this statement to cover people who provide unpaid care to a member of their family or to another person, and who work in partnership with social workers to deliver a service. It should be recognised that students and staff may also be, or have been service users and/or carers. In providing services, social workers should engage with service users and carers in ways that are characterised by openness, reciprocity, mutual accountability and explicit recognition of the powers of the social worker and the legal context of intervention. Service users and carers are required by the four care councils to be integrally involved in all aspects of the design, delivery and assessment of qualifying honours degree programmes.

4 Defining principles

4.1 As an applied academic subject, social work is characterised by a distinctive focus on practice in complex social situations to promote and protect individual and collective well-being. This underscores the importance of partnerships between HEIs and service providers to ensure the full involvement of practitioners, managers, tutors, service users and carers with students in both academic and practice learning and assessment.

4.2 At honours level, the study of social work involves the integrated study of subject-specific knowledge, skills and values and the critical application of research knowledge from the social and human sciences, and from social work (and closely related domains) to inform understanding and to underpin action, reflection and evaluation. Honours degree programmes should be designed to help foster this integration of contextual, analytic, critical, explanatory and practical understanding.

4.3 Contemporary definitions of social work as a degree subject reflect its origins in a range of different academic and practice traditions. The precise nature and scope of the subject is itself a matter for legitimate study and critical debate. Three main issues are relevant to this.

- Social work is located within different social welfare contexts. Within the UK there are different traditions of social welfare (influenced by legislation, historical development and social attitudes) and these have shaped both social work education and practice in community-based settings including residential, day care and substitute care. In an international context, distinctive national approaches to social welfare policy, provision and practice have greatly influenced the focus and content of social work degree programmes.

- There are competing views in society at large on the nature of social work and on its place and purpose. Social work practice and education inevitably reflect these differing perspectives on the role of social work in relation to social justice, social care and social order.

- Social work, both as occupational practice and as an academic subject, evolves, adapts and changes in response to the social, political and economic challenges and demands of contemporary social welfare policy, practice and legislation.

4.4 Honours graduates in social work should therefore be equipped both to understand, and to work within, this context of contested debate about nature, scope and purpose, and be enabled to analyse, adapt to, manage and eventually to lead the processes of change.

4.5 The applied nature of social work as an academic subject means that practice is an essential and core element of learning. The following points clarify the use of the term 'practice' in the statement.

- The term 'practice' in this statement is used to encompass learning that not only takes place in professional practice placements, but also in a variety of other experiential learning situations. All learning opportunities that bear academic credit must be subject to methods of assessment appropriate to their academic level and be assessed by competent assessors. Where they form part of the curriculum leading to integrated academic and professional awards, practice learning opportunities will also be subject to regulations that further define learning requirements, standards and modes of assessment.

- In honours degree programmes covered by this statement, practice as an activity refers to experiential, action-based learning. In this sense, practice provides opportunities for students to improve and demonstrate their understanding and competence through the application and testing of knowledge and skills.

- Practice activity is also a source of transferable learning in its own right. Such learning can transfer both from a practice setting to the 'classroom' and vice versa. Thus practice can be as much a source of intellectual and cognitive learning as other modes of study. For this reason, learning through practice attracts full academic credit.

- Learning in practice can include activities such as observation, shadowing, analysis and research, as well as intervention within social work and related organisations. Practice-learning on honours degrees involves active engagement with service users and others in practice settings outside the university, and may involve for example virtual/simulated practice, observational and research activities.

4.6 Social work is a moral activity that requires practitioners to recognise the dignity of the individual, but also to make and implement difficult decisions (including restriction of liberty) in human situations that involve the potential for benefit or harm. Honours degree programmes in social work therefore involve the study, application of, and critical reflection upon, ethical principles and dilemmas. As reflected by the four care councils' codes of practice, this involves showing respect for persons, honouring the diverse and distinctive organisations and communities that make up contemporary society, promoting social justice and combating processes that lead to discrimination, marginalisation and social exclusion. This means that honours undergraduates must learn to:

- recognise and work with the powerful links between intrapersonal and interpersonal factors and the wider social, legal, economic, political and cultural context of people's lives

- understand the impact of injustice, social inequalities and oppressive social relations

- challenge constructively individual, institutional and structural discrimination

- practise in ways that maximise safety and effectiveness in situations of uncertainty and incomplete information

- help people to gain, regain or maintain control of their own affairs, insofar as this is compatible with their own or others' safety, well-being and rights

- work in partnership with service users and carers and other professionals to foster dignity, choice and independence, and effect change.

4.7 The expectation that social workers will be able to act effectively in such complex circumstances requires that honours degree programmes in social work should be designed to help students learn to become accountable, reflective, critical and evaluative. This involves learning to:

- think critically about the complex social, legal, economic, political and cultural contexts in which social work practice is located

- work in a transparent and responsible way, balancing autonomy with complex, multiple and sometimes contradictory accountabilities (for example, to different service users, employing agencies, professional bodies and the wider society)

- exercise authority within complex frameworks of accountability and ethical and legal boundaries

- acquire and apply the habits of critical reflection, self-evaluation and consultation, and make appropriate use of research in decision-making about practice and in the evaluation of outcomes.

5 Subject knowledge, understanding and skills

Subject knowledge and understanding

5.1 During their degree studies in social work, honours graduates should acquire, critically evaluate, apply and integrate knowledge and understanding in the following five core areas of study.

5.1.1 **Social work services, service users and carers**, which include:

- the social processes (associated with, for example, poverty, migration, unemployment, poor health, disablement, lack of education and other sources of disadvantage) that lead to marginalisation, isolation and exclusion, and their impact on the demand for social work services

- explanations of the links between definitional processes contributing to social differences (for example, social class, gender, ethnic differences, age, sexuality and religious belief) to the problems of inequality and differential need faced by service users

- the nature of social work services in a diverse society (with particular reference to concepts such as prejudice, interpersonal, institutional and structural discrimination, empowerment and anti-discriminatory practices)

- the nature and validity of different definitions of, and explanations for, the characteristics and circumstances of service users and the services required by them, drawing on knowledge from research, practice experience, and from service users and carers

- the focus on outcomes, such as promoting the well-being of young people and their families, and promoting dignity, choice and independence for adults receiving services

- the relationship between agency policies, legal requirements and professional boundaries in shaping the nature of services provided in interdisciplinary contexts and the issues associated with working across professional boundaries and within different disciplinary groups.

5.1.2 **The service delivery context**, which includes:

- the location of contemporary social work within historical, comparative and global perspectives, including European and international contexts

- the changing demography and cultures of communities in which social workers will be practising

- the complex relationships between public, social and political philosophies, policies and priorities and the organisation and practice of social work, including the contested nature of these

- the issues and trends in modern public and social policy and their relationship to contemporary practice and service delivery in social work

- the significance of legislative and legal frameworks and service delivery standards (including the nature of legal authority, the application of legislation in practice, statutory accountability and tensions between statute, policy and practice)

- the current range and appropriateness of statutory, voluntary and private agencies providing community-based, day-care, residential and other services and the organisational systems inherent within these

- the significance of interrelationships with other related services, including housing, health, income maintenance and criminal justice (where not an integral social service)

- the contribution of different approaches to management, leadership and quality in public and independent human services

- the development of personalised services, individual budgets and direct payments

- the implications of modern information and communications technology (ICT) for both the provision and receipt of services.

5.1.3 **Values and ethics**, which include:

- the nature, historical evolution and application of social work values

- the moral concepts of rights, responsibility, freedom, authority and power inherent in the practice of social workers as moral and statutory agents

- the complex relationships between justice, care and control in social welfare and the practical and ethical implications of these, including roles as statutory agents and in upholding the law in respect of discrimination

- aspects of philosophical ethics relevant to the understanding and resolution of value dilemmas and conflicts in both interpersonal and professional contexts

- the conceptual links between codes defining ethical practice, the regulation of professional conduct and the management of potential conflicts generated by the codes held by different professional groups.

5.1.4 **Social work theory**, which includes:

- research-based concepts and critical explanations from social work theory and other disciplines that contribute to the knowledge base of social work, including their distinctive epistemological status and application to practice

- the relevance of sociological perspectives to understanding societal and structural influences on human behaviour at individual, group and community levels

- the relevance of psychological, physical and physiological perspectives to understanding personal and social development and functioning

- social science theories explaining group and organisational behaviour, adaptation and change

- models and methods of assessment, including factors underpinning the selection and testing of relevant information, the nature of professional judgement and the processes of risk assessment and decision-making

- approaches and methods of intervention in a range of settings, including factors guiding the choice and evaluation of these

- user-led perspectives

- knowledge and critical appraisal of relevant social research and evaluation methodologies, and the evidence base for social work.

5.1.5 **The nature of social work practice**, which includes:

- the characteristics of practice in a range of community-based and organisational settings within statutory, voluntary and private sectors, and the factors influencing changes and developments in practice within these contexts

- the nature and characteristics of skills associated with effective practice, both direct and indirect, with a range of service-users and in a variety of settings

- the processes that facilitate and support service user choice and independence

- the factors and processes that facilitate effective interdisciplinary, interprofessional and interagency collaboration and partnership

- the place of theoretical perspectives and evidence from international research in assessment and decision-making processes in social work practice

- the integration of theoretical perspectives and evidence from international research into the design and implementation of effective social work intervention, with a wide range of service users, carers and others

- the processes of reflection and evaluation, including familiarity with the range of approaches for evaluating service and welfare outcomes, and their significance for the development of practice and the practitioner.

Subject-specific skills and other skills

5.2 As an applied subject at honours degree level, social work necessarily involves the development of skills that may be of value in many situations (for example, analytical thinking, building relationships, working as a member of an organisation, intervention, evaluation and reflection). Some of these skills are specific to social work but many are also widely transferable. What helps to define the specific nature of these skills in a social work context are:

- the context in which they are applied and assessed (eg, communication skills in practice with people with sensory impairments or assessment skills in an interprofessional setting)

- the relative weighting given to such skills within social work practice (eg, the central importance of problem-solving skills within complex human situations)

- the specific purpose of skill development (eg, the acquisition of research skills in order to build a repertoire of research-based practice)

- a requirement to integrate a range of skills (ie, not simply to demonstrate these in an isolated and incremental manner).

5.3 All social work honours graduates should show the ability to reflect on and learn from the exercise of their skills. They should understand the significance of the concepts of continuing professional development and lifelong learning, and accept responsibility for their own continuing development.

5.4 Social work honours graduates should acquire and integrate skills in the following five core areas.

Problem-solving skills

5.5 These are sub-divided into four areas.

5.5.1 **Managing problem-solving activities:** honours graduates in social work should be able to plan problem-solving activities, ie to:

- think logically, systematically, critically and reflectively

- apply ethical principles and practices critically in planning problem-solving activities

- plan a sequence of actions to achieve specified objectives, making use of research, theory and other forms of evidence

- manage processes of change, drawing on research, theory and other forms of evidence.

5.5.2 **Gathering information:** honours graduates in social work should be able to:

- gather information from a wide range of sources and by a variety of methods, for a range of purposes. These methods should include electronic searches, reviews of relevant literature, policy and procedures, face-to-face interviews, written and telephone contact with individuals and groups

- take into account differences of viewpoint in gathering information and critically assess the reliability and relevance of the information gathered

- assimilate and disseminate relevant information in reports and case records.

5.5.3 **Analysis and synthesis:** honours graduates in social work should be able to analyse and synthesise knowledge gathered for problem-solving purposes, ie to:

- assess human situations, taking into account a variety of factors (including the views of participants, theoretical concepts, research evidence, legislation and organisational policies and procedures)

- analyse information gathered, weighing competing evidence and modifying their view-point in light of new information, then relate this information to a particular task, situation or problem

- consider specific factors relevant to social work practice (such as risk, rights, cultural differences and linguistic sensitivities, responsibilities to protect vulnerable individuals and legal obligations)

- assess the merits of contrasting theories, explanations, research, policies and procedures

- synthesise knowledge and sustain reasoned argument

- employ a critical understanding of human agency at the macro (societal), mezzo (organisational and community) and micro (inter and intrapersonal) levels

- critically analyse and take account of the impact of inequality and discrimination in work with people in particular contexts and problem situations.

5.5.4 **Intervention and evaluation:** honours graduates in social work should be able to use their knowledge of a range of interventions and evaluation processes selectively to:

- build and sustain purposeful relationships with people and organisations in community-based, and interprofessional contexts

- make decisions, set goals and construct specific plans to achieve these, taking into account relevant factors including ethical guidelines

- negotiate goals and plans with others, analysing and addressing in a creative manner human, organisational and structural impediments to change

- implement plans through a variety of systematic processes that include working in partnership

- undertake practice in a manner that promotes the well-being and protects the safety of all parties

- engage effectively in conflict resolution

- support service users to take decisions and access services, with the social worker as navigator, advocate and supporter

- manage the complex dynamics of dependency and, in some settings, provide direct care and personal support in everyday living situations

- meet deadlines and comply with external definitions of a task

- plan, implement and critically review processes and outcomes

- bring work to an effective conclusion, taking into account the implications for all involved

- monitor situations, review processes and evaluate outcomes

- use and evaluate methods of intervention critically and reflectively.

Communication skills

5.6 Honours graduates in social work should be able to communicate clearly, accurately and precisely (in an appropriate medium) with individuals and groups in a range of formal and informal situations, ie to:

- make effective contact with individuals and organisations for a range of objectives, by verbal, paper-based and electronic means

- clarify and negotiate the purpose of such contacts and the boundaries of their involvement

- listen actively to others, engage appropriately with the life experiences of service users, understand accurately their viewpoint and overcome personal prejudices to respond appropriately to a range of complex personal and interpersonal situations

- use both verbal and non-verbal cues to guide interpretation

- identify and use opportunities for purposeful and supportive communication with service users within their everyday living situations

- follow and develop an argument and evaluate the viewpoints of, and evidence presented by, others

- write accurately and clearly in styles adapted to the audience, purpose and context of the communication

- use advocacy skills to promote others' rights, interests and needs

- present conclusions verbally and on paper, in a structured form, appropriate to the audience for which these have been prepared

- make effective preparation for, and lead meetings in a productive way

- communicate effectively across potential barriers resulting from differences (for example, in culture, language and age).

Skills in working with others

5.7 Honours graduates in social work should be able to work effectively with others, ie to:

- involve users of social work services in ways that increase their resources, capacity and power to influence factors affecting their lives

- consult actively with others, including service users and carers, who hold relevant information or expertise

- act cooperatively with others, liaising and negotiating across differences such as organisational and professional boundaries and differences of identity or language

- develop effective helping relationships and partnerships with other individuals, groups and organisations that facilitate change

- act with others to increase social justice by identifying and responding to prejudice, institutional discrimination and structural inequality

- act within a framework of multiple accountability (for example, to agencies, the public, service users, carers and others)

- challenge others when necessary, in ways that are most likely to produce positive outcomes.

Skills in personal and professional development

5.8 Honours graduates in social work should be able to:

- advance their own learning and understanding with a degree of independence

- reflect on and modify their behaviour in the light of experience

- identify and keep under review their own personal and professional boundaries

- manage uncertainty, change and stress in work situations

- handle inter and intrapersonal conflict constructively

- understand and manage changing situations and respond in a flexible manner

- challenge unacceptable practices in a responsible manner

- take responsibility for their own further and continuing acquisition and use of knowledge and skills

- use research critically and effectively to sustain and develop their practice.

ICT and numerical skills

5.9 Honours graduates in social work should be able to use ICT methods and techniques to support their learning and their practice. In particular, they should demonstrate the ability to:

- use ICT effectively for professional communication, data storage and retrieval and information searching

- use ICT in working with people who use services

- demonstrate sufficient familiarity with statistical techniques to enable effective use of research in practice

- integrate appropriate use of ICT to enhance skills in problem-solving in the four areas set out in paragraph 6.2

- apply numerical skills to financial and budgetary responsibilities

- have a critical understanding of the social impact of ICT, including an awareness of the impact of the 'digital divide'.

Index

CANTERBURY CHRIST CHURCH UNIVERSITY